Leveling the Playing Field

LEVELING THE PLAYING FIELD

How the Law Can Make Sports
Better for Fans

PAUL C. WEILER

HARVARD UNIVERSITY PRESS
Cambridge, Massachusetts
London, England
2000

Library of Congress Cataloging-in-Publication Data

Weiler, Paul C.
  Leveling the playing field : how the law can make sports better for fans /
Paul C. Weiler.
    p. cm.
  Includes index.
  ISBN 0-674-00165-6 (alk. paper)
  1. Sports—Law and legislation—United States   I. Title.
KF3989.W45   2000
344.73′099—dc21   99-087304

To Nat and Sid Darwin

PREFACE

As a teenager I was strongly committed to playing as well as watching sports. But at the end of a far from stellar season with my midget hockey team in my native Canada, the coach took me aside and said, "Son, if you're hoping for a professional career, you should start hitting the books, not just the pucks!"

Following that advice not only got me into college at the University of Toronto but also won me a sports bonus. As a high school graduation gift, my dad took me down to New York to watch my hero Mickey Mantle and the Yankees win the World Series against the Milwaukee Braves. A few years later I went to study at Harvard Law School, and while in the Boston area I spent considerable time at the old Boston Garden: both watching Red Auerbach coaching Bill Russell and his Celtics teammates to yet another NBA title and listening to the last-place Bruins fans praying for Bobby Orr to get old enough to turn pro.

After some years spent teaching law in Toronto and chairing the Labor Board in British Columbia, I returned to Harvard Law School as a professor on Labor Day weekend of 1978. And in what is probably the fastest conversion I have ever experienced, it took only four weeks for me to switch my lifetime allegiance from the Yankees to the Red Sox in that season's historic pennant race. That is why I was moaning rather than cheering when Bucky Dent's pop fly went over Fenway's Green Monster as a fair rather than a foul ball, costing my Sox that sudden-death playoff game.

Back in those days I was teaching the basic subjects of labor and torts, and no one at Harvard thought there was anything legally special about sports to warrant a law school course on the subject. A year later I began to learn the truth on that score, when four of my labor law students said they wanted to write their final-year theses on how the law was and should be shaping the players market in the four major sports.

The late-1970s absorptions by the NHL and the NBA of their respective WHA and ABA rivals gave us Boston fans the benefit of watching such all-time greats as the WHA's young Wayne Gretzky coming to play the Bruins, and the ABA's Julius Erving playing against the Celtics, who had just picked up Larry Bird from college. As someone who regularly went to those games—then just for fun, not for research—I had the good fortune to be introduced by my Harvard colleague Alan Dershowitz to Red Auerbach, by then president of the team. Sitting just a couple of rows behind us, Red often educated me about how teams should play their games.

At around that same time a growing number of HLS students were asking me to create a sports law forum that would bring in major figures to enlighten us about what the law was doing in the industry. I agreed to begin that program only when Auerbach accepted my invitation to be co-chair. Red would say at the beginning of each session, "The professor will teach you about the law in the courts and the books, and I will teach you about the law on the courts and the streets."

Red and I spent a half-dozen years in that venture, one that let my students learn a lot from major league guests in this field. By the late 1980s my HLS students had persuaded me—and I had persuaded my dean Jim Vorenberg—that there was more than enough intellectual content in this field to justify granting academic credit for a course in sports and the law. But given the wide array of moral as well as economic challenges generated by sports for lawyers, we needed a text that offered students in-depth presentations of them. Again I had the very good luck, when I was down in New Orleans, of running into one of the pioneering law professors in this field, Gary Roberts. Soon the two of us were collaborating on *Sports and the Law,* which depicts the historic and legal setting for the sports industry and poses all of the key public policy issues raised not just in professional leagues but also in college athletics, professional tours, and international games (especially the Olympics).

In the field of sports law I have devoted almost all of my efforts to teaching and writing about the issues (and watching and enjoying the games), rather than to participating in the legal contests. One reason I did not get more deeply involved in the practice of sports law was that I was asked by my present dean, Bob Clark, to create a new course on entertainment law and write its text, *Entertainment, Media, and the Law.* Teaching and writing about the way the law shapes this industry provided many helpful perspectives on both the similarities and differences between entertainment and sports. I will be noting a number of the comparisons in this book.

Perhaps it was my move into the entertainment field that stimulated me to write a rather different depiction of the key issues here than what I had presented in my earlier scholarly works, such as *Governing the Workplace* and *Medical Malpractice on Trial*. These new fields require books aimed at a broader audience. In *Leveling the Playing Field* (as in its forthcoming entertainment counterpart *Speech for Fun and Profit*) I do offer serious judgments about the major legal policy questions posed by these industries. But *Leveling* is written in a fashion that allows fans to understand what must be done to make the games better for them, not just for owners and players. And those academics or practitioners who would like more legal and economic details and references can take comfort in the fact that these are all available in the Weiler and Roberts text *Sports and the Law*.

When I began my professional life, I never dreamed that its focus would shift from labor and personal injury law in the 1980s to entertainment and sports law in the 1990s, just as Harvard was naming me its Friendly Professor of Law. I wonder if my long-ago hockey coach could ever have expected that after following his advice to "hit the books, not just the pucks," I would end up writing not just about the law of "work and torts" but also about the law of "fun and sports."

CONTENTS

Leveling the Playing Field

SPORTS ON TRIAL

American fans rarely open the sports section of the newspaper or turn on the sports news without reading or hearing about a lawsuit. The legal battles may involve individual players (ranging from Casey Martin to Latrell Sprewell), team owners (like Al Davis or George Steinbrenner), or, most often, leagues and the players' associations. Sometimes they involve broad sports organizations such as the International Olympic Committee (IOC), which, for example, made an instant decision in Nagano, Japan, to bar from future Olympic Games any athletes found to have smoked marijuana, but which was reluctant to take action against cities that had won the chance to host the Games by channeling money into the pockets of IOC members.

The popular impression that there is a litigation frenzy in sports is fairly accurate. Sports is one of the two industries that are now most inundated with lawyers and lawsuits; the other is entertainment. But few of us realize that many of the films we watch also generate legal disputes. For example, almost no fans knew that the hit film *Jerry Maguire* produced a lawsuit by Reebok soon after it reached the screen, or that settlement of that suit required changing the movie's ending on home video and television.* By contrast with sports, these entertainment suits and their outcomes are almost always buried in the back pages of the general press or covered only in trade journals such as *Variety* and *Billboard*.

---

* Reebok thought it was getting a script that had Cuba Gooding Jr. literally saying early in the movie, "Fuck Reebok," but at the end (after winning the Super Bowl for his team) making a commercial saying, in effect, "Love Reebok." But when Tom Cruise saw fans' reactions to the test screening, he had that last scene dropped, leaving the ending with him embracing his lover and her child, rather than with Gooding embracing Reebok. Needless to say, Reebok did not like having put up around $3 million to secure that not-so-loving role, so its lawyers persuaded Sony's to restore the Gooding ending to *Jerry Maguire* (after Gooding, not Cruise, had won an Oscar for his performance).

1

Thus it is just the insiders in the movie, television, and music businesses who are aware of the difference the law makes in their working lives.

Americans have a love-hate relationship with lawyers. Sometimes we celebrate the lawyer as Sir Galahad fighting to protect downtrodden individuals against oppressive powers that be: think of Gregory Peck in *To Kill a Mockingbird*. The more common image of lawyers is the one conveyed by the title of the Jim Carrey movie *Liar, Liar*. By the end of this book, after having traced the ways in which the law has transformed the world of sports, we will see that the lawyer's role is much more complicated than it appears in either of those scripts.

The reason the law is built right into the design of sports—for better or for worse—can be seen from the fundamental contrast between sports and entertainment. At first glance, the two would seem to be part of the same family. From the point of view of fans, spectator sports are as much a part of our leisure lives as movies and television. That is why entertainment conglomerates like Time Warner, Disney/ABC, and Rupert Murdoch's Fox are now regularly acquiring teams like the Braves, the Angels, and the Dodgers to make sure they have games to broadcast on their television and cable channels.

Yet beneath the surface these two branches of our leisure lives have qualitatively different characters. The essence of the worlds of movies, television, theater, music, and trade books is captured in the phrase "speech for fun and profit." This feature regularly brings into play such bodies of law as the First Amendment, copyright, contracts, and international trade to determine *who* can say *what* in front of *whom*, whether in a film, a play, or a book.

Much of that same law also applies to sports "products" once they appear on television or become attached to merchandise. However, the true essence of sports is athletic competition, a fierce struggle by players and teams pushing each other to new heights—Michael Jordan leaping even higher above the rim, Mark McGwire slamming the ball even farther over the wall. But the very existence of a game to play, let alone a championship race to savor, requires that the participants cooperate off the field to create a fair and balanced match-up on the field.

That is why any sports venture must have a league or other body to establish rules for the game that make the contests challenging to players and attractive to spectators. Making such rules is often not an easy job. For example, the National Collegiate Athletic Association (NCAA) and the United States Golf Association (USGA) have been facing similar dilemmas: should they put serious limits on the power of aluminum bats and titanium clubs to preserve the challenge for players trying to hit a home run in a ballpark or score a birdie on a golf course that cannot itself expand with the technological power of these sports weapons? And in a team sport like baseball, by contrast with an individual sport like golf, an even bigger challenge is how to design the team lineups and league schedules in a manner that leaves fans never knowing for sure who is going to win the immediate game or the season championship.

The privately fashioned law of each sport is complex. The NCAA Manual, for example, runs to over 500 pages and is just about as easy for fans to read as the Internal Revenue Code. The National Football League (NFL) and National Basketball Association (NBA) versions of the salary cap for their players are equally Byzantine. That is why the senior officials in sports—including league commissioners and leaders of players' associations—almost always ascend to their positions from legal careers.

There is, however, a fundamental legal and social problem posed by such centralized authority in sports. Once club owners or colleges have come together to form an NFL or an NCAA, that organization becomes the single dominant major league in its branch of sports. This gives it strong monopoly power to wield in dealings with players, fans, and taxpayers—and the history of sports displays a number of abuses of such power.

One egregious example was the decision by NCAA members in the early 1990s to place a $16,000 cap on salaries any school could pay to what the NCAA called "restricted earnings coaches," in order to avoid a "catastrophic cost spiral" in their "non-profit" sports business. One victim of this new NCAA rule was Pete Gaudet, who had previously been paid around $70,000 a year as an assistant coach of Duke University's basketball team, the Blue Devils. Gaudet's salary was slashed to less than a quarter of that amount during the 1994–95 season, even though he stepped in to replace the Blue Devils' ailing head coach, Mike Kryzyzewski—who was paid around $1 million for *not* coaching that year.

A less obvious use of this power took place in the NFL in 1998, when the league auctioned off the franchise that would return the Browns to Cleveland for $530 million, nearly four times the previous top price for any expansion franchise in sports. This exponential growth in team value had two major sources. First, the NFL had used its central control over the broadcasting of team games on television to secure a $2.2 billion annual deal from the competing networks like NBC versus CBS. Second, the NFL owners had used their control over scarce new franchises to extract from Cleveland taxpayers $250 million in subsidies to build a luxurious facility to house the new Browns. And just a year later the NFL raised the expansion record to $700 million, when the Houston billionaire Bob McNair outbid the Los Angeles billionaire team (which included Tom Cruise) with the help of $200 million contributed by local Texas taxpayers to replace what had once been their Eighth Wonder of the World, the Astrodome.

Such apparently exorbitant price hikes cannot, however, justify applying to sports the same legal standards that govern the rest of our economic or leisure lives. Again, comparing sports with the entertainment industry illustrates the point.

Television networks cannot come together in a central body that submits a single low bid for NFL (or NCAA Final Four) broadcast rights, any more than they can for any other type of programs. We would be shocked, for example, if the National Association of Broadcasters (NAB) were to initiate a spring "draft" of new TV shows being offered by producers, allotting the most attractive program to the network with the lowest Nielsen ratings. Back in the early 1990s there was a fierce network bidding war for the "free agent" David Letterman, a war that CBS finally won by signing Letterman for $14 million a year (much more than was then being paid to any athlete). Although entertainment is the field in which the industry salary cap first appeared—in Hollywood in the early 1930s—no one would now suggest that it was either moral or legal for networks or studios to collectively impose such a cap on their performers' pay. And it would be even more unthinkable to see either the Motion Picture Association of America (MPAA) or the NAB install a new commissioner-czar who wielded the power to ban from all movies or television shows any performers who had engaged in illegal and immoral behavior such as using drugs or abusing spouses—even though this too is something that was done half a century ago, to the "Hollywood Ten" Communists.

The fundamental interdependence of participants in sports, by contrast with those in movies or television, explains (but may not entirely justify) the organizational differences between these industries. If a late-night TV viewer wants to enjoy David Letterman, he turns on his local CBS channel without having to worry about how the equally high-priced Jay Leno or lower-priced rivals on other channels are doing. Likewise, nobody thought it affected the quality of moviegoing in 1998 that *Titanic* had cost $210 million to produce while its Oscar rival *The Full Monty* had been made for just $3 million. And if movie fans that winter did not have terribly fond opinions of Woody Allen and his relations with Mia Farrow and her children, they could easily avoid watching Allen as the misogynist in *Deconstructing Harry*, and simply go to see, for example, fresh-faced Matt Damon playing a very different kind of person in *Good Will Hunting*. But in the summer of 1998 baseball fans had no choice but to watch Time Warner's very talented and high-paid Atlanta Braves playing the suddenly low-talent, low-paid Florida Marlins, while Boston Red Sox fans who had booed the wife-beating Wil Cordero out of town the previous year had to put up with Cordero when he came back to play at Fenway Park for the Chicago White Sox.

It is this intrinsic "joint product" quality of sports that requires a central organization to set rules about who is eligible to play and how the available talent is to be distributed among teams to ensure balanced competition. If properly designed, these governing rules can significantly enhance the excitement and appeal of the game for fans. But these rules also determine the shares of sports revenues that go to the various participants. The fact that league organizations tend to be dominated by team owners—whether individuals such as George Steinbrenner or giant companies such as Time Warner—creates an obvious tendency to tip the economic balance in the owners' favor, even if doing so works against, rather than for, the quality of the games being played.

During the first century of organized sports in this country—from the 1850s to the 1950s—players and fans occasionally tried, unsuccessfully, to use public law to address their concerns about the way leagues were using their private power. Then, starting in the 1960s, the situation changed dramatically. Players in all professional sports organized into unions, gaining the right under labor law to bargain with owners and (if necessary) to strike in order to win freer and fairer treatment on the job. Players also learned how to file suits under antitrust law. And players themselves have not been the only beneficiaries of such suits: the "restricted earnings" college coaches like Pete Gaudet won $55 million in their class-action suit against the NCAA. And even some team owners have gone to court to sustain actions of which their fellow owners disapprove: Al Davis when he moved the Raiders from Oakland to Los Angeles and later back to Oakland; Jerry Jones when he sold Nike the right to use the slogan "Texas Stadium: Home of the Cowboys."

Using public laws to contest private league rules has paid off for both players and owners (and, needless to say, for sports lawyers). But has it improved the lot of the public—supposedly the major beneficiaries of laws fashioned by our elected representatives? That is my principal focus in this book: how the law can level the playing field in sports for the public—not just as fans, but also as taxpayers.

I have found these issues to be far more complex than I could ever have imagined when I came to Harvard Law School 20 years ago. After two decades of reflecting on the problems and the options, I have finally made up my mind about the actions that should be taken by owners and players' associations, by courts and administrative agencies, and especially by Congress. My verdicts do not cover just the financial markets for players, franchises, and television deals. They also address the moral challenges confronting the NCAA and the IOC as well as the NFL and Major League Baseball (MLB). For example, should Pete Rose have been banned from baseball for life because he placed bets with bookies on his Reds (to win their games), while Steve Howe was allowed to return to play for the New York Yankees even after his seventh strikeout with cocaine? Should the Nebraska Cornhuskers have reinstated their star running back, Lawrence Phillips, so he could lead them to the college football title over the Florida State Seminoles, even though Phillips had severely battered another Nebraska student, his ex-girlfriend, earlier in the season? Which role model should sports authorities feel the greatest responsibility to display to young American fans? We will start by seeing how the law should treat players who choke their coaches, and we will close by deciding how to level a playing field in which teams now squeeze billions of dollars out of the pockets of taxpayers.

I

THE INTEGRITY
OF SPORTS

1

MISCONDUCT
ON THE FIELD

In the summer of 1997 the Bay Area's Golden State Warriors had fallen
on hard times after giving up several star players. To try to turn the
team around, the Warriors hired P. J. "Butch" Carlesimo as their new
coach. Carlesimo's college and professional clubs had been quite successful, partly because of his often tough, abrasive, even foul-mouthed
exchanges with his players. But when his new team got off to a terrible
1–14 start in the 1997–98 season, Carlesimo's relations with the Warriors deteriorated—especially his relationship with Latrell Sprewell, a
player who had blossomed into an All-Star under the mellower style of
Rich Adelman, Carlesimo's predecessor.

The animosity between Sprewell and Carlesimo literally came to a
head on December 1 in a closed practice session. The coach upbraided
Sprewell for lackluster effort, and eventually ordered him off the floor.
When Sprewell refused to leave, Carlesimo moved toward him. They
shouted profanities at each other, and Sprewell said, "Butch, if you don't
trade me, I'm going to kill you!" Then he grabbed Carlesimo's neck and
squeezed it for several seconds, until other players pulled him away.
Even after 15 minutes in the locker room, Sprewell was still very angry.
He went back out on the court, told Carlesimo he hated him, and took a
swing at the coach, grazing his cheek. This time Sprewell was escorted
out of the building.

When the practice was over, Carlesimo met with team management,
who decided to suspend Sprewell for at least ten games. After that decision was announced to the press the following day, both the National
Basketball Players Association (NBPA) and Sprewell's agent said that
they would accept this penalty (and the accompanying loss of $940,000
in salary), and that Sprewell would also apologize to Carlesimo. How-

ever, the next day the Warriors' owner Chris Cohen decided that a better move for his team would be to terminate Sprewell's entire four-year, $32 million contract, relying on the standard contract ban on players' engaging in "acts of moral turpitude."

The Warriors took this step against Carlesimo's advice, whose validity was immediately confirmed when word filtered out that other NBA teams (in particular, the San Antonio Spurs) wanted to sign the suddenly available Sprewell to fill an important shooting guard gap in their playoff-contender lineups. To head that off, NBA Commissioner David Stern announced on December 4 that Sprewell would be suspended from playing for any club in the league for a full 82 games (representing $8 million in lost salary) in order "to preserve the integrity of and maintain public confidence in" the NBA. Stern surely did not believe that Sprewell had been trying to *murder* Carlesimo. However, with the media characterizing Sprewell's behavior as among the "most infamous, most outrageous acts in the history of sports," Stern said that "a sports league does not have to accept or condone behavior that would not be tolerated in any other segment of society."

The NBPA immediately filed a grievance on Sprewell's behalf, and the arbitrator, John Feerick, came down with a mixed verdict. First, he held, the fact that Sprewell had still been emotionally angry and upset, rather than cooled-down and cold-blooded, in his second assault on Carlesimo meant that the Warriors did not have "just cause" for finding that he had committed the kind of deliberate act of moral turpitude that would justify termination of a guaranteed contract. Second, Feerick concluded that Commissioner Stern had gone too far in imposing an 82-game suspension, and that 68 games was the more appropriate length for preserving the integrity of basketball. NBPA Director Billy Hunter celebrated a "victory that is shared by Latrell and the other 400 members of our union," while Stern lamented the unduly "charitable" decision by the arbitrator as meaning that only in the NBA could an employee "choke your boss and hold your job."

Spitting in the Umpire's Face

To help us understand the true nature of the issues in Sprewell's case, let us look at some other notorious examples of misbehavior by players, beginning with Roberto Alomar, who spat in an umpire's face. On the final weekend of baseball's 1996 regular season, Alomar, the Baltimore Orioles' All-Star second baseman, got into a heated argument with an umpire, John Hirschbeck, about a called third strike. After Hirschbeck said something that Alomar considered demeaning of his Puerto Rican mother, the player spat in the umpire's face. American League President Gene Budig immediately suspended Alomar for five games, a punishment that would keep him out of the Orioles' playoff series with the Cleveland Indians. However, the MLB Players Association quickly filed an appeal on Alomar's behalf, which prevented any suspension from starting until the following spring, after Budig conducted a full-blown hearing. This kept Alomar in post-season play, enabling him to hit the 12th-inning, 5th-game home run that clinched the opening playoff series for the Orioles over the Indians.

Alomar apologized to Hirschbeck and also donated $50,000 to a foundation set up to combat the disease that had killed Hirschbeck's young son. Nevertheless, Americans demonized Alomar. Many fans were appalled by what they considered very lenient treatment of behavior that the Hall-of-Famer Joe Morgan called "the most despicable act by a baseball player, ever." *Sports Illustrated* said that a five-game penalty the following April, rather than that October, was "ludicrous, galling, appalling—choose your adjective!" And the one issue that the 1996 Vice Presidential opponents Al Gore and Jack Kemp (a former Buffalo Bills star quarterback) agreed about in their October television debate was that baseball needed to institute much faster and tougher suspensions of misbehaving athletes to provide the proper role models for American youth.

The *Sprewell* and *Alomar* cases pose questions about the appropriate penalties for misbehavior: for example, should players be suspended for 5 games for "spitting" and 82 games for "choking"? But with respect to *when* the suspension should take place, I believe it would be in the best interests of baseball (and other sports) to have *all* player suspensions served during the regular season rather than the playoffs. (The one exception would be suspensions for infractions that were designed to win playoff games by cheating in them: for example, using a corked bat.) This would ensure that the punishment was actually borne by the player who was guilty of misconduct, rather than by his team and its fans. Baseball fans watching the 1996 Orioles-Yankees games were better off when they knew that each club had its best talent out on the field, as the Yankees won this American League playoff series on their way to the World Series title. By contrast, recall what happened when the NBA punished players for fighting during the 1997 and 1998 playoffs. In 1997 the New York Knicks lost Patrick Ewing and thus lost their series to the Miami Heat, and in 1998 the Heat lost Alonzo Mourning and thus lost that series to the Knicks.

Not only would a policy of regular-season suspensions minimize the harm inflicted on innocent teammates and fans, it would also increase the financial penalty imposed on guilty players. Players' salaries are paid for regular-season play, and playoff awards and bonuses now represent only a tiny fraction of the pay of stars such as Alomar, Ewing, and Mourning. Clearly, the most effective (as well as most equitable) deterrent for players' misconduct is one that is directly targeted at a guilty player's own pockets, rather than at his team's big-game performance.

I was stunned to learn from the Alomar case, though, that current MLB rules in fact generate exactly the opposite result. When Alomar did sit out the first five games in April 1997, the Orioles (and their fans) lost the value of his services for those early-season games. However, the Orioles were required to pay Alomar his salary for those games because of an arbitration victory the MLB Players Association had won for Larry Walker three years before. While Walker was leading the Montreal Expos to first place in 1994 (before the players' strike brought that season to an end), he charged the mound after being hit by a pitch, setting off a brawl among players and getting himself a four-game suspension. But when the case got to arbitration it turned out that MLB clubs had long been paying their players during suspensions by the league for misconduct on (rather than off) the field. Thus the arbitrator concluded that even the cost-cutting Expos were bound by that "past practice" reading of the standard player's contract, and the team had to pay Walker $88,000 for the four games he had missed.

Roberto Alomar began the 1997 season not only by shaking hands with John Hirschbeck and offering him another apology but also by donating to charity the $180,000 in pay to which the *Walker* precedent legally entitled him for the five games of his suspension. That form of personal atonement displayed Alomar's true character, in spite of his admittedly unseemly behavior the previous September. It did not, however, address this underlying flaw in baseball's current regime for ensuring the quality and integrity of the game. If only to protect its members who play by the rules and do not physically attack their opponents, in the next round of baseball negotiations the Players Association should agree to amend its collective agreement so that the penalty for misbehavior on the field no longer takes the form of a paid vacation. But baseball (and other sports) should also revise their rules so that players' suspensions are served during the regular season when their salaries are being paid, rather than in critical playoff series when the team and its fans most need the fractious players' services.

How Long a Suspension?

Even without pay, Alomar's 5-game suspension for spitting in the face of an umpire does seem too soft. However, Sprewell's eventual 68-game suspension (with $6.4 million in lost pay) seems far too harsh, especially when compared with these other NBA precedents:

- During the 1994–95 season, Vernon Maxwell of the Houston Rockets received a 10-game suspension after going into the stands and hitting a fan who had been heckling him.
- During the 1996–97 season, Dennis Rodman of the Chicago Bulls was suspended for 11 games for kicking a cameraman in the groin after stumbling over him by the side of the court.
- During the 1977–78 season, Kermit Washington of the Los Angeles Lakers received a 26-game suspension (60 days) for slugging Rudy Tomjanovich of the Houston Rockets in the face. Tomjanovich had been trying to act as peacemaker in a set-to between Washington and the Rockets' Kevin Kunnert. Washington's blow knocked Tomjanovich to the floor, where he fractured his skull, ending his All-Star playing career.

Numerous other physical confrontations between NBA players and their coaches (as well with teammates) have not produced team contract terminations or league suspensions.*

Surprisingly, in the flood of stories about the *Sprewell* case, no one

---

* A week after the Sprewell-Carlesimo confrontation, two Washington Wizards players, Rod Strickland and Tracy Murray, got into a fierce fight (over a woman) at the team's hotel in Charlotte. Several hours later they showed up heavily bandaged to play (and lose to) the Charlotte Hornets. A few days later the Wizards announced that the team was fining the players $25,000 each, and everyone seemed to find this a sufficient penalty for that violent event.

ever mentioned an even more notorious incident of players' violence, one that took place in baseball back in 1965. Juan Marichal of the San Francisco Giants and Sandy Koufax of the Los Angeles Dodgers were pitching against each other in an important pennant race game. While Marichal was occasionally throwing the ball near Dodger batters, Koufax was not retaliating against the Giants. Thus, when Marichal was at the plate, the Dodgers' catcher John Roseboro grazed Marichal's head with a ball he was supposedly throwing back to Koufax. Marichal turned around and slugged Roseboro on the head—but with his bat, not his fist. After a fierce brawl among all the players, Marichal was thrown out of the game while Roseboro was carried off the field with a concussion. For that egregious misbehavior, Marichal was fined $1,750 by the league and suspended for eight games (and he eventually paid $7,500 to settle Roseboro's tort suit). No one suggested that Marichal should be suspended longer for his destructive blowup. Indeed, Marichal and Roseboro were reconciled by the time Marichal was installed in the Hall of Fame.

Numerous distinctions were offered between *Sprewell* and the other NBA cases. One was that Sprewell had launched not one but two attacks on Carlesimo, which, in Commissioner Stern's view, made the second a "clearly premeditated assault." However, the arbitrator concluded that these two attacks, only 15 minutes apart, were part of the same heated confrontation.

Another argument offered in favor of the harsher punishment of Sprewell is that there is a fundamental difference between a player's attacking the head coach (or another management figure), and attacking players, other employees, or fans. I find rather troubling the claim that the "boss" is entitled to greater protection from assaults by employees than anybody else in American life. In any case, such a policy would merely have given the Warriors the freedom to terminate Sprewell's contract. It would not have justified the league's banning Sprewell from playing for any other club that believed he would have a more amicable as well as more productive relationship with its coach.* Evidently that was the

---

* Suppose, for example, that during the 1996–97 NBA season the Bulls' Dennis Rodman, rather than kicking a cameraman during a game in front of the fans and television cameras, had kicked the Bulls' coach, Phil Jackson, during a team practice. And suppose that, as punishment, the Bulls had then fined Rodman the $940,000 that the Warriors initially fined Sprewell. Not only would the Bulls' owner Jerry Reinsdorf never have terminated Rodman's contract (espe-

verdict of the New York Knicks when they traded some valuable talent to the Warriors to secure Sprewell at the start of the NBA's 1999 "lockout" season. Ironically, this lockout by the owners cost Sprewell the extra 14 games and $1.6 million in salary he had been awarded by Arbitrator Feerick in this apparent NBPA legal "victory."

Tyson versus Holyfield

What is truly distinctive about the *Sprewell* case is vividly displayed by a comparison of Sprewell's actions with those of Mike Tyson. In June 1997 Tyson bit off part of the ear of Evander Holyfield while they were fighting for the heavyweight championship. The Nevada Boxing Commission imposed on Tyson a one-year ban, similar to what Sprewell had received from the NBA commissioner. But consider these differences between Tyson's actions and Sprewell's: Tyson inflicted a very painful injury on Holyfield; he did this as part of his effort to win the fight; he did it in front of a worldwide audience of boxing fans who had paid up to $50 to see the fight on pay-per-view TV; and he cost these fans the chance to see the fight go on to a legitimate competitive ending. Clearly Tyson deserved (and received) a far harsher penalty than those given to Alomar for spitting on an umpire, to Maxwell for hitting a fan, and to Rodman for kicking a cameraman. It is less clear that Tyson deserved more punishment than Marichal, who knocked out Roseboro by slugging him on the head with his bat, let alone Washington, who fractured Tomjanovich's skull while Tomjanovich was trying to break up a fight.

Each of these offenses shared critical features with Tyson's but not with Sprewell's: they all involved a player attacking someone who was not part of his own team, and they all took place in public view during the game rather than behind closed doors during a practice. The penalties meted out by league commissioners should be significantly more severe for players who strike fans (or opposing players) during a public game than for players who strike their coach (or teammate) during a private practice or trip. My bottom-line verdict, then, is that both Commissioner Stern and Arbitrator Feerick got it wrong in the *Sprewell* case.

cially against Jackson's advice), but I cannot believe that Commissioner Stern would have suspended Rodman for the full season, depriving the Bulls of a key asset with which to retain its NBA championship that year.

Choking one's coach (or other supervisor) should be considered a violation of the "morals" language in an individual employment contract (a principle that the NBPA accepted in the new 1999 wording of the "behavior" clause in standard player contracts). However, that kind of private battle within the team should not be grounds for the commissioner to bar the player from any other club in the league because his presence supposedly threatens the "integrity of and public confidence in the game."

2

HONORING CIVIL RIGHTS
IN SPORTS

When golf was first appearing in American life in the late 19th century, Mark Twain characterized this sport as a "good walk spoiled." A century later the powers that be in the golf world, convinced that their game was now the *best* kind of walk, believed the sport was in danger of being spoiled by a cart. This "threat," though, came from a player who attracted widespread popular sympathy and support: Casey Martin. But the fact that sports fans loved Martin as much as they detested Latrell Sprewell does not mean that his case presented a less complex challenge to the law and morality of sports.

One reason Martin began playing golf as a child was that he was born with a rare disabling condition—Klippel-Trenauney-Weber (KTW) syndrome—that precluded most other athletic activities. Malfunctioning veins in his right leg obstructed the circulation of blood, and his calf muscles gradually atrophied. In spite of the obstacles (including severe pain) caused by this condition, Martin's golf blossomed to the point where he was able to lead the Stanford University golf team to the NCAA title (even before Tiger Woods became his roommate and teammate), and to make the Academic All-America team for all college athletes.

During Martin's time in college, his KTW syndrome steadily worsened. He was in constant pain, and the condition made it dangerous as well as difficult for him to walk. Especially after Martin embarked on a professional athletic career, his situation posed a major question for the sports authorities. Should the rules of the game be modified to allow someone with a disabling condition to ride a cart rather than walk the course?

The NCAA reached an affirmative verdict on this score after a thorough medical examination of Martin's condition and an assessment of the essential features of golf, his chosen sport. But the reaction of the PGA Tour was negative, leading another disabled American, Bob Dole, to quip that PGA now seemed to stand for "Please Go Away!" Although players on the Senior Tour (aged 50 years and up) were permitted to use golf carts and all golfers were occasionally required to do so for logistical reasons during regular and Nike Tour events, PGA authorities refused to carve out a special exception from their general no-cart rule for someone with Martin's condition. So in late 1997 Martin went to court to challenge that PGA stance under the Americans with Disabilities Act (ADA). He soon secured the legal relief he wanted. In 1998 Martin was regularly riding a cart both on the Nike Tour and during an occasional regular Tour event; he was even able to return to the San Francisco Bay Area to compete with Tiger Woods in that year's U.S. Open. However, backed by golfing stars like Arnold Palmer, Jack Nicklaus, and Fred Couples, PGA Tour Commissioner Tim Finchem appealed the trial judge's ruling as an unacceptable intrusion on the integrity of golf.

The Tour did not, of course, contest the medical basis for Martin's claim that he was suffering a severe physical disability of the type covered by the ADA. The PGA's concern was that a legal directive altering its no-cart rule would give a competitive advantage on the course to the golfer who was riding rather than walking.

Historical Treatment of Blacks in Sports

Leaving aside for the moment the question of whether it is appropriate for golf to have a Casey Martin riding a cart while his competitors like Tiger Woods must walk, let us consider the more fundamental claim of the Tour that the rules of its game should be exempt from the ADA and other civil rights laws. Even fans who were personally sympathetic to Martin felt qualms about seeing the PGA Tour (and other sports) subjected to any government regulation or private litigation about what happened on the course (or the field). Surprisingly, in discussions of this broader issue in the newspapers or over the air, there was little mention of the past treatment of civil rights by the PGA and other sports authorities.

When the Professional Golfers Association was created in 1916, its charter limited membership to the "Caucasian race." Even as late as the 1950s, Negro League stars such as Ted Rhodes and Charles Sifford were still not allowed to compete against PGA stars such as Ben Hogan and

Byron Nelson. But the 1950s also saw the courts begin to use the Constitution—as interpreted by the Supreme Court in *Brown v. Board of Education*—to strike down rules by state *public* boxing authorities that prohibited "Caucasians" from boxing "Negroes." But it was not until the early 1960s, when Congress was preparing to subject *private* organizations to a new Civil Rights Act, that the PGA relented and gave black golfers the right to play on the Tour. It was this early application of civil rights law to entities like the PGA Tour that paved the way for Tiger Woods to become the star of the Tour in the late 1990s. Similarly, in the early 1970s, Congress refused, despite pressure from the NCAA and its supporters, to exempt sports from a new law requiring equal treatment of women in education. This law, Title IX, has produced not just a flourishing of athletic competition among American women but a new and popular professional sport—women's basketball (which may soon be followed by women's soccer).

Baseball, "America's national pastime," is the sport in which this invidious feature of our national history is best known. Unlike the rules of the PGA, Major League Baseball's constitution did not have an explicit "Caucasians only" clause. Indeed, MLB's first commissioner, Kenesaw Mountain Landis, insisted in 1942 that "there is no rule, formal or informal, or any understanding—unwritten, subterranean, or sub-anything—against the hiring of Negro players by the teams of Organized Baseball." In truth, though, there was a tacit agreement among the owners, enforced by Commissioner Landis, that no team would break the barrier to black players. This was a time when Negro Baseball League stars like Josh Gibson, Butch Leonard, and Satchel Paige were regularly besting their MLB counterparts in privately organized off-season exhibition games. But rather than bring those future Hall-of-Famers into MLB to turn around long-time last-place clubs such as the St. Louis Browns, owners and general managers were instead recruiting one-armed white players like Pete Gray. In the early 1940s Landis reportedly blocked the sale of the Philadelphia Phillies to a group headed by Bill Veeck when he heard that Veeck was planning to restock the Phillies with talent from the Negro League. Essentially the same organized exclusion of black players took place in the National Football League—this one initiated by George Preston Marshall after he had bought the Boston Redskins and moved them south to Washington, where Redskin fans stood respectfully for the playing of "Dixie" before the kickoff.

The major change in this situation was precipitated, not by enactment of a law, but by the death of Commissioner Landis in 1944 and his replacement by a senator from Kentucky, Albert "Happy" Chandler. Chandler's view was that "if a black boy can make it to Okinawa and Guadalcanal, hell, he can make it to baseball!" Thus Chandler did not allow the other owners to block Branch Rickey and his Brooklyn Dodgers from signing Jackie Robinson and bringing him to the majors in 1947, the year the Dodgers lost the World Series to the Yankees in the seventh game. Meanwhile, Bill Veeck had acquired the Cleveland Indians, to which he also brought Larry Doby in 1947 and Satchel Paige in 1948, when Paige was 42. That year Doby and Paige were instrumental in winning the Indians what is still their most recent World Series title.

Racial Diversity in Present-Day Sports

In racial matters, the ethics of American society, including sports, had dramatically improved by 1997—the golden anniversary of Jackie Robinson's appearance at Ebbets Field and the same year Casey Martin was seeking to introduce a very different antidiscrimination standard into golf. However, true to the general "revolution of rising expectations," current social values have us looking for even broader protection of a larger array of historically disadvantaged groups—not just blacks but women, the elderly, and the disabled.

As we shall see, it is often very difficult to decide how to apply broad civil rights standards (especially in the ADA) to the world of sports while preserving its distinctive need for a level playing field. At the same time, the fact that sports organizations such as the PGA Tour almost always wield monopoly power means that we cannot comfortably rely on social and market pressures to ensure that the sports establishment will adhere to such community values. The same reasons that each sport requires a single body with the *authority* to define and enforce the rules of the game also mean that such a body must not enjoy full legal *autonomy* regarding the treatment of minorities who have been excluded from the game.

It is encouraging that professional sports, especially baseball, have become our greatest success story in the racial integration of the American work force. Black athletes now make up approximately 80 percent of NBA players, 66 percent of those in the NFL, and 17 percent of those in MLB. Concern is often expressed about that disparity between the NBA and the NFL on the one hand and MLB on the other, especially since the black share of MLB rosters dropped from about one-third in the late 1970s to one-sixth in the late 1990s. However, that concern is misplaced. Not only is the 17 percent black share of baseball players significantly larger than the 12 percent black proportion of the adult population, but the sharp increase in opportunities and salaries in professional basketball and football has changed the athletic focus of many young black Americans. Equally important, the reason blacks have a smaller share of MLB rosters is not that whites have a larger share: the latter (at 58 percent) have fallen far below their overall population distribution. The reason is that Hispanics now represent one-quarter of MLB players, whereas in the 1970s they were less than 5 percent. And it now appears that Asians have begun to take the same trail blazed by African Americans over the last half-century and by Hispanic Americans (and Dominicans and Cubans) over the last quarter-century.

Given the importance of racial and ethnic diversity in the moral example that sports offers Americans, an event like the 1998 All-Star Game seems a great accomplishment. It was so not just because the numbers of white, black, and Latino players seemed large enough for each group to stock its own All-Star lineup. Even more, it was so because everyone watching knew that Mark McGwire, Ken Griffey Jr., Sammy Sosa, and the others had made it to the game because of their personal accomplishments and fan appeal: they had been neither excluded nor included because of their racial or ethnic origin.

Yet some observers would still have raised questions about the fact that both managers in that All-Star Game were white. This is a visible illustration of the apparent systemic underrepresentation of blacks and Hispanics in the ranks of MLB managers and NFL and NBA head coaches. Blacks currently fill less than 20 percent of head coaching positions in the NBA, 10 percent in the NFL, and 13 percent in MLB (though baseball has a long-time Hispanic manager of the Montreal Expos, Felipe Alou, and also a new manager of the Milwaukee Brewers, Davey Lopes, who is both African American and Hispanic American). In most American industries, this minority share of high-paying management positions would seem to be a victory rather than a defeat in the battle against racial exclusion. (Again to use the motion picture industry for comparison, a black movie director like Spike Lee is far more a statistical exception than an NBA head coach like Lenny Wilkens.) However, since the vast majority of managers and coaches come from the ranks of players, the gap between the 80 percent black share of NBA players and the 20 percent black share of NBA head coaches persuades many observers that the leagues and their commissioners should adopt official affirmative action standards and programs that would bring these figures closer together.

Few issues in present-day American public life evoke more heated debate than "affirmative action" (at least in the sense of hiring preferences tied to racial distribution). In this domain as in others, the experience in sports provides American fans and citizens with valuable illustrations of what should and should not be done on this score.

Needless to say, in the past blacks were just as deliberately excluded from major league coaching as from playing. But even after Jackie Robinson and his successors had made it clear to club owners and fans how valuable black players (and later Hispanics and Asians) were to the teams on the field, it took considerably longer to make similar progress in managerial positions in the dugout. Until the early 1990s there had been only five black managers in the history of MLB—the first being Frank Robinson, who began managing the Cleveland Indians in 1975. Football was even worse, with its racial barrier to black head coaches not broken until 1989, when the Oakland Raiders installed Art Shell in that position.

These exclusions were certainly not part of a league effort to reserve managerial and coaching ranks for "whites only," as had been done to players in team sports until the mid-1940s and on the PGA Tour until the early 1960s. Rather, the stark underrepresentation of blacks among managers and coaches was due to owners' stereotypes about blacks' intellectual skills in management (by contrast with their physical skills in play), and to the resulting lack of role models for black players who were considering whether to try for careers in management once their playing days were over. It is precisely this type of racial vacuum that affirmative action programs can and should be designed to fill, even after explicitly negative discrimination has been eliminated.

However, a look at the situation of managers and coaches in professional sports today suggests that there is no longer a tangible need for the types of race-based preferences that now spark heated controversies in educational and employment settings. A significant number of blacks have been hired to fill managerial and head coaching positions. Of course, like their white counterparts, blacks in these positions not only get hired but also regularly get fired when their teams lose. But before Cito Gaston lost his job after his Toronto Blue Jays fell to last place in 1997, he had been honored for managing the Blue Jays to Canada's first two World Series victories in 1992 and 1993. Meanwhile, Dusty Baker had won two Manager of the Year awards with the San Francisco Giants; Dennis Green, Ray Rhodes, and Tony Dungy had received similar plaudits for reviving their respective NFL teams; and the NBA Hall-of-Fame player Lenny Wilkens had surpassed Red Auerbach as the coach with the most team victories in NBA history.* Perhaps even more important in the long run, blacks now fill a substantially larger share of big-league assistant coaching positions: 30 percent of the total in the NBA, 20 percent in the NFL, and approximately 15 percent in MLB (where another 11 percent of assistant coaches are Hispanics being groomed to follow in the footsteps of Felipe Alou and Davey Lopes).

This current sports situation provides a welcome corroboration of what has long been my scholarly view about the appropriate scope and limits of full-blown "affirmative action" in the sense of special racial preferences and standards. It is a mistake, on the one side, to assume (as do critics of affirmative action) that to give a black person something of an edge (that is, a preference) in competing for a historically white position is to inflict on his white competitor the same exclusionary treatment that Josh Gibson and Butch Leonard experienced from baseball in the 1930s. On the other side, it is a mistake for the proponents of such

---

* College basketball witnessed a similar success story in the spring of 1998. The barriers to African-American head college coaches had already been broken by such greats as John Thompson, who with Patrick Ewing won Georgetown its first major NCAA championship in 1984. But back in the 1960s the University of Kentucky's Adolph Rupp had been not only the all-time leader in college basketball team victories and NCAA titles but also sad testimony to the racial history of America (including its sports). For example, just before losing the 1966 NCAA championship to an all-black Texas Western team, Rupp was quoted as saying that he would never add a "coon" to his all-white lineup. In the summer of 1997 Kentucky's head coach (and NCAA winner) Rick Pitino left the university to set the new record in head coaching salaries with the Boston Celtics. As Pitino's successor, Kentucky appointed its first black head coach, Orlando "Tubby" Smith, who had been an assistant to Pitino at Kentucky before going on to successful stints as head coach at Tulsa and Georgia. In the spring of 1998 Smith became the first coach to win an NCAA title in his first season with a team, proving once again that African Americans win championships off the court as well as on it.

preferences intended to undo the effects of past racism to assume that it is legitimate to practice such affirmative discrimination until we have secured and maintained the designated numbers and proportion of minorities in the positions in question. Instead, our aim should be to create a critical mass of minorities occupying and succeeding in positions from which they have historically been excluded. We want to drive home the message that these kinds of Americans have both the talents (as viewed by employers) and the opportunities (as viewed by minorities) to succeed in these roles.

Because of the special "winner takes the lion's share" nature of the sports marketplace, once these practical as well as formal barriers to minorities have been removed, there is little or no danger that a racially prejudiced owner will choose to install a less talented white, rather than a more talented black, as manager or head coach, and thus risk letting the team lose the pennant race. Notwithstanding their invidious history of racial discrimination, baseball and other sports are now perhaps the best starting point for declaring victory in the wars about race. We should commit ourselves to the principle that it is the quality of each candidate's talent, not the color of his skin, that determines who will secure the scarce and ever more lucrative positions both on the field and in the dugout.

Treatment of Disabled Athletes

While in racial matters we may favor a "color-blind" policy, in a situation like that of Casey Martin we cannot readily aspire to a "disability-blind" posture, whether in the broader society or even in the sports world. Disabling conditions such as Martin's KTV syndrome affect not only their victims' ability to live but also their ability to play. The question facing sports and legal authorities, then, is whether the normal rules of the game should be altered to accommodate such special physical conditions. Indeed, in addressing particular athletic disabilities, sports authorities have occasionally felt it necessary to alter their rules to the disadvantage, not the advantage, of the affected athletes. Let us consider the way boxing authorities dealt with Tommy Morrison.

When he beat George Foreman to win the World Boxing Council's (WBC) heavyweight title in the early 1990s, Morrison was characterized as "The Great White Hope" for boxing. After losing that title to Lennox Lewis in October 1995, Morrison sought to revive his career with a fight in Las Vegas in early 1996. Promoter Don King's plan was to match up Morrison with Mike Tyson (who had been released from prison in 1995) in what seemed to be a potential "pot of gold" on pay-per-view TV. However, when Morrison took the random blood test that the Nevada Boxing Commission required of fighters, he turned out to be HIV-positive. The Nevada Commission forced the cancellation of the pending bout, and, along with other state boxing authorities, Nevada adopted a rule prohibiting HIV-positive fighters from boxing in that state.

Tommy Morrison was simply the latest in a series of star athletes who discovered in the 1990s that they were HIV-positive, thus driving home to Americans the much broader scope of an affliction that during the 1980s was viewed largely as a product of homosexuality. One of the most tragic was Arthur Ashe, who had been the Jackie Robinson of tennis during the 1960s. Ashe had become a national idol when he broke the racial barrier to what was then seen as an upper-class as well as whites-only sport, then went on to win at Wimbledon and other major tennis tournaments. Some time after he retired from play, Ashe underwent an operation during which he was given a blood transfusion with HIV-infected blood. The news was finally made public in the early 1990s when Ashe's condition had evolved into full-blown AIDS, and he passed away shortly afterward.

At around the same time, NBA fans were shocked to learn of the HIV-positive condition of Earvin "Magic" Johnson. Magic is clearly one of the top half-dozen players in the history of basketball, and a personality who, along with Larry Bird and then Michael Jordan, turned the NBA into one of America's most popular leagues. In the fall of 1991 Johnson learned that he had become HIV-infected from one of his many sexual encounters with women, and he voluntarily retired from the game. A few months later Magic changed his mind and returned to lead the U.S. "Dream Team" to victory at the 1992 Olympic Games in Barcelona. However, when Johnson reported to the Lakers training camp that fall, his return was met with significant opposition from many NBA players—most vociferously, from Karl Malone—who were worried about the danger to themselves if they happened to collide with Magic in play.

These concerns seemed to get some validation when the news came out in 1994 that Greg Louganis, perhaps America's greatest diver ever, had been HIV-positive during the 1988 Olympics in Seoul, South Korea, when he had again won the gold medal in both platform and springboard diving. The disclosure of his condition six years later raised qualms among his 1988 competitors, who recalled that during one practice in Seoul Louganis had struck his head on the diving board and shed some of his infected blood into the swimming pool. The Louganis saga helped influence boxing commissioners in Nevada and other states to keep HIV-positive fighters out of the ring.

We now know enough about AIDS to permit a more reasoned appraisal of the dangers, if any, that HIV-positive athletes pose to their competitors. The actual risk of contracting HIV comes from unprotected sex, contaminated needles, and other means of direct transmission of one person's bodily fluids into another's body (a risk that doctors did not know about when Ashe had his operation in the early 1980s). In athletic competition, then, the only real danger arises when one bleeding player comes into contact with another bleeding player, such that the infected player's blood can go directly into the other's system. Recognizing these facts of life, the NBA initiated the current league procedure of stopping the game at the first opportunity after a player has begun to bleed, and removing the player from the floor until after the bleeding has stopped and the wound has been bandaged. This accommodation is what allowed NBA fans and players (especially Karl Malone) to welcome Magic Johnson back in 1996 for one final stint on the court with the Lakers.

The nature of a sport may, however, place some limits on a league's ability to modify its rules to protect the athletes while also preserving the integrity of the game. To some, boxing may seem to be a rather egregious illustration of this special need for "integrity." (This sentiment is felt especially by those who would like to outlaw a sport in which even championship bouts occasionally witness one fighter *killing* the other, as Sugar Ray Robinson did to Jimmy Doyle in 1974.) But there has never been a reported case of HIV transmission taking place during a boxing match, and only two of the more than 20 million cases of HIV discovered in the world have been identified as by-products of bloody fistfights. Still, the fact that no case of HIV infection through boxing has yet been documented is no guarantee that it could not happen in the future. Boxing is a sport in which both contestants regularly bleed at the same time; moreover—unlike football players, for example—boxers do not wear uniforms or helmets that would offer them some protection against injury and infection.

One possible way to address this problem would be to change the rules of the "game"—perhaps by interrupting a fight if one boxer begins to bleed, and calling off the match if the bleeding cannot be stopped quickly. This is exactly the plan that Tommy Morrison and his promoter adopted when Morrison made a brief return to the ring in late 1996 in a match held in Tokyo and shown in America on pay-per-view. If either boxer's bleeding required ending the fight, the one who was ahead on points was to be declared the victor. Happily for Morrison these rules never came into play, because he knocked out his opponent in the first round, pocketed $500,000, and then retired from boxing.

In the spring of 1998 the U.S. Supreme Court ruled (in a case involving dentistry, not sports) that the HIV-positive condition is a form of disability whose victims can have a right to protection under the ADA. So any successor to Tommy Morrison who wants to continue boxing after contracting HIV is likely to file suit to strike down the current state rules that exclude him from this sport.

In my view, this will be a difficult legal judgment call. For better or for worse, the kind of professional boxing that fans expect to see involves two fighters battering each other until one is unconscious. Thus, calling off the match because one or both happen to be bleeding seems to violate the very essence of this sport. On the other hand, boxing has no single authority establishing and enforcing the basic rules of the game. Instead, a host of authorities around the world compete to license matches for their locality (say, in Tokyo rather than Las Vegas), and a host of private bodies (like the WBC) compete to designate the match as a battle for *their* championship. In turn, the managers and promoters of the two boxers negotiate the terms of an event whose principal audience is on worldwide television.

Thus, if the opponent of a future Morrison is fully informed of the risk of a deadly infection, and if viewers are fully informed of the risk of an aborted match, it is not clear why this kind of ad hoc boxing deal should be legally barred from the ring. However, if boxing were finally to become a true sport with a central authority, then I do not believe the ADA should be read as overriding the key feature of this sport—that the two boxers have to fight to the end.

Casey Martin's Cart

With the *Morrison* boxing case as background, we are in a better position to appreciate the complexities of the *Martin* golf case and its interplay of the PGA's private law and the public ADA law. By contrast with race, physical disabilities may well require special treatment in sports, whether for purposes of exclusion or inclusion. The central legal question is how far we can go in offering equal opportunities to the disabled athletes without sacrificing the essential (not merely the historical) features of a sport.

Everyone agrees that Casey Martin needs a cart to have *any*, let alone an *equal*, opportunity to play on the PGA Tour: walking that distance is something he can no longer do. However, the ADA does not require that an organization offer an accommodation to the disabled that would alter the fundamental nature of its program. For example, no lawyer would ever have suggested that the Tour de France, the major event in cycling, was required to allow Lance Armstrong to use a motorcycle to race for 2,200 miles around the Alps, in order to accommodate the testicular cancer that Armstrong had developed in 1996 and that had spread into his lungs and brain. Happily for that sport as well as the Armstrong family, Lance's doctors were able to restore his athletic, not just his personal, health so that he won the 1999 Tour in the most enchanting sports accomplishment of that year.

Unhappily for Martin, there has never been a chance that his doctors could remove his KTW disability. Given that fact of life, the basic thrust of the Tour's legal argument, backed by testimony from Arnold Palmer, Jack Nicklaus, and especially Ken Venturi, was that golf (like cycling) is inherently "a game of stamina." The example they all cited was the 1964 U.S. Open. On what was then the 36-hole final round of the Open, the temperature was nearly 100 degrees and the humidity was oppressive. On the 17th hole Venturi was advised by his doctor (who was treating his illness) to stop playing in order to avoid the risk of dying. Venturi decided, instead, to take some tablets and accept the risk, and he walked the next 19 holes to win his first major golf tournament by one stroke. As Palmer put it, preserving the PGA Tour's "walking rule" was essential to "inject the element of fatigue into the skill of shot-making." Thus, the PGA claimed, to allow a disabled golfer such as Martin to ride instead of walk would give him the equivalent of a one- to two-stroke advantage in scoring.

Although Judge Thomas Coffin was correct in finding much more myth than reality in that argument, the situation is more complicated than was portrayed in popular views on both sides. It is true that golf is a game of stamina. But the kind of exhaustion that comes into play in competition is much more psychological than physical, and even a player's physical fatigue is far more the result of swinging the clubs than of walking between shots. The distance that a golfer must walk to play 18 holes is approximately five miles, and he walks that distance over a five-hour stretch; in other words, he covers about one mile an hour, while stopping every two or three minutes. When amateur golfers play, either just for pleasure or in club competitions, some regularly ride in carts and others walk. In that situation no one claims that the rider should give a stroke or two edge to the walker. And one major difference between professional and amateur competitions is that the walking professional golfer has a caddie to carry his clubs, rather than having to carry or pull them himself.

There is, however, an occasional exception to this rule: for example, a round that is being played in 100-degree heat on a very hilly course. Near the end of that kind of round, not only are players feeling exhausted, but their scores are likely to be rising. Venturi's famous 1964 victory is no longer a directly relevant illustration, because the U.S. Open's special 36-hole final round has now been reduced to 18 holes (to make the finish of their tournament more attractive to television viewers and fans on Sunday afternoon). Even that year, the principal source of Venturi's physical problem was the combination of heat, humidity, and the resulting dehydration; in fact, that day a number of spectators sitting in the stands experienced essentially the same problem as Venturi. The oppressive weather would also affect a golfer riding a cart, especially the kind that Martin uses, which has no shading roof.

Even with those qualifications, it is likely that a golfer riding a cart on a very hot and humid day and over a very hilly course would have some modest advantage. But on a normal day and course, riding a cart imposes a *disadvantage*. The best corroboration of that point can be found on the PGA's own Senior Tour. All but a handful of the Senior Tour members choose to walk rather than to ride because they have found that walking casually from shot to shot—with a caddie carrying their clubs—leaves them better prepared physically and mentally for the next shot. (Walking also gives spectators a more attractive view of the players, a factor that Jack Nicklaus admitted in his testimony was the principal reason for the PGA's special no-cart rule.) By contrast, a golfer who rides must always climb into his cart after each shot, and then climb out of the cart to take his next shot. These steps involve the use of some energy—as well as some pain for Martin—and also some disruption in concentration on the hole and the next shot. It is this regular disadvantage of having to ride a cart to accommodate his disabled condition that persuaded me that it is legally and morally fair to afford Martin the occasional (but still modest) advantage that he gets from riding a cart on a very hot day and a very hilly course.

This is one lesson I would draw from the cases we have seen so far: to preserve the moral appeal of the game, the authorities must take their time to think through the complexities of the issues in order to reach the right verdict, rather than react hastily to the emotional reactions of players, owners, and fans to offer an instant decision.

The *Sprewell* case would have been handled much better for basketball had the Warriors' owner and Commissioner Stern taken the time afforded by the initial ten-game suspension to work out with NBPA Director Billy Hunter the final disposition of the case. In the *Martin* case, the PGA Tour did have the luxury of a full-blown trial to reflect on the issues. After hearing all the evidence, but before the trial judge had rendered his verdict, the Tour should have moved to modify its cart rules while working out with Martin the specific limits on cart design and use. After all, many of the 14 million seriously disabled Americans have at some time played golf, and they still follow the Tour. Surely almost all of them, along with millions of others, empathized with Martin and his condition. The image and appeal of professional golf would have been enhanced if Tour authorities had been the ones who embraced Martin as a new role model for their sport in 1998, just as they had done with Tiger Woods in 1997, rather than reluctantly abiding by the judge's order while pursuing their appeal. Just as I was finishing this book in the fall of 1999, Martin won a spot on the next year's Tour. As fans of both golf and civil rights, let us hope that the PGA does not win a legal ruling that its commissioner then uses to tell Martin, "Please Go Away."

3

THE DEADLIEST SIN
IN SPORTS

When spring training began in 1989, Pete Rose stood at the pinnacle of baseball. The Cincinnati Reds star seemed guaranteed election to the Hall of Fame when he became eligible in 1992; in fact, many believed Rose had a fighting chance of being the first Hall-of-Famer ever elected by unanimous vote, an honor not even conferred on Babe Ruth or Jackie Robinson. Rose's topping of Ty Cobb's record for most base hits in a career had attracted even more national attention in 1985 than had Hank Aaron's outstripping of Babe Ruth's career home run total in 1974 or Cal Ripken's passing of Lou Gehrig's record for consecutive games played in 1995.

But Rose occupied an even more special place in the hearts of baseball fans because of his style of play. Physically, Rose lacked superstar assets: he wasn't strong enough to hit many home runs, or fast enough to steal many bases. But he more than compensated for these natural limitations with his motivation and tough-mindedness. As a 1963 rookie Rose was quickly dubbed "Charlie Hustle" because of his trademark head-first slide and his sentiment that he'd "walk through hell in a gasoline suit to play baseball." And while that go-for-broke style contributed a great deal to Rose's 4,256 career hits, his personal statistical favorite was his all-time career high of 1,972 team *wins*.

Rose was the team leader of several other future Hall-of-Famers, including Johnny Bench and Joe Morgan, who made up the Cincinnati "Big Red Machine" that won the 1975 and 1976 World Series. Then free agency came to baseball, permitting Rose to move to the Philadelphia Phillies at what was briefly a record-setting baseball salary. While in Philadelphia Rose inspired a talented but historically underachieving Phillies team to win its first World Series in 1980, and *Sporting News* named Rose its Player of the Decade. When Rose returned to Cincinnati in the early 1980s, not only to chase and surpass Ty Cobb's record but also to be baseball's first player-manager in decades, his home-town admirers expressed their adulation by renaming the road to Riverfront Stadium "Pete Rose Way."

However, hidden from both these adoring fans and from MLB authorities was the darker side of Rose's character. Of his several personal vices, the most malignant was his addiction to gambling. Rose began gambling as a youngster, betting at the racetrack with his father. By the time he was a highly paid star in the free agent market, Rose was betting tens of thousands of dollars weekly on a host of sports. Though he occasionally won big money, like most compulsive bettors Rose usually lost significantly more than he won.

Even his million-dollar annual salaries were not large enough to sustain Rose's lavish standard of living and also meet his gambling debts. He was able to trade on his name and his fame to avoid paying off at least some of these losses to bookies who enjoyed socializing with him. More important, a new source of cash had recently emerged—autographing. Players' autographs sold especially well at card-signing shows, where a popular headliner like Rose could command a $25,000 fee for a single appearance. But Rose insisted that his payment for such an appearance be delivered in cash, in a paper bag, so that he could avoid disclosing it to the Internal Revenue Service on his tax return.

Another major mistake was that Rose carried on much of his off-the-field betting with fellow members of a Gold's Gym conditioning center, people who were involved in the local drug trade. It was an FBI investigation of drug activity at the gym that brought to the Bureau's attention Rose's own illegal activities. After determining that Rose was not involved in cocaine dealing, FBI officials decided that his regular betting with bookies was not a crime significant enough to justify use of scarce law enforcement resources. Instead, they passed on to the IRS their information about the income that Rose had not been reporting. But by early 1989, when Rose and the Reds were heading south for spring training, the FBI's findings were being leaked to the media and to the commissioner's office.

At this time the commissioner's office was being vacated by Peter Ueberroth, who had been mainly preoccupied with the economics of baseball—in particular, how to secure higher profits for the owners by orchestrating a collusive agreement among teams *not* to bid higher for free agents. Unluckily for Pete Rose, Ueberroth's successor, the former president of Yale Bart Giamatti, was far more passionate about baseball's tradition and morality than about its money. Thus when word filtered out that Rose was not just betting illegally through bookies (a venial baseball sin) or betting on *baseball* games with these bookies (a mortal but redeemable sin), but actually betting on his own team's games, Giamatti saw this as the deadliest of all sins in baseball.

Like any other human authority, a commissioner can mete out punishment for such "sins" only if he can establish that they took place. Having clear proof would be especially important in dealing with a baseball legend like Rose. Giamatti and Deputy Commissioner Fay Vincent brought in as baseball's first "special prosecutor" John Dowd, Vincent's Yale Law School classmate, a former head of the Justice Department's Organized Crime Unit. Dowd had to deal with a fundamental difference between Rose's gambling and other kinds of misconduct by players, such as Roberto Alomar's spitting at an umpire or Latrell Sprewell's choking his coach. Gambling is a classic "victimless crime." Such private and voluntary transactions between consenting parties typically leave little or no corroborative evidence. Instead, just as with sexual charges against a U.S. President, the MLB's special prosecutor needed testimony from one party to the offense who had agreed to turn the other in. As it turned out, Dowd was able to secure such a sworn affidavit from Rose's principal bookie, Ron Peters. Peters said that Rose would call almost every day during the season to place bets on several baseball games, usually $2,000 a game. With only one exception that the bookie could recall, Rose always included the Reds game in his bets; without exception, Rose always bet on the Reds to win.

In order for Dowd to extract this crucial affidavit from Peters, Giamatti had to agree to send a letter on Peters's behalf to the judge presiding over the bookie's criminal prosecution. Giamatti wrote that Peters had been "candid, forthright, and truthful" with Dowd, and that he had provided "significant and truthful cooperation" in MLB's investigation of Rose. On its face this kind of letter, signed by Giamatti before he had ever heard from Rose on the issues, was incompatible with Giamatti's obligation as commissioner to conduct the MLB process "like judicial proceedings, and with due regard for all the principles of natural justice and fair play." Instead, Giamatti had endorsed the veracity of Peters the accuser without having even listened to Rose the accused.

The reason Giamatti took that step and Vincent and Dowd endorsed it was that they all assumed the letter to the judge in the *Peters* case would be confidential (as such documents normally were). But unfortunately for the commissioner, the judge, Carl Rubin, was a long-time fan of the Reds and especially of Pete Rose. Judge Rubin sent a copy of Giamatti's letter to Rose's lawyer Reuven Katz and also called a press conference to condemn Giamatti for "carrying out a vendetta against Pete Rose."

Judge Rubin's own actions attracted significant criticism, forcing him to step down from the *Peters* case. However, he had handed Rose's legal team the "smoking gun" they were looking for to try to block action by Giamatti. Unlike an Alomar or a Sprewell, Pete Rose had no right to have an arbitrator scrutinize the judgment of the commissioner, because he was a manager, and managers are not members of a union with the protections of a collective agreement. But Rose's lawyers could and did go to court, seeking a ruling that Giamatti's statement of his opinion in the case had denied Rose the "natural justice and fair play" he was entitled to as a matter of general contract principle. This move set off a summer-long litigation battle between Giamatti's and Rose's legal teams about whether the Ohio state courts or the federal courts had jurisdiction over this issue. Although the commissioner's office did win that jurisdictional contest, the merits of the case would still have to be resolved by a federal district judge from Ohio, the home of Rose and the Reds, not from New York, the site of the MLB commissioner's office.

By the end of the summer of 1989 Rose and Giamatti decided to give up their litigation and instead settle the underlying dispute. The best that Rose could have won from even a successful lawsuit was a judicial directive that replaced Giamatti with a neutral arbiter of this case. Moreover, by this time Rose had conceded that he regularly bet with bookies on sports events, though, he insisted, not on any baseball (let alone Reds) games. But historical precedents made such an admitted association with bookies a violation of the catch-all "best interests of baseball" provision in MLB Rule 20. Equally important, Rose's legal team was having to focus its time and its client's resources on dealing with the IRS, which had tightened its noose around Rose's neck for failing to report his cash earnings from baseball card shows, cash that Rose had been spending instead with the bookies. Consequently, Rose agreed to accept a ruling by the commissioner that he was "permanently ineligible" to work in baseball; at the same time, the commissioner agreed that Rose would eventually have a right to apply for reinstatement.

At his own press conference following the signing of the agreement, Rose apologized for his behavior and said that he was looking forward to his daughter's birthday a year later, when he would be applying for reinstatement. However, at the commissioner's press conference, Giamatti said that he believed Rose had bet on Reds games, and that in doing so he had stained and disgraced the game. Giamatti even told the sportscaster Howard Cosell, in a private phone call that same day, that by banning Rose he was "ridding baseball of a cancer." By that point the opinion of fans and reporters across the country was in much that same vein.

This battle, however, left no winners—except for the Reds' owner, Marge Schott, who replaced Rose as manager with Lou Piniella and saw her Reds win the 1990 World Series over the Oakland Athletics. Only a week after his press conference, Giamatti died of a heart attack, to which the enormous strain of the Rose affair was undoubtedly a contributing factor. That winter Rose pleaded guilty to evading taxes on nearly $400,000 in unreported baseball card revenues, and he went to jail for several months. The rules for admission to the Hall of Fame were changed to bar induction to the Cooperstown shrine of anyone on baseball's permanent ineligibility list. Both Fay Vincent, Giamatti's friend, colleague, and successor as commissioner, and Bud Selig, who later had Vincent removed from office and then took his place, made it clear that on their watches Rose should not expect reinstatement to the good graces of the game.

The Black Sox Give Birth to the Commissioner

The source of popular support for the ban on Rose was an event that had taken place 70 years earlier: the 1919 World Series, which saw the Chicago White Sox dubbed the Black Sox because of their corrupt behavior. Indeed, this case gave rise not only to the anti-gambling rule violated by Rose but also to the commissioner's position and authority wielded by Giamatti.

The seeds of the Black Sox scandal had been sown in 1918 by Hal Chase. Chase was the top first baseman of the era, who in 1914 was the target of bidding and litigation wars between the White Sox and the Buffalo team in the Federal Base Ball League. The following year, after the Federal League folded, Chase returned to MLB, this time with the Cincinnati Reds. But in August 1918 he was suspended by his player-manager, the future Hall-of-Famer Christy Mathewson, because of reports that he had suggested to his teammates that they throw a few games—games on which Chase had bet against the Reds. That winter the National League president, John Heydler, held a hearing and concluded that Mathewson had misinterpreted mere "joking" remarks by Chase. Two years later a lawsuit involving another Reds player, Lee Magee, conclusively established that Chase and Magee had been fixing Reds games in 1918. In the meantime Chase had been picked up and later released by the New York Giants and their manager, John McGraw. But by that time he had served as a go-between for White Sox players and certain gamblers who were hoping to fix the 1919 World Series.

That season the Chicago White Sox, led by "Shoeless" Joe Jackson, their batting champion, and Ed Cicotte, their star pitcher, had replaced the Boston Red Sox as the top team in baseball. However, Jackson, Cicotte, and other White Sox stars were significantly underpaid relative to other MLB players, because they were now tied by baseball's reserve system to the owner of the White Sox, Charles Comiskey, known as the "cheap stingy tyrant." That situation made these players receptive to Chase's suggestion that they accept an offer from some of his gambler friends to throw that fall's World Series for $100,000. Jackson, who was paid only $6,000 by Comiskey for hitting .351 that year, was to get $20,000 from the gamblers, and Cicotte, who earned a mere $5,000 for winning 29 games, was to get $10,000.* Following that deal, the Sox lost the 1919 Series to the Cincinnati Reds by five games to three.

Even before the Series began, there were rumors floating around that the "fix is in," generated by the huge wave of betting money suddenly flowing in on the underdog Reds. Notwithstanding the innuendoes in

---

* From Cicotte's point of view, taking the bribe was also a payback for what Comiskey had done to him. In addition to his $5,000 salary, Cicotte's contract offered a bonus payment if he won 30 regular-season games. But after Cicotte reached 29 victories and the White Sox clinched the AL pennant, Comiskey told his manager to keep Cicotte on the bench rather than give him a shot at winning 30 games or more. This was tantamount to a contract "fix" by the owner, subverting what should have been a fair bet and a well-earned payoff for a great pitching season.

newspaper commentary that winter, no one in baseball followed up on the issue: neither Comiskey, nor American League President Ban Johnson, nor the owners' National Commission (of which the chairman, August Hermann, happened also to be the owner of the Reds). Not until September 1920 did the story break wide open, when several of the Sox players were called before a Chicago grand jury in another case. Young, uneducated, and without legal counsel, they admitted to the deal with gamblers for the 1919 Series. It was after one of those grand jury sessions that Jackson emerged from the courtroom to hear a young boy uttering the famous lament "Say it ain't so, Joe!"

The eight White Sox players who had admitted their involvement in the fix were both suspended from baseball and criminally prosecuted in the summer of 1921. So were several of the gamblers, though not the kingpin, Arnold Rothstein of New York (later the model for a major character in F. Scott Fitzgerald's *The Great Gatsby*). Several of the indicted gamblers did not even show up for trial—including Hal Chase, who had decamped to California and its "outlaw" league, and whom that state refused to extradite to Illinois. As the trial was to begin, it turned out that the players' signed confessions had disappeared. Apparently Chicago's departing district attorney had taken along many key documents from the grand jury hearing when he left for New York to work for Rothstein. In the absence of signed statements, and with the players now testifying that they had not been involved in any gambling scheme, a Chicago jury acquitted them all.

No such break for the players was forthcoming from baseball, which had recently installed its first commissioner. The Black Sox scandal had precipitated the MLB owners' decision to establish a centralized authority over their game. The owners' first choice for the position was former President William Howard Taft, but Taft turned the job down in favor of the Chief Justiceship of the Supreme Court. The owners' second choice was Kenesaw Mountain Landis, a Chicago-based federal district court judge who had endeared himself to MLB when he held in abeyance the initial antitrust suit filed by the Federal League until the parties settled it with the dissolution of that league. Previously, Landis had made his name as the "trust-busting judge" who had dared to impose a then-huge $30 million antitrust fine on John D. Rockefeller's Standard Oil. However, in the course of the Federal League case, Landis expressed concern about subjecting his favorite sport to the constraints of an antitrust regime that might "tear down the foundations of the game so beloved to thousands—as a national institution."

When the owners offered Landis the position of commissioner, he accepted it, but only after they agreed to pay him $50,000 a year and to adopt his wording of the commissioner's total authority—over owners, managers, and players—to ensure the best interests of the sport. Labeled by *Sporting News* the "absolute ruler of the game," Landis made clear his attitude toward the Black Sox even before their trial began: "There is absolutely no chance of any of them [being allowed] to come back to Organized Baseball. They will remain outlaws!" Landis stuck to that resolve even after the Chicago jury's acquittal, and his ruling went unchallenged by the players.

When another gambling scandal arose in 1926, this one involving the all-time greats Ty Cobb and Tris Speaker, Landis used the same authority to spell out an anti-gambling rule for baseball, the rule that is still in force today. The events leading to this scandal had also taken place back in September 1919, when the White Sox had clinched the 1919 American League pennant, Tris Speaker's Cleveland Indians had secured second place, and Ty Cobb's Detroit Tigers were battling the New York Yankees for third place. Seven years later the story came out that Cobb, Speaker, and several of their teammates had met before a late-season series between the two teams and agreed that the Indians would let the Tigers win the games so that the Tigers could collect the third-place finisher's share of the World Series pie. Apparently, the players had also decided that since they knew who was going to win the games, they might as well place some bets on them.

The source of the revelation in 1926 was Dutch Leonard, who had been a teammate of Cobb's on the 1919 Tigers as well as a participant, he alleged, in the game-fixing/betting deal with Speaker and his teammates. But shortly before Leonard blew the whistle, Cobb, by then the Tigers' player-manager, had sent Leonard down to the minors. This act may have incited Leonard to make up these charges as revenge (though he was implicating himself as well). In those days the commissioner did not appoint special prosecutors like John Dowd to investigate the validity of such charges. Rather, Landis told the press and the public that in his own best judgment neither Cobb nor Speaker had been fixing games. However, because there was significant evidence of players' betting on those games, Landis announced his new MLB rule: any player, manager, or owner who bet any money on a baseball game would automatically be suspended for a year, and anyone who bet on a game involving his own team would be banned from baseball for life.

This account reveals the ultimate irony of the Pete Rose saga: Rose's place in baseball's pantheon of heroes seemed assured after he had surpassed the all-time hits record set by Ty Cobb. But Rose lost his place in the Hall and became baseball's most notorious outcast (much more so than Shoeless Joe Jackson) because of his violation of the anti-gambling rule that Cobb had helped generate, which is still posted in every MLB clubhouse.

The Gambling Problem in Sports

After the commissioner's announcement of MLB's new anti-gambling Rule 21(j), the amount of gambling—at least visible gambling—among baseball's participants dropped sharply. Part of the reason was that Landis rigorously was enforcing the rule, as illustrated by what he did to a team owner, William Cox of the Philadelphia Phillies. Cox had bought the Phillies in 1943 when Landis helped block the sale of the team to Bill Veeck after learning of Veeck's intention to hire players from the Negro League. Only one year later, though, Landis learned that Cox regularly placed small bets on his Phillies to win their games. Landis immediately ordered Cox to sell the Phillies and get out of baseball.

This strong anti-gambling posture was not limited to Landis. His successor as commissioner, Happy Chandler, had a profoundly different view about the value to baseball and the country of Jackie Robinson's entrance into our national pastime. But just as Robinson was to begin his 1947 rookie season with the Dodgers, Chandler announced that Dodgers manager Leo Durocher was being suspended for a year because of his close association with the notable gambler (and movie star) George Raft. Two decades later, in 1979, Commissioner Bowie Kuhn barred both Mickey Mantle and Willie Mays from any official connection with MLB when they agreed to play public relations roles (largely on the golf course) for the new casinos in Atlantic City.

Peter Ueberroth, who had a somewhat more relaxed attitude toward gambling than Kuhn and his predecessors, removed the ban on Mays and Mantle shortly after he replaced Kuhn in the commissioner's office. But the Pete Rose case revealed how strongly Ueberroth's successor, Bart Giamatti, felt that gambling was a threat to the integrity of the game.

Giamatti's deputy and eventual successor, Fay Vincent, was even more passionate about this issue. For example, in 1990, after learning that the Yankees' owner George Steinbrenner had used inside information obtained from an inveterate gambler, Howard Spira, in a contract dispute with the Yankees' star Dave Winfield, Vincent forced Steinbrenner to give up his control over the baseball (though not the business) side of the Yankees for several years.

It is fair to say that Vincent, along with the general public, reacted emotionally rather than rationally to the Steinbrenner case. There is no threat to the integrity of baseball when an owner happens to get (or even buy) valuable information about a player from a gambler, as long as the owner is not betting with that gambler. Indeed, in a 1991 case involving Lenny Dykstra of the Philadelphia Phillies, Vincent let Dykstra off with just a one-hour lecture and one year of probation for having bet and lost around $100,000 in off-season play in an illegal (and criminally prosecuted) poker operation in Dykstra's home state of Mississippi.

Of course, by contrast with Dykstra, Steinbrenner at the time was labeled by magazines like *Newsweek* "the most hated man in baseball." Moreover, by the 1990s there was a players' union and a labor agreement that gave Dykstra a right to challenge the commissioner's decisions before neutral arbitrators, an avenue not available to Shoeless Joe Jackson and his Black Sox teammates in the 1920s. And by the time of the Dykstra case, notwithstanding the outcries over Pete Rose and George Steinbrenner, gambling by major league players no longer seemed to pose a serious danger to the game.

For example, in the late 1990s MLB Security Director Kevin Hallinan investigated Albert Belle and concluded that although Belle had lost something like $300,000 from his sports bets, all of these bets had been placed on sports such as professional football or college basketball, and none on baseball games (let alone those of Belle's own Indians or White Sox). Bud Selig, then acting commissioner, decided that no action at all was necessary to protect the integrity of the game. Of course, that $300,000 in gambling losses seemed like small change next to Belle's five-year, $55 million free agency contract, which had lured him from the Indians to the White Sox (on the way to the Orioles).

A gambling scandal that engulfed Boston College at that same time evoked a sharply different reaction. During the 1996 college football season it came out that several players on the BC Eagles (together with many of their classmates) were regularly betting on sports events. These bets, which tended to be in the $25–$50 range (though occasionally were as high as $1,000), were placed with professional bookies, each of whom employed a Boston College student as his "runner" to collect the bet money and then deliver the winnings. Some bets were placed on the World Series, others on NFL games, and still others on college football. Two were identified as bets on the BC Eagles to *lose* a game to Syracuse, which they did. (One of those two bettors did not play in that game; the other was in the game for only one play.) When this practice was discovered, the college suspended all of the betting players (one of whom was the son of the boxing promoter Don King) for having violated NCAA rules. These rules bar players from betting with anyone on any game involving their school's teams, not simply a team they play on, as well as from betting with a bookie on anything at all, such as the World Series or the Super Bowl.

Most people consider this broad-based NCAA rule justified because of the kinds of college gambling scandals that emerged a year after the BC incident—though with qualitatively different behavior by players. A few former basketball players from Arizona State and Northwestern were discovered to have accepted money from gamblers to "shave" the points by which their teams won or lost games during the 1994 season, while four Northwestern football players had done the same thing to win bets they had placed on their own games.

Both the appeal of betting on sports and the incentives to fix games were greatly enhanced by the invention in the 1940s of a new betting technique, the point spread. People who bet on baseball games (or horse races) have to pick a team to win, and the inequalities in players' talent are dealt with by variations in the odds and thus the payoffs on the teams (or horses). However, the fact that many points are scored in football, and even more in basketball, facilitates the use of the point spread in those sports. The favored team has to win by a minimum number of points in order for those betting on it to collect. The point spread is attractive to gambling fans because it sustains the excitement of the game long after the win-loss outcome has been settled. Unfortunately this technique also makes it easier for professional gamblers to bribe players to affect the betting outcome: players on the favored Arizona State team, for example, could agree simply to shave the number of points by which they would win, without sacrificing their team's prospects for victory.

The first point-shaving scandals in college sports came to light in 1951. One incident involved players at several New York schools, particularly City College of New York, which in 1950 had become the only college ever to win both the NCAA and NIT tournaments in the same year. The scandal took on a national dimension when the same kind of misconduct was uncovered on the part of the All-Americans Alex Groza and Ralph Beard. These two players had taken their Kentucky Wildcats to consecutive NCAA titles in 1948 and 1949, and in between had led the United States team to victory in the 1948 Olympic Games.

One gets some sense of the relative status of college and professional basketball at that time from the fact that, when Groza and Beard graduated in 1949, the NBA agreed to create for them and their Kentucky teammates (known as the "Fabulous Five") a new franchise to be owned by the players. For two years Groza and Beard were first-team NBA All-Stars, and their Indianapolis team was a success both on the court and at the box office. So it was shocking to fans as well as threatening to the NBA when, in the autumn of 1951, Groza and Beard were indicted and pleaded guilty to having accepted bribes to shave points in their college games. The trial judge thought this crime merited a sentence of just three years' probation. But because Groza and Beard had so profoundly violated the integrity of basketball, NBA Commissioner Maurice Podoloff barred them from the NBA for life and insisted that they dispose of their franchise interests within 30 days.

Shortly afterward Podoloff followed the lead of MLB's Commissioner Landis and ruled that the NBA prohibited players from even betting on, not just fixing, team games. Jack Molinas had been an All-American basketball player for Columbia University. As the first-round pick of the Fort Wayne Pistons in the 1953 NBA draft, Molinas signed what was then the highest-paying rookie contract ever, $9,500 for that season. Unfortunately, Molinas had a penchant for betting on games, a habit he had started as a youth with the neighborhood bookie, Joe Hacken, who operated near the Molinas family's Coney Island bar. While playing in Fort Wayne for the Pistons (who had not yet moved to Detroit), Molinas would occasionally call Hacken to bet on the Pistons to win games he felt confident about. But when someone tipped off Commissioner Podoloff and he was able to document Molinas's betting, Podoloff expelled Molinas as a "cancer that had to be excised from the game."

The Gambling Problem in American Life

The late 1990s posed complex questions about what attitude either sports or government authorities should take toward players' gambling. Since Molinas's expulsion from basketball in the 1950s, a dramatic transformation has taken place in the role of gambling in the lives of Americans. Yet it is still illegal for a Pete Rose or a Boston College Eagle to place a bet with a bookie on any game—not just his own. The powers that be in sports have persuaded Congress to preserve their games as the sole exception to the current social and legal stance toward gambling.

American colleges now produce the highest levels of gambling anywhere, including gambling on sports. Surveys conducted in the early and late 1990s reveal that 75–85 percent of college athletes are betting on something, and that 25–35 percent are betting on sports (including some betting or even shaving points on their own games). The athletes' appetite for gambling simply reflects the behavior of the entire student body: around 85 percent of college students gamble at least occasionally, and 23 percent do so at least once a week. Not surprisingly, male students (47 percent) are far more likely than female students (14 percent) to bet on athletic events. More important, nearly 10 percent of the male students (and 2 percent of the female students) show symptoms of being "pathological gamblers," with some betting an average of $100 a day. Gambling now tops drinking and smoking, let alone use of illegal drugs, as the favored indulgence for adolescent Americans.

It is stunning to look at the way gambling has evolved in American society. Back in the early 1960s Americans were legally wagering approximately $2 billion a year. By the mid-1970s that proportion had grown to $18 billion a year, raising some serious social concerns. But by the late 1990s we were legally betting around $640 billion a year. Various estimates, including some by the FBI, put the amount wagered *illegally* in the $100 billion range, bringing the gambling total to around $740 billion.

These figures include just the amounts wagered in commercial gambling ventures—whether legal casinos or illegal bookies—not the sums that Americans bet privately on the Super Bowl or the NCAA March

Madness. In that private context, what one person loses and pays, the other wins and keeps, so there is no net expenditure. By contrast, in commercial gambling part of the money wagered is retained to cover the expenses and profits of the organization operating the business—overall, approximately 8 percent.

That figure indicates that Americans now *spend* about $50 billion annually on legal gambling and another $10 billion on illegal gambling. To illustrate the significance of these figures in our lives, Americans spend around $6 billion a year for admission to sports events, and around $7 billion a year for admission to movies.

This dramatic increase in the gambling share of our personal expenditures is largely due to the transformation of our legal posture toward this form of entertainment. At the beginning of the 1960s virtually all gambling operations were illegal. The only exceptions of consequence were betting on horse races, which required being at the racetrack (for example, at Churchill Downs for the Kentucky Derby), and betting at the casinos that Benjamin "Bugsy" Siegel had launched in Las Vegas in the 1940s. Then came the first fateful public policy decision: in 1963 New Hampshire instituted a state lottery as a source of government revenues, so as to preserve its traditional opposition to "compulsory" income or sales taxes by using instead "voluntary taxation through the sweepstakes." Now 37 states have adopted lotteries for a host of purposes, with the state's take tending to be about 40–50 percent of what Americans fork over at their neighborhood lottery stores. In the mid-1970s New Jersey decided to give a boost to its economy as well as its tax revenues by following Nevada's lead and permitting casinos to open in Atlantic City, a location that was far more accessible to the large urban population. Twenty-four states now have legalized casino operations, many of them on rivers or lakes bordering their neighboring states. In the late 1980s the combination of a 1987 Supreme Court decision (*Carbazon*) and a 1988 federal law (the Indian Gaming Regulatory Act) gave Native American tribes a broad right to open casinos on their reservations. There are now nearly 300 tribal gambling ventures around the country, and the Foxwoods Casino in Connecticut, operated by the Mashantucket Pequots, is reportedly the largest-grossing gambling enterprise in the world.

These legal changes made two important practical differences. First, gambling is now easily accessible throughout the country, with just two states, Hawaii and Utah, still making it entirely illegal (and Utah borders Nevada). In the early 1960s the only way Americans could experience the pleasures of a casino was to use their vacation time and money to fly to Las Vegas or Monte Carlo. Now over 90 percent of the population is within a four-hour drive of a casino, the same distance that many sports fans travel for weekend baseball or football games. In fact, during the 1993 Bulls-Knicks playoff series, Michael Jordan created a splash in the media when he rented a limousine to take his father and friends down to Atlantic City for some late-night gambling after the games were over. Meanwhile, states like New York have eliminated the need to go to the racetrack by instituting off-track betting sites with simultaneous broadcasts of the races. Horse racing is one of the very few sports at which live attendance has decreased over the past several decades, but meanwhile its annual betting amounts have risen sharply, to more than $15 billion.

Not only have governments made gambling more accessible, they have also made it far more popular. They have done so partly by licensing casinos, but even more by running lotteries. When someone wins a big lottery prize (one prize in 1998 hit $300 million for a single Powerball contest), the family's sudden good fortune is a lead item in television and newspaper stories. The prospect of such a life on Easy Street entices many more people to try their luck in the lottery; and when they lose there, to expand their efforts to slot machines in the casinos, and so on.

In almost any other context, this surge would be considered a great success story. For example, the upswing over the last quarter-century in the number and size of sports leagues, game attendance, and television and cable broadcasts has been gratifying to American fans. Presumably the 80-odd percent of adult Americans (including Michael Jordan) who gamble also appreciate the pleasure they experience when they bet in casinos, lotteries, and elsewhere.

However, the surge in gambling (unlike that in sports) has generated something of a social problem along with great personal pleasure. Recall the case of Pete Rose, who was betting tens of thousands of dollars every week with his bookies. Rose was one of an estimated 3 million Americans who are totally addicted to gambling—who cannot stop wagering continuously on their favorite gambling activity, in spite of the risks this creates in their professional careers and personal lives. Unlike the case of smoking, for example, the source of this addiction is psychological rather than physiological. Some people are simply unable to resist the emotional urge to try to win, if only to make up for past losses. Indeed, the competitive pressures generated by this kind of game are similar to some things we are going to see within the world of sports itself.

The incidence of such "pathological" or "compulsive" gambling is significantly higher among adolescents than among adults, and highest of all among American college students, whose families usually have to pick up the bills for their losses. The consequences of such losses are such that even a highly paid player-manager like Pete Rose may feel compelled to evade his taxes in order to pay his bookie: that is why Rose ended up in jail rather than in the Hall of Fame. Approximately 40 percent of white-collar crime (private fraud as opposed to public tax evasion) is now attributable to addicted gamblers, who also account for a substantial proportion of personal bankruptcies, family conflicts, and even suicides. The additional social price that American taxpayers now pay for the surge in personal pleasure in gambling is conservatively estimated to be $5–$6 billion a year.

Legal Bars to Betting on Sports

In sports, it was gambling that precipitated the creation of the commissioner's office and its role in preserving the moral integrity of the game. Sports leagues have also secured substantial financial benefits from this addition to the entertainment market. Indeed, it was a state lottery, the "voluntary sweepstakes tax" devised by New Hampshire in the 1960s, that was used by Maryland in the mid-1990s to lure the Browns from Cleveland to play in a new publicly financed stadium in Baltimore. And because it is lower-income Americans who invest the highest proportion of their income in efforts to strike it rich through the lottery, they were the ones who conferred on Art Modell that $300 million windfall increase in the value of his NFL franchise.

Leagues gain a much broader benefit from betting because of the way it enhances the fans' interest in the game itself. Like the players on the field, fans celebrate their own victory if they have displayed the necessary talent (and luck) in picking the winner. The impact of the point spread on Super Bowl television ratings vividly demonstrates this connection. Super Bowl games are often quite one-sided contests, with the favored team regularly trouncing the underdog. But huge numbers of fans have bets riding on the game (even if only with a friend), and most bets include the point spread that equates competitive balance on this score, if not out on the field. The spread keeps fans watching even lopsided games right to the end, when they learn whether they have won their bets. As the NFL was negotiating its current $2.2 billion-a-year television contracts, it certainly profited from the fact that Americans annually bet billions of dollars on football games. The same payoffs were being pocketed by other leagues (and the NCAA) and also by television networks and newspapers which devote part of their sports coverage to "expert" advice about which teams to bet on (given the spread and/or the odds).

And yet, with the historic exception of horse racing, sports remains the major domain of *illegal* gambling in this country. Of course, it is not illegal for family members or friends to bet among themselves on the games they are watching together. But that kind of private betting falls far short of satisfying the current appetite for gambling on sports. Making a personal bet on who will win the Kentucky Derby or the Super Bowl is cheaper than betting with a parimutuel operator or a bookie, because the bettors do not have to pay the 10 percent take by operators or bookies. But such friendly private bets are possible only if the bettor knows someone else who is willing to bet the same amount of money on the same game and with the same odds or point spread, but for the opposite team. The usual absence of this legal option explains why the vast majority of the $100 billion that Americans now gamble on sports each year is bet through illegal channels (including many office pools).

Four decades ago all forms of gambling, with the exception of racetrack betting, were illegal in every state but Nevada. Not surprisingly, Nevada was also the first place to legalize betting on sports, and this facet of its gambling operations now generates approximately $2 billion in annual wagers in the state. Few other states were prepared to take that step in the 1970s and 1980s, although Delaware, for example, occasionally used "picks" of games as the basis for its weekly lottery. But by the 1990s there was a distinct possibility that other states would follow Nevada's lead here, as they had with casinos, and permit not only off-track betting on races but also accessible betting on all sports through a local taxable entity. The professional leagues and the NCAA reacted by going to Washington and persuading Congress to pass the 1992 Professional and Amateur Sports Protection Act, which now effectively prohibits any state other than Nevada from legalizing betting on sports, supposedly in order to preserve the morality of the games.

This federal gambling prohibition has had no discernible impact on the nearly $100 billion bookie industry; in fact, like most "criminalizing" measures, it has produced some negative side effects. Some college students are now spending time as lawbreaking bookies or runners, thus making it easier for their classmates (including athletes) to violate the law by placing such bets on games. After this initiation, the small but sad percentage of gamblers who become addicted to this illegal activity will feel more comfortable about violating other laws in order to pay off their betting losses—as Pete Rose did with the federal tax laws and Arizona State's Steven Smith did by shaving the points on his team games. And in the 1990s, in an effort to avoid rather than to evade federal law while satisfying this strong and growing consumer demand for betting on sports, entrepreneurs began to use the Internet to offer this service.

It has long been a violation of the federal Interstate Wire Act to make a telephone call from one state to another—say from Massachusetts to Nevada—to place a bet on a sports event. But in the mid-1990s a number of operations appeared in the Caribbean, licensed by governments in Antigua and elsewhere, which invite Americans to place those same bets through their computers. The customer uses his credit card or a bank transfer to open a gambling account with such a firm. He can then use this account to place bets until it is depleted. Within a mere couple of years, the Internet share of the gambling business passed the billion-dollar mark. Given the increasing presence of the Internet in American life and culture, one can well imagine our overall gambling activities approaching the trillion-dollar range in the next few years. To try to head that off, a proposal is now pending in Congress for an Internet Gambling Prohibition Act, which would make it a crime for Americans to use their computers to place bets on sports events with someone in another country as well as in another state. Passage of this bill not only was endorsed by the Report of the National Gambling Impact Study Commission but has been backed by organizations like the NCAA, the Nevada-based American Gaming Association, the Christian Coalition, and Ralph Nader's Citizens' Group—odd bedfellows indeed.

Reflection on this problem has convinced me that gambling over the Internet does call for government action, but that carefully designed regulation would be far more productive than traditional blanket prohibition. Betting via home computers is going to expand the dangers as well as the dimensions of gambling, especially among high school and college students, who are most likely to be compulsive bettors unable to pay for their losses. At the same time, now that the technology of computer-based betting is becoming well known, making it illegal would simply send the process underground, with bookie locations around the world that no longer depend on runners. Our society would be better off with the carefully licensed and regulated computer betting operations that now exist in Antigua as well as in Nevada.

However, Americans may want the law to protect them not only from others, such as unscrupulous operators, but also from themselves—from a gambling addiction. If so, we are going to have to add a key feature to our sports gambling laws, and the Internet ventures suggest the possible solution. People should be allowed to gamble—not just on sports like the World Series or racing's Triple Crown, but also at casinos or on lotteries—only after they have obtained a license to do so. This license—bearing a photo of the user—should not be granted to those below a designated age. It should also serve as a "gambling credit card," the sole source of funds permitted to be used at legal gambling sites. In casinos as well as in Internet gambling, individual credit or bank cards are now a major source of cash for betting; my proposal would also make this licensed credit card the source of *restraints* on betting. With this kind of device, the federal government could establish a maximum level of funds that any individual could use and lose in betting in a given year; the dollar limits would reflect the individual's IRS-documented income and assets. So a person who bet and lost his limit too early in the season would have to wait until the next year before indulging in that aspect of his favored sport—although he could continue to watch and enjoy the games.

This kind of licensing-regulatory regime would, of course, be both an intrusion on the personal freedom of the typical moderate gambler and no full guarantee of protection for or from the compulsive gambler. Moreover, as our current criminal (and athletic) war on drugs has demonstrated, placing legal barriers in the way of personal indulgence can create an illegal underground market to satisfy that indulgence. That is why Americans now spend far more money making illegal bets with bookies than legally attending the games.

I believe that, if the 95 percent of Americans who bet on sports events in a non-compulsive fashion were able to do this legally, the bulk of the illegal market would wither away. The current regime that was sought by sports leagues and established by governments gives us the worst of both worlds. One arm of our government is vigorously promoting gambling as an exciting "sport" in casinos and lotteries, attracting large numbers of Americans to this activity and addicting a few. But when these gambling fans want to place a bet on their favorite real sports event rather than at a legal roulette wheel, another arm of government tells them they can do that only if they can find an illegal bookie. If excessive gambling (either on sports or in casinos) is judged to be a social problem, we need a more rational and consistent approach, designed to ameliorate rather than aggravate the harms of this behavior—in which, legally or not, people will continue to engage. To protect our society from the dangers of betting, whether on sports or elsewhere, what we need is a gambling *cap*, not a criminal ban.

What about Players Who Gamble?

Some serious reflection by sports authorities on their own experience with compulsive gamblers might eventually change their prohibitionist attitude toward betting on sports. However, though *USA Today* did a poll that found two-thirds of Americans saying "it should not be illegal for Americans to bet on sports events," law reform in this domain is unlikely to happen in the near future. Thus, within the current legal regime, what policy should leagues themselves adopt about gambling by their players? What action should a commissioner take toward a Shoeless Joe Jackson who appeared to have fixed the 1919 World Series, or toward a Pete Rose who regularly bet on his own Reds to win, or toward a Lenny Dykstra who played in illegal poker games?

Contrary to Joe Morgan's assertion that Roberto Alomar's spitting in the face of an umpire was "the most despicable act by a baseball player, ever," the throwing of the 1919 World Series by the White Sox deserves that dubious honor. Even shaving the score, let alone throwing the game, should be the "capital offense" in sports, and should result in banishment of the offender from the game.

The very essence of athletic competition assumes that both sides are fighting as hard as they can to win, and thereby spurring each other on

to higher and higher levels of athletic achievement. To maintain the popularity of any enterprise among its customers—to keep attracting sports
fans to spend their money to watch the games—there must be no hint
that the product is tainted. It was no accident that the Black Sox scandal
gave birth to centralized commissioner authority in sports. Although an
individual team might be tempted to ignore misconduct by its own star
player, the other members of the league would suffer the much greater
harm of a tainted product. And just as a bank may fire an employee it believes has fixed the books even if the prosecutor is unable to prove this
in the criminal courts, so also Commissioner Landis was justified in barring Shoeless Joe Jackson from baseball when Landis made the reasonable judgment that Jackson had at a minimum accepted money to throw
the games.*

Happily, game-fixing is no longer a real risk in professional sports,
precisely because of the new economics of the game. Remember that
back in 1919 Jackson made $6,000 for hitting .351 and Ed Cicotte made
$5,000 for winning 29 games. Players with statistics like these would
now be paid $10–$15 million a season. The $100,000 spent by gamblers
to bribe the top players on the 1919 pennant-winning White Sox would
be just pocket change to current stars. Thus, it would cost present-day
gamblers at least $200 million to persuade the stars on a pennant-
winning team to risk their incredibly lucrative careers by throwing the
World Series, and that level of investment would make no economic
sense. Ironically, it may have been the MLB Players Association's winning of free agency bidding by owners for players' services that made it
impossible for gamblers to bid for *non*-services by the same players.
Bribing of athletes (by people who are already breaking the law by betting on the games) is now feasible only in college sports, where the players must live with an NCAA ban (not a mere cap) on salaries.

Of course, the more money that professional team owners pay their
players, the more likely it is that at least some of the players will spend
part of that money on gambling, including gambling on sports. The

---

* There is serious debate over whether Jackson (by contrast with Cicotte) did in fact try to
lose the 1919 World Series, in which he set a long-standing record of twelve Series hits. Apparently Jackson received only part of the $20,000 he was promised, so he changed his mind about
throwing the Series. However, that a star player had been involved in a gamblers' plan to fix the
World Series, and that he had not revealed the scheme to the authorities until after the action of
his teammates, seem to be sufficient reasons for the commissioner to expel him from the game.

long-ago outcry over the Black Sox and the continuing outrage at point-shaving in college basketball have led sports authorities, especially in baseball, to view betting on a game as tantamount to fixing the game. This is what prompted Bart Giamatti to banish Pete Rose from baseball for betting on the Reds, and what impelled Fay Vincent to punish George Steinbrenner for merely associating with a compulsive gambler. But this identification of gambling with fixing a game is misguided. Throwing a game is and should be considered the capital offense in sports. Betting on a game—even one's own game—should not be treated as equally heinous.

It is important to understand that there is no inherent link between fixing and betting on a game. Consider an episode from the spring of 1993. While televising a heavyweight fight, HBO's cameras and microphones accidentally picked up the highly rated boxer Ray Mercer offering money to his journeyman opponent, Jesse Ferguson, to ease up during the match, in order to protect Mercer's $2 million deal to fight Riddick Bowe for the championship later that year. That fix attempt had nothing to do with betting. And remember that MLB's ban on players' betting on their own team's games stemmed from the Ty Cobb–Tris Speaker incident, in which Speaker's Indians were apparently letting Cobb's Tigers win so that the Tigers could beat out the Yankees for third place in that year's AL race. The bets on these games by Cobb, Speaker, and their teammates were simply afterthoughts.

Whatever the reason for fixing a game—whether it be friendship, draft positions, bribes, or bets—the harmful result is the same. Fans are denied what they have invested their hearts as well as their money in: an honest effort by both sides to do their best to win a match whose outcome is supposed to be unknown beforehand.

Not only may players throw a game for reasons other than gambling, but the fact that players have bets riding on a game by no means implies that the game is fixed. Certainly if a player bets a substantial amount of his money *against* his team, this financial incentive to play poorly makes his bet the functional equivalent of a fix, and it should be treated accordingly. But in the massive media coverage of the Pete Rose saga, no one—including Commissioner Giamatti—ever focused on the fact that Rose was always betting on his Reds to *win* their games. Instead, Giamatti and everyone else assumed that this kind of betting threatened the integrity of the game as seriously as did the throwing of the 1919 World Series.

Other examples illustrate the fallacy in that identification. Golfers often have money riding on their club matches, yet no one would dream of saying that these bets create a risk that the player will give away the match (and thus his money) to the opponent. The same is true of an owner, trainer, or jockey who places a bet on his own horse at the Churchill Downs track window before the Kentucky Derby. Even in professional team sports, although players are prohibited from betting on their team to win, they regularly negotiate contracts that pay large bonuses if the team wins, say, the World Series or the Super Bowl. Team management actually prefers these bonus incentive clauses to fully guaranteed contracts, because the "bet" that the player is thereby making on his team's performance constitutes exactly the kind of incentive to win that teams want their players to feel.

Even though, from an economic perspective, betting on one's own team with a bookie generates the same productive incentive as "betting" with the team's owner, betting with a bookie is still illegal. Perhaps the league's concern is that players who bet on their games may end up owing a lot of money to bookmakers engaged in a criminal enterprise. Once players have incurred such a debt to a criminal organization, they may be unable to resist the creditor's pressure to fix their games. The object of MLB rules, then, may be to prevent players (or managers) from falling into the hands of low-life characters, as Pete Rose did with the bookie–drug dealer Ron Peters.

This is a more plausible rationale for baseball's anti-gambling policy, though again, the current finances of professional sports virtually eliminate it as a realistic concern. But it cannot justify the extremely harsh sanction imposed on Rose (or on the NBA's Jack Molinas) for betting on their own teams to win games. To the extent that there is a criminal threat, it comes from whom the player is betting with, not which event he is betting on.

Recall that the Phillies' Lenny Dykstra ran up debts of over $100,000 while playing in an illegal poker operation during the 1990–91 off-season. Yet for that offense Dykstra got only a sharp talking-to and a year's probation from MLB Commissioner Vincent—just a year after Pete Rose was expelled from the game and banned from the Hall of Fame for running up a similar debt with his bookie. An even starker illustration comes from basketball. Shortly after this Dykstra case it was learned that Charles Barkley, then with the Philadelphia 76ers, and Mark Jackson, then with the New York Knicks, were occasionally betting $500 against each other on the outcomes of Sixers-Knicks games. If those bets had happened in baseball, MLB Rule 21 would have required that both players be placed on the permanent ineligibility list, even though their behavior posed absolutely no threat to the integrity of their game. Fortunately for both the players and the fans, NBA Commissioner David Stern displayed his customary practical sense and simply fined the players $5,000 each and told them not to play such "in our face" games anymore.

If only to avoid an uproar from fans about the integrity of the game, baseball and other sports are not going to relax their time-honored rule that no player can bet on his team's games. (One rationale now offered for the rule is that it prevents players from using their "inside information" to place bets just on those games they feel confident their teams will win—though, of course, this was *not* what Rose was doing.) But, for the reasons I have discussed here, MLB should stop treating betting as a capital offense and save expulsion for those who fix games. Even for bets placed with illegal bookies, suspension for a year or so would surely be a harsh enough penalty to send players and managers the message that if they do not comply with this rule they risk a severe financial and reputational loss. In defense of this proposal, let me offer one more incident of gambling in sports, a case I never saw mentioned in coverage of the Rose story.

In the early 1960s Paul Hornung was an NFL star of great magnitude. He had won the Heisman trophy while quarterbacking at Notre Dame, then had led the Green Bay Packers to several NFL championships while winning Most Valuable Player honors for himself. So the country was shocked to hear in the spring of 1963 that Hornung was being suspended for the fall season. League authorities had discovered that Hornung was regularly placing bets on his Packers team—always to win—and they were making him sit out the season in order to preserve public confidence in the integrity of professional football. As promised, Commissioner Pete Rozelle reviewed the case a year later, and lifted the suspension after determining that Hornung had abandoned his gambling habits and connections. Hornung returned to the game and eventually took the Packers to victory in the first-ever Super Bowl and himself to football's Hall of Fame.

Like Pete Rose as an MLB manager in the late 1980s, Paul Hornung and other NFL players in the early 1960s did not have a union and a labor agreement that enabled them to challenge commissioners' decisions in front of an arbitrator. Hornung did, however, have the benefit of a strong competing league, the American Football League, which almost certainly would have hired him—perhaps to play with the rookie Joe Namath for the large-market New York Jets. Whatever the reasons for Commissioner Rozelle's decision, did its moderation impair public confidence in the integrity of professional football? These numbers may provide the answer: in 1963 each NFL team received approximately $400,000 through the league's single television contract; in 1999 each team took in $75 million generated by tens of millions of fans watching games on four different networks. Perhaps before permanently banning Pete Rose to try to protect the integrity of baseball, Commissioner Giamatti should have heeded a message from Oliver Wendell Holmes, America's greatest legal thinker: "A page of history is worth a volume of logic!"

4

THE SPORTS WAR
ON DRUGS

The 1998 Winter Olympics in Nagano, Japan, produced several "firsts." The American team won the first-ever gold medal in *women's* hockey. Snowboarding, a popular pastime on the ski hills, also made its first appearance in the Games. A Canadian, Ross Rebagliati, won that first snowboarding gold medal, but the award was immediately in jeopardy when his post-race drug screen turned out positive for marijuana. Rebagliati quickly appealed, contending that the traces of "pot" in his system must have been absorbed from second-hand smoke at a going-away party thrown for him by his friends in Whistler, British Columbia. Then, when the International Olympic Committee Court of Arbitration looked more closely at the rules for skiing competition, they found to their dismay that marijuana was not on the list of prohibited drugs.

So while Rebagliati was able to take his gold medal back to Whistler for a celebratory party, IOC officials quickly convened a meeting to amend their rules. They decreed that the use of any "social" drug, including marijuana, would disqualify athletes from participating in any future Olympic event, beginning in Sydney in the year 2000. The Olympic authorities always seem to respond much more quickly and vehemently to athletes taking drugs than to IOC members taking bribes from cities.

While gambling has become a major component of American economics and personal lives, it is only a minor problem among athletes, at least at the professional level. Commissioners focus so intensely on the occasional behavior of a Pete Rose because of the historic threat that gambling is felt to have posed to the integrity of the game. Meanwhile, use of drugs like marijuana and cocaine has become the most common offense filling American courts and prisons, moving in exactly the opposite direction from legalized gambling. And the news often features stories of athletes—professional as well as student—who are arrested by the police and disciplined by the league or school for use of illegal "recreational" drugs.

It was in fact the fate of an athlete, Len Bias, that most dramatically focused America's attention on the "war on drugs." Bias had been a basketball star at the University of Maryland. His family's neighbor Arnold "Red" Auerbach had advised him to remain in college for his senior year to ensure that he would be a lottery pick in the 1986 NBA draft. Auerbach's Celtics were lucky enough to secure the second lottery pick that year and used it to select Bias. The day after the draft, Bias flew up to Boston to be introduced to the media and fans, who considered him an ideal addition to a Celtics team with such future Hall-of-Famers as Larry Bird, Robert Parrish, Kevin McHale, and Bill Walton. But late that night, after Bias had flown back to Maryland, he and his college roommates celebrated his future not only with alcohol but also with cocaine. The next morning Bias was dead of convulsions and a heart seizure.

The death of Len Bias precipitated an alliance between President Ronald Reagan and the Democratic (Boston-based) Speaker of the House, Tip O'Neill, to pass the federal Anti–Drug Abuse Act. Bias's fate provided the President and his wife, Nancy, with their single most vivid example for driving home to Americans why they must "just say no" to drug use, as well as for convincing employers to "just say yes" to drug testing of their personnel. The NCAA quickly accepted this request from the Reagan administration and its drug czar, William Bennett. It decided not only to prohibit use of illegal drugs by student athletes but also to institute random drug testing of athletes to detect and deter any such use (though there were no such rules or tests for other college students). And both before and since Bias's death, players' associations in basketball and other professional sports have regularly bargained with owners about the appropriate league policy regarding drug use and drug testing.

Another type of drug made headlines after the 1990 Summer Olympics in Atlanta, where the Irish swimmer Michelle Smith surprised and delighted her fans by winning three gold medals. Smith's miraculous surge in performance aroused a great deal of suspicion; when President Clinton phoned to congratulate her, he added, "Sorry for all that crap the media are giving you. I have to put up with this all the time." As it turned out, both the President and Smith faced much more media "crap" in 1998. She was expelled by the International Swimming Federation for failing a drug test targeted not at cocaine but at "performance-enhancing" anabolic steroids.

Bodies regulating amateur sports, such as the NCAA and the IOC, act unilaterally on issues such as athletes' use of drugs, with no meaningful influence from the athletes themselves. In professional leagues, though, the players have organized themselves into unions that negotiate about league constraints on the players' personal lives, as well as their economic rewards. By contrast with gambling, the drug "problem" in sports arose in the 1970s, after unions were established in all the major sports. And the positions taken by the players' associations about drugs often evoke as much popular concern as do free agency and soaring salaries.

Seven Strikes and Still Not Out

Steve Howe had been the star pitcher on both his high school and college baseball teams, and he was the first-round draft pick of the Los Angeles Dodgers in the 1979 MLB draft. By opening day of 1980 Howe was in the Dodgers' lineup as a reliever, and by the end of the season he had become their stopper, winning the National League's Rookie of the Year award. Howe's career flourished over the next two years. He helped take the Dodgers to the 1981 World Series, in which he saved the deciding game in the Dodgers' victory over the New York Yankees, and in 1982 he pitched in the All-Star game.

But behind these glory-filled headlines Howe's personal life had begun to unravel. Howe had started drinking in high school, occasionally at a bar with his father, and continued at college. When he reached the majors as a highly paid but still immature 22-year-old, he discovered that cocaine had become the drug of choice for those in the fast lane. Cocaine had become so popular in the late 1970s and early 1980s in part because its users experienced few harmful side effects in return for the big rush this (pre-crack) coke gave them. Although cocaine is not physically addictive like heroin, a small fraction of users do become psychologically addicted to the cocaine experience. Unfortunately for him and his family, Steve Howe's background and personality made him a prime candidate for that sad fate.

Though Howe was pitching very well in both 1981 and 1982, he was also mixing more and more cocaine use with his alcohol bouts. His increasingly erratic behavior during the 1982 season, including one occasion when his wife, Cindy, hired a private investigator to try to find him during a five-day binge, made the Dodgers aware of their star pitcher's problem—though team officials were still not sure how much was due to coke and how much to liquor. At the urging of his wife, his agent, and his team, Howe agreed to spend several weeks that fall at the Meadows in Arizona, a rehabilitation center to which the Dodgers had earlier sent Howe's teammate Bob Welch to be treated for alcoholism. Howe's comparatively brief stay at the Meadows did nothing to change his weakness for cocaine; it simply brought his condition into public view. Undoubtedly these news stories helped the Dodgers win their salary arbitration fight with Howe that winter and hold his salary at $325,000.

The 1983 season was a roller-coaster ride for Howe. On the field, he pitched well enough to post his lowest-ever ERA of 1.44. Off the field, his performance was anything but a success, landing him in another rehabilitation center for the month of June. When Howe returned to the active roster, the Dodgers docked him a month's pay, an action that established the first drug suspension on his record. A second well-publicized suspension at the end of the season cost the Dodgers the services of their ace reliever during the 1983 playoffs, which they lost to the Philadelphia Phillies. Yet another failed drug test in the off-season brought Commissioner Bowie Kuhn into the picture. Kuhn announced Howe's suspension for the entire 1984 season. The combination of mounting debts and no salary expected for the following year forced Howe to file for personal bankruptcy that winter. His drug-related shortcomings as both husband and father led his wife to file for divorce.

Fortunately for Steve, Cindy Howe eventually relented and took her husband back. The Major League Baseball Players Association (MLBPA) also took up his cause as part of its broader attack on Kuhn's evolving drug policy. Although the Players Association succeeded by mid-1984 in getting Howe off the suspended list and back into rehabilitation, neither Howe, his family, nor his doctors could wean him from his dependence on drugs as a "chronic addicted user" (to quote the Dodgers' drug consultant's verdict).

Steve Howe's extraordinary talent—his ability to pinpoint a 95-mile-an-hour fastball under the late-inning pressures of close games—made a number of teams eager to take a chance on him: the Dodgers in early 1985, the Twins at the end of 1985, the Texas Rangers in 1987, and teams in the California League, the Mexican League, and even the Japanese League at points in between. But Howe's inability to control his craving for cocaine resulted in his continually failing drug tests, eventually bringing his suspension total to six. When Howe told his wife he was going to the corner store for a quart of milk, she was never sure whether he would return in 20 minutes or 3 days. Indeed, on one occasion when Cindy herself was going out to shop, she had to chain Steve to a fence in their back yard to stop him from going off on yet another drug binge.

With his baseball career apparently behind him, Howe and his family relocated to the Flathead Valley in Montana, where he ran a small construction business. At first he continued his drug indulgence. However, after an all-night soul-searching session with a pastor friend, he decided to kick it for good. For the first time in a decade, Howe was successfully fighting his drug addiction, with the help and support of twice-weekly prayer groups.

Thus, by the 1989–90 off-season, Howe was ready to try baseball one more time. He and the MLBPA entered into extended negotiations with Commissioner Fay Vincent. After drug and medical specialists had examined Howe and given him a clean bill of health, Vincent agreed to let him have one last chance. He could pitch in the minor leagues in 1990 and the major leagues in 1991. This reinstatement decision required Howe to participate in a drug aftercare program and submit to regular drug testing. Vincent emphatically warned Howe that he would be immediately expelled from baseball in the event of a positive drug test.

Steve Howe's return to the big leagues with the New York Yankees was the Cinderella story of 1991. The strength of his performance that summer was exhibited in the contract the Yankees gave him that fall: a $600,000 guaranteed base salary in 1992 plus another $1.7 million in easily achievable bonus incentives. Howe returned to Montana secure in the belief that simply by pitching reasonably well for a single full season, he could ensure a comfortable future for Cindy and their children.

But on December 19 disaster struck. Howe tried to buy a gram of cocaine from a supplier who turned out to be an undercover agent for the federal Drug Enforcement Agency, which had been trying to ensnare drug dealers in that region of Montana. Howe's criminal lawyers marshaled a number of legal strategies on behalf of their client—in particular, trying to suppress a statement he made at the time of his arrest to the effect that he was simply trying to buy cocaine "to have one last party before spring training." Thanks to this deft defense, Howe received fairly lenient treatment from the criminal justice system: three years' probation, a $1,000 fine, and 100 hours of community service in Montana.

More draconian treatment awaited Howe within the baseball justice system—in particular, under the official MLB drug policy that had been formulated by the commissioner's office. The basic tenet of the drug policy was elementary: "There is no place for illegal drug use in Baseball." Any use, possession, or sale of illegal drugs would be subject to discipline that could be as stringent as permanent expulsion from the game, especially for those who, "despite our efforts to treat and rehabilitate them," continued to use illegal drugs. Vincent concluded that it would be in the "best interests" of baseball to "extinguish [Howe's] opportunity to play" after he had "squandered" so many opportunities to prove that he could comply with MLB's "unequivocal" drug policy. So Howe received the first-ever lifetime ban from the game for drug use. Referring by analogy to the ban imposed on Pete Rose two years earlier by Commissioner Giamatti, Vincent said that severe sanctions had to be imposed on Howe "in order to maintain a meaningful deterrent . . . [that] will protect baseball from the kind of threat represented by individuals who cannot deal with the temptations of gambling and of substance abuse."

Unlike Pete Rose, however, Steve Howe had an avenue of appeal from the merits of the commissioner's ruling. The Players Association immediately lodged a grievance under its collective agreement with Major League Baseball. The hearing before baseball's labor umpire George Nicolau precipitated a fierce battle between Vincent and the Yankees which temporarily pushed the Howe grievance to the sidelines. With the Yankees not wanting to lose their star reliever, both their general manager, Gene Michael, and their manager, Buck Showalter, testified on Howe's behalf. They said that because drug use was a sickness, not a crime, people like Howe required treatment, not punishment. Vincent was livid when he heard about this testimony. He called the Yankee officials into his office and told them they were in danger of losing their jobs for undermining an MLB drug policy that was "not subject to dissent." When they replied that they had testified in accordance with their personal conscience and principles, Vincent reportedly snapped back, "You should have left your conscience and your principles outside the hearing room."

Word of these exchanges leaked out to the press and generated a Players Association charge against Vincent and MLB for violating the labor law that prohibits intimidating witnesses when they testify on behalf of workers. In light of this public outcry, Arbitrator Nicolau adjourned the hearing, telling each side to appoint a specialist in drug addiction to examine Howe and review his case history.

The importance of the new evidence became crystal clear when Nicolau finally issued his decision in November 1992. Nicolau agreed that baseball had an institutional interest in keeping its workplace free of drugs and in dealing with "the pressures brought to bear on Baseball by those who see the 'athlete-as-hero.'" However, he believed that giving fair consideration to the situations and needs of individual players was equally important. Both of the nationally recognized drug specialists engaged in the case agreed that since birth Howe had been suffering from attention deficit hyperactive disorder, which had put him at a high risk of substance abuse as an adult. The disorder required a kind of drug dependency treatment—including stringent year-round drug testing every other day—that Howe had never received. Therefore, Nicolau concluded, the "yet another chance" that Vincent had supposedly offered to Howe to return to baseball drug-free had not had "a fair shot at success."

But what about Vincent's other argument, that Howe had to be permanently expelled in order "to deter repeated drug use by others . . . [because] a less severe sanction would have sent the wrong message to players who [would] view anything short of a lifetime ban as a license to take up and repeatedly use drugs"? Nicolau's first response was that Howe had already lost nearly $2 million in salary and bonuses in the 1992 season alone: the arbitrator believed this penalty was a "clear warning that drug use will continue to be treated with severity." Moreover, baseball had made steady and substantial progress toward a drug-free environment since the initial appearance of the problem in the early 1980s. At this point Steve Howe's repeated drug use was very much the exception rather than the rule.

The arbitrator's bottom-line verdict was that a lifetime ban was excessive punishment. Howe was to be reinstated after serving a suspension for the last 17 weeks of the 1992 season, but only on condition that he participate in a rigorous aftercare program involving drug tests every second day—all year round—for the rest of his baseball career. Any positive test result would "constitute just cause for his permanent removal from the game."

By the time Nicolau rendered his decision, Vincent had been knocked out of the commissioner's office by Bud Selig and other owners and was on his way to baseball exile in Oxford, England. But he could not resist telling the press that Nicolau's decision was a "joke" in ordaining that the seventh offense was not enough, but that an eighth would be. Vincent predicted that when Howe slipped again, the Players Association would invent new excuses and ask for a ninth chance. "It's a daisy chain," Vincent railed; "you never get to the end of it!"

The Yankees, much more optimistic than Vincent, quickly put together a lucrative offer to sign Howe to a two-year, $4 million contract before he and his agent could test the waters of the free agent market. This action outraged Charles Rangel, a congressman from the district in the Bronx where Howe would be pitching in Yankee Stadium, who was chairman of the House Committee on Narcotics Abuse and Control. Rangel complained: "By offering Steve Howe—someone who has had more drug suspensions than a cat has lives—a lucrative contract, you have just told all the little boys in New York to go against the advice of their fathers . . . who have told them 'Drugs are bad for you. Do not touch them.' From you they get a conflicting and very disturbing message—'Drugs are bad, unless you can pitch, hit, or steal bases.'"

As it turned out, Howe's remaining career with the Yankees was quite successful, with no recurrence of drug use. But when he was finally released by the Yankees in 1996, Howe was arrested again—this time for having a loaded .357 Magnum in his luggage when he and his family were boarding the plane to fly back to Montana. Apparently neither Acting Commissioner Bud Selig nor Congressman Rangel believed that players' breaking gun laws required baseball to take action to protest this other message that fathers often send their children.

Labor Battles over Drugs

In 1982, a decade before the *Howe* verdict, Willie Wilson, star center fielder for the Kansas City Royals, was caught up in a federal drug enforcement net. Wilson was convicted of *attempting* to possess drugs, and was the only person in the entire country who was sentenced to jail that year for this federal offense. The federal magistrate told Wilson that he was receiving this sentence because he was "a national hero who occupied a special place in our society." Imposing a tough penalty on him was necessary to deter such behavior by others who "hold you out as a role model in their lives." Commissioner Bowie Kuhn echoed this judicial opinion when, after being released from jail, Wilson was suspended for the entire 1984 season.

The arbitrator of Wilson's grievance against Kuhn's ruling accepted the basic MLB premise that the league could legitimately penalize players for use of illegal drugs as something that was contrary to the "best interests" of baseball: "Because baseball players are highly skilled, well compensated, and constantly visible, they deserve and receive national attention . . . and their drug involvement . . . constitutes a serious and immediate threat to the business that is promoted as our national pastime." But the arbitrator concluded that a more fitting penalty for a first offense of drug possession was a mere one-month suspension at the beginning of the 1984 season. So Wilson was able to return to the Royals on May 16 in a game at Chicago's Comiskey Park, at which some White Sox fans unveiled a welcoming banner that quipped, "Willie: Coke is it."

The *Wilson* case displayed the way a collective labor agreement with neutral arbitration exposes league policies established by the commissioner to challenge by baseball players (but not by managers, like Pete Rose). Football, though, followed a different path, beginning with a case in the late 1970s. At that time drug use by athletes was attracting media and public attention. A ten-part series in the *Washington Post* entitled "Drugs and Sports" painted an alarming picture of the problem and sought to generate a response from the governing sports bodies. Interestingly, the focus of that *Post* exposé was entirely on performance-enhancing drugs, including the then-new anabolic steroids, as well as amphetamines, the principal concern in those years. Cocaine and marijuana received only casual mention as "recreational" drugs that athletes were using in their leisure time. As MLB's Willie Wilson and Steve Howe, the NBA's John Lucas and Michael Ray Richardson, and the NFL's Don Reese and Randy Crowder were all about to learn, attitudes toward drugs would change profoundly in the 1980s.

Reese and Crowder were among the top defensive players on Don Shula's Miami Dolphins when they were arrested in the spring of 1977 by undercover Miami police officers: the two had been trying to buy a large stash of cocaine to supply to someone they thought was a friend. After pleading guilty to criminal charges, Reese and Crowder were sentenced to serve a year in the Dade County (Florida) Stockade, from which they were not released until August 1978.

At that point NFL Commissioner Pete Rozelle announced that the league would also take disciplinary action against the two players. He told them that, as NFL players, they occupied "a unique position in the public's perception . . . which requires at least minimal standards of personal conduct—on the field and off," including no "criminal involvement with illegal drugs." The grievance proceedings initiated by the NFL Players Association (NFLPA) on behalf of Reese and Crowder differed in two striking ways from the *Wilson* case. The legal difference was that the football arbitrator interpreted the NFL labor agreement as conferring upon the commissioner the unreviewable discretion to deal with conduct that he believed was "detrimental to the integrity of, or public confidence in, the game of football." The practical difference was that the penalty Rozelle levied on the two players who had been convicted and jailed for *trafficking* in cocaine was a contribution of $5,000 apiece to a drug rehabilitation center in South Florida.

Unfortunately, unlike Crowder, Reese turned out to be a personal loser even after his reinstatement in football. He began using free-base cocaine (the predecessor to crack), and his play deteriorated sharply. By early 1982, having decided to leave football, Reese appeared in *Sports Illustrated* with a bleak account of how his life had been destroyed by the "cocaine cloud that is now over the entire league."

Sports Illustrated's "Special Report on the 'Cocaine Cloud'" came at a critical point in the evolution of the public mood about drugs. Overall levels of cocaine use had risen sharply since the mid-1970s, and the far more dangerous smoked variant of cocaine, crack, had just made its appearance on the nation's streets. The summer of 1982 also happened to be the time when the NFL leadership was sitting down to negotiate a new collective agreement with the Players Association.

Those football negotiations produced a lengthy strike about the players' quest for salary standards, something that Rozelle and the NFL owners then thought was too "socialist" an idea. The negotiations did, however, lead to a relatively amicable agreement about a new drug plan that was part of the eventual strike settlement in December 1982.

The drug program had two principal components. First, the players accepted drug testing of everyone as part of their pre-season physical examination, when urine and blood were already being sampled for medical reasons. Second, the owners agreed to limit further drug testing to situations in which a team doctor had "reasonable cause" to suspect that one of his players was using drugs. This compromise constituted the first drug program mutually adopted by players and owners in any sport.

The following year saw professional basketball take the next step, in response to an even more strongly felt need. While there had been much popular suspicion of drug use among NBA players, the first public acknowledgment of such use came in early 1982.

John Lucas had been a two-sport All-American at the University of Maryland. In tennis he was a teammate of Jimmy Connors on the U.S. Junior Davis Cup team. An even bigger star in basketball, he was selected by the Houston Rockets as the top pick in the 1976 NBA draft. After starring as the Rockets' point guard for two seasons, Lucas was awarded by Commissioner Larry O'Brien to the Golden State Warriors as compensation for the Warriors' loss of the free agent Rick Barry to the Rockets. Lucas led the Warriors for two years, but his play began to deteriorate in 1980 when he developed a serious cocaine problem. Eventually the Warriors sent him to the Washington Bullets in the hope that living and playing near his family as well as his college coach and mentor, Lefty Driesel, would snap him out of his drug-related slump. But this ploy was unsuccessful, and Lucas finally had to seek rehabilitation and publicly acknowledge his drug addiction.

Soon after the Lucas case, stories surfaced about a number of other NBA players with drug problems, including such All-Stars as John Drew of the Atlanta Hawks, David Thompson of the Denver Nuggets, and Michael Ray Richardson of the New Jersey Nets. All these players were black. This was not surprising, because 80 percent of NBA players were (and still are) black. The issue of race posed a problem for the league, however, because of two popular misconceptions: that drug use was principally a black phenomenon in this country, and that a large percentage of NBA players were indulging in cocaine. This presented a serious marketing obstacle for the NBA, in an era when even with stars such as Magic Johnson, Julius Erving, and Larry Bird on the court, the league was unable to get even its championship *finals* broadcast on prime-time television.

This time it was the Players Association, led by the future Hall-of-Famer Bob Lanier, that took the initiative and proposed an immediate ban of any NBA player found using or distributing heroin or cocaine—though *not* marijuana. This apparently harsh rule was accompanied by an elaborate treatment program for players like Lucas who voluntarily came forward and admitted to their drug problem. On the first occasion, treatment would be provided while the player was paid his full salary; on the second, pay during treatment would be cut in half; and only on the third occasion would the permanent ban be imposed. Even that drastic "permanent" sanction allowed for reinstatement after two years if there was persuasive evidence that the player had become drug-free. The Players Association held firm on the limits of drug testing, though, and the NBA owners eventually agreed that individual players would be tested only if a jointly appointed independent expert was satisfied that there was reasonable cause for doing so.

The NBA's new drug program was part of a 1983 collective agreement that contained an even more notable innovation—a salary-sharing system that imposed a cap on what teams could bid for other teams' free agents. When this pioneering agreement was made public in the fall of 1983, Bob Lanier wrote an op-ed piece for the *New York Times* setting out the rationale for "The Players' War on Drugs." The vast majority of players wanted to fight this war, he explained, because they were tired of "being tarnished with the brush of 'all being hopheads'" on account of the behavior of just a few of their league-mates. In addition, now that the players had agreed to take a 53 percent share of the league's revenues, they had just as great a need as the team owners to reinforce "the fans' perception that the players will be playing at all times at their highest possible skill levels"—the key to greater attendance at games, higher television ratings, and more marketing opportunities. Finally, the predominantly black membership of the Players Association, knowing they were idolized by kids in the inner cities, accepted their "responsibility as role models" to send a "loud and clear message" against drug abuse.

To complete the first cycle of bargaining about drugs in sports, in early 1984 the new leader of the MLB Players Association, Donald Fehr, negotiated an even more elaborate drug policy with Lee MacPhail, the head of the owners' Player Relations Committee. Both sides agreed that the particular targets of concern would be cocaine and heroin rather than marijuana (or alcohol). Drug testing of individual players would be permitted only at the direction of a jointly appointed panel of three experts when they found reasonable cause to believe that a player was abusing drugs. If the player tested positive, he could be sent into treatment for 30 days at full pay, then another 30 days at half pay, and finally for another 30 days at the major league minimum salary.

This rather rare "win-win" accord in baseball was, however, short-lived. The shattering news of Len Bias's death from cocaine hit the American public at a critical time. The use of illegal drugs had soared by the mid-1980s, and the annual number of deaths attributed to cocaine and heroin had passed the 5,000 mark. Among the other athletes who became drug fatalities was Don Rogers, the Pro Bowl safety of the Cleveland Browns, who died from smoking crack at a party the night before his scheduled wedding. In addition, yet another drug scandal was rocking baseball: a Philadelphia drug dealer disclosed that he had regularly supplied drugs to players including Dave Parker, Keith Hernandez, Lonnie Smith, and Claudell Washington. Led by *Time* and the *New York Times*, the media painted a gloomy picture of baseball, declaring that the sport faced the worst crisis since the 1919 Black Sox scandal. They called on MLB's new commissioner, Peter Ueberroth (*Time's* 1984 Man of the Year), to emulate Judge Landis and do what was necessary to restore the integrity of the game.

Ueberroth was happy to oblige. At the same time that the commissioner was covertly initiating baseball's new "collusion" policy that no owner would bid on another team's free agents, he exercised the owners' right to terminate the previous year's negotiated drug accord, which allowed drug testing only if an independent expert judged that a player had a drug problem. Ueberroth sought instead to grant President Reagan's request to make sports the role model for American business: regular testing was to be required of *all* players to prevent the initial occurrence of any such ugly spectacles.

The commissioner sent each player a letter warning that "baseball is in trouble" because "the shadow that drugs have cast is growing larger and darker by the day." With "baseball's reputation at stake," dramatic action was needed "to restore our good name and preserve baseball's place as the national pastime." Ueberroth was aware, of course, of the players' long-standing objection to randomized drug testing as an invasion of the privacy of innocent as well as guilty players. His response was that testing for drugs was no more significant an intrusion on privacy than what players experienced when they put their bodies and bags through the metal detectors at airports.

The players were not convinced that this brief automatic check at the airport was a fair analogy to someone watching them urinate into a bottle whose contents were then subjected to chemical examination. In order to outmaneuver the MLBPA, Ueberroth orchestrated a successful effort by the clubs to insist that every new contract signed that winter include an agreement by the individual player to submit to drug testing. The MLBPA promptly filed and won a grievance attacking the validity of such a clause under the provisions of baseball's Basic Agreement, which permitted individually negotiated contract terms only if they conferred a "benefit" on the player. As a result of Ueberroth's termination of the 1984 Fehr-MacPhail agreement, MLB's drug policy and the penalties for violations became subject to arbitral review, producing the results we saw in the *Howe* case.

NBA Commissioner David Stern was able to resist the political and media pressure and stand by the more narrowly tailored drug program negotiated with Bob Lanier in 1983. NFL Commissioner Pete Rozelle, by contrast, decided to follow Ueberroth's lead, setting off yet another labor battle. But when Paul Tagliabue became NFL commissioner in 1990 his sport achieved a happier ending.

The football world had been racked by its own drug scandal after the 1986 Super Bowl. The New England Patriots, who had initially thrilled their fans by reaching the Super Bowl for the first time in the team's history, left the fans dejected by a 46–10 thrashing by the Chicago Bears. Two days later the *Boston Globe* shocked the region with a front-page exposé of an allegedly serious drug problem among the Patriots. Star players such as Irving Fryar, Raymond Clayborn, and Kenneth Sims were implicated, and the *Globe* writers suggested that drug use was the reason the team had blown the Super Bowl. It turned out that during pre-season testing 7 of the more than 50 players on the Patriots roster had tested positive for drug use—5 of them for marijuana and 2 for cocaine. But regular testing of those players during the season had shown them all to be free of drugs. Moreover, great season performances by Fryar, Clayborn, Sims, and the others had put the Patriots in the Super Bowl against the Bears before they succumbed to those "Monsters of the Midway."

Commissioner Rozelle, however, responding to a media outcry that did not include all these facts, sat down with NFLPA Executive Director Gene Upshaw in the spring of 1986 to work out a more sophisticated drug program than the one they had created four years earlier. The two sides were able to agree on some essential points. Drug testing would be centralized and standardized within the commissioner's office rather than left to individual teams like the Patriots. If a player tested positive for drugs, a three-step league response would be implemented: after the first positive test, supervised treatment and regular testing in the future; after the second, a four-game suspension without pay (which in the NFL means loss of a quarter of a season's salary); and after the third, a blanket ban from the game, though with the possibility of application for reinstatement in the future, as allowed by the NBA.

The sticking point, as always, was spot drug testing of all players, prior users or not. Even though the NFL was party to an existing collective agreement with the NFLPA containing a somewhat different drug program, Commissioner Rozelle unilaterally instituted his own plan in early July 1986. Besides the established pre-season drug test, he added a requirement that every player submit to two random drug tests at some time during the season. This earned Rozelle wide applause for taking steps to deal with what the general public perceived as a major crisis of drugs in sports. Not only had the Patriots' Super Bowl scandal erupted a few months earlier, but Len Bias and Don Rogers had died from using drugs only a couple of weeks before Rozelle's announcement.

The Players Association, of course, did not applaud: instead, it filed a grievance under the football labor contract. Its lawyers faced the challenge of the *Reese/Crowder* precedent, in which the arbitrator had concluded that the commissioner had an unreviewable authority to take action against individuals whose conduct threatened "the integrity of, or public confidence in, the game of football." In this case, though, the arbitrator struck down the drug-testing features of Rozelle's new program. His rationale was that once the owners had explicitly agreed with the players on one policy—here, on just a single pre-season drug test as part of the routine physical exam—this agreement implicitly precluded the owners, through their commissioner, from unilaterally adopting a different policy on the same subject. So, like their baseball counterparts, the football players were able to use their labor law resources to foil a commissioner's effort to respond to the nationwide mid-1980s crisis atmosphere surrounding drug use.

However, as we shall see in Part II of this book, by the end of 1989 the NFL players had decided to renounce all their rights under labor law so as to be able to assert their rights under antitrust law and challenge the NFL's long-standing restraints on player free agency. That action by the players restored the owners' freedom to institute a policy of random drug testing if they wanted to do so. But by the beginning of the 1990s two things had changed: Paul Tagliabue had succeeded Rozelle as NFL commissioner, and the general public had begun to have second thoughts about broad drug testing.

One of the public's concerns related to the flaws that were being discovered in the operation of testing programs, including the NFL's system of pre-season testing, which had produced false positives for players such as the Chicago Bears star defensive end Richard Dent. Another concern related to what Tagliabue himself characterized as a "journalistic Molotov cocktail, mixing two of the country's most volatile issues—drugs and racism." No tangible evidence supported a media charge that the NFL was targeting its drug penalties at black players and had deliberately covered up positive drug tests of three white quarterbacks. But this story struck a chord in the minority community, which was painfully aware that, as national studies showed, although black Americans had only a slightly higher statistical likelihood than whites to use drugs, blacks were four times as likely to be arrested on suspicion of drug offenses. So Tagliabue realized that if he rushed to take advantage of the opening left by the legal transformation of the Players Association, he risked having the NFL's "war on drugs" portrayed as a "war on blacks." Instead, he chose not to use that legal opening to implement Rozelle's 1986 plan for random drug testing of all players for illegal "recreational" drugs such as marijuana and cocaine.

The Current State of the War

After settling the NFL's long-time battle over the reserve system and bringing both free agency and a hard salary cap to football, Tagliabue and Upshaw went on to reach an amicable agreement on a drug program. Players who use drugs that are illegal under public law are also judged to be in violation of the league's Policy and Program of Substances of Abuse. But there is no program for regular random testing of all players for potential use of these substances. With the adoption of similar policies by the NHL (after settlement of the 1994–95 labor dispute and lockout) and the NBA (in the settlement of their similar labor battle in 1998–99), the owners and players in all the major professional team sports have now reached a consensus on essentially the same approach to players' use of illegal drugs.

The situation in nonprofessional sports is fundamentally different with respect to both the development and the current scope of anti-drug programs. Recall the 1998 snowboarding case: after learning that Olympic snowboarders were not barred from using marijuana, the IOC immediately changed its rules to make use of that drug a disqualifier for all participants in future Olympic Games. The same kind of instant step had already been taken by the NCAA. At their 1986 convention, NCAA members had voted to make use of marijuana or cocaine by student athletes grounds for ineligibility, and to institute random drug testing for all student athletes. There were no representatives of college athletes at that convention with either a voice or a vote on this major step.

In the 1990s a number of local public school boards adopted the same policy for all their student athletes. Then, in a 1997 decision involving the *Vernonia School District* case, the U.S. Supreme Court ruled that even though drug testing amounted to "search and seizure" governed by the Fourth Amendment, there was sufficient "reasonable cause" to justify testing high school athletes. Ironically, a year later the Supreme Court ruled that there was no reasonable justification for requiring drug testing of all electoral candidates (that is, *political* athletes); and relying on that *Chandler* decision some lower courts have barred public schools from randomly testing their teachers (including the coaches). I suspect that the Court would be even less inclined to permit random drug testing of all judges. Of course, the Constitution does not govern "private actors" such as professional leagues or even the NCAA. The fundamental policy question posed by the history recounted here is whether athletes (professional or not) should be singled out for such anti-drug programs. Answering this question is the aim of the next chapter.

5

ATHLETES AS
ROLE MODELS

The biggest reason for the resurgence of interest in baseball in the late 1990s was the phenomenal number of home runs being hit. Fans became most "homer happy" in 1998 as they watched Mark McGwire competing with Sammy Sosa to see who would replace Roger Maris as our home run record-holder. McGwire ended up breaking Maris's record of 61 home runs with 70 that season.

Everyone knows how close Sosa came to McGwire in 1998 (with 66 homers) and how close both came again in 1999 (with 65 and 63, respectively). What few fans realize, though, is that neither McGwire nor Sosa came close to breaking Babe Ruth's *true* home run record. Suppose we were to do the same kind of adjustment for home run inflation that we regularly do for economic inflation, for example, to calculate the real rise of the Dow Jones Index from the 1920s to the 1990s. In order for a McGwire or a Sosa (or Ken Griffey Jr.) to break Ruth's *real* home run record from the 1920s, he now has to hit more than 150, not just 60, home runs over the season. Put those figures together with the fact that Ruth was a pitcher of Hall-of-Fame quality for the Red Sox when they won their last World Series in Fenway Park back in 1918, before their owner, Harry Frazee, sold Ruth to the Yankees. It should now be clear why Babe Ruth was our greatest athlete in any sport in the past century.

A number of factors have contributed to the surge in home run hitting over the last several decades. One is the change in the design and quality of balls and bats, the same as has happened to the balls and clubs or racquets in golf and tennis. Another is the size and shape of new ballparks, which have not only more luxurious seats but also walls that are easier to reach. In addition, the umpires have altered the strike zone to force pitchers to put the ball in a spot where it is easier to hit it a long way.

Finally, the bodies of hitters are dramatically different than they were back in the 1920s.

There are a host of reasons why athletes are now in so much better shape. For our purposes here, the issue is whether such additional body strength (and speed or endurance) has been created by a kind of drug not targeted by the war on drugs—the performance-enhancer. The latest such substances to appear on the scene were Androstenedione ("Andro") and Creatine. It was the news of McGwire's use of Andro in 1998, along with use by other players such as José Canseco and Jeff Bagwell, that made this a best-selling pill for youngsters wanting to follow that same path to glory. While the athletic pioneer with Creatine was Brady Anderson, who used it to turn himself into a 50–home run lead-off hitter, even more famous Creatine users have been Sammy Sosa, John Elway, who quarterbacked the Denver Broncos to Super Bowl Championships in 1998 and 1999, and Michael Johnson, the record-setting track and field star of the 1990s.

In late 1999 baseball authorities were still considering whether to make the use of Andro a sports offense (and no one was suggesting doing anything about Creatine). At least with Andro, the NFL has adopted a very different position, consistent with football's change of focus when Paul Tagliabue was installed as commissioner in 1990. Following the trail blazed by the International Olympic Committee beginning at the 1972 Olympics in Munich, the NFL is now targeting its drug control efforts as much at performance-enhancing drugs like steroids (or Andro) as at mind-altering drugs like cocaine. That same priority was displayed in the original drug control program proposed to the NCAA in 1985, triggered by the scandal of steroid use by many American athletes at the 1983 Pan-American Games in Caracas, Venezuela. At the NCAA's January 1986 convention, marijuana and cocaine were added only as an afterthought to the testing and banning of steroids and amphetamines.

A decade earlier the *Washington Post's* series "Drugs and Sports" had also focused principally on amphetamines, making only casual references to athletes' use of marijuana or cocaine. Amphetamines were colloquially known as "speed" because of their acceleration of the body's circulatory and respiratory systems. While they had a number of accepted medical uses, including as diet pills, these tablets had also become a common way to fight the fatigue felt by college students studying all night before their final exams, by truck drivers on long-distance hauls, or, in sports, by cyclists and marathon runners. In the NFL amphetamines were used to pump up players' aggressive instincts, especially among linemen, for whom control and rhythm were not as important as they were for quarterbacks. But even though amphetamines enhanced athletic performance in the short run, they created a significant risk of harm in the longer run. For example, their "speed-up" of the heart and liver occasionally resulted in cardiac convulsions or coma.

By the 1980s the performance-enhancing drugs of choice for athletes were anabolic steroids, intended to make their bodies both stronger and faster. Steroids are a synthetic substitute for the male hormone testosterone. The synthetic form was designed to provide more of the muscle-building (anabolic) effect of testosterone while minimizing its masculinizing (androgenic) effect. Steroids were first developed as a mode of treatment for certain diseases, but the principal market for them soon was made up of athletes such as weightlifters, shotputters, and football players.

As a high school football player in the late 1960s, Lyle Alzado was too undersized to get a college athletic scholarship. But when he discovered the magic of steroids—his favorite was Dianabol—Alzado became an All-Pro defensive lineman who led the Denver Broncos to a Super Bowl appearance in 1977 and the Los Angeles Raiders to a Super Bowl victory in 1982. Later, in a 1991 *Sports Illustrated* cover story revisiting the problem of drugs in sports, Alzado depicted himself as a stark example of why athletes should *not* use steroids: he was dying of lymphomatic cancer of the brain.

The Alzado story was a dramatic example of the athletic advantages of steroids, but not a particularly accurate portrayal of their dangers. It is scientifically improbable that the type of cancer afflicting Alzado was the product of steroids. Indeed, one of the challenges posed by steroids, as well as their successors of the 1990s, human growth hormone (HGH) and erythropoietin (EPO),* is that while sharply altering the body chemistry is likely to create some serious health risks, it is diffi-

---

* The main athletic benefit of HGH is enhanced strength, a big plus for, say, offensive line blockers, while EPO is taken for enhanced endurance, of special value in cycling. The 1998 Tour de France cycling scandal began when French police and Tour authorities discovered that entire teams were using EPOs, the same drug that had killed five cyclists on the Dutch team a decade earlier. Happily, after the Tour authorities had installed the most intensive drug-testing program in sports history, the 3 blood tests and 15 urine tests applied to Lance Armstrong in the 1999 Tour de France disclosed no illicit substance at all in his system as he was restoring the drama and appeal of this sport.

cult to document precisely what and how serious those risks are. Making such determinations requires epidemiological studies that follow matched groups of users and nonusers of steroids, HGH, or EPO for two to three decades. This is the research procedure that led to the discovery of the dangers of another "miracle" substance—asbestos. Unfortunately, by the time the truth about asbestos was known and safeguards adopted in the 1960s, millions of American workers had already been exposed to the substance on the job, and hundreds of thousands were fated to die as a result. Not until the 1990s was it scientifically established that steroids can lead to conditions such as heart disease and liver cancer.

What about Andro and Creatine? Creatine is an amino acid powder, and Andro is a testosterone-producing pill; both enhance weight, strength, and muscular ability. Both Andro and Creatine are categorized as legal "dietary supplements" under the federal Food and Drug Act, which was significantly relaxed in 1994: this was some time after anabolic steroids had been classed as "controlled substances," illegal to use without a medical prescription. Athletes' use of Andro has been prohibited by Olympic and college sports authorities, as well as by the NFL, but not yet by any other professional team sport. Because of the physiological nature of this substance's effects, it will be another decade or two before epidemiological studies can document whether Andro poses risks to the body similar to those of steroids and amphetamines.

On the other side of that athletic coin is the immediate performance-enhancing value of steroids, amphetamines, HGH, EPO, and now Andro and Creatine. After the news broke in 1998 about the boost that Creatine had apparently given Elway during the Broncos' Super Bowl chase, and the one that Andro had given McGwire in his quest for the home-run record, over-the-counter sales of those substances soared, especially sales to high school athletes. The Andro phenomenon is an eerie reminder of the steroid revelations that surfaced at the 1988 Olympic Games in Seoul, with the rise and fall of Ben Johnson. In the early 1980s this Canadian sprinter was good but not great. Then he began using steroids to accelerate his training, and by 1988 he not only had beaten America's Carl Lewis in the 100-meter Olympic finals but had run what is still the fastest-ever time of 9.79 seconds. And awaiting victory by Johnson at the Olympics were more than $10 million in endorsement deals.

Two days later Johnson tested positive for steroids and lost it all—gold medal, record, and $10 million endorsement bonus. But he had already demonstrated to athletes around the world that such a substance could transform a middle-level runner into the world's fastest human being, at least as long as he could conceal his use of the drug. Of course, exposure to such a drug cannot be "hidden" from the body, and it may eventually reveal itself in a life-threatening disease. However, unlike workers exposed to asbestos at a naval shipyard or a construction site, many athletes feel that the "pot of gold" for winning in their sport is large enough to justify betting that they will not be the ones to suffer from those health hazards. A 1995 poll of aspiring Olympians found more than half saying that they were prepared to accept *dying* from a performance-enhancing drug in five years, if it would guarantee their winning a gold medal now.

Because of the inherent interdependence of participants in sports, sports authorities should impose much tougher constraints on athletes' use of steroids than on their use of cocaine. Both cocaine and steroids do generate some risk of physical harm or death; and by contrast with the use of loaded guns, for example, their immediate physical impact is felt by those who choose to use them, not by other people. The intoxicating or addicting features of recreational drugs may still justify broad legal prohibitions designed to protect occasional drug abusers from inflicting harm on themselves, and thus on their families and society. However, reflecting on the Ben Johnson case reveals that performance-enhancing drugs like steroids actually impose much of their harm on *other* athletes who would prefer not to use the drugs.

When Johnson used steroids to dramatically improve his speed and performance at the 1988 Olympics, he also inflicted significant harm on the health and well-being of his present and future competitors. The same was true of the Irish swimmer Michelle Smith when she used HGH (and Andro) to allow her to surprise everyone by winning not one but three gold medals at the 1996 Olympics. Johnson's rivals such as Carl Lewis and Smith's rivals such as Janet Evans faced a Prisoner's Dilemma: either concede the Olympic golds to Johnson and Smith, or put their own lives and limbs at risk by using the substances themselves. After all, world-class athletes devote their lives to a sport in order to become champions, not just graceful losers. If use of performance-enhancing drugs becomes widespread, no one gets any special advantage from them. In that case, everyone is left worse off because of toxic exposure whose harmful consequences are likely to appear only after these athletes have left sports and the public eye.

One special characteristic of sports is the need to preserve wholehearted competition among teams for the benefit of fans. That is why leagues must have and enforce rules barring players from throwing games or shaving points. Less obvious, but also crucial, are rules designed to create *fair* competition; in particular, to protect athletes against the pressure to sacrifice too much to win. Pursuit of this objective led Paul Tagliabue, after he became football commissioner in 1990, to establish in the NFL the first anti-steroid policy in professional sports.

But it is not enough for a sports authority simply to put on its books a rule that prohibits use of a substance like steroids. Effective enforcement of that rule is essential. Otherwise, when the governing body announces its ban on performance-enhancing drugs, most athletes will comply voluntarily, expecting their competitors to be doing so as well. But if enforcement is lax, a few athletes are likely to get away with breaking the rule and thereby beating their rivals on the field. So if we cannot achieve the ideal—effective control of unscrupulous rule-breakers—the second-best option may be to repeal the rule entirely, fully inform competitors of the risks of steroid use, and let the athletes decide whether or not to take their chances.

In my view, systematic drug testing of all athletes is the best option. It was this IOC procedure that uncovered Ben Johnson's breaking of the rules and thus cost him his dramatic victory at Seoul. The most graphic illustration in the 1990s involved Chinese swimmers. After the Chinese team hired an East German coach in the mid-1980s, its swimming performance suddenly blossomed: China garnered a substantial number of gold medals at the 1988 and 1992 Olympic Games, and 12 of the 16 golds at the 1994 World Championship in Rome. But only a few months later, tests administered without warning to the Chinese team at the Asian Games in Hiroshima disclosed a host of drug users: by 1998, 27 of the team's top swimmers had been banned from international competition. That nation will have to reclaim its position in this sport by complying with, rather than violating, these key rules of the game.

However, the principal value of performance-enhancing drugs like steroids (unlike that of amphetamines) is realized in off-season training cycles. If the athlete ceases using steroids for a sufficient period before competing—something Ben Johnson failed to do before Seoul—the drugs (but not the benefits) will disappear from the athlete's system before testing at the event. To address this problem, the IOC and other international sports authorities have expanded their programs to have the tester suddenly appear unannounced at the athlete's door to administer the test. It was this procedure that revealed Michelle Smith's use of HGH and Andro in the middle of the 1998 winter in Ireland, after she had tested negative during the 1996 summer games in Atlanta. Recognizing that same need for a safe and level playing field in football, the NFL Players Association has agreed that its members be subject to random testing for steroids and the like even during the off-season.

The steroids debate provides yet another illustration of what is special about sports, and of why the NFL and the NCAA have made the right judgments on this score. Leagues must ban players' use even of legal performance-enhancing substances like Andro, as well as of illegal counterparts like steroids. Players who use these substances create a significant risk not just for themselves but also for their competitors and successors, who face strong pressures to follow that same path in order to excel in their sport. And random year-round drug testing must accompany the ban to ensure that no players can get away with violating those rules.

Accepting the wisdom of this policy is one thing: implementing it is another, rife with difficult issues. Any testing process will make an occasional mistake with a false positive finding, and thus players must have a meaningful procedure for challenging and correcting such results. Since I cannot explore such operational questions in any detail here, I will simply note and compliment the carefully tailored procedural design that the NFL players and owners have worked into their Policy on Anabolic Steroids and Related Substances. Needless to say, the rather authoritarian policymaking processes of the NCAA and the IOC have performed less impressively on this score. The fact that professional athletes have organized into a union gives them not only the leverage to defend their personal interests but also the potential to devise win-win solutions with the owners to problems facing their sport.

Performance-Detracting Drugs

Once a players' union has agreed to a policy of testing all its members for performance-enhancing drugs, testing the same urine sample for recreational drugs imposes no added intrusion upon players' *physical* privacy. This returns us to a question that has been debated for the past two decades, in sports and elsewhere: Should players be tested and punished for use of drugs like cocaine and marijuana in their private lives? During the 1998 NBA labor dispute, the owners were strongly committed to finally adding marijuana to the league's anti-drug policy, along with cocaine and heroin (though no such effort was made for anabolic steroids, let alone Andro). The Players Association eventually agreed to that move, in part because some of its veteran members (like Karl Malone) were endorsing it, and in part because the players' bargaining priority was to preserve the "Larry Bird" salary cap loophole that will be discussed in Part II. Thus use of marijuana by an Allen Iverson (who was arrested for possession after police found marijuana in his car) is now illegal under NBA rules as well as federal law.

There is, of course, a fundamental difference between the effects of steroids and those of marijuana on the sports themselves. Steroids enhance the performance of players who take the risk and use them, whereas marijuana may detract from the performance of players who indulge in it. Clearly, recreational drugs can be a danger to the players who use and abuse them, as evidenced by Len Bias's death. But Bias's use of cocaine, or Iverson's use of marijuana, imposes no direct harm on their competitors (like Malone) who choose not to use those substances. In light of this, if George Steinbrenner and his Yankees were willing to take their chances with Steve Howe in spite of his penchant for cocaine, why should Commissioner Vincent have judged it so vital to ban Howe from the Yankees' bullpen?

Perhaps it is because recreational drugs tend to reduce rather than enhance players' performance. When that happens, indulging in these drugs denies fans what they expect and are paying for—a contest that matches up athletes playing at the very peak of their physical and emotional capacity. So it may be that athletes whose ability is sapped by cocaine use do not belong on the field, and thus that the commissioner, to protect fans' faith in the integrity of the contest, must bar these players from going out there.

However logical it may appear on the surface, this defense of leagues' anti-drug policies simply will not wash. In fact, Steve Howe's final drug incident occurred in the off-season, when he was trying to buy cocaine for one final party in Montana before heading off to spring training in Florida. And though some players undoubtedly use cocaine *during* the season, a host of other recreational indulgences are equally likely to hamper an athlete's ability to play at his best. One highly visible example is when a player like the Chicago Bears' William "the Fridge" Perry eats so much that his weight balloons up near 400 pounds. Yet no commissioner would ever dream of randomly *weighing* all the players in the league to judge whether they were staying fit enough to play at top form so as to give fans their money's worth.

Players are much more likely to indulge themselves by overdrinking than by overeating. With the help of Jim Bouton's famous diary, *Ball Four,* baseball fans now know how often Mickey Mantle and Billy Martin of the Yankees drank until late in the night following a game, even with another game facing them the next day. Sadly, decades later both Mantle and Martin died as a result of their alcohol addiction: Martin from an auto crash, Mantle from cancer of the liver. Indeed, a significant number of athletes have died from alcohol use right in the middle of their careers. Yet no one is pushing the commissioner's office to institute random alcohol tests to check for hangovers that leave players unable to play at their best. And if anyone did make such a suggestion it would immediately be vetoed by the league authorities, whose major advertisers are beer companies like Anheuser-Busch and Miller.

The fact is that commissioners do not institute blanket bans on performance-reducing behavior because it is individual team management that is best equipped to identify and respond to this concern. Just like excessive drinking or eating, excessive use of cocaine can cause a player's performance to deteriorate to a level below what the fans expect and the club is paying him for. But these concerns about performance would never lead a team to adopt a flat rule that made any use of cocaine (not to mention marijuana) an automatic reason for getting rid of a player, no matter how valuable that player's performance still was. Not only would such a policy cost the team too much talent, but much of that talent would end up with other clubs. So though the New York Giants were well aware that Lawrence Taylor was regularly using drugs during the 1980s, the team would never have cut him from its roster because of it; doing so would have cost the Giants their 1987 and 1991 Super Bowl victories, as well as Taylor's 1999 installation in the Hall of Fame.

A stark example occurred late in the 1991 baseball season. Otis Nixon was having a great year for the Atlanta Braves in center field, at bat, and on the base paths, in spite of using cocaine. However, his cocaine use was detected by a random urine test, a league procedure to which he was subject because of prior cocaine incidents. Applying MLB policy, Commissioner Vincent suspended Nixon for the rest of the 1991 season. Though the Braves were able to win that year's National League pennant without Nixon, his absence cost them the World Series, which was won by the Minnesota Twins. Nixon would surely not have made the baserunning blunder committed by his replacement, Lonnie Smith, in a late inning of the seventh Series game, a mistake that cost Atlanta that city's first-ever championship in any sport. The best evidence of how the Braves assessed Nixon's value to the team in spite of his drug weakness was the fact that the following winter they outbid the California Angels to sign Nixon to a lucrative three-year deal that kept him in Atlanta. Indeed, Nixon remained in the majors for the rest of the 1990s, even after reaching the age of 40.

The free market verdict is clear: if the aim of a sports drug policy is to secure a high quality of performance by players, direct dealings between individual teams and players can get that job done. The appropriate method is to have the players' contracts permit the team to release a drug-abusing player without having to pay his expected salary. Even in the absence of an explicit contract provision targeting drug use—which clubs are most likely to negotiate with a player when they already have reason to suspect such behavior, as in Nixon's case—the standard commitment by the player to "keep himself in first-class physical condition" can and should be interpreted in this fashion. This contract language was used by the Pittsburgh Pirates as the basis of a favorable settlement of a lawsuit they had filed against Dave Parker: after making Parker the first million-dollar-a-year MLB player, the Pirates had seen his performance plummet in the early 1980s after he became addicted to cocaine.

If there is any doubt about this, the labor agreements in professional sports should explicitly give teams the relief they need (and spell out for players the incentives they must feel) to avoid poor performance on the field as a result of drug use off the field. The availability of such contractual protection for individual teams from excessive use of cocaine (or alcohol) would mean that the league would not impose an absolute ban on even casual player use of just one of such substances.

Illegal Recreational Drugs

Even though occasional cocaine use does not detract from a player's performance, and alcohol abuse is at least as harmful on this score as cocaine abuse, a fundamental distinction between the two substances still holds. Recreational use of cocaine and marijuana, unlike that of alcohol, is illegal in this country. So the true rationale for a league policy that treats a player's indulgence in cocaine or marijuana as qualitatively different from his indulgence in alcohol or tobacco is the felt need to protect the morality—or at least the moral image—of the game. Many fans as well as commissioners do not want to see their favored sport identified with law-breakers.

In reflecting on that morality argument, though, it is crucial to consider three underlying questions. Why were cocaine and marijuana (and not alcohol and cigarettes) made illegal in the first place? Why should athletes (and not, say, television performers) be singled out for suspension or expulsion from their industry for possession of illegal drugs? Finally, why has drug use (and not domestic abuse) been singled out as the form of illegal off-the-field behavior that attracts the most stringent league sanctions?

With respect to the first question, clearly we cannot delve into the complex details of America's current drug policies and controversies. However, a quick look at some of the basic facts is helpful. Sports has had a major impact on the broader debates about public drug policy, just as is true with gambling. Perhaps the single event that deserves the most "credit" for the intensity of our current war on drugs was the sudden death of Len Bias, which triggered bipartisan enactment of the Federal Anti–Drug Abuse Act.

The dimensions of this war are staggering. Back in the early 1970s about 325,000 Americans were in prison or jail at any one time. We now have over 1.8 million Americans behind bars, the highest number of any country in the world. The most important source of criminal arrest and incarceration is enforcement of the drug laws. Around 600,000 Americans are now arrested every year just for *possession* of marijuana (as happened to Allen Iverson and several other NBA players), and a majority of current federal prisoners are drug offenders. Indeed, early release of people who may have killed or raped someone is occasionally needed to free scarce prison space for new arrivals serving mandatory lifetime sentences for certain drug convictions. America now spends $75–$80 billion in government funds each year to try to win this drug war.

Are we winning? Overall rates of drug use have dropped significantly from the high points they had reached in the mid-1980s. But approximately 20 million Americans still smoke marijuana at least occasionally, and 4 million use cocaine. And a 1997 NCAA survey of college athletes found that although cocaine use had dropped from 17 percent in 1985 to 2 percent in 1997 (and steroid use from 4 percent to 1 percent), marijuana use had fallen only moderately, from 35 percent to 28 percent. Perhaps, then, the reason both NBA Commissioner David Stern and the NBA star Karl Malone were eager in 1998 to make marijuana use illegal under NBA law was in order to send a more powerful anti-drug message to future NBA aspirants and their college and high school classmates.

In reflecting on the value of this anti-drug war, it is useful to compare smoking marijuana with smoking cigarettes, and drinking alcohol with using cocaine. The differences are stark in the marijuana-tobacco comparison. Approximately 60 million Americans now smoke cigarettes, the vast majority are addicted to this recreational drug, and a significant number—now about 420,000 a year—will die as a result. By contrast, though over 100 million Americans have smoked marijuana over the past three decades, this substance has not been found to be physically addictive, and there is no scientific evidence that it kills any of its users (though overindulgence in this drug does occasionally disrupt their personal and professional lives).

Proponents of criminalizing marijuana—even when they acknowledge those facts—emphasize that this drug often leads to use of the more dangerous cocaine. True, cocaine users are more likely than not to have tried marijuana first. Interestingly, though, the single biggest lead-in to illegal drug use is cigarette smoking. Of people who have never smoked cigarettes, only 7 percent have ever used any illegal drug; of those who occasionally smoke cigarettes, 68 percent have used illegal drugs; and of pack-a-day smokers, fully 79 percent have tried one or more illegal drugs.

So maybe the real message that sports authorities should be sending to our government is that the NBA star and Players Association president Bob Lanier was right to accept the recommendations of public and scientific commissions in the 1970s and early 1980s to decriminalize marijuana. Unfortunately, our political authorities have not followed the lead of Lanier's (and Stern's) original 1983 drug policy (nor MLB's similar but short-lived 1984 accord). Instead, they have expended huge amounts not just of taxpayer dollars but also of people's lives (spent in jail) to combat the least dangerous of all mind-altering drugs, whether legal or illegal. Even if some marijuana users do go on to try cocaine (after starting with tobacco), the more rational measure for segregating the two would be to regulate rather than prohibit marijuana. The most sensible strategy for containing excessive use of marijuana would be to levy a tax on marijuana sales, a measure that would place financial rather than criminal obstacles in the way of those who were tempted to overindulge. In fact, adoption of a "sin" tax on marijuana might finally persuade Congress to enact a similar tax on cigarettes, as a more effective antidote than lawsuits to the nation's most addictive and most dangerous recreational drug.

The comparison between cocaine and alcohol is much closer and more complicated than that between cigarettes and marijuana. Cocaine use now produces around 8,000 fatalities annually—including some well-known athletes. Alcohol use, in contrast, leads to more than 100,000 deaths every year: approximately half of these are from diseases such as the liver cancer that killed Mickey Mantle; the other half are attributable to drunken behavior, as was the auto accident that ended Billy Martin's life.

Indeed, not only have players such as Fred Washington of the Chicago Bears, Stacy Toran of the Los Angeles Raiders, and Pelle Lindbergh of the Philadelphia Flyers killed themselves while driving under the influence of alcohol; other intoxicated players such as Charles Smith of the Boston Celtics, Craig Mactavish of the Boston Bruins, and Reggie Rogers of the Detroit Lions have struck and killed innocent victims. Even piloting a boat while drunk can be deadly. At a 1993 spring training party for Cleveland Indians players, Tim Crews became intoxicated; then, while boating home at dusk, Crews ran into an unlighted dock, killing himself and his teammate Steve Olin and seriously injuring Bobby Ojeda. Finally, a rarely mentioned fact about the Len Bias case is that, on his late-night return from Boston to the Maryland campus, Bias began celebrating by doing some serious drinking with his roommates. It was only later that the students pulled out their stash of cocaine, and it was actually the combination of the two drugs that killed Bias, something that is true of many other cocaine deaths.

Needless to say, the law no longer "prohibits" use of alcohol, which now accounts for approximately 50 percent of homicides, 40 percent of auto fatalities, 30 percent of other accidents (such as in boats or on motorcycles), and 30 percent of suicides. And the same soft stance toward alcohol is taken by sports authorities, as illustrated by another case involving Lenny Dykstra of the Philadelphia Phillies, whose poker-playing problems were discussed in Chapter 3. In the spring of 1991 Dykstra was convicted of drunk driving after getting into an accident while driving home from a party. The accident injured both Dykstra and, much more severely, his passenger and Phillies teammate Darren Daulton. Commissioner Fay Vincent decreed that Dykstra's own painful injury and the criminal fines levied on him were more than enough punishment for his dangerously illegal behavior, and thus baseball would impose no further penalties. What a stark contrast to Vincent's reaction to Steve Howe's cocaine conviction the following year for behavior that endangered only Howe.

Illegal use, not just abuse, of alcohol continues to be a significant problem in this country. Recall the NCAA's survey findings that while cocaine use by college athletes had fallen from 17 percent to 2 percent, marijuana use had dropped just from 35 percent to 28 percent. That same survey found that drinking by college athletes had decreased even more marginally, from 88 percent to 81 percent, and that 61 percent of male athletes indulged in binge drinking. When student athletes under the age of 21 drink alcohol, they violate the law. Yet the NCAA has never made illegal use of alcohol grounds for suspension, let alone required random testing, as it now does for illegal use of marijuana.

The mere fact that some alcohol use is illegal or dangerous hardly warrants the restoration of Prohibition. Just as with gambling, the vast majority of Americans who drink do so only occasionally, moderately, and for the pleasure it brings to their lives. It would be a mistake to restore the legal ban on anyone's use of alcohol simply to protect future Mickey Mantles and Billy Martins from the fatal consequences of their overuse. However, as with marijuana, it might well be a good idea to establish a more substantial tax on alcohol, and not just to help pay for the billions of dollars of annual social costs of alcohol abuse. Such a tax would also reduce, at least to some extent, the levels of excessive drinking, because it would make this recreational activity more expensive (though among athletes this would be felt just by those in college, not by those in the professional ranks).

Should the same policy be adopted for cocaine? Proponents of legalization should recognize that, unlike marijuana, cocaine is more dangerous than alcohol (though not more dangerous than tobacco). While current fatality rates from alcohol are much higher than those from cocaine, the gap is much smaller than the 30-fold difference in number between those who use alcohol (130 million) and those who use cocaine (4 million). Prohibition in the 1920s did succeed in cutting alcohol use in half and alcohol-related deaths by two-thirds; it is quite likely, then, that legalizing cocaine would substantially *increase* the number of current users, and thence the potential risks to their lives.

The tough policy call is whether substantially increasing the level of legal cocaine use would also reduce the percentage of dangerous use: not just by ensuring a safer substance (unlike the fatal dose Len Bias inhaled) but also by cutting back on the large number of homicides, robberies, and other crimes that flow out of the current criminal drug-dealing culture. In my view, the most sensible and moderate step would be to relax—perhaps even remove—the stiff criminal punishments now imposed on personal users. The law should focus its efforts on dealers who create the danger for others, rather than on users who endanger only themselves.

Here again, sports authorities might consider serving as a role model for the Drug Enforcement Agency. Only if athletes are found to be providing cocaine to others should they be barred from the game by the league. This would leave it up to the individual team to decide whether or not a player should be fired for merely using the drug, according to whether it damages his play (as it did to Dave Parker with the Pirates, but not to Otis Nixon with the Braves). The basic scientific fact is that cocaine is harmful only when taken in excess, and is much less addictive than alcohol, let alone tobacco. And yet in our current war on drugs the prevailing legal view is that we must destroy the users (via long-term jail sentences) in order to save them. A valuable lesson that American sports fans—and public authorities—should draw from Steve Howe's full career is that extremism in the war on drugs is *not* a virtue, and moderation in that struggle is not a vice.

Athletes as Role Models?

It is not likely that American lawmakers will moderate, let alone legalize, our public restraints on drug use in the foreseeable future. (Lately it seems that only an athlete-turned-politician, Governor Jesse "The Body" Ventura, has been calling for true "Reform" of our marijuana ban.) This leaves open the question of whether the leagues should relax rather than toughen their own treatment of players who use either marijuana or cocaine. After all, the penalties imposed on players by sports authorities for these drug offenses are often far harsher than the ones they receive from criminal authorities. Recall that while Steve Howe received a $1,000 fine from the criminal judge for possession of cocaine, Commissioner Fay Vincent strongly criticized Arbitrator Nicolau for imposing too "moderate" a baseball punishment of approximately $2 million in earnings lost by Howe on account of his suspension. Is there something about athletes that warrants such treatment within their profession, particularly regarding drug use?

The double standard for sports and other professions is vividly illustrated by the position taken by Disney/ABC toward a pair of cases arising in 1997. That summer, the Anaheim Angels' second baseman Tony Phillips was arrested for buying cocaine from an undercover drug agent. While criminal charges were pending, the Angels sought to suspend Phillips, but they were blocked from doing so by arbitration precedents that required players to be convicted before being banned from the field of play. Michael Eisner, the head of Disney/ABC, which owns the Angels, strongly criticized that baseball rule. Eisner and his Disney colleagues believed that much faster and tougher action was required from baseball authorities to reassure fans (including children) that they were watching a game being played in a fully "drug-free" zone. By contrast, only two months after making his irate comments about Phillips and the evil of drugs in sports, Eisner signed ABC's *Home Improvement* star, Tim Allen, to the highest-paying contract in television history—$1.25 million an episode, or about $30 million a season. No mention was made to the media of the fact that Allen had once served 28 months in prison for *trafficking* in cocaine.

The list of entertainment performers who have spent time in jail for drug offenses is a long one, going back at least to Robert Mitchum's conviction for marijuana use in 1949, and including such stars as the "Godfather of Soul" James Brown, Kelsey Grammer of *Cheers* and *Frasier,* Sean Penn, and Robert Downey Jr. And like the athletes Len Bias and Don Rogers, a number of notable actors have died from drug overdoses: John Belushi, River Phoenix, and Chris Farley from *Saturday Night Live,* to name a few.

Of course, just as the Angels did with Phillips at the end of the 1997 season when his contract had expired, movie studios and television networks do occasionally release performers whose popular image has been tarnished by drug use or other misbehavior. However, in the highly competitive entertainment marketplace, this is a rather rare step. And it would be unthinkable—as well as illegal—for members of the Motion Picture Association of America or the National Association of Broadcasters to agree collectively to ban any drug user from appearing on the screens in movie theaters or family rooms, to ensure that entertainment provides proper role models for American viewers.

Why, then, should a Tony Phillips or a Steve Howe be barred from appearing on the screens as well as on the fields of baseball through such collective action by MLB owners, which include studio/networks such as Disney/ABC with its Angels, Twentieth Century Fox with its Dodgers, and Time Warner with its Braves? As Willie Wilson of the Kansas City Royals said in the early 1980s after receiving a stiff jail sentence (for merely *attempting* to possess drugs) from a judge concerned about baseball players as role models for children, "All I signed a contract to do is play baseball. I didn't sign a contract to take care of anyone else's kids or to be a role model for anyone else." A decade later Charles Barkley echoed those sentiments when he said in a Nike ad, "I'm *not* a role model. I am paid to wreak havoc on the basketball court, not to raise someone else's kids." But the fallacy in both Wilson's statement and Barkley's ad is that the very reason athletes are now paid such huge amounts by advertisers (around $600 million a year) is precisely that they do operate as important role models, especially among younger fans and potential customers.

Why have athletic superstars such as Michael Jordan or Tiger Woods earned an order of magnitude more in endorsement deals (though not in performance contracts) than do even hugely popular movie stars like Tom Cruise or Leonardo DiCaprio? I believe the reason is that movie fans identify with the *characters* portrayed by actors like Cruise (the feisty sports agent in *Jerry Maguire*) or DiCaprio (the poor but valiant lover in *Titanic*); sports fans, in contrast, identify directly with Jordan and Woods as real people whom they have witnessed playing on the court or golf course. Considering how many athletes are portrayed in advertisements, it is clear that sports stars have become special role models in American life.

However, that fact does not by itself seem to justify collective restraints on the services of even "immoral" players. Recall the NBA episodes in which Sprewell choked his coach and Rodman kicked the cameraman. The Converse shoe company then exercised its right to terminate its endorsement deal with Sprewell, but it did not do the same to Rodman. And a year later another company, And 1, signed Sprewell to a new deal because of his new rogue appeal in the sports shoe market. It would be considered unconscionable as well as illegal for all the manufacturers of any one product (let alone all the corporate sponsors of every product) to agree among themselves—rather than let each decide for itself—that a player's public image had been fatally compromised by his illegal behavior on or off the court.

This brings us back to the fundamental difference between a sports league and an association of either motion picture producers or athletic shoe makers. When Disney places Tim Allen on its ABC network or Converse displays Dennis Rodman on its shoe advertisements, this action affects the perception and prospects only of that company's product, not of those of its counterparts like NBC or Nike. In contrast, when the Anaheim Angels released Tony Phillips for cocaine use once his 1997 season contract had expired, not only did this leave Phillips free to sign with the Blue Jays for the 1998 season, but he was also able to come back to Anaheim with the Jays to play the Angels in Edison Field. The "joint product" character of sports, the feature that shapes so many of the distinctive issues of the *economics* of the game, puts a unique spin on the challenges to the *morality* of the game. Any individual owner may be willing to risk slightly dimming the moral luster of his team by signing up a lawbreaker who also happens to be a game winner. But what if that player's character is so unsavory that his presence on the fields or courts around the league appears to cast a shadow over the moral appeal of the game as a whole? Only one team gets the benefit of the player's efforts to win the championship, but all may be tainted by his participation over the course of the season. If the image of the league is worth protecting from that threat, the necessary action has to be taken by its central authority.

Drug Use versus Domestic Abuse

Of course, the monopoly power of a central league authority over its sport creates opportunities for it to do the wrong as well as the right thing. After all, for the first half of this century the authorities in baseball (and other sports) used their power to protect the "integrity" of their game by ensuring that no team would add talented black players to its roster. And in 1947, when Jackie Robinson was finally breaking the racist barriers in baseball, the major movie studios were creating an analogous political barrier. Through their Motion Picture Association of America (MPAA), the studios collectively agreed that none of them would hire even Oscar-winning members of the Hollywood Ten or other members of the Communist Party to write, direct, or appear in a movie.

How can we use the power of such central authorities to protect just the integrity of the game rather than the selective (and sometimes prejudicial) feelings of the powers that be? The leagues have to commit themselves to a broader principle: any kind of seriously illegal behavior by players must receive the same response from their sport as does a drug offense.

A notable illustration of this problem is another college case, this one involving the running back Lawrence Phillips of the University of Nebraska. As the 1995 college football season started, Phillips was the Heisman Trophy favorite, a position he reinforced by rushing for more than 200 yards and four touchdowns to lead the Cornhuskers to victory against Michigan State. The following night, though, Phillips climbed up an outside wall and through the window of the apartment of his teammate Scott Frost, where he found his ex-girlfriend (another Nebraska basketball player) Kate McEwen. He grabbed McEwen by her hair and dragged her down three flights of stairs until he was stopped by Frost and neighbors in the building who had been awakened by her screaming. McEwen was rushed to the hospital by ambulance, and Phillips was hauled off to jail by the police.

Nebraska's football coach, Tom Osborne, immediately suspended Phillips from the team and told him to go to class rather than to practice. A few weeks later, after Phillips had pleaded "no contest" to the assault charge and been placed on probation, Osborne brought him back on the team as the Cornhuskers were moving into the key part of their season. That New Year's Day Phillips was again a college football star, rushing for 165 yards and three touchdowns as Nebraska whipped Florida in the Fiesta Bowl to win the national title. Seven months later the St. Louis Rams picked Phillips early in the first round of the NFL draft. While the Rams did not get much benefit from their $5 million deal with Phillips,

Kate McEwen received a good share of that money in settling her tort suit against her assailant. The question remains whether Phillips reformed his behavior off as well as on the field while playing in Europe before his return to the NFL in the fall of 1999.

In terms of the larger issue of sports policy we are considering here, the significant fact in the Phillips case is that the NCAA took *no* action against him. Recall that in 1986 the NCAA established a very rigid policy regarding players' drug use. This policy requires both penalties for athletes who are found using marijuana, for example, and random tests of all players to detect anyone using such substances. But the NCAA has never seen fit to establish a similar policy governing brutal assaults by athletes such as Phillips (who was only one of several of those Nebraska national champions who had attacked women). So also in a professional sport like baseball: while the MLB authorities have suspended Darryl Strawberry and Dwight Gooden for extensive periods because of their drug use, the league did not even reprimand the two for their assault offenses (including Strawberry's attacks on both of his wives).

From any fair-minded perspective, athletes' assaults on women are a far greater source of personal and social harm than their use of cocaine, let alone marijuana. Indeed, a key reason Congress passed the 1994 Violence Against Women Act was that, among women aged 15–44, assault by a spouse or domestic partner is the leading cause of injury, claiming more victims than do auto accidents, rapes, and muggings combined. At present, around 100 criminal charges of physical abuse of women are lodged every year against professional and college athletes. Among the athletic celebrities who have run afoul of these laws (though not of their sports authorities) are Barry Bonds, José Canseco, Scottie Pippen, Robert Parrish, John Daly, and, most notorious of all, Mike Tyson, who not only raped his date Desirée Washington but had previously battered his wife, Robin Givens. One disturbing study of college students found that male athletes, who make up only 3 percent of the male student body, accounted for 19 percent of the sexual assaults reported to school (though not necessarily to criminal) authorities.

What causes this propensity for misbehavior among some athletes? It is less the result of the tough and aggressive attitudes generated by play on the field than of the celebrity status and indulgence that players enjoy off the field. Almost all of the reported sexual assaults by athletes involved women who were either their long-time domestic partners or their immediate dates. It is precisely because athletes are so used to having women say yes to whatever they want that a few react violently when one woman says no. Indeed, in the 24 hours before Desirée Washington said no to Mike Tyson and then was raped by him, two other women had given Tyson the sex that he was always looking for.

When athletes are accused of such assaults they are more, not less, likely than non-athletes to be arrested by the police and charged by a district attorney; however, they are also more likely to be acquitted by a jury, which means that the overall ratios of investigation to conviction are roughly the same. Contrary to many commentators, I do not believe this is because juries are unwilling to convict star athletes—as Mike Tyson and his lawyers learned. At least some of the acquittals stem from false accusations generated by the celebrity status of athletes, such as the "date rape" charges filed against the Dallas Cowboys Michael Irvin and Erik Williams in the middle of the 1996 NFL playoffs. The bigger part of the explanation is revealed in a notorious case involving Warren Moon.

Moon was not drafted by any NFL team when he graduated from the University of Washington in 1977. After an outstanding apprenticeship period with the Edmonton Eskimos in the Canadian Football League, he returned to the United States to become a star, the first great black quarterback in professional football history (and one of the all-time greats of any race). Not only was Moon named the NFL's 1989 Man of the Year, but in 1994 *USA Today* honored him as America's "most caring athlete." So fans around the country were shocked to learn what happened on the evening of July 18, 1995, just before NFL training camps were to open. Houston police received a 911 call from Moon's young son saying that his father was hitting and choking his mother. The police broke up this domestic assault, which even had Moon in his car chasing his wife out on the highway. The couple made up the next day, with Warren apologizing for his "tremendous mistake" in losing control in an argument, apparently over his infidelity and her spending. Felicia Moon said that "after many hours of prayers, tears and consultations with my husband, I feel safe in his presence."

In the normal case, the husband's contrition and his wife's forgiveness would persuade the district attorney not to bring criminal charges against a first-time domestic assault offender. However, the massive public attention that such incidents involving athletes attract, with headlines on the front page as well as in the sports section, means that offices like that of the Houston district attorney feel compelled to prosecute a Warren Moon. But as also often happens in these cases, when Felicia Moon testified on behalf of her husband rather than in support of the prosecution's charge, the jury acquitted Moon. (Later some jury members commented that there is "some sort of slapping in most marriages," and that a first offender such as Moon "needs another chance.") And in fact the very same factors that make criminal authorities feel compelled to press these charges—the athletes' professional status and popular renown—also encourage the abused wives to support their spouses in court. Acquittal may well preserve their marriage, but even if it doesn't, it will at least maintain the husband's athletic career and thus the wife's share of that career's financial rewards.

From a broader public policy perspective, this understandable response of the victims of abuse can aggravate rather than ameliorate the social problem. Not just Warren Moon's wife but also Lawrence Phillips's ex-girlfriend could obtain compensation for the harms they suffered only if their assailants' playing careers and high salaries continued. But if we want to protect potential future victims of sexual violence, it is crucial that the most visible offenders, athletes, be punished at least as severely as other abusers—precisely because this is the best way to send out the message that ordinary Americans need to receive.

After all, when players use an illegal drug like cocaine, most of the time they do not suffer any harm, and even if they do, it is harm they inflict on themselves alone. By contrast, when a player assaults his wife or rapes his date, he inflicts pain and often serious injury on a woman who has not consented to any such action. The most fundamental flaw in the policies of professional—and college and international—sports authorities toward players' off-the-field offenses is that their major priority has long been to combat recreational drug use rather than violent domestic abuse.

Happily, in the summer of 1998 the NFL took a crucial step toward a truly moral approach to players' misbehavior. Exercising the authority that was first formulated in the *Reese/Crowder* drug use case in the late 1970s, Commissioner Paul Tagliabue proclaimed that "engaging in violent criminal activity is unacceptable and constitutes conduct detrimental to the integrity of and public confidence in the NFL." In order to avoid not only "potential tragic consequences for the victim" but also "alienating the fans on whom the success of the League depends," the commissioner announced, any player *charged* with such a crime would have to immediately undergo "clinical evaluation and appropriate coun- seling." Under this policy, if the player admits to or is *convicted* of a vio- lent crime (specifically including "crimes of domestic violence" as well as illegal possession of "deadly weapons"), he is subject to the same kind of league discipline as a drug offender. The first NFL player to get such a penalty was Lawrence Phillips, who received a substantial fine from Tagliabue when he returned to the NFL in 1999, a penalty that was im- posed for Phillips's second domestic abuse offense but his first while in professional football (with the Dolphins in 1998). For any sports au- thority (such as the NCAA) that considers it vital to the integrity of its game to control the behavior of players (or coaches or other employees) off the field, the NFL's new approach should serve as the role model.

A Principled Approach to Immoral Behavior

Let us now return to the problem of drug use, the subject of national de- bates over the last quarter-century about the morality of this behavior by ordinary Americans as well as athletic stars. The challenges here are even more complex than they were with the gambling behavior we ex- amined earlier. Indeed, when we reflect about gambling and drug use together (as we rarely do), we discover a troubling illustration of how unsystematic our social policy approaches are—more prejudicial than principled. One arm of our government is actively encouraging Ameri- cans to indulge in, and occasionally become addicted to, gambling in ca- sinos and lotteries (even if not on sports events), while another arm of government fills our prison space with those who indulge in recreational drugs.

In the world of sports, it is both legitimate and necessary to adopt a more proactive and tough-minded policy toward performance-enhanc- ing drugs like steroids than toward recreational drugs, precisely because of the harmful pressure that a player's use of performance enhancers in- flicts on *other* players competing in the same sport. Mark McGwire's use of the potentially harmful Andro to help him become baseball's home- run record holder should *not* put an asterisk beside that record, because he was clearly complying with the current rules of the game. But even though McGwire told us that he stopped using Andro in the 1999 sea- son, baseball should change its rules for all future players. McGwire's celebrated success had already made him a much more powerful role model for young American athletes and fans thinking about which substances to use, than, say, Steve Howe became when he was prosecuted for possession of cocaine.

With respect to recreational drugs, as I have already made clear, I believe we made a major public policy mistake by putting marijuana in the same illegal situation as cocaine. Not only is an Allen Iverson's smoking of marijuana an order of magnitude less dangerous than a Len Bias's inhaling of cocaine; it is also far less so than a Mickey Mantle's drinking of alcohol—let alone any player's smoking of cigarettes. Legalizing—and taxing—marijuana would be a far more sensible policy than prosecuting people for its use.

Even with respect to cocaine, whose distribution (if not possession) I believe should remain illegal, a significant sports policy issue remains. Should a player's off-the-field use of this drug be grounds for suspension (or even banishment) by the league, or should it simply be a reason for the player's own team to release him if his drug use undermines his performance on the field? The fact that athletes, especially in professional sports, have become major role models in American life justifies the leagues' taking action to protect the morality, not just the image, of the game. However, the bottom-line test of whether a league is truly committed to that moral standard is whether it treats physical abuse of women as an offense at least as serious as use of drugs (or illegal possession of guns). So far the only sports authority that passes this morality test is the National Football League.

6

THE MORAL IDEAL
FOR AMERICAN SPORTS

The anti-violence policy instituted by NFL Commissioner Paul Tagliabue is the most principled effort to date by a sports authority to promote the moral integrity of the game. As we move into the 21st century of sports, I hope this will be the role model followed by our other leagues—including the NCAA—in treating athletes' domestic abuse just as seriously as their drug use.

Many fans may view this moral challenge as confirmation that every sport needs to have a commissioner in charge of everything happening in the game—the kind of independent and powerful commissioner that MLB owners first created in 1920 in response to the Black Sox scandal. As a federal judge put it in one of the rare challenges to a decision by the first MLB commissioner, Kenesaw Mountain Landis, the owners had "endowed the Commissioner with all the attributes of a benevolent but absolute despot, and all the disciplinary power of a proverbial paterfamilias."

My views on that score are rather mixed. We definitely do need commissioner-like authority for administering and enforcing the rules of the game. The present-day need is strongest in boxing, which has integrity problems far deeper than Mike Tyson's biting Evander Holyfield's ear (for example, boxing associations being bribed to give fighters world championship ratings). That is why I would like to see Congress significantly expand Senator John McCain's Muhammad Ali Boxing Reform Act of 1999 by establishing a National Boxing Commission in charge of designating which fights are truly championship matches and who should be the referees and judges who decide who wins those bouts (perhaps even using instant replay).

At the same time, we must recognize that in team sports, at least, the commissioners have always been selected (and dismissed) by the own-ers of the teams in each sport; this is also true of the universities that make up the NCAA that governs college sports. The usual pick in pro-fessional sports is someone who previously was the league's lead lawyer, such as Paul Tagliabue or David Stern. But now baseball has again been the pioneering sport by installing the first-ever owner in the commis-sioner's office—Bud Selig of the Milwaukee Brewers.

I do believe Selig was the right choice for this position. However, the fact that he is a team owner (with his daughter running the Brewers) provides the most graphic illustration of why there must be public limits on such private authority. In sports, as anywhere else in American life, the law cannot give the representative of the owners of the business an unreviewable power to make decisions with major consequences for others who have no role in picking and paying the commissioner. We now face that same challenge under international law in developing the appropriate vehicle for public scrutiny of the fateful decisions made by the private International Olympic Committee—such as why one city has won the race for a future Olympic Games.

In the rest of this book we shall be exploring the economics of sports. What should the players market be like, both to ensure fair treatment of players and to enhance competitive balance in the sport? How can we best serve the interests of fans who want access to the game without hav-ing to pay unjustifiably high prices—especially in taxpayer-funded sta-dium deals? It is not plausible to assume that the right answers on these and other economic scores will always be coming from the commis-sioner's office.

What about the morality of the game, which we have been exploring throughout Part I? Certainly, we have come a long way from those "good old days" when Commissioner Landis used his absolute but not-so-benevolent despotic authority to reserve our national pastime for "whites only." Indeed, baseball now appears to be the most racially and ethnically diverse of all American professions. And not only has the lon-ger-lasting "Caucasian only" PGA Tour at last embraced stars of color such as Tiger Woods, but with the help of the law, Casey Martin has viv-idly displayed to his fellow disabled Americans that reasonable accom-modation can be made to at least some of their needs without detracting from the integrity of the game.

The sports message is somewhat more mixed with respect to behavior off the field—in particular, drug use and domestic abuse. Notwithstanding our massive expenditure of public funds and personal freedom in the war on drugs, there has been only a modest drop in American use of marijuana (as opposed to the dangerous cocaine). Perhaps it is now time for government and sports authorities to draw upon the lessons provided by athletes as well as scientists. While players like Allen Iverson are arrested for possession of marijuana, their use of this substance does not seem to have generated anything like the harm inflicted by legal cigarettes and alcohol (for example, on Mickey Mantle), let alone by illegal cocaine (for example, on Len Bias). Indeed, if we were to substitute a marijuana tax for a marijuana ban, we would be able to free up more time for criminal and sports authorities to combat the substantial harm that athletes (and non-athletes) inflict on other people via domestic abuse, date rape, and other violent behavior.

What about gambling, the widespread social activity that gave rise to the 1919 Black Sox scandal and then to the Office of the Commissioner? Certainly Americans are now greatly attracted to the pleasures of gambling, as evidenced by how many billions of dollars are now being spent with casinos, lotteries, racetracks, and sports bookies. Several million members of this huge gambling population do, however, face essentially the same risk of pathological harm as abusers of cocaine and alcohol. That is why I believe we need Congress to institute something like an individual gambling cap—a dollar limit on how much money anyone can bet annually. This is one way in which we could control the risks of this brand of entertainment while still preserving its pleasures.

In sports, league authorities have displayed much the same inconsistencies as governments in their response to gambling. Commissioners regularly advocate the use of state lotteries to finance new stadiums and channel the financial rewards of these luxurious facilities into the pockets of team owners. Leagues as a whole have also benefited from the way betting on games enhances their appeal and profitability: certainly commissioners do not object to game odds and point spreads being prominently displayed on sports pages and television screens. However, the leagues (including the NCAA) have used their influence with Congress to make sure that one key form of gambling remains illegal—placing a bet on a game with a business. That is why American fans, including many college athletes and their classmates, now channel billions of dollars into the hands of criminal bookies rather than into legally regulated business operations like the Foxwoods Casino and the Churchill Downs racetrack.

And as Pete Rose learned, MLB authorities remain committed to Commissioner Landis's rule that anyone who places a bet on his team, even to win its games, faces a lifetime ban from baseball. By contrast with a player like Steve Howe, there are no meaningful checks and balances on the exercise of the commissioner's authority over a manager like Rose. So when Commissioner Bart Giamatti was deciding how to deal with Rose's betting, he felt no need to emulate NFL Commissioner Pete Rozelle's more moderate response to the same kind of misbehavior by the Packers' Paul Hornung. Perhaps the new brand of owner-turned-commissioner, Bud Selig, will see the value of a more balanced approach to this volatile issue in baseball, especially if Rose were to finally acknowledge that he had been betting on his Reds to *win* their games. If so, the Hall of Fame will at last admit the sport's all-time leader not just in personal hits but also in team wins—Pete Rose.

II

OWNERS VERSUS PLAYERS

7

SHOW US
THE MONEY

As we enter a new millennium, the year 2000 seems likely to be the first in a while without a fierce labor battle in a major league. But throughout the 1990s American fans had love-hate feelings toward sports. League attendance levels were higher than ever before, and the soaring value of sports television deals displayed how large and committed an audience there was for games coming over the air. But each of the major sports had been rocked by a big labor dispute in that decade, resulting in a stoppage of play, a lawsuit, or a combination of the two, and we are quite sure there will be numerous replays in the coming decade. Fans feel quite upset about the apparent effect of these money battles on the integrity and quality of the games being played.

When the same people go to a movie or watch a television program, they rarely think about the amount of money being paid to a Tom Cruise or an Oprah Winfrey to put their works on the screen. However, with *USA Today* printing annual league payrolls and ESPN's *Sports Center* regularly discussing them, the people watching games are usually aware of—and often appalled by—the huge salaries that teams now pay their players. The resentment felt by the people in Boston when the future Hall-of-Famer Roger Clemens left the Red Sox for a large pay increase from the Blue Jays was dwarfed by the outrage of Clevelanders when the Browns' owner Art Modell moved the entire team to Baltimore (there to be known as the Ravens) to cash in on a huge taxpayer-financed bonanza. Nevertheless, most fans, along with the media, believe that the seemingly greedy owners are driven to such actions by their need to meet the gargantuan payrolls created by even greedier players.

Fans' immediate concern about player free agency and astronomical salaries focuses on the way these skew the competitive balance between small-market and large-market teams. But the more fundamental concern is that this constant pursuit of more and more money is corrupting the role of sports in American life. Unlike movie fans, who actually celebrate the record-setting box-office returns of a film like *Titanic,* sports fans have traditionally viewed their favorite sports as a crucial part of American culture, more akin to religion than to business. A game like baseball is felt to be much more a part of the American heritage than the fine arts, and who wins the Super Bowl far more important than who wins the Oscars.

This "sacred" stature of sports explains why people so lamented the loss of the 1994 World Series to a players' strike, and were so anxious about the prospects of losing the NBA Championship and the NHL Stanley Cup to owner-imposed lockouts. Most fans assume that rising salaries are the reason ticket prices have gone up so much—such that a family of four now spends around $250 to go watch a regular-season NFL (or NBA or NHL) game.

The principal culprits in the assault on this central feature of American life are usually believed to be the leaders and lawyers of the players' associations. These are the people who have waged the sports wars over the past several decades to try to force the owners to pay more money to their associations' members—money that the owners say must come from ticketholders and taxpayers. While the average American was quite supportive of the strike of United Parcel Service (UPS) workers in the summer of 1997, by which the Teamsters union was trying to improve the situation of low-paid, part-time workers, the following summer people were not at all sympathetic toward the NBA players, who were engaged in a seven-month battle with the owners to avoid a "hard" cap on salaries that had already reached $2.6 million for the average player.

The 1990s was the most tumultuous decade to date in sports labor relations, culminating in the first NBA games ever missed because of a labor dispute. A brief look at the conflicts in each sport during that decade will offer us a window into the evolution of sports labor relations over the entire century. More important, it will give us a basis for judging how the players and owners in the 21st century should address these surprisingly complex challenges to professional sports—especially in Major League Baseball, which may well be embarking on an even bigger battle than those in the past.

Basketball

On July 1, 1998, Commissioner David Stern announced that the NBA owners were locking the players out of the basketball courts. This action was taken, even though team practice and play were not scheduled to begin for months, to prevent players from either receiving any up-front salary payments under their current contracts or signing lucrative new deals as free agents. The owners' aim was to force the players and their union to accept the league's favored salary cap design. Not until January 6, 1999, with the owners about to vote to shut down the entire season, were the two sides able to negotiate all night to reach a settlement. This deal did place a ceiling on how much money could be paid to individual players, but it still has not done that for the total payrolls of individual teams.

The NBA was the league in which the salary cap first appeared in sports, at a time when professional basketball was in a financially precarious state. In the early 1980s fans had to stay up until after the 11 P.M. local news to watch taped network broadcasts of an NBA *championship* series featuring such all-time greats as Magic Johnson, Julius Erving, and Larry Bird. Even the players acknowledged that something had to be done to curb the impact of the emerging free agent system on payroll levels, which were putting a number of franchises on the endangered species list.

So in the spring of 1983 the NBPA's long-time leader, Larry Fleisher, negotiated with Commissioner Larry O'Brien and his soon-to-be successor David Stern a pioneering version of a salary cap. Each team was given the same payroll budget, calculated as an agreed-to percentage of the league's Basketball Related Income (BRI). However, a key exception was written into that payroll cap so that it would *not* govern the amount that a team like the Boston Celtics could use to re-sign its own stars like Larry Bird, as opposed to luring free agents from other teams. It is this "Larry Bird" exception that led sports law aficionados to dub the NBA's version a "soft" rather than a "hard" cap.

By the mid-1990s the financial consequences of this soft cap design were quite apparent. Although the formal cap figures had soared along with basketball's popular appeal, from $3.1 million in 1983–84 to $15.9 million in 1993–94, players' average salaries had gone from $250,000 to

$1.8 million, which put the average team payroll at nearly $25 million. So the NBA owners began their five-year effort to eliminate Larry Bird as a cap loophole (while bringing him back as a coach).

This effort triggered battles not only between owners and players but also among the players themselves. The players' union in basketball had always used antitrust litigation rather than strike action—something that also happened in the summer of 1994. This time, though, the NBPA got the bad news from the federal Second Circuit—in a case known as *Buck Williams* after the NBPA president—that as long as players were part of a labor union they had no right to sue under antitrust law. Thus, just after Hakeem Olajuwon and his Houston Rockets had beaten Patrick Ewing and his New York Knicks in the seventh game of the 1995 championship series, Williams and the NBPA's new executive director, Simon Gourdine, signed a deal with David Stern. The cap figure shot up from $16 million in 1994–95 to $23 million in 1995–96, but the cap was to be hardened by a 100 percent "luxury tax" imposed on any team whose payroll exceeded the designated amount. In future, any club that wanted to follow the lead of the Knicks, who were about to pay Patrick Ewing $18 million for the 1995–96 season (almost all of it above the cap), would have to pay an additional $18 million to the league to be divided up among the team's competitors. Everyone assumed that the prospect of such a huge surcharge would discourage any significant exceeding of the designated payroll figures.

That is why the tentative settlement set off a big struggle among the players. Some of the stars, like Olajuwon and David Robinson, favored its terms, but others like Patrick Ewing did not. The biggest name against the tax was Michael Jordan, who had just decided to return to basketball rather than continue trying to raise his batting average in baseball. Ewing and Jordan, along with their agent, David Falk, began a move to decertify the NBPA under labor law, in order to restore the players' right to sue the owners under antitrust law. Faced with that possibility, the owners backed off and restored the full Larry Bird exception for veteran free agents, though they did impose a hard cap on individual salaries of rookies during their first three years in the league.

By 1998 Jordan had returned the NBA title to Chicago for three years in a row, and was earning $33 million a year for his efforts (while the total team payroll was $62 million). Meanwhile, Ewing was getting $21 million from the Knicks and had succeeded Williams as NBPA president, with Billy Hunter installed as the new executive director. The formal payroll limit, based on 48 percent of BRI, was supposed to be $27 million that year, but the payroll average had actually reached $33 million, or 57 percent of BRI. The owners' gravest concern was generated, not by veteran stars like Jordan and Ewing, but by 20-year-old Kevin Garnett's six-year, $126 million contract with the Minnesota Timberwolves, only three years after he had left high school to play in the NBA. True, the NBA owners had just negotiated new television deals with NBC and TNT that raised annual network payments from $275 million to $660 million, beginning in the 1998–99 season. However, that summer Stern and the owners decided to exercise their option to terminate the collective agreement and lock the players out in order to jettison the Larry Bird exception.

This time, contrary to the advice offered by Gene Upshaw, the head of the NFL Players Association (NFLPA), Ewing and Hunter decided not to decertify their union and sue under antitrust, although they tried, unsuccessfully, to persuade Arbitrator John Feerick that the owners could not stop paying guaranteed salaries during a lockout. Six months later, with the prospect of a totally lost season staring everyone in the face, the parties finally reached a compromise settlement that added some more salary constraints, although it preserved the Larry Bird exception for players re-signing with their current teams.

Under the NBA agreement the formal salary cap remained at 48 percent of BRI. But by 2002, the fourth year of that labor contract, 10 percent of all players' salaries were to be paid into an escrow account: if total league payrolls then topped 55 percent of BRI, the escrow account would be used to reimburse the owners. And not only was the salary cap for individual rookies extended from three to four years for future Kevin Garnetts, but the first-ever salary cap was imposed on future veterans like Patrick Ewing. As of 1998–99, the maximum that could be paid to Scottie Pippen, for example, was $14 million a year.

For these veterans, the NBA actually widened the Larry Bird gap between what a free agent's own team and any other team could pay for his services. There was no difference between the maximum amounts in the first year, but after that the "home" team could offer the player six more years with 12.5 percent guaranteed annual increases, while other teams could offer no more than five years with 10 percent annual increases. The two sides also agreed to a "Michael Jordan" exception permitting players to receive a 5 percent increase over their current salaries, however large those salaries might be. Notwithstanding that prospect of a $35 million salary, Jordan decided to retire after the settlement, and the Bulls' owner Jerry Reinsdorf decided to dismantle this dominant major league team of the 1990s. Time alone will tell whether life without Jordan but with this new labor deal will make the NBA better off in the future.

Football

The NBA owners did not succeed in establishing the hard salary cap on all free agent signings that the NFL owners enjoyed. Ironically, in football that cap had been won by the *players*—in 1993, as a victorious ending of six years of striking and litigating against the owners.

In 1987 the NFLPA leader Gene Upshaw—formerly a Hall-of-Fame offensive lineman for the Oakland Raiders—decided that it was time to eliminate football's long-standing version of the player reserve system. Originally dubbed the Rozelle Rule after the commissioner who created it in the early 1960s, this system allowed a player to become a free agent after his contract expired; however, it also required any other team wanting that player not just to pay him for moving, but also to compensate the team that was losing him. The level of compensation, in the form of draft picks, specified in the 1977 collective agreement was so steep that only one "free" agent was able to move from one NFL club to another in the next decade. That league practice did not have such a depressing effect on players' mobility and salaries in the mid-1980s, because Donald Trump and his partners in the United States Football League (USFL) appeared on the scene with both money and interest in bidding for attractive football talent. This inter-league competition helped boost average NFL salaries from $90,000 in 1982 to $205,000 in 1987. But with the demise of the USFL and the unlikelihood that any other league would emerge to compete in the market for football players, Upshaw and the NFLPA set out to bring meaningful free agency inside the NFL.

Their effort to do so through a players' strike early in the 1987 season produced the biggest defeat ever suffered by a players' union. Besides lining up replacement players among those who had been cut at training camps, Rozelle and the NFL owners offered a standing invitation to NFLPA members to cross the picket line to play and be paid during these games. This was an offer that more than 200 of the Association's 1,500 members felt they could not refuse, including such superstars as Joe Montana, Tony Dorsett, Steve Largent, and Lawrence Taylor, as well as the Heisman Trophy winner Doug Flutie, who was hoping for a career in the NFL now that the USFL had folded. While attendance at the replacement games dropped sharply and television ratings sagged significantly, the NFL's per-game profits actually increased because their payrolls were now so much lower. Recognizing these economic facts of life, Upshaw decided to concede defeat after the third replacement game, and he sent all of the NFLPA members back to work.

Unable to win through player solidarity and self-help, Upshaw turned to the Association's lawyers for legal help. A lawsuit was filed in the name of NFLPA President Marvin Powell of the New York Jets, seeking to use the Sherman Antitrust Act to deliver true free agency to football. Two years later, though, the NFLPA got some bad news from an Eighth Circuit judicial panel: as long as the players were represented under labor law by a union that had agreed at the bargaining table to a version of the Rozelle Rule restraints, they could not use antitrust law to attack those restraints in court, even years after the collective agreement had expired.

In response to that judicial message, the players voted to turn the Association into a body that could just sue their employers under antitrust law, rather than bargain with them under labor law. This new "non-union" NFLPA had its lawyers file another suit on behalf of eight high-ranked players headed by the New York Jets' star running back, Freeman McNeil. It took two more years of legal infighting before the *McNeil* case came to trial in the late summer of 1992. But when it did, the eight-member jury—all women who said they were *not* dedicated football fans—concluded that although a sport needs some limits on players' movement in order to preserve competitive balance on the field, the NFL's plan was far too restrictive of the players' ability to secure their fair market value off the field.

The NFLPA then expanded its case into a class-action suit filed on behalf of all 1,700 NFL players, with the lead plaintiff being the Eagles' star Reggie White. Though the ultimate legal outcome (especially on appeal) was not a foregone conclusion, the new NFL commissioner, Paul Tagliabue, realized that the league would be better off if it reached a compromise with the Players Association and its lawyers, rather than risk everything with the judges. Happily, such a compromise was finally reached in early 1993.

As part of the deal, the NFL owners paid the players a total of $195 million to settle all but one of their outstanding lawsuits. More important, the parties negotiated a seven-year collective agreement that was signed by the Association after it was reconstituted as a union. Under this new pact all veteran players would be able to experience full-blown free agency in 1993 and again in 1999. In the intervening five years, a cap—and also a floor—would be imposed on the total payroll permitted for each team. As in the NBA version, the payroll figures were based on the players' agreed-to share of the NFL's Designated Gross Revenues (DGR).

That first-ever season of NFL free agency sent Reggie White, the biggest star available that year, from the large-market Philadelphia Eagles to the small-market Green Bay Packers, who with White's help won the Super Bowl three years later. Meanwhile, average NFL salaries rose from $490,000 in 1992 to $650,000 in 1993, a leap from 56 percent to 67 percent of DGR, or more than enough to trigger the salary cap for 1994. This advent of the salary cap prompted team owners to enlist the services of corporate finance and tax lawyers—"capologists"—who would be skilled at avoiding (rather than evading) the cap restraints. Indeed, the Browns' owner Art Modell reportedly quipped, "Our first draft choice is going to have to be from the Harvard Law School." Football's real pioneer was Carmen Policy, who, as president of the San Francisco 49ers, restructured the team's 1994 payroll in a way that left enough room under the cap to bring in players like Ken Norton from the Cowboys, Richard Dent from the Bears, and Deion Sanders from the Falcons. While Steve Young was voted the league's Most Valuable Player for taking that year's Super Bowl back from Dallas to San Francisco, everyone recognized that Policy was the league's MVP *off* the field.

By 1998 Policy had left the 49ers to become a key member of the group that was restoring professional football to Cleveland, after Art Modell had used "franchise free agency" to move the city's cherished Browns to Baltimore in pursuit of a huge stadium subsidy *without* a cap. That same year, after Tagliabue had negotiated a record-setting $2.2 billion television deal, he and Upshaw extended football's hard cap contract and labor peace through 2003, with average salaries in 1999 reaching the $1.1 million mark.

Hockey

While that hard salary *cap* was being installed in football in 1994, a strong effort was being made to create a pioneering hard salary *tax* in hockey. This was a very good time for the National Hockey League. That spring Mark Messier had led the New York Rangers to their first Stanley Cup in over fifty years, an event that produced a *Sports Illustrated* cover image of the NHL going up and the NBA going down. Though that NHL-NBA comparison was questionable, hockey attendance and media coverage in the United States had risen impressively in the early 1990s, with NHL teams recently planted in San Jose, Dallas, Tampa Bay, and Miami. At the same time, players' average salaries had shot up from $180,000 in 1987–88 to $570,000 in 1993–94—more than trebling in just five years. This meant that, notwithstanding all the good news, a labor dispute was brewing between NHL owners and players, one that would cost the fans as well as the battling parties an even bigger chunk of their 1994–95 season than what the NBA would lose in 1998–99.

Until the 1990s hockey imposed essentially the same kind of restraints on player free agency as did football, though in hockey a neutral arbitrator rather than a league formula determined the appropriate level of compensation owed by the team signing a player to the team losing him. Then in 1992, when Bob Goodenow replaced Alan Eagleson as executive director of the National Hockey League Players Association (NHLPA), hockey players went out on strike for the first time, for ten days on the eve of the 1992 Stanley Cup. This work stoppage ended only when the owners granted largely unrestricted free agency to players who had reached age 31. The high pay negotiated by those exceptional free agents, and the bootstrap effect of these figures on the awards won by younger players in salary arbitration (a practice that originated in hockey, not baseball, back in 1970), sent hockey salaries soaring in the early 1990s.

The 1992 NHL settlement did give the owners the right to reopen the agreement after two years. The new NHL commissioner (and former NBA executive vice president), Gary Bettman, took this step shortly after he was installed in office. Besides pushing for the elimination of salary arbitration, Bettman wanted to use a tax, ranging from 100 to 200 percent, to enforce the same kind of limits on payrolls that had been established by football's cap. When the players refused to agree to such a

hard tax, the NHL owners set the precedent for the NBA owners by locking the players out at the start of the 1994–95 season to try to get them
to yield on this issue.

Unlike many of their NFL counterparts back in 1987, all the top NHL
stars, including the highly paid Wayne Gretzky, Mario Lemieux, and
Mark Messier, remained committed to their union's cause on behalf of
their successors like Eric Lindros, Jaromir Jagr, and Paul Kariya. By early
January the entire season was in grave jeopardy. At that point Bettman's
negotiating team finally gave up on the salary tax idea, and Goodenow's
team gave the owners some concessions on salary arbitration and free
agency, as well as the first hard cap ever imposed on individual *rookie*
salaries. The owners reluctantly approved this settlement by a 17–9
vote, thus saving the 1994–95 season and the Stanley Cup, which went
to the New Jersey Devils for the first time.

Under this no-tax deal, average NHL salaries reached the $1.4 million
mark by the 1999–2000 season, rising from around 40 percent of league
revenues in the late 1980s to 70 percent in the late 1990s. In the absence
of either salary taxing or revenue sharing, the franchises in Quebec,
Winnipeg, and Hartford moved to the somewhat larger markets of Denver, Phoenix, and Raleigh-Durham respectively. Though Bettman had
again reserved the right of the owners to reopen the agreement after
three years, the league decided instead to extend the contract to 2004.
The more cooperative relationship between Bettman and Goodenow and
their respective constituencies had helped the NHL expand into four
new markets (as well as the 1998 Winter Olympics), and then secure a
240 percent increase in its television package with ABC-ESPN. It is not
at all unlikely, though, that in 2004 hockey will be racked by a labor battle even bigger than the one in 1994.

Baseball

Baseball's labor dispute of the 1990s was even more visible and contentious than those in other sports. Besides a host of legal claims that the
owners and players made to the courts, the National Labor Relations
Board (NLRB), and the Congress, Major League Baseball experienced
the longest and most costly strike in sports history—one that dragged
on for more than 200 days from August 1994 to April 1995. Even President Clinton became involved, trying unsuccessfully to settle the dis-

pute one wintry night in the Oval Office. While a ruling by a federal district court judge ended the work stoppage just before the 1995 season, it took another two years for the owners and players to resolve their underlying economic differences. When that new baseball contract was finally signed, it made the 1997 season the first to generate a salary tax in any sport.

This scenario actually began back in the summer of 1992, when the owners decided to reopen their collective agreement with the MLB Players Association (MLBPA). Average baseball salaries had just topped a million dollars for the first time, up from less than $500,000 in 1989. But aggregate attendance figures and television revenues for baseball were also rising significantly during that period. Thus the independent Economic Study Committee on Baseball, commissioned to probe beneath the surface of these figures and trends, concluded that baseball's problem lay not so much in player free agency as in revenue disparity among teams: say between the large-market Yankees and Dodgers and the smaller-market Brewers and Pirates. The committee pronounced that baseball needed more equal sharing of league revenues if teams like the Pirates were ever going to be able to keep stars like Barry Bonds at home.

Not surprisingly, George Steinbrenner was unenthusiastic about this "socialist" idea of "donating" a sizable share of his Yankees' revenues to less affluent teams like Bud Selig's Brewers. However, in 1993 the small-market clubs used a form of collective self-help to bring Steinbrenner around, along with the Braves' Ted Turner, the Dodgers' Peter O'Malley, and other large-market owners. The Brewers, Pirates, and other small-market clubs announced that they would be locking out of their home stadiums the television announcers and cameramen of the visiting Yankees, Braves, and other teams, who were there to send those games to TV screens back home. Even if the Yankees and Braves had responded with a similar lockout of the Brewers' and Pirates' broadcasters, those smaller-market teams would have had much less to lose in television revenues. Spurred by the threat of a TV lockout, the baseball owners finally signed a revenue-sharing pact among themselves, but with a key condition attached. Before that revenue sharing could come into play, the players would have to agree to a salary cap, following the NFL's hard model rather than the NBA's soft version.

In June 1994 the owners' Player Relations Committee finally presented the owners' salary cap proposal to the Players Association. The crucial element was that half, but no more than half, of MLB revenues would be spent on player payrolls. Although that 50–50 sharing had obvious popular appeal, it was not terribly attractive to the players. Allocating half of the league's designated gross revenues to player costs (benefits as well as salaries) would actually produce a significant *cut* in player salaries, which had already passed the 50 percent mark and were still rising.

Unlike their counterparts in basketball and other sports, the players in baseball faced a special legal barrier to launching an antitrust challenge to owners' restraints on free trade in players' services. Since team owners could use their special antitrust exemption to impose the cap they wanted during the following winter's off-season, the players voted to go on strike in August to try to change the owners' minds. Unfortunately, this cost America's national pastime what seemed likely to be the greatest season ever. Attendance was the highest in history, averaging more than 31,000 a game on the way to passing the 70 million mark (double the total attendance in the mid-1970s just before the advent of free agency in baseball). Fans wanted to see players like Ken Griffey Jr. closing in on a 61-homer season, and Tony Gwynn on a .400 batting average, with pitchers like Greg Maddux and Randy Johnson enjoying equally great years on the mound. Interestingly, the best team that season was the low-paying (though not small-market) Expos, whose winning percentage topped even that of the high-paying and definitely big-market Yankees.

Though baseball fans had become quite familiar with players' strikes (or owners' lockouts) over the previous quarter-century, this was the first labor dispute ever to cost a major league its championship series. By mid-September, when Bud Selig announced that there would be no World Series that year, he and his colleagues realized that Don Fehr and his MLBPA members were not going to accept an NFL-like salary cap. So the baseball owners decided to follow the same bargaining path the NHL owners were taking that fall, and try for a salary tax instead. But the first tax rate proposed—more than 100 percent on any payrolls above the designated level—had no more appeal to the players than a hard salary cap. The owners were just as unenthusiastic about the players' proposal of a flat 1.6 percent tax to be levied on all team payrolls and team receipts, with the tax money used to fund the sharing of revenue among the clubs.

Throughout the autumn the parties did make some progress at the bargaining table with the help of the notable labor mediator William Usery, who had been recruited for this role by President Clinton. By mid-December the baseball owners and players had each put forward a proposal for a graduated tax applied to payrolls at different levels above the league average. Although the two sides now both subscribed to the concept of taxation, they were still a substantial distance apart on their actual figures; it was clear that considerably more time and effort would be needed to reach a settlement. Thus the owners decided to take two steps to increase the pressure felt by the players to make a greater compromise at the table.

First, MLB authorities instituted their most recent salary *cap* proposal, placing a firm ceiling on any player contracts that could be signed by teams that winter. Next, the owners prepared to start the upcoming season with replacement players, who would be invited to spring training along with any major leaguers willing to cross the MLBPA picket line. As in the NFL strike, the teams clearly had the right to use replacements in scheduled games that were being struck by their regular players. Needless to say, MLB owners were not about to exercise their further right to replace striking stars such as Griffey, Gwynn, Maddux, and Johnson *permanently*.

By contrast with their football counterparts back in 1987, the stars in baseball all made it clear that they were firmly committed to their association's cause, even if it cost each of them $5 million or more in salary. The greatest individual sacrifice would be made by the Baltimore Oriole Cal Ripken Jr., whose fourteen-year mission to break Lou Gehrig's all-time record for consecutive games played was due to be accomplished during the 1995 season. Ripken, recognizing that he had been the beneficiary of similar efforts by Catfish Hunter, Reggie Jackson, Brooks Robinson, and other stars of the 1970s who had fought for player free agency, declared that he was willing to give up that historic moment in his (and baseball's) life in order to protect future players from a salary cap (or its tax equivalent).

It would be up to baseball fans to render the verdict about how much aesthetic and economic value there was in seeing replacement players on the field. But it was the legal authorities who would determine whether and when the owners could unilaterally impose a cap on all team payrolls. While the NLRB was assessing charges of unfair labor practice filed by the MLBPA, the owners and players continued to whittle away at the gap between them at the bargaining table. The owners eventually reduced their proposal to a 50 percent tax on payrolls above $44 million, while the players upped their offer to 25 percent on payrolls above $50 million. In a meeting with the two sides at the White House, President Clinton recommended that they agree to binding arbitration rather than continue the strike over these economic issues; the players agreed, but the owners refused. Then on Friday, April 2, at the request of the NLRB, a federal judge, Sonia Sotomayor, ruled that the owners' unilateral imposition of their cap was illegal because the parties had not yet reached an "impasse"—a legal deadlock—on that score. The next day the players announced that they were ending their strike, and on Sunday morning the owners canceled the replacement games that were scheduled to begin that night. Three weeks later the regular major league players at last began to play ball.

This intervention by the Labor Board and Judge Sotomayor put an end to baseball's 234-day strike, a stoppage of play that was more than twice as long as the 103-day lockout in the NHL. Because no replacement games had been played in April, the people in Baltimore were able to celebrate Cal Ripken playing his historic record-setting game in September, and Atlanta could cheer the Braves as they won the city's first World Series title that October. However, baseball still had an unresolved bargaining dispute, which continued to cost both sides economically. Average attendance dropped 20 percent in the 1995 season to slightly over 26,000 a game, and overall team revenues slipped even more. Average players' salaries went down by more than $100,000 for the first time in many years, and were likely to drop even further as existing guaranteed contracts expired.

It was not until August 1996 that the two sides finally reached a contract settlement: the key feature was a 33 percent tax imposed on the amount by which the top five team payrolls exceeded the sixth highest. It took three more months before the rebellious owners were prepared to ratify that deal; what finally convinced them was seeing the deal's opponent Jerry Reinsdorf and his White Sox sign the Cleveland Indians' free agent Albert Belle to a record-setting five-year, $55 million contract. Shortly afterward Commissioner Selig reconvened the MLB owners, and they decided that even a "soft" salary tax was better than no tax at all on a Reinsdorf (or a Steinbrenner).

This extremely soft tax turned out to be much less advantageous to the owners than what the players had been offering at the table in the spring of 1995, let alone what an arbitrator would have awarded had the MLB owners accepted President Clinton's recommendation that they take that route. The 1997 season, the first under the new labor contract, witnessed a considerable increase in fans' interest and attendance, but also a 20 percent increase in average salaries, to over $1.3 million. With around $55 million as the payroll tax base that year, the New York Yankees topped the tax ranks by paying $4.4 million in tax on their $68 million in salaries. The following year the Yankees' payroll jumped to $72.5 million for a team that won an unprecedented 125 games on the way to a World Series sweep; but their tax dropped to $650,000, as the payrolls of the Orioles and other league-leading teams went up even more. The Yankees' taxes did go up somewhat in 1999, when the team became the first in any sport to top the $90 million payroll mark, but for other high-paying clubs like the Braves this MLB tax was still a very modest price to pay for making it to the last World Series of the century.

From 1997 through 1999, with rare exceptions—notably the White Sox in 1997, the Orioles in 1998, and the Dodgers in 1999—the highest-paying clubs were also the best-playing teams on the field. The significance of pay for performance was most dramatically illustrated by the fate of the Florida Marlins. In 1997 this five-year-old team with the fifth-highest payroll won the World Series in the seventh game against the Cleveland Indians. Shortly after celebrating that unprecedented ascent to the top by an expansion team, the Marlins' owner Wayne Huizenga announced that he planned to sell the team, but only after drastically reducing its payroll commitments. By the end of the 1998 season the Marlins' roster was being paid a total of less than $10 million, and the team had come very close to breaking the record for the *worst* win-loss percentage in baseball history.

Although this "downsizing" of the Marlins horrified South Florida fans, it did help Huizenga sell the franchise for his $150 million asking price—$60 million more than he had paid six years earlier. It also drove home the message of how far baseball still is from designing a level financial playing field. Early in the 21st century, sports fans are likely to witness replays of these intense battles between players and owners not just in baseball but also in the other major sports.

8

SPORTS JOINS
THE UNION

Understandably, Americans have trouble empathizing with the labor cause of major league players who claim to be underpaid for performing in a game that everyone else has always played for fun. By the end of the 1990s the average major league player was earning over $1.4 million a year, 35 times the $41,000 average of 25 years earlier. (These overall averages are calculated by adjusting each league's own average by both its number of teams and the size of its rosters.) The athletes' real salaries, after controlling for inflation, had risen nearly tenfold. During that same period the real hourly earnings of the average American worker— who pays to watch these millionaire players—had gone *down* by about 5 percent.

Athletes are not the only ones who have experienced such a surge in both absolute and relative earnings. The last quarter-century has witnessed a dramatic change in the American economy: it is now one in which "the winner takes the lion's share." Even Michael Jordan's 1997–98 total of $80 million in basketball salary and endorsement fees was dwarfed by the $200 million that Oprah Winfrey makes annually in the broader entertainment industry. Chief executive officers of major U.S. corporations are now averaging $5 million in total pay, nearly 200 times what the ordinary employee is making.

A large part of this explosion in executive earnings comes in the form of company stock options. This same period has seen an unprecedented rise in stock prices, with the Dow Jones Index moving from under 1,000 to above 11,000 (a 300 percent gain in real value). And the value of sports franchises has climbed even faster than that of general corporate stock. For example, George Steinbrenner and his partners bought the Yankees for $10 million in 1973, and they received a valuation of $600 million in their 1999 merger deal with the New Jersey Nets. But while in the general business world the rise in stock prices and executive earnings was propelled in part by a decline in real hourly pay for 120 million working Americans, exactly the opposite trend has taken place with players' real earnings, now up nearly 1,000 percent.

Baseball provides a revealing glimpse of the trends in players' pay over the last half-century. In 1947 the average baseball player earned $11,000 a year, a little more than four times the pay of the average American worker. In 1967 the average player earned $19,000, about 3.5 times the $5,500 average for workers. In 1973 baseball salaries had jumped to $36,000, but workers too had generally experienced a large gain (to $9,500), leaving the player-worker ratio still a little under the 1947 level. But by 1999 the average baseball player was earning $1.57 million, while the average worker earned just $28,000: a ratio of 56 to one. So although the gap between CEOs' and workers' earnings is still much larger, the ratio of baseball players' pay to that of workers has been rising much faster.

One explanation for these salary gains by professional athletes is an institution that is available both to players and to other workers, though not to CEOs: the labor union. Viewers of the 1996 movie *Jerry Maguire* were left with the impression that it was the agent, played by Tom Cruise, who was able to show Cuba Gooding, as his football player client, the money. In the real worlds of football, baseball, and other sports, it is the union leaders like Gene Upshaw and Don Fehr who must be given the credit (or, by some, the blame).

That was once equally true for ordinary American workers. By the late 1940s the wages and benefits of approximately 40 percent of the private-sector work force were negotiated by their union representatives at the bargaining table with employers. In the period 1947–1973 the American economy was experiencing an unprecedented 3 percent annual increase in productivity, and the leverage of collective bargaining enabled the ordinary employee to secure a somewhat larger share of this expanding gross national product: real pay per hour worked approximately doubled during those years. But since the early 1970s union representation of American workers has plummeted to less than 10 percent of the private sector. While during that same period annual growth in productivity has also dropped, from 3 percent to 1 percent, even that more modest economic growth rate should have permitted a rise of nearly 30 percent in real pay. Yet the average employee's real hourly pay actually dropped by around 5 percent during that time, thus permitting financial returns for investors and executives to soar.

In the late 1940s neither baseball nor any of the emerging major sports were unionized; this explains in part why the players' share of total baseball revenue fell to less than 13 percent by 1956. The players did create their own associations in the mid-1950s to try to discuss various issues—such as minimum salaries and retirement pensions—with the owners. However, Bob Feller, Bob Cousy, and other leaders of those initial organizing efforts took great pains to ensure that these bodies were *not* real unions seeking to challenge owners' control over the sports labor market. Eventually, in the late 1960s, the players moved toward full unionism in order to secure real concessions on benefits. But it was not until the early 1970s that the players' unions focused on the owners' long-time reserve systems and the way they shaped the players market. It was this collective action by players that set off the salary spiral that has transformed professional sports since that time.

Early Days of
the Big Leagues

Baseball historians still debate who first invented our national pastime. Was it Abner Doubleday in Cooperstown in 1839, Alexander Cartwright on the Elysian Fields in Hoboken in 1846, or someone else who deserves the credit? Happily, we do not need to confront that issue here. Everyone does agree that the first fully professional team was the barnstorming Cincinnati Red Stockings, created in 1869, and that the first professional organization was not a league of owners but the National Association of Professional Base Ball *Players* (NAPBBP), fashioned principally by the athletes who wanted to make their living in that sport. The NAPBBP was a loose confederation of teams, rosters, and schedules that did culminate in a championship series. Players' salaries averaged about $1,000, roughly four times what the average worker was earning then. In 1876 the principal investors in the NAPBBP redesigned the association as the National League of Professional Baseball *Clubs* (NL). This new name captured the changes in the organization: not only was there now a more tightly drawn schedule of games, but there would soon be a sharp divide between the club owners and the players who now worked for them. Meeting in September 1879, the National League owners created the first reserve system, agreeing not to bid for and sign up players who were on another team's protected roster.

It was not this reserve clause but rather a salary cap established by the owners in the mid-1880s (a $2,000 maximum salary for any player) that sparked the first organization of athletes as employees. John Montgomery Ward was both a pitcher and a shortstop for the New York Giants, and in his spare time was studying law at Columbia. (Ward is the only player in major league history to win more than 100 games as a pitcher and also have more than 2,000 hits as a batter; even Babe Ruth did not surpass both of these marks.) As a star player with some knowledge of the law, Ward was able to organize his fellow players to form a Brotherhood of Professional Base Ball Players. The Brotherhood tried to get the NL owners to loosen their salary cap, but the owners instead expanded it into a rigid salary scale for all players. This hard-line response from the owners moved the Brotherhood members to create a new Players League, one that took on the National League in 1890.

Ward won the key judicial ruling that barred NL owners from using the reserve clause in every player's contract to block players from moving to a new *league*. He then persuaded the majority of the players, including such standouts as Connie Mack and Charles Comiskey, to be part of the Players League, which attracted significantly more fans to its games than the National League. However, with players' salaries shooting upward, the investors who provided the financial backing for the Players League accepted the invitation of their NL competitors to close down the new body and merge into the National League. Interestingly, 1890 was also the year in which Congress enacted the Sherman Antitrust Act. But this reinstallation of the National League monopoly, and the resulting sharp drop in players' salaries in 1891, proved to be just the first of many occasions when antitrust scrutiny was *not* applied to this kind of "combination" of baseball owners.

Two replays of that Brotherhood/Players League saga took place in the next quarter-century. By 1900, with players' salaries and employment conditions remaining stagnant, the players, led by the star pitcher Clark Griffith, organized a new Protective Players Association. But it was quickly rendered redundant when a new league appeared on the scene. Ban Johnson transformed his minor Western League into an American League (AL), which moved into eastern metropolitan centers like New York, Boston, and Philadelphia, and signed up more than a hundred players from the National League—not just top players like

Griffith, but also a player-manager, John McGraw. After the American League consistently outdrew the National League at the gate, the NL owners felt compelled to enter into a new Major League Baseball Agreement, signed in 1903.

Not surprisingly, one critical provision of this agreement had all of these new league partners subscribing again to the reserve clause.* Inserting that feature into their standard player contract probably left it unenforceable in court against a rival league, as the NL Phillies learned when the AL Athletics and then the AL Indians took away the Hall-of-Famer Napoleon Lajoie. However, owners could readily reinforce the system within their new MLB, through the league's head office. This return of baseball's monopoly was not challenged by the administration of President Theodore Roosevelt, which, at least at the outset, was mainly using antitrust law to attack collective action by workers (through their new American Federation of Labor) against businesses.

Over the next decade the popularity of baseball soared—total attendance in 1910 was 7.25 million, up from 3.9 million in 1901—but players' salaries did not. Another players' group was organized in 1912, this time precipitated by a major controversy involving Ty Cobb. During a Detroit Tigers game in New York, Cobb went into the stands and beat up a spectator who had been heckling him. After AL President Ban Johnson suspended Cobb for ten days, the Tigers refused to play in the next game. When they were fined for this, all the MLB players reacted by forming the Baseball Players Fraternity.

This third effort at self-help by players was again overtaken by a new competing league, Federal Base Ball, which began in 1913 and by 1915 had lured more than 200 players away from MLB. Even players who eventually stayed in the AL or the NL, including Ty Cobb, Honus Wagner, and Walter "Big Train" Johnson, used the threat of league-jumping to extract large pay increases, and the overall MLB salary average more than doubled.

---

* There was no initial agreement to hold a World Series. So after the AL champions, the Boston Pilgrims (predecessors to the Red Sox), beat the NL champion Pittsburgh Pirates in a privately arranged championship series in 1903, the next year's NL champion New York Giants (managed by McGraw) refused to play the Boston team and risk losing. This led to an amendment of the MLB agreement a year later, in which both the NL and the AL committed their champions to the World Series. Not until ninety years later did another World Series fail to be played, this time because of the 1994 players' strike.

This was also the era in which President Woodrow Wilson, assisted by his top legal advisor, Louis Brandeis, piloted through Congress the Clayton Act of 1914, which amended the Sherman Antitrust Act in several important respects. One of these changes gave private parties the right to sue for antitrust violations, and triple damages if they won. When MLB owners used a combination of contract lawsuits and generous new deals to try to preserve their reserve system against players' movement, Federal Base Ball responded with an antitrust suit. Judge (and future MLB commissioner) Kenesaw Mountain Landis decided to sit on this case rather than press it forward, and as had always happened earlier, the MLB and Federal Base Ball owners met in late 1915 and settled their fight. The two sides agreed to disband Federal Base Ball and bring in a number of its principal investors as owners of existing AL or NL teams. (One of them, Phil Weegham, took over the Chicago Cubs so that he could move the team to his brand-new ballpark, now known as Wrigley Field.) The remaining Federal Base Ball investors were bought off with a $700,000 payment by MLB to settle the antitrust suit.

One of the latter group of investor-owners, Ned Hanlon of the Baltimore Terrapins, objected to the deal and sought to challenge it under antitrust law. This *Federal Base Ball* case produced an opinion written by Supreme Court Justice Oliver Wendell Holmes that said baseball was totally exempt from the federal antitrust law. Whether because of this special status under the law or the economics of the game, Major League Baseball has not faced a competitive league in more than 80 years. And it took another four decades after *Federal Base Ball* before the players again organized themselves into an association that would address their dissatisfaction with the owners' practices.

In the broader market for sports fans, of course, Major League Baseball has faced significant challenges from professional leagues in other sports. The first was football, a sport developed by Ivy League colleges in the 1870s.* By the 1880s college football had become a major feature of

---

* Like baseball, football sparks a debate among historians. Should the first American-style game be credited to the Princeton-Rutgers match in 1869—which appears to have been what most of the world does call football, but what Americans label soccer? Or was it a Harvard-McGill game in the early 1870s, modeled on English-style rugby, which permitted players to use their arms as well as their feet to advance the ball up the field?

American leisure life in the fall. The first professional teams emerged in the 1890s; typically they were barnstorming clubs modeled on baseball's Cincinnati Red Stockings, as the Green Bay Packers were in their early days. The seminal league event took place in 1920 in an automobile showroom in Canton, Ohio, where George Halas and several others agreed to create the American Professional Football Association. The group placed eight teams in small midwestern cities, at a franchise fee of $25, and installed the American sports great Jim Thorpe as the league's first president.

Over the next few years the league, renamed the National Football League, expanded into New York, Chicago, and other large cities, though it was still organized as a loose confederation of teams and schedules, with its games rarely drawing more than a few hundred spectators. That is why Tim Mara was able to acquire the New York Giants football franchise for $500 in early 1925, shortly after Colonel Jacob Ruppert had gained sole ownership of baseball's Yankees for $3 million. Luckily for Mara, he secured the Giants just before the event that was to transform the popular appeal of the NFL. After Harold "Red" Grange graduated from the University of Illinois and signed up to play for the Chicago Bears, 70,000 New York fans turned out to see the Bears play the Giants in the fall of 1925.

The next quarter-century was a turbulent period for the NFL, with franchises regularly being added and then folding. In an attempt to control the players market in football, the league took two steps: it added baseball's reserve clause to its standard player contract, and, in 1935, it developed the first draft in sports. The draft was designed to eliminate competitive bidding among NFL teams for incoming college stars.* But right after World War II the NFL faced another league competitor for fans as well as players—the All-American Football Conference (AAFC). Indeed, Paul Brown's creation of the AAFC Cleveland Browns led the NFL Rams to move from Cleveland to Los Angeles to become the first major league team in the West. But the Browns so dominated the AAFC

---

* As an illustration of the economic level of professional football at that early stage, the number-one pick in the first NFL draft was Jay Benswanger, who that same year had won the first-ever Heisman Trophy as a star player at the University of Chicago. Yet Benswanger decided to pursue a professional career in business rather than in football. Even in the early 1950s another Heisman Trophy winner, Dick Kazmaier from Princeton, chose to work on Wall Street rather than play in the NFL.

that the new league's attendance declined even in Cleveland. This imbalance led the AAFC to dissolve after the 1949 season, and the Browns, the San Francisco 49ers, and the Baltimore Colts moved over to the NFL. In their first NFL season, the Browns traveled to Los Angeles to defeat the Rams and win the 1950 NFL championship.

During the NFL-AAFC struggle, Commissioner Bert Bell and his NFL owners realized from the experience of baseball that they could not effectively enforce their reserve system in court to block players from moving to a rival league. However, in order to give their current players an incentive to stay put, they established a "blackballing" policy: any player who left the league was barred from returning. After the AAFC folded, the NFL enforced that rule against Pete Radovich, who had moved from the Detroit Lions to the Los Angeles Dons. When Radovich's lawsuit reached the Supreme Court, the Justices told the owners in football that they did not enjoy the special antitrust exemption that the Court had conferred on baseball.

In the 1870s, at the same time as American football was being developed, the game of ice hockey was emerging in Canada and becoming the country's national sport. In 1893 Governor General Lord Stanley (the official sent by Queen Victoria to oversee what was still a British colony) donated a Stanley Cup to be awarded to the Canadian amateur hockey champion. By the early 1900s professional teams and leagues had been created, and from 1912 on the Stanley Cup was awarded to the professional champion. The National Hockey League (NHL) came into being in 1917; originally based in eastern Canadian cities, it expanded into the United States in the 1920s. By the 1940s the NHL was the sole major hockey league. Although almost all of the players were Canadian, four of the six remaining franchises were located in the United States. In fact a single person, James Norris, owned both the Detroit Red Wings and the Chicago Blackhawks and effectively controlled the New York Rangers, who played in his Madison Square Garden.

Sports historians all agree that the game of basketball was invented in 1892 by James Naismith in a YMCA in Springfield, Massachusetts, as an enjoyable form of exercise that could be played indoors during the New England winter. Basketball quickly followed the lead of football and became a prominent feature of the college sports scene (unlike baseball, which was played in late spring and summer when college classes had ended). The first professional basketball ventures were also barnstorming teams, exemplified by the Harlem Globetrotters. Numerous leagues were created and folded in the first half of the 20th century. One was the National Basketball League (NBL), which, like the NFL, was originally based in small midwestern cities. Another was the Basketball Association of America (BAA), which was formed in 1946 with teams in eastern cities, such as the New York Knickerbockers, the Boston Celtics, and the Philadelphia Warriors. After the Minneapolis Lakers (with the basketball great George Mikan) were induced to move from the NBL to the BAA in 1948, the two leagues agreed to merge the following year into a National Basketball Association (NBA). This new league started out in 1949 with 17 teams, but by 1957 it had been reduced to 8 clubs, which served as the base for the fourth major league to be firmly established in the sports marketplace.

The Emergence of Players' Unions

By contrast with Major League Baseball, the NFL, the NBA, and the NHL have all experienced serious challenges from rival leagues since the 1960s. Also unlike the story of baseball, the early history of the other sports was devoid of any efforts by players to deal collectively with the owners. In the 1950s the situation changed, and players' self-organization burgeoned in all four sports.

Actually, MLB witnessed a brief organizing effort in 1946. In the spring of that year the lawyer Robert Murphy took it upon himself to create the American Baseball Guild, an organization through which players could seek to exercise their rights under the 1935 National Labor Relations Act to bargain collectively with the owners about salaries and benefits. Murphy signed up a significant number of players as members of the Guild; but even though he had once been a lawyer for the National Labor Relations Board (NLRB), Murphy was not able to convince the NLRB that baseball was subject to federal labor laws any more than it was to antitrust laws.

Denial of NLRB jurisdiction did leave Murphy with the option of using state labor law, which would apply to an individual team located in the state. So the Guild filed a certification petition in Pennsylvania on behalf of the Pittsburgh Pirates. The MLB owners were able to fend off that organizing effort by quickly adopting the recommendations of the Yankees' co-owner Larry MacPhail. In late July 1946 all MLB players were told that they were going to get a minimum $5,000 salary, a pension plan, and living expenses during spring training (a benefit still known as "Murphy money"). In addition, Commissioner Albert "Happy" Chandler's office set up a new system to permit players to address their concerns directly with the owners. Each team would have a player representative, who in turn would pick a representative for each league. These two league-wide representatives would meet periodically with the owner representatives on the MLB executive council. This kind of action by employers on the eve of a certification vote would be a gross violation of present-day federal labor law, but back in 1946 it did the job of persuading the Pirates (including the rookie Ralph Kiner) to vote "No" to Guild representation.

Over the next several years some major changes took place in the economics of baseball. Once World War II had ended, America was eager to relax at the ballpark: in 1948 attendance at MLB games was up to 21 million from 10 million in 1939, and in the minor leagues it rose to 42 million. The 1948 World Series winner was the Cleveland Indians, two of whose star players were Larry Doby and Satchel Paige, who had followed the trail blazed in 1947 by the Brooklyn Dodgers' Jackie Robinson, ending the exclusion of black players from Major League Baseball. By 1953, as television sets found their way into more and more American homes so fans could follow the sport without going out to a game, MLB attendance sagged to 14 million. But as baseball proved to be a popular show on television, the teams soon began collecting substantial revenue from this new source.

That gain was not, however, reflected in players' salaries and benefits. The share of all MLB revenues devoted to players' payrolls dropped from 25 percent in 1946, when the Guild appeared on the scene, to 13 percent a decade later. Realizing that this was happening, the AL and NL player representatives, Allie Reynolds and Ralph Kiner, met with representatives from individual teams at the 1953 All-Star Game; the group decided to hire a lawyer, Norman Lewis, to represent them in discussions with the owners. But the MLB owners refused to let Lewis into that winter's executive council meetings. The player representatives responded by creating the Major League Baseball Players Association (MLBPA), signing up most of the players at spring training, and electing Bob Feller as the first MLBPA president. At that year's All-Star Game, the new commissioner, Ford Frick, and the owners relented and agreed to negotiate with Lewis: the outcome was a pension plan that promised the players 60 percent of the television revenues from the World Series and the All-Star Game.

An analogous development occurred in football. At the January 1954 Pro Bowl, a secret organizational meeting of players took place, led by the Browns' offensive lineman Abe Gibron, and involving such big-name stars as Kyle Rote and Frank Gifford of the Giants, Norm Van Brocklin of the Rams, and Eddie LeBaron of the Redskins. The players waited for over a year before going public with their NFL Players Association (NFLPA), and it took another two years before Commissioner Bell and owner representatives would meet with them. Though the league signed no binding contract with the players, the owners agreed to establish a $5,000 salary minimum as well as pension and disability benefits for players.

In basketball it was Bob Cousy and Bob Pettit who led the players' effort to create a National Basketball Players Association (NBPA) in the mid-1950s. Though NBA owners agreed to talk to the players about a pension plan, they never actually did anything about it, as we shall see, until after the players took action at the 1964 All-Star Game.

The hockey players' effort fared even worse than that. The Detroit Red Wings' star Ted Lindsay ran into the Cleveland Indians' Bob Feller at a social event and learned about the pending pension/television sharing deal that the MLBPA's lawyer Norman Lewis had negotiated with the baseball owners. Inspired by this example, Lindsay met with Doug Harvey of the Montreal Canadiens, Fernie Flaman of the Boston Bruins, and several other players at the 1956 NHL All-Star Game. This group created the NHL Players Association (NHLPA), with Lindsay as its first president and Lewis as its lawyer. But unlike the baseball owners, the hockey owners refused to recognize and deal with their players' association. When the NHLPA and Lewis filed a $3 million antitrust suit against the owners, James Norris sent Lindsay from Norris's first-place Red Wings to his last-place Chicago Blackhawks. Norris said he did so because Lindsay was "over the hill," even though "Terrible Ted" had just made the All-Star team for the eighth time, as a member of hockey's greatest-ever forward line with Gordie Howe and Alex Delvecchio. Under pressure from the Red Wings' general manager, Jack Adams, Howe persuaded his teammates to drop out of the NHLPA; players on the other teams soon followed suit. The owners responded by establishing a

$7,000 minimum salary and a modestly improved pension plan, and by creating an owners-players council to meet twice a year in conjunction with the meetings of the NHL Board of Governors.

———————

In all these organizational efforts of the 1950s, the leading players saw themselves as creating "players' associations," not "labor unions." Bob Feller and Norm Van Brocklin, Bob Cousy and Ted Lindsay were seeking just face-to-face relationships with the owners through which to address such issues as pension plans and minimum salaries. The players assumed that the traditional reserve system was essential to the integrity and quality of their games, and that membership in large and powerful labor organizations was incompatible with their self-image as those responsible for this key part of American culture, rather than just workers in a money-making business.

During that same period the athletes' counterparts in the entertainment world felt no such compunction about being unionized; they were quite content to reap the benefits of collective bargaining with their employers. Movie stars such as Jimmy Stewart and Elizabeth Taylor and television stars such as Jackie Gleason and Lucille Ball had at least as much popular appeal as a Mickey Mantle or a Johnny Unitas, and they were paid far more handsomely. It was at the end of the 1950s that the head of the Screen Actors Guild, Ronald Reagan, led his colleagues out on the longest strike in Hollywood history—in which the actors won a sizable share of the "residual rights" fees that studios earned when their movies were shown on the new entertainment medium, television.

A labor leader like Ronald Reagan was much more important to the economic welfare of actors than even a top agent, for reasons dating back to the 1930s. When the movie industry moved out to Hollywood at the beginning of the 1920s, Actors' Equity, the union of Broadway actors, sought to represent its members when they traveled west to make movies. The studios, through their Motion Pictures and Producers Association (MPPA), responded by creating a "company union," the Academy of Motion Picture Arts and Sciences. The existence of the Academy led actors, and also writers, directors, cinematographers, and other brands of film talent, to feel that their employment interests were better served by an "in-house" academy created and run by their employers than by an "outside" labor organization such as Actors' Equity.

However, when the Depression hit Hollywood in the early 1930s, the major studios banded together to institute both an immediate salary cut and a permanent salary cap. Assisted by Academy officers, the studios set out to sell the idea of a salary cap to federal officials, promoting it as the best way to preserve the financial viability of the movie industry under the National Industrial Recovery Act (NIRA) that President Franklin Delano Roosevelt had persuaded Congress to enact in the first hundred days of his administration. But when word filtered out about what the studios were doing, James Cagney, Gary Cooper, Groucho Marx, Mae West, and other major actors got together in their Beverly Hills homes and created the Screen Actors Guild (SAG) and its counterparts, the Screen Directors Guild and the Screen Writers Guild. The first SAG president, Eddie Cantor, went to Georgia in 1933 to spend Thanksgiving with FDR and his wife, Eleanor; he regaled them with tales about moviemaking and managed to persuade the President to pull the plug on the MPAA-Academy salary cap.

Two years later Congress replaced the NIRA with the National Labor Relations Act (NLRA), the law that finally gave American workers an enforceable right to bargain collectively with their employers. The Hollywood guilds quickly took advantage of this new law to secure recognition from the studios and to negotiate labor contracts that established both basic pay and benefits for all performers and defined the negotiating framework for individual deals. (The Academy, now out of the labor business, turned to lighter matters, such as the Oscars.) It is this labor setting that permits a Tom Cruise to extract from Sony Entertainment a $20 million up-front salary guarantee plus a share of the gross revenues of the sports movie hit *Jerry Maguire*. And it was his role as president of SAG that made Ronald Reagan the kind of political figure who would later be elected Governor of California and President of the United States (where, paradoxically, he was not known as a champion of labor). But while professional baseball had come into being 40 years before the movie industry, it was not until the 1960s, 30 years after true unionism arrived in Hollywood, that the baseball players—and those in football, basketball, and hockey—would follow that same path.

An important early step in this direction was taken in basketball. In the early 1960s Bob Cousy's successor as NBPA president, Tom Heinsohn of the Boston Celtics, asked his friend Larry Fleisher, then a student at Harvard Law School, to prepare his tax returns (as well as those of John Havlicek and several other Celtics teammates). When Fleisher graduated in 1962 and went off to New York to set up a law practice, Heinsohn hired him as the part-time director and lawyer for the Association, which became based in Fleisher's office. For the next 18 months Fleisher tried unsuccessfully to persuade the NBA owners finally to do what they had promised Cousy years earlier: set up the pension and benefit plans that had been established in other sports. After getting nowhere with the owners, Fleisher decided it was time to play hardball. Just as the 1964 All-Star Game was about to get under way, with television cameras focused on the parquet floor of the Boston Garden, Fleisher had all the stars—such as Wilt Chamberlain and Bill Russell, Elgin Baylor and Oscar Robertson—sit in their locker rooms for 15 minutes until Commissioner Walter Kennedy came in to tell them that the owners had firmly committed themselves to implementing the pension plan. Three years later the NBPA secured the first signed labor agreement in sports.

This was also a time when full-blown unionism was appearing in football. In early 1966 a quarterback bidding war began between the NFL and AFL rival leagues, with clubs in each looking for stars like John Brodie and Joe Namath. To free themselves from these competitive pressures in the players market and other financial arenas, the two leagues negotiated a pact that would create a new NFL, divided into a National Football Conference (NFC) and an American Football Conference (AFC), whose champions would meet in an annual Super Bowl. Pete Rozelle beat out his AFL rival for the job of commissioner of this newly amalgamated NFL.

The owners were able to persuade members of Congress to slip into another 1966 bill a special exemption of this merger from antitrust law (in part by promising to award New Orleans the expansion franchise that had long been sought by two congressional powers from Louisiana, Senator Russell Long and Representative Hale Boggs). Because this would bring to a grinding halt the sharp rise in football salaries—which had doubled to $25,000, the highest in any sport—the players became seriously interested in real union representation. Indeed, the Cleveland Browns' defensive back Bernie Parish began to organize players into an affiliate of the Teamsters called the American Federation of Professional Athletes. The prospect of having to deal with a branch of

Jimmy Hoffa's Teamsters convinced Commissioner Rozelle to embrace the in-house NFLPA as a better option for the owners. But shortly afterward, when another young law graduate, Ed Garvey, became executive director of the NFLPA, he got the association certified as a union bargaining agent by the NLRB and took football down a different labor-relations path than the one Rozelle had anticipated.

That threat of the Teamsters on the horizon also helped bring a brand of unionism to hockey a decade after the owners had aborted Ted Lindsay's NHLPA. Several players on the Stanley Cup–winning Toronto Maple Leafs, such as Carl Brewer, Bobby Baun, Billy Harris, and Bob Pulford, had begun to use the recent University of Toronto Law School graduate (and hockey fan) Alan Eagleson for a variety of personal legal services. Thanks to this connection, Eagleson was hired by the family of hockey's next superstar, 18-year-old Bobby Orr, to negotiate Orr's first contract with the Boston Bruins. Eagleson's client got a record-setting $25,000 salary and $25,000 bonus. Brewer and his teammates then sent Eagleson to talk to players on the Bruins and other teams, to persuade them to secretly sign up for a revival of the NHLPA. Meanwhile, the NHL was in the final stages of its first big expansion, into six new cities for the 1967–68 season. With no warning, Eagleson announced in June 1967 the creation of a new NHLPA, with Bobby Pulford as its president. NHL President Clarence Campbell had heard that the Teamsters' new sports arm was also courting the players; the owners had no trouble deciding that it would be preferable to deal with Eagleson than with Hoffa.

The most important event in the evolution of labor unions in sports was then taking place in baseball, though more by accident than by design. By the mid-1960s the Phillies star and MLBPA president Robin Roberts and his executive board (which included Jim Bunning, now a U.S. senator as well as a Hall-of-Famer) had decided that the MLBPA needed a full-time executive director. The executive board wanted the association's part-time lawyer and director, Robert Cannon, to play that role. The baseball owners were pleased with that choice, because Cannon had been a defender in Congress of such baseball traditions as the reserve system, and he even had aspirations to succeed Ford Frick as baseball commissioner. The owners went so far as to agree to use $150,000 of their television revenues to pay for the MLBPA executive director's salary, staff, and office expenses. (If the MLBPA had been considered a "labor organization" like the Teamsters, this employer financing of its director would have been illegal under the Taft-Hartley and Landrum-Griffin Acts.)

However, Cannon declined the invitation to move from Milwaukee to New York to take the job, so Roberts offered it to Marvin Miller, who had been chief economist for the United Steelworkers of America. For the first time athletes would be represented by someone with real experience in union representation and collective bargaining. Before he would accept the position, Miller spent the spring of 1966 in Florida and Arizona, visiting every team's training camp to see whether the players themselves wanted someone like him in that role. After receiving a strong endorsement from the players, he agreed to take the job. Unlike the other MLBPA directors, Miller was an economist and not a lawyer, but he quickly filled that gap by hiring another Harvard Law School graduate, Dick Moss, as general counsel, to shape the players' legal strategy.

For the first several years after players' unions came to the sports world, their bargaining with the owners focused on the same old issues—minimum salary, pension plans, and working conditions—that players and owners had tussled with in the past. But the presence of a real union did make a huge difference in the kinds of gains that players could secure even here. In baseball, for example, Larry MacPhail's original minimum salary had risen from $5,000 in 1946 to $7,000 in 1966; but Miller more than doubled the amount to $15,000 in 1972, and nearly quadrupled owners' annual contributions to players' pensions, from $1.8 million to $6.5 million. But before the unions could have the impact on players' salaries that has caused them to reach their present astronomic heights, they would have to tackle the player reserve systems in their respective sports. Needless to say, Marvin Miller and his counterparts in the other players' associations would not be able to eliminate this long-standing feature of the sports world simply by paying a call on President Nixon, as the SAG's Eddie Cantor had done with FDR. The path to free agency for players was to be much more arduous.

9

OPENING THE
FLOOD-GATES

The summer of 1998 saw the unanimous passage by Congress of the Curt Flood Act, a bill jointly sponsored by conservative Republicans like Orrin Hatch and Strom Thurmond and liberal Democrats like Patrick Leahy and Daniel Moynihan. Sadly, this legislative effort took place just after Curt Flood died of cancer. The objective of the bill was to resolve a legal struggle launched by Flood three decades earlier, an attack on baseball's special exemption from antitrust law. The terms of the legislative amendment had actually been negotiated by lawyers for Major League Baseball and the MLB Players Association, as part of the settlement of that sport's major labor dispute. But like almost everything involving baseball and the law, even this bipartisan proposal faced major political obstacles. Ironically, for Congress to be able to pass such a law, it had to design the bill so that it covered just those who needed its protection the least and excluded those who needed it the most.

The *Flood* Case

In the late 1960s Curt Flood was at the peak of his career, as center fielder for the St. Louis Cardinals team that won the seventh game of the 1967 World Series against Carl Yastrzemski's Boston Red Sox, and then lost the seventh game of the 1968 World Series to Dennis McClain's Detroit Tigers. Though the Cardinals' top players were the future Hall-of-Famers Bob Gibson and Lou Brock, Flood was certainly in the upper ranks of the game. Indeed, a 1968 *Sports Illustrated* article ranked him as the best center fielder of the time, and the magazine's cover featured a self-portrait that he had done in his new avocation (and off-season business) as artist and photographer.

After the successful 1968 season (albeit with a disappointing ending), Flood asked the Cardinals' owner Gussie Busch for a substantial salary hike, from $90,000 to $120,000 a year. Instead of a raise, Flood received the bad news that he had been traded to the Philadelphia Phillies as part of a package that also featured the Phillies' star hitter Dick Allen. In any other walk of life, such a fate would be unthinkable: in television, for example, ABC could never have traded its *Home Improvement* star, Tim Allen, to NBC to replace ABC's retiring *ER* lead, George Clooney. Yet in baseball as well as other professional sports, trades—even sales—of players to other clubs and distant cities had been standard operating procedure ever since the leagues were created a century earlier.

But in the 1960s the traditional ways in which American organizations did business were being challenged in many domains. Curt Flood decided to become the first athlete to tackle such treatment by the owners. In a letter to Commissioner Bowie Kuhn, he stated: "I do not feel that I am a piece of property to be bought and sold irrespective of my wishes." Kuhn agreed with Flood that "as a human being, you are not a piece of property to be bought and sold." However, as a baseball player, Flood had signed a contract with the Cardinals that gave them the right to sell his services to another club.

The only way for Flood to stay in St. Louis with his family without having to give up his baseball career was to attack the reserve system that had made trading players a common practice in the sports world. In Flood's view, the only way the Cardinals had secured his agreement that he could be traded was by exclusively "reserving" him for itself, so that it could include the standard trading term in his contract on a nonnegotiable "take it or leave the league" basis.

Flood's legal team, headed by Arthur Goldberg, faced some major hurdles in its challenge to that reserve system.* The most plausible under-

---

* Marvin Miller, executive director of the MLBPA, agreed to provide financial as well as moral support for Flood's challenge to this baseball tradition. To file the suit and argue the case, Miller picked Goldberg, who had been chief counsel for Miller's Steelworkers Union in the 1950s. In the early 1960s Goldberg was made Secretary of Labor by President Kennedy, and then appointed to the Supreme Court. However, President Johnson lured him off the Court to serve as U.S. Ambassador to the United Nations and defend to the world the American role in Vietnam. Johnson promised Goldberg that after the war was won he would be reappointed to the Court. But the war was still going on in 1969 when President Nixon replaced Johnson in the Oval Office, and thus Goldberg had to go back into private practice. *Flood* was the case that took Goldberg back to the Supreme Court, this time on the other side of the bench.

pinning of the *Flood* case was to be found in the Sherman Antitrust Act of 1890. This antitrust regime—which bans both "combinations in restraint of trade" and "monopolistic" behavior—was designed to preserve a freely competitive marketplace for goods and services. As we shall be exploring throughout this book, the merits of league restraints on the sports market pose much more complex and hotly debated questions than do studio restraints in the entertainment market, for example. However, Flood's lawyers faced a huge preliminary problem they would not have had if Flood had played football, basketball, or hockey: Did antitrust law even apply to baseball?

The original source of that problem was the Supreme Court's decision in the *Federal Base Ball* case mentioned in the previous chapter. In 1915 the owners of MLB and Federal Base Ball teams had resolved their fierce competition for baseball players and fans by agreeing to disband the Federal League, bring in a number of its investors to own and operate existing MLB teams, and pay the others off from a $700,000 settlement of an antitrust suit filed against MLB for using the reserve system to try to block players from switching leagues. Ned Hanlon, the owner of the Federal League's Baltimore Terrapins, was unhappy with this deal, particularly because he had been denied the chance to buy the struggling St. Louis Cardinals and move them to Baltimore. Hanlon filed his own antitrust suit and was awarded $240,000 at trial. This verdict was appealed to the Supreme Court, and, in a brief and cryptic opinion written by Justice Oliver Wendell Holmes, the Court ruled that although baseball was a "business," one that involved "exhibitions . . . made for money," this business was not the type of "commerce among the states" that permitted federal (rather than just state) regulation of its affairs.

Back in that 1920s legal environment, such a judicial conclusion was not entirely implausible. It was, after all, an era in which the Supreme Court was regularly giving a narrow interpretation to the Interstate Commerce Clause of the Constitution, the source of congressional regulatory authority over businesses of any kind. By the late 1950s, though, the Court had overturned all of its earlier precedents in this area and explicitly ruled that antitrust governed Broadway theater production (in the *Shubert* case), championship boxing (in *International Boxing Commission*), and baseball's major team sports competitor, football (in the *Radovich* case). However, in another 1950s decision, *Toolson*—involving a baseball player whom the Yankees were keeping in the minor leagues rather than giving him a chance to play for teams like the St. Louis Browns that probably needed him—the Court refused to touch *Federal Base Ball*. As the Justices admitted in *Radovich*, if they were "considering the question of baseball for the first time on a clean slate, we would have no doubts" that this sport was also governed by antitrust law; but that old *Federal Base Ball* precedent meant that only Congress could rectify this "error or discrimination, if any there be."

What made Arthur Goldberg think there was a strong chance that the Supreme Court would finally change its mind for Curt Flood and other baseball players in the early 1970s? The basis for his optimism was that Goldberg's former Court colleagues had developed a far more adventurous legal philosophy than that of the 1950s. After all, the Court was about to take a major constitutional step in *Roe v. Wade*, the crucial abortion case that was being debated inside Court chambers at the same time as *Flood*. So when Goldberg persuaded the Court to accept *Flood* as one of the tiny number of appeals it hears each year, many observers assumed that *Federal Base Ball* was about to experience the same fate as many other outmoded judicial precedents. However, as soon as Goldberg and others began to read the first section of the *Flood* opinion, with its worshipful history of "The Game,"* they realized this legal step had not been taken. A majority of the Court was still unwilling to touch baseball's reserve system and its long-standing immunity from federal antitrust scrutiny.

The Union Tackles the Reserve System

The Supreme Court's acquiescence in *Flood* was clearly inspired by the Justices' reverence for our traditional national pastime, and by their feeling that allowing players to move freely from team to team in the same

---

* Justice Blackmun, author of the *Flood* opinion, first rendered his verdict that it was Alexander Cartwright who had given birth to baseball in the 1840s. Blackmun then listed 70 or so notable players, from Ty Cobb and Babe Ruth on down—the names that "packed the diamond and its environs and that have provided tinder for recaptured thrills." When Blackmun's first draft opinion was circulated to his colleagues, Justice Thurgood Marshall noted that no "Negro players" were included on the list. Although Blackmun quickly added Jackie Robinson, Roy Campanella, and Satchel Paige, Marshall still dissented on the legal issue, saying that he wanted to bring to baseball the antitrust "Magna Carta of free enterprise . . . as important to the preservation of economic freedom . . . as the Bill of Rights is to the protection of our fundamental personal freedoms."

league would threaten the quality and integrity of the game. In *Radovich,* by contrast, the NFL had blacklisted a player who, at the end of his contract with an NFL team, had sought to move to the new AAFC, not just to another NFL city and team. As we shall see in the next chapter, the Supreme Court ruled that antitrust law covered the NFL and its league restraints on players. This meant that the NFL could not, for example, threaten John Brodie of the San Francisco 49ers with such action when he agreed to sign a contract with an AFL team in 1966, just before the two leagues merged. But from the players' point of view, giving owners in the only major baseball league sole control over where anyone could play was the most egregious rule of the game. After receiving this third—and likely to be final—verdict from the Supreme Court on this score, the players realized they would have to tackle the problem through their union rather than through the courts.

The first instrument used by the MLBPA was arbitration, a role that had been transferred from the commissioner to a "neutral" party in the 1970 baseball labor agreement. Just four years after that agreement came a player's grievance that was legally narrow but economically explosive. The pitcher Jim "Catfish" Hunter had risen to baseball glory: he won 20 games four years in a row, led the Oakland Athletics to three consecutive World Series championships, and in 1974 was picked as the American League's Cy Young Pitcher of the Year. But in that same season the owner of the Athletics, Charles Finley, had withheld part of Hunter's $100,000 salary because of a complicated tax question posed by the terms of their contract. After pitching the A's to yet another World Series victory that October, Hunter exercised the option available under the standard player contract to leave a team if it had not paid him his full salary. Finley, with the support of Commissioner Kuhn, argued that losing a star player was too harsh a penalty to impose on a team involved in such a complex salary/tax dispute; but baseball's labor arbitrator, Peter Seitz, after reading the contract language as the parties themselves had written it, disagreed.

No one in baseball had the slightest inkling of how much money Hunter was about to make as the first star player ever to become a free agent. In December there was a spirited auction for his services. Though the highest bidder was Ray Kroc, owner of the San Diego Padres (as well as McDonald's), Hunter accepted George Steinbrenner's offer to sign with the Yankees for $3.75 million over five years. The $750,000 annual figure was a staggering increase over Hunter's previous $100,000 salary, and the multi-year contract guarantee was also unprecedented.

Catfish Hunter's financial bonanza graphically displayed to his fellow baseball players how lucrative free agency could be for them. (When Hunter passed away in 1999 from Lou Gehrig's disease, current fans were also reminded of how valuable an asset Hunter proved to be for Steinbrenner's Yankees, whom he led to their only two World Series victories in two decades.) Still, the specific route that Hunter had taken in freeing himself from the Athletics would rarely be available to anyone else. But the MLBPA's general counsel, Dick Moss, had developed a legal theory for achieving free agency that would have much broader applications, and Marvin Miller persuaded the Dodgers' Andy Messersmith to serve as the test case.

Messersmith had led the Dodgers to the World Series in 1974, winning 20 games with seven shutouts. However, after losing the Series to Hunter and the A's, the Dodgers offered Messersmith only a modest salary increase, and the owner, Peter O'Malley, adamantly refused to give this young player a no-trade clause in his contract. Messersmith refused to sign a new agreement, but rather than hold out he played the 1975 season under the standard contract that was unilaterally renewed by the Dodgers. At the end of another very good season (for Messersmith, if not the Dodgers), Dick Moss took this case to Arbitrator Seitz, who made a much more momentous decision than the *Hunter* ruling of the previous fall. Seitz ruled that when Messersmith chose to play that year at the Dodgers' option, but without signing a new contract (containing yet another option), he then became an unrestricted free agent. While Messersmith did not reap anything like Hunter's financial windfall, he did get a three-year, $1 million contract with the Atlanta Braves and their brand-new owner, Ted Turner.

From a strictly legal point of view, the *Messersmith* decision seems as dubious as *Flood*. The option clause in Messersmith's contract—as in all standard player agreements—gave the club the right to "renew the contract for the period of one year on the *same* terms." But Seitz said that this option clause was not a "term" to be included in the renewed contract, because otherwise owners could keep renewing "in perpetuity." But even that arbitral stretch of the phrase "same terms" simply left Messersmith contractually free to play in another league, for example in Japan. The second obstacle he faced was a provision in the agreement among the MLB teams themselves, which stated that the only club that could deal with a particular player was the one "with which he is under contract . . . *or* by which he is reserved" (as Messersmith certainly was by the Dodgers). Seitz removed this obstacle by saying that "or" here really meant "and": "no contract, no reservation!" Any other reading, he said, would be "incompatible with . . . freedom of contract in the economic and political society in which we live and of which the professional sport of baseball ('the national pastime') is a part."

Most people give the *Messersmith* decision the credit (or the blame) for opening the door to free agency in the world of sports. But this is incorrect. While the MLB owners were not able to get the *Messersmith* reading of their prior language overturned in court, they were free to get it rewritten before any harm was done to them. Messersmith was the sole free agent during the 1975–76 off-season, though after reading about his award more than half the players chose to play out their options during the 1976 season. More important, though, the collective agreement between the two sides had expired at the end of 1975, a week after Seitz announced his verdict, so the parties would have to renegotiate it in any event.

Miller and the players were willing to place some limits on free agency—in particular, to have it kick in only after the player had put in a few years in the major leagues. The owners, however, wanted free agency to begin only after 8–10 years of play, and even then in a somewhat restricted form. In order to pressure the players to accept that position, the owners locked them out during spring training. Then came another fateful step. After 17 days of lost spring training games, Commissioner Kuhn ordered the owners to lift the lockout "for the good of the game." This action by the commissioner removed any economic pressure on the players to compromise at the table. By midsummer the owners had agreed to a new four-year agreement essentially on the Players Association's terms: largely unrestricted free agency after six years, with salary arbitration available to players after two years. The era of true free agency in sports was about to begin.

Baseball's Battles Continue

The saga of baseball has provided ample proof that antitrust law is far from the only lever that players can use to secure a better deal from the owners. During the decade when *Flood* was being litigated and *Messersmith* arbitrated, average annual baseball salaries were steadily rising (in tandem with the overall economy): from $19,000 to $52,000. The Players Association was focusing its bargaining efforts on minimum salary levels, pensions, and working conditions that were common to every player. But when the union turned to reshaping the setting for negotiating individual players' contracts and secured free agency as the basic premise, salaries suddenly jumped from $52,000 in 1976 to $76,000 in 1977 (with Reggie Jackson leading the way) and went on up to around $200,000 by 1981.

But there has never been a simple, across-the-board removal of all restraints on the baseball players market that would leave every player completely free to deal with any club as long as he did not have a signed contract term with just one of them. Right from its inception in 1976, free agency in baseball has been limited to players who have put in six full years of service in the major leagues. Paradoxically, in the 1976 labor negotiations it was the maverick owner of the Oakland Athletics, Charles Finley, who tried to convince the other owners that if they were going to make *some* of the players free agents, they should free up almost all the players. The MLBPA leader Marvin Miller later confessed that he was delighted that the other owners had refused to listen to Finley, because Miller believed the free agent market would serve players best if only a small amount of blue-chip talent was available at any one time to the large number of teams pursuing it. And restricting the market this way would serve the interest of all players, not just of the veteran stars who were the subject of free agent bidding wars, because the resulting new salary figures would be passed along to most of their teammates through salary arbitration.

Salary arbitration alone could not significantly enhance overall salaries; its role, instead, was to eliminate discrepancies in the treatment of specific players by their teams. In 1974 and 1975, when salary arbitration was operating in the context of the reserve system, the spread between the team and player proposals averaged $10,000–$15,000. In the 1990s the average spread exceeded $1 million. The reason was that the salary levels set by free agents served as the economic parameters for the arbitrators' judgments. One key precedent was the $700,000 arbitration award secured by Bruce Sutter in 1980, after he had won the Cy Young Award in his fourth year as the Chicago Cubs' closer. Counsel for the

MLBPA persuaded the arbitrator to use Nolan Ryan's new salary as the benchmark for Sutter's: Ryan's agent had just negotiated the first million-dollar free agency contract for his client's move to the Houston Astros. Two years later, in 1982, Fernando Valenzuela rode that rising salary wave into the first million-dollar arbitration award, after only *two* seasons with the Dodgers.

Ever since this breakthrough baseball agreement of 1976, it is the owners who have pushed for changes in the system and the players who have fought to preserve the status quo. The next contract battle took place in 1980–81. Any team that lost a free agent received a draft pick from the club that signed him, but such a pick was of rather skimpy value in baseball. Thus the owners sought compensation in the form of major league players, though they were prepared to exclude the top 15 players on each team's roster.

The owners' basic argument was that a team deserved real compensation for losing one of its player "assets," since clubs made a significant investment in training and developing this talent. The players' response was that they were "people, not property," who were entitled to the fundamental right of all Americans to move and work wherever they wanted at the end of any contract they had signed. When the clubs announced that they would establish this new player-for-player compensation system at the end of the 1981 season, the players voted for a mid-season strike to block them from doing so.

Before going on strike, though, the MLBPA tried to get the owners to show them the teams' financial records. But neither the owners nor a federal judge could be convinced that the players had any right to check whether baseball really was facing a fiscal crisis caused by soaring salaries, as Commissioner Kuhn had been telling the media. The judge ended his ruling on June 10, 1981, with the injunction, "PLAY BALL!!! So ordered." But the players went on strike instead, shutting down the season for 51 days.

At the outset of the strike the owners appeared strong and united, buttressed by $50 million in strike insurance coverage from Lloyd's of London. When the insurance fund began to run out, though, so did the owners' resolve. By the end of July they felt compelled to accept Marvin Miller's subtle but crucial variation on their proposal. Any team losing a high-quality free agent would be entitled to be compensated with another player, though only from among those below the top 24 on each team's roster. However, that player would not necessarily come from the signing team's roster, but from a pool of all eligible players on all the teams that had asserted the right to bid for free agents. This rather remote prospect of losing a player who was just a bench-warmer anyway turned out to be no deterrent to bidding for free agents: average players' salaries nearly doubled from slightly under $200,000 in 1981 to slightly over $370,000 in 1985, when this agreement expired.

The new compensation rule had only one notable effect: it was the reason Tom Seaver won his 300th game in Yankee Stadium rather than in Shea Stadium. Seaver, a future Hall-of-Famer and the greatest of all New York Mets, was left unprotected by the Mets in the winter of 1984 because they thought no one would pick him: Seaver's pitching career was winding down, but he was still drawing a high salary. But when the Toronto Blue Jays signed the Chicago White Sox reliever Dennis Lamp that winter, the White Sox took Seaver from the Mets roster as compensation. Pitching for the White Sox, Seaver revived his career with a flourish. On August 4, 1985, he won his 300th game in New York, but he was in town to play against the Yankees rather than for the Mets.

Seaver reached this milestone the day before yet another baseball strike—which fortunately lasted just two days, the shortest-ever work stoppage in sports. Both sides were prepared to make a quick compromise settlement. One element suggested by the owners' chief negotiator, Lee MacPhail, was to go back to giving teams that lost a free agent a draft pick from the team that signed him, rather than a future Tom Seaver from any team in that free agent market. The other change reflected the fact that the MLBPA's negotiators now believed that at least some teams were experiencing real financial difficulties. (Unlike Bowie Kuhn in 1981, the new commissioner, Peter Ueberroth, insisted that the clubs open their books to the MLBPA and its economic expert, Roger Noll.) The players' union thus agreed to delay a player's right to salary arbitration (which usually produced a pay increase of roughly 100 percent) until after he had spent three, rather than two, years in the majors. Marvin Miller publicly criticized Don Fehr, the new MLBPA leader, for making this concession, which allowed owners to cap their younger players' salaries for an extra year.

Unfortunately, the prospects of a more cooperative relationship were soon crushed by the owners, under the guidance of Commissioner Ueberroth. The ink was barely dry on the 1985 settlement when the owners reached a private understanding that they would not bid on any free agent whose current team wanted to keep him. For the next three years star players such as Jack Morris, Kirk Gibson, Tim Raines, and Lance Parrish failed to attract a single outside offer in the free agent market. Andre Dawson, who desperately wanted to leave the Montreal Expos, eventually got an offer from the Chicago Cubs, but only when his agent publicly gave the Cubs a contract signed by Dawson that left the salary amount blank. After apologizing in writing to the owners' Player Relations Committee, the Cubs gave in to their fans and signed Dawson for less than half of what the Expos had been paying him. For that price Dawson got to play on the grass of Wrigley Field, where he was the 1987 Most Valuable Player.

This radical change in the legal rules of the game substantially slowed salary growth, as the elimination of bidding for free agents rippled through the entire salary structure. Whereas in prior years the salaries of free agents and other veterans had gone up by 15–20 percent, in 1986 and 1987 salaries *declined* by 6 percent and 15 percent respectively, and almost always in one-year contracts. If employers in any other industry had taken this kind of collective action, it would have instantly produced an antitrust lawsuit for "conspiracy in restraint of trade." Given the *Flood* and *Messersmith* precedents in baseball, this action instead produced multiple arbitration proceedings over whether the owners had violated a labor agreement that barred them from "acting in concert" in individual contract negotiations.

After hearing voluminous testimony from both sides, the arbitrators rejected the owners' argument that it was only by pure coincidence that George Steinbrenner and Ted Turner, for example, had suddenly stopped bidding for any free agent stars. Not only did the owners have to pay damages for the salary amounts already lost by the players whose free agency prospects had been affected by the owners' collusion, but these players were immediately freed from their contracts to have another chance at free agent bidding. The first to move was Kirk Gibson, going from the Detroit Tigers to the Los Angeles Dodgers, where he was the 1988 National League MVP and hit the breathtaking tenth-inning home run off Dennis Eckersley that began the Dodgers' World Series sweep of the Oakland A's. Three years later Jack Morris followed much the same path from the Tigers to the Minnesota Twins, for whom he won the seventh game in their 1991 World Series victory over the Atlanta Braves.

In the meantime, prodded by the new commissioner, Fay Vincent, the owners finally agreed in 1990 to settle these cases by paying the estimated $280 million that had been lost by players during the three years of collusion. In addition, as part of the 1990 contract renegotiations, the owners agreed to change the anti-collusion contract provision to replicate the antitrust remedies of *treble* damages plus all legal costs (and to slightly expand eligibility for arbitration).

The baseball experience dramatically illustrates how a background legal regime—even one privately created by the parties involved—can shape economic outcomes. Overall baseball salaries rose modestly from $370,000 in 1985 to $430,000 in 1988, reflecting both the results of the owners' collusion and their transmission through salary arbitration. But after the collusion ended in 1988, free agency bidding sent average salaries soaring to $1.1 million by 1994. Little wonder that Commissioner Bud Selig and the owners were determined that summer to put a hard cap on team payrolls (although they ended up with a rather soft salary tax).

How Far to Roll Back *Flood*

Baseball's experience since then with its salary tax—one that is imposed just on the high-paying, not the low-paying teams—is the reason we are likely to have a replay of that sport's labor battles when the current contract expires at the end of 2001. Many fans would like to return to the Curt Flood era, when players had no right to either free agency or salary arbitration, and thus owners had no need for either a salary cap or tax. But the economic realities and needs of the sports world are much more complex than they appear even to faithful readers of the sports pages. That is why I am soon going to spend two chapters spelling out my diagnoses and prescriptions for the players market in sports.

As we have already seen with morality issues, the experience in sports can provide a number of revealing lessons for citizens and lawmakers about what to do in the broader society. What economic lesson should America draw from what has happened in the baseball labor market? Remember that when baseball players decided in 1967 to join together in a real union to bargain with the owners, their average salaries were around $19,000, less than four times the overall American average. By 1999, though, baseball players were averaging nearly $1.6 million, more than

55 times what the ordinary American worker was being paid. The vast bulk of that change took place after the Supreme Court in *Flood* had "just said no" to the players' using antitrust law to challenge the owner's actions. But because of the solidarity that baseball players have always displayed in their common cause, they have done even better through "self-help" than their counterparts in other sports have been able to do with plenty of "court help."

The message that worker-fans can draw from this baseball experience is that if they want to end the *real,* let alone the *relative,* decline in their own pay, they are going to have to unionize and bargain collectively, rather than simply accept "take it or leave it" offers from employers. But before that kind of self-help can seem feasible in the present-day labor market, these same fans are going to have to focus some of their efforts as voters in securing congressional action to make our labor laws more supportive of ordinary workers. After all, these are the people who are likely to be *permanently* replaced if they ever dare to go out on strike, a risk that has never been faced by major league athletes like John Elway or Cal Ripken even when owners have found substitutes to fill their positions during a strike.*

In the current political environment, Congress has been more inclined to enact bills like the one jointly promoted by the MLB owners and players that would make only "Major League Players . . . covered under the antitrust laws." If Curt Flood were alive he might well feel distressed as well as honored by the Curt Flood Act of 1998, because of what it left out rather than what it put in. As requested by the major league owners and players, the Curt Flood Act explicitly cautions that nothing in it should be construed as making antitrust law applicable to whatever baseball owners do in their dealings with communities about franchise location, or with minor league teams and players, or even with

---

* I am not going to spend any of the scarce pages in this book detailing my views about labor law reform, something I have done in several other books. I do want to make it clear, though, that I advocate a principled approach to the law of the workplace, one that also calls for removal of some unjustified legal obstacles now placed in the way of employers. Baseball provides an illustration of such obstacles, in the "bargaining in bad faith" charges that were upheld against the owners in the 1994 negotiations. Having started bargaining for a salary cap in June of that year, the owners should not have had to face judgment by the NLRB that an "impasse"—a deadlock—had still not been reached by December, a judgment that meant the owners were not then legally free to establish the cap themselves as free agent bargaining was about to get under way, with the players being equally free under labor law to collectively refuse to sign contracts in that salary cap setting.

major league umpires. Indeed, the danger of such an express limitation in this congressional act is that it might well restrain the courts from continuing what some are now doing—confining baseball's antitrust exemption to the historic reserve system that was the actual focus of the *Flood* case and most of its predecessors.

The starting point for that judicial effort was a lawsuit filed against the National League owners for blocking the move of the San Francisco Giants to the Tampa Bay area in 1992. The effort might have borne fruit in George Steinbrenner's 1997 suit against MLB Properties for trying to restrain the New York Yankees' merchandising deal with Adidas, had that suit not been settled. Baseball owners must not be insulated from *any* judicial scrutiny (even the kind now applied to football owners, for example) of the way they have shaped league and team relations with television networks, merchandising companies, and local communities.

On the surface, at least, more complex questions seem to be posed by relations between major and minor league baseball. Major League Baseball and the minor league alliance, the National Association of Professional Baseball Leagues, are parties to a Professional Baseball Agreement (PBA) designed to further the interests of the two constituencies. However, since neither fans nor players have had any role in shaping the terms of this agreement, it is unlikely that their independent and sometimes conflicting interests vis-à-vis the owners are reflected in the PBA. A revealing example of the exclusion of fans' interests is the PBA provision that prohibits introducing minor league teams into locations that major league clubs have designated as their exclusive territory. In the early 1990s, for example, this rule allowed the New York Mets to block the establishment of a minor league club on western Long Island. As a result, those suburban Long Island fans had to go into New York City to watch a Mets (or Yankees) game at major league prices of $15–$50 a ticket, rather than staying closer to home and watching a minor league game for $5–$10 a ticket.

What about minor league players? Major league owners have secured that territorial priority over the minor leagues (one that allowed MLB's expansion Colorado Rockies to dislodge the Triple A Denver Zephyrs) in return for bankrolling the entire players' payroll of their "farm clubs." In fact, minor league players are actually employees of the major league teams, and they are the only players still fully governed by baseball's historic reserve system.

That system begins with a June draft of high school graduates and third-year college players, a draft that only recently was capped at 50 rounds. The drafted player must sign a standard contract that effectively binds him to his drafting club for up to seven years in the minors—by which time his major league prospects and bargaining leverage are almost always minimal. The relative situation of minor league players is now worse, not better, than it was back in the early 1950s when George Toolsen unsuccessfully sought to have the Supreme Court free him from the Yankees' farm system so that he could play for a talent-starved club like the St. Louis Browns (now the Baltimore Orioles).

How has minor league baseball fared overall? In the late 1940s there were more than 450 minor league teams drawing more than 40 million fans to their games—a team average of 90,000 a season. Then television arrived in American homes, drastically reducing the demand for minor league baseball. By the late 1950s attendance had plummeted to around 15 million, where it remained for the next 20 years. At the end of the 1970s the average price paid for a Class A team was $10,000; individuals tended to buy and operate these teams primarily as a gesture for their local communities. Then came the resurgence in interest in minor league (as well as major league) baseball among baby boom families who did not feel like staying home every night to watch television. By the late 1990s total minor league attendance had reached 35 million, an average of about 200,000 a season for each of the nearly 175 teams. The value of a Class A franchise is now around $5 million, and Triple A teams—the top-of-the-line minors—sell for over $10 million.

Has this success of minor league franchises improved the financial situation of minor league players? Back when Toolson filed his suit in the early 1950s, Triple A players earned slightly over $3,000 a year, about one-quarter of the average for major league players. By the late 1990s the typical Triple A salary was about $25,000, less than one-fiftieth of the major league average. Unlike their major league counterparts (but like the typical American worker), minor league players are not unionized, so they have been unable to secure decent salary scales and benefits. But unlike the rest of the labor force, minor league players lack a competitive market for their services that would ensure them anything near the appropriate economic return for their talent at this stage in their careers.

The current legal situation clearly works to benefit both the minor league owners, who pay nothing at all for the talent they are using, and the major league owners, who can contain the cost of the talent they are developing. These restraints on minor league salaries also enhance the economic situation of major league players: the less money that has to be paid to minor leaguers by their common employer, the more money is available for major league players to tap through their collectively bargained instruments of free agency and salary arbitration. Of course, the major leaguers who end up with multi-million-dollar contracts were themselves once minor leaguers, and they may well say that their short-term minor league sacrifice was worth it for that longer-term bonanza. However, only a small fraction of minor leaguers ever play a single game in the majors, and a large proportion of those who do get to the big leagues do not even make it to the fourth year, when a salary-arbitrated contract kicks in, let alone to the seventh year, when players reap the benefits of free agency. This kind of distribution of the financial benefits of the soaring popularity of minor league ball can be justified only if we believe that the winner really *should* take the lion's share.

I doubt that many Americans think the aim of our legal policy should be to make the wealthy even wealthier at the expense of the vast majority of citizens who are not even part of the well-to-do. Once we understand what has been happening, it should be clear why baseball's antitrust exemption should not insulate from judicial scrutiny the baseball owners' agreement that keeps minor league games—which ordinary Americans might find easier to afford and enjoy than major league games—out of major league cities. As for the players market, if Congress had been moved by socioeconomic principle rather than by political lobbying, it would have seen fit to remove the special *Flood* barrier to minor league as well as major league players.

The distinctive characteristics of sports may justify some kind of reserve system constraining the way players rise from the minors to the majors; we will look at this issue soon. But from a broader institutional perspective, the people who have to be convinced of the value of such a system should be the players (perhaps through an expanded union of minor as well as major league players), or at least a neutral judicial body, rather than just the owners, who clearly are reaping the benefits of their own rules. If Congress wants to open the gates to a freer and fairer players market, it should give serious attention to the minor league successors to George Toolson, not just to future major league Curt Floods.

10

WHAT ANTITRUST DID
FOR PLAYERS

When the Supreme Court was rendering its *Flood* judgment in the early 1970s about whether antitrust law should apply to baseball and its reserve system, the Justices were clearly concerned about the as-yet-unknown impact that free market principles might have on the national pastime. Now that we have had a quarter-century of experience with antitrust in the other sports, the Court and Congress can make a much more informed judgment on this score. Is there a difference in the quality as well as the economics of the game when player-owner relationships are shaped by antitrust as well as labor law?

Antitrust Appears in the Players Market

It was in the late 1950s that the Supreme Court, in *Radovich v. NFL,* first ruled that leagues in sports other than baseball were not exempt from the Sherman Antitrust Act. Pete Radovich had been an All-Pro guard with the Detroit Lions in the early 1940s. After going off to fight in World War II, he returned to find that his father, who lived in Los Angeles, was very ill. Radovich asked the Lions to trade him to the Los Angeles Rams so that he could be near his father (in those days before easy air travel). When the Lions refused, Radovich decided to leave them and go play for the Los Angeles Dons in the newly created All-American Football Conference.

Four years later the NFL and the AAFC decided to settle their turf war; as a result, the Cleveland Browns, the San Francisco 49ers, and the Baltimore Colts were absorbed into the NFL. But before making that deal the NFL authorities had blacklisted Radovich and other players who had moved to the AAFC, forbidding them to come back to play (or work) for any NFL team. In 1957, only four years after reaffirming baseball's special exemption in *Toolson,* the Supreme Court ruled that Radovich could sue the NFL under antitrust law for this boycott of his services; the league eventually settled the case for a substantial sum.

One practical difference from the *Toolson* (or *Flood*) case was that Radovich was challenging a league policy that blocked and punished players for leaving their current team to move to another league, not just to another club in the same league. Indeed, just a couple of years after *Radovich,* when the new American Football League appeared on the scene, the NFL lawyers had to make it clear to players that their standard contract did not contain a perpetually renewable option that would block them from jumping to the AFL. And the result of that inter-league competition was that average NFL salaries jumped from $10,000 in 1960 to $25,000 in 1967, significantly more than Curt Flood's colleagues were averaging in baseball.

Faced with these financial consequences of their bidding wars for players like John Brodie and Joe Namath, the NFL owners decided to merge with the AFL. All of the existing AFL teams were incorporated in what became a two-conference league with a Super Bowl, and two new franchises were added as part of the deal. One was the Cincinnati Bengals, created by Paul Brown after he had been ousted from his position as founding father of the Cleveland Browns (by the Browns' new owner, Art Modell). More important for the league's performance *off* the field was the New Orleans Saints. This new team brought professional sports to Louisiana for the first time, and in return Senator Russell Long and Representative Hale Boggs tucked into an unrelated tax bill a late-night amendment giving the NFL-AFL merger the congressional blessing necessary to make it immune from antitrust challenge. This sudden restoration of the owners' monopoly power in football forced the players to turn their association into a real union that could engage in collective bargaining with the league, in the hope of undoing the damage that had suddenly been done to their previously competitive players market.

The presence of unions in basketball and hockey made similar league mergers far more difficult after competitors had entered these two sports: the American Basketball Association (ABA) in the late 1960s and the World Hockey Association (WHA) in the early 1970s. Rightly assuming that *Radovich* would make antitrust applicable to basketball as well as to football, the NBA amended its reserve clause to make it clearly give teams no more than a one-year option; however, just as in the NFL, if the player chose to move to another team within the same league, the NBA commissioner would award compensation to the team losing him. This enabled the ABA to attract established NBA stars like Billy Cunningham and Rick Barry, as well as to pursue new prospects who had not finished college, like Artis Gilmore, Spenser Haywood, and Julius Erving, or perhaps had not even attended it, like the path-breaking Moses Malone. By the early 1970s the bidding war between the NBA and the ABA had sent basketball salaries soaring even higher than had football's in the early 1960s—from $20,000 in 1967 to $90,000 in 1972.

Thus the owners of the two leagues soon began talking about a merger. When word of these conversations filtered out, the players filed an antitrust suit in the name of NBPA President Oscar Robertson. And, revealing the difference that union organization could make in the political as well as the legal and industrial relations spheres, the NBPA's executive director, Larry Fleisher, went to Washington and persuaded the Senate Judiciary Committee to withhold from basketball the statutory authorization of a merger that had been granted to football just five years earlier—unless the owners agreed to relax the operation of their reserve system *within* the league.

Unlike football and basketball, hockey had maintained its traditional reserve system, in which players were effectively committed for life to the team with which they signed their first contract. Bobby Orr, for example, made such a commitment to the Boston Bruins when, at the age of 14, he began to play for a "midget" team in his home town of Parry Sound, Ontario—an amateur club that was sponsored by the Bruins. The NHL teams sent their lawyers out to enforce the league's perpetually renewable option clause and block the moves of such hockey stars as Bobby Hull, Gerry Cheevers, and Derek Sanderson to WHA clubs bidding for their services. The WHA responded with an antitrust suit filed in the name of the Philadelphia Hockey Club, and District Judge Leon Higginbotham gave the WHA the injunctive relief it was looking for.

The NHL owners modified their rules to adopt the NFL/NBA version of a one-year team option, after which the player would be free to move to another team. However, if that switch was to another team in the NHL rather than to the WHA, it would not really be "free." Rather, the NHL owners agreed among themselves that the player's signing team would have to compensate his former team with some combination of current

players, draft picks, and/or money. Notwithstanding this major constraint on players' mobility within the league, the existence of the option
of moving to the WHA (along with salary arbitration) caused average
NHL salaries to leap from $19,000 in 1967 to $44,000 in 1972—only
half as high as NBA salaries, but significantly higher than those in either
the NFL or MLB.

The players in football and baseball, of course, did not have the benefit of inter-league competition for their services. As in baseball, the new
football players' union, the NFLPA, devoted its first few years to bargaining (and occasionally striking during summer training camp) over issues such as pensions, disability benefits, payment for exhibition games,
and other standard terms of employment for all players. In 1972, when it
first attacked the NFL's Rozelle Rule constraint on free agency, the route
the Association followed was antitrust litigation rather than labor negotiation. And by contrast with Curt Flood in baseball, football's lead
plaintiff, NFLPA President John Mackey, was the winner in court.

The trial judge in *Mackey* (and those in *Robertson* and several other
trials going on at that time) found that requiring the team signing a "free
agent" to pay large compensation to its league partner which was losing
him placed an unreasonable restraint on the market for players' services.
By late 1976 the Eighth Circuit had rendered in *Mackey* the first appellate verdict on that score. According to the court, while this kind of
inflexible reserve system might serve the interest of owners in containing player costs, it did not meet the interest of players in a competitive
labor market, and it had not even been shown to serve the fans' interest
in seeing a more competitive game on the field.

Labor Negotiation Trumps Antitrust Litigation

But while *Mackey* won the litigation battle in football that *Flood* had lost
in baseball, the NFLPA and its executive director, Ed Garvey, lost the
collective bargaining war that the MLBPA's Marvin Miller had won in
baseball.* The football union, unlike its baseball counterpart, was facing

* John Mackey suffered a personal defeat. Besides his role as NFLPA President, Mackey was
the dominant tight end of his era—probably the best ever. He combined the strength and
blocking ability of his predecessor standout Mike Ditka of the Chicago Bears with the speed
and pass-catching talent of his successor Kellen Winslow of the San Diego Chargers. However,
in large part because of his efforts on behalf of his fellow players in both the 1972 lawsuit and a

a major institutional crisis. It had suffered a severe industrial relations defeat when it called a strike in the summer of 1974 to try to loosen up free agency through direct negotiations with the owners. The strike failed when player after player crossed the picket line and went to training camp for fear of losing their jobs to competitors who had gotten to camp earlier. Meanwhile, the NFLPA was running up huge legal expenses in its attempt to secure full free agency via the *Mackey* litigation. Moreover, the absence of any collective agreement after 1974 meant not only that the clubs did not have to provide pension and disability benefits to players but also that the players did not have to pay union dues—and fewer than 20 percent were doing so voluntarily. So in an effort to save their organization, Ed Garvey and the other Association leaders settled both the *Mackey* case and the free agency issue in a new five-year collective agreement that restored union security and improved minimum salaries and across-the-board benefits.

The price was a new version of the Rozelle Rule for compensating teams that lost free agents. The compensation would consist just of draft picks: no more veterans would be subjected to such free agency "trades." In addition, the number and quality of draft picks were spelled out in advance in the labor contract—ranging from none for players offered less than $47,000 to two first-round picks for players offered more than $200,000. Garvey's expectation was that teams hoping to add valuable free agents to their rosters would be much more likely to bid if they knew beforehand what the total price would be, rather than having to face uncertainty about what the commissioner would award.

As it turned out, football's new reserve system had a considerably more chilling effect on bidding for free agents than even the former Rozelle Rule. During the ten-year span of the next two collective agreements, only one "free" agent who was subject to draft pick compensation actually shifted to a new team: the St. Louis Cardinals' Norm Thompson moved to the Baltimore Colts. For example, the Chicago Bears' Walter Payton, well on his way to the NFL's all-time rushing rec-

---

six-week strike in the summer of 1974, Mackey was both released early by the Colts' new owner, Bob Irsay, and excluded from the NFL Hall of Fame by Commissioner Pete Rozelle. Not until Rozelle had been replaced by Paul Tagliabue was Mackey given his rightful place in the Hall of Fame—ironically, in tandem with the NFL owners' other legal pariah, Al Davis of the Raiders.

ord and football's Hall of Fame, did not receive a single offer from another team when he became a free agent in 1981.

In hindsight, the NFLPA made two mistakes in negotiating the design of this severely restrictive free agency for veterans. The salary test for how many draft picks were owed should have been how much the current team—not the bidding team—had offered to pay the player. In addition, at least in cases where no outside bid was made, the player should have had a right to neutral arbitration of a fair salary that would be paid by his prior team, which still "owned" him. True, even with this huge obstacle to players' mobility, average NFL salaries did jump from $55,000 in 1977 to $90,000 in 1982, a generous increase by comparison with what the ordinary sports fan was earning. But baseball players, who after *Flood* had no antitrust chips to play at the bargaining table, were still able to secure a far more attractive combination of largely unrestricted free agency and salary arbitration. As a result, average baseball salaries soared from $52,000 to $241,000 in that same period, even though the NFL's popularity, television revenues, and franchise values were all rising far faster than MLB's.

A similar development took place in hockey. As noted earlier, after its antitrust defeat at the hands of the WHA, the NHL had modified its standard contract to free its players to move to a rival league. However, when a player wanted to move to another club within the NHL, the owners agreed among themselves that the team signing a free agent would pay compensation to the team losing him (with a neutral arbitrator selecting one of the two "final offers" made by the clubs). In order to insulate that restraint on the intra-league market from antitrust challenge by the players, the owners felt they needed the consent of the NHL Players Association. In 1975 the NHLPA's founder and leader, Alan Eagleson, did approve this system in return for an increase in veterans' pension benefits (from $500 to $750 a month). The reason the players accepted this deal was that competition from the WHA was more than enough to keep players' salaries rising. This part of the labor agreement was terminable by the players in the event of an NHL-WHA merger, and Eagleson publicly vowed that he would never accept such a merger without free agency appearing within the new and larger league.

In the spring of 1978, though, the NHL and WHA owners did agree to the functional equivalent of a merger: the WHA disbanded and the NHL took in the Quebec Nordiques, Winnipeg Jets, Hartford Whalers, and

Edmonton Oilers (with Wayne Gretzky). After the new NHL president, John Ziegler, made it clear that the owners were not prepared to budge on free agency, Eagleson decided to blink rather than to strike or sue. The players agreed to maintain heavily restricted free agency in the enlarged NHL, in return for the owners' raising promised pension benefits from $750 to $1,000 a month. Just as in football, the removal of almost all competition for players' services initiated a slide in relative hockey salaries (relative to professional athletes, not ordinary workers). Thus, while average NHL salaries had reached $96,000 in the 1977–78 season, significantly higher than baseball's $76,000 (even after a full year of baseball free agency), by the early 1990s hockey salaries averaged just over $200,000 and baseball's over $1 million. The 1992 labor negotiations finally produced a modest amount of unrestricted free agency for players aged 31 or more and/or those with 10 years of service who were earning less than the league average. The combination of even this limited free agency with salary arbitration sent average hockey salaries to $1.4 million by the 1999–2000 season.

Meanwhile, in basketball, NBA owners and Commissioner Larry O'Brien wanted to end the *Robertson* litigation and secure a merger with the ABA. They knew they needed the consent of the players because they were not going to get the blessing of Congress. Thus NBPA Director Larry Fleisher (and its new president, Paul Silas) secured a far better deal for basketball players than Eagleson had done for hockey players or Garvey for football players.

The ten-year NBA settlement worked out in early 1976 would take free agency through two stages. For the first five years, free agent moves would generate compensation awarded by the commissioner, but subject to judicial review to ensure that the award was no more than fair market value. In 1981 real free agency would come to basketball, with no compensation to the prior team, though that team would have a right of first refusal. This was the price the owners had to pay to end their decade-long battle with the ABA, absorb the latter's New Jersey Nets, Indiana Pacers, San Antonio Spurs, and Denver Nuggets, and bring such stars as Julius Erving, Moses Malone, and Artis Gilmore into a single dominant league.

Thus five years after labor law had brought free agency into baseball, antitrust law accomplished the same thing in basketball. And whereas average hockey salaries rose from $96,000 in 1977–78 to $112,000 in

1982–83 (less than inflation), basketball salaries leaped from $143,000 to $246,000 in that same period. But that largely unrestricted free agency model was short-lived in basketball, soon constrained by a collectively bargained salary cap.

The idea of a salary cap—more accurately, a payroll share—had actually been put on the sports agenda in 1982 by NFLPA Director Ed Garvey and President (and Oakland Raiders' All-Pro lineman) Gene Upshaw. Garvey and Upshaw had become disenchanted with the compensation system (draft picks as compensation for the loss of free agents) they had negotiated as the successor to the Rozelle Rule. They were also skeptical about the value of even less restricted free agency, especially in a sport like football in which almost total revenue sharing among the clubs reduced the owners' financial incentive to spend large salaries on top-flight players in order to win games and championships. Garvey's view was that if there was to be "socialism among the owners" there should be something similar for the players. This should, however, take a more rational form than the kinds of individual contracts negotiated by owners with agents, especially for early draft picks, who often did not fulfill their promise.

The NFLPA proposed, instead, that the players be guaranteed a fixed percentage of the game's total revenues: their opening bid was a 55 percent share, but Garvey was prepared to come down from there. About two-thirds of that money would be distributed according to a seniority-based wage scale: the longer one played, the higher one's salary. The remaining third would be paid out on the basis of individual performance that season, according to incentive formulas collectively negotiated by the league and the Association. From the perspective of Garvey and Upshaw, both players and owners would gain from this system, with the only losers being players' agents.

The salary cap was too radical an idea for the NFL owners at that time. The league's negotiator, Jack Donlan, told Garvey that his "'percentage of the gross' concept is anathema to American business." In that turbulent bargaining round, the two sides eventually worked out a fixed dollar guarantee for the players as a whole, but with the bulk of the money to be spent by teams individually negotiating contracts with their players (and agents). After football's first-ever regular-season strike, one that began with the third game of the season and lasted for 55 days, the parties eventually settled for a league commitment that the owners would spend $1.3 billion during the 1983–1986 seasons. While a minimum salary-and-benefits structure was established that did channel somewhat more of the guaranteed money toward senior players, most of the money would be spent on contracts that were individually negotiated without any meaningful free agency and competition for the players' services.

Shortly afterward Garvey retired from sports and went into government, while Upshaw retired from the Raiders and succeeded Garvey as director of the NFLPA. Meanwhile, their salary cap idea did come to fruition in basketball. In the early 1980s the NBA was experiencing the following traumas: telecasts of its finals (featuring Larry Bird, Magic Johnson, and Julius Erving) were tape-delayed until late at night; many fans suspected that most (black) players were using drugs; and a bidding war for players between big- and small-market clubs was endangering the existence of several franchises (and thus the jobs they provided). That is why in their 1983 labor negotiations NBPA Director Larry Fleisher and President Bob Lanier were quite prepared to agree with NBA Commissioner Larry O'Brien and his about-to-be successor, David Stern, that a salary cap should be superimposed on their current free agency system.

While the NBA owners had originally wanted not just a *cap* but a *cut* in the permitted level of salaries, the eventual deal set the amount at roughly the existing levels—53 percent of designated gross revenues, or $3.1 million a team. And this NBA version of the "soft" cap limited only the amount that teams could spend on new players, whether rookies or free agents. Clubs could take in such a new player only if they got below the cap or used a salary slot vacated by an existing team member through release or retirement. However, no limits were placed on the amount that a club like the Celtics could pay to re-sign a star like Larry Bird, whose contract was then expiring. Equally important, the system was more accurately described as salary *sharing* rather than salary *capping*. Besides the collectively bargained ceiling imposed on the total amount that a team could pay its player roster, there was a floor that had to be met in the payrolls of traditionally low-paying (and poorly performing) clubs like the Indiana Pacers, whose payroll was then just over $1 million.

The Labor Exemption Comes to Sports

We have now witnessed the somewhat ironic role that the law can and does play in sports. Baseball players, the ones who were told by the Supreme Court in *Flood* that they had no antitrust rights, successfully used collective bargaining under labor law to secure the first and still the least restricted free agency system in any sport. Football, hockey, and basketball players, who have known ever since *Radovich* that antitrust law does govern their sports, took significantly longer to secure a somewhat less free players market. And the reason is a labor exemption from antitrust whose current judicial design is a by-product of sports litigation.

This labor exemption doctrine has a complicated legal history that cannot be retraced in any detail here. Suffice it to say that the fundamental problem was that while the Sherman Antitrust Act bans "any [unreasonable] combination in restraint of trade," the National Labor Relations Act gives employees the right to organize themselves into unions that negotiate collective agreements that protect workers from competitive pressures in the labor market. In the mid-1960s the Supreme Court finally rendered a pair of decisions, *Pennington* and *Jewel Tea,* that sought to accommodate the legal status of these "restraints of trade in labor." The swing vote opinion was written by Justice Byron White—who in his football career had been both college All-American and NFL Hall-of-Famer "Whizzer" White.

The *Pennington* and *Jewel Tea* judgments came down just as real unionism was appearing in sports, but with the players' associations planning to use antitrust as well as labor law to tackle the league's historic restraints on the players market. The first such union-supported antitrust suit was baseball's *Flood* case. There Justice Thurgood Marshall noted, in his dissent to the majority's preservation of baseball's unique and outmoded exemption from antitrust, that MLB owners might well be able to use the labor exemption to protect their century-old reserve system from antitrust attack. As evidence, he cited a just-published article by a Yale law professor, Ralph Winter. According to Winter's piece, "Superstars in Peonage," the *Flood* litigation was a case of "the right teams playing the wrong game in the wrong [legal] arena."

Just a few years later, a divided Sixth Circuit panel applied the antitrust exemption in the 1979 *McCourt* case. Dale McCourt, NHL Rookie of the Year with the Detroit Red Wings, was awarded by the arbitrator to the Los Angeles Kings when the Wings signed the Kings' free agent All-Star goaltender Rogatien Vachon to a six-year, $1.9 million contract. Even though Alan Eagleson and the NHLPA had only reluctantly accepted this clear obstacle to players' movement as the price of higher pension benefits secured from the owners, that consent by the players' union protected the owners from antitrust litigation by dissident individual players.

By the late 1980s, then, the circuit courts had rightfully concluded that leagues should be insulated from antitrust suits filed by players challenging league restraints that may have been designed to benefit the owners, but that had the *consent* of the players' union as part of a broader "win-win" labor deal that also served the interests of the players (who do get to vote to ratify labor agreements). The tougher legal call concerned the availability of the labor exemption simply because the union was *present* on the scene, even though it did not consent to what otherwise would be an illegal restraint of trade in the players' services. That question in turn could be subdivided into two situations. One was when the players' union had consented to the restraint when it was originally created (like the NFL's compensation for free agents or the NBA's salary cap) but the collective agreement had now expired and the union wanted this feature removed. The other situation was when the owners unilaterally added to the earlier restraint (tightening up the NBA cap) or created a brand-new one (an NFL salary cut) after reaching an impasse in bargaining with the union. Sports negotiations in the late 1980s and mid-1990s produced what are probably the final judicial verdicts on all of these scores.

By that time professional basketball was enjoying huge success on the playing court. Average NBA salaries had more than doubled in the five years of the salary cap, reaching $510,000 in the 1987–88 season. The immediate reason for such escalating salaries was that NBA revenues had risen proportionately. The creative 1983 labor agreement may have had something to do with that—not just the salary cap protection for small-market teams, but the drug program developed by NBPA President Bob Lanier and his fellow players. The major contributor, though, was soaring fan interest in spectator sports—at the gate, on television, and now in merchandising. Similar revenue gains were being experienced in baseball and football (though not yet in hockey). But the NBA revenue streams were rising the most because of the talent that had been added on the floor—with Michael Jordan and Patrick Ewing joining Magic Johnson and Larry Bird. There was now no question that NBC would be broadcasting NBA championship games during prime time.

The NBPA's leader, Larry Fleisher, had always been ambivalent about the salary cap. He had accepted its original justification: the need to give NBA owners more financial assurance in the game's troubled state in the early 1980s. Now that professional basketball had such rosy prospects, Fleisher, NBPA President Junior Bridgeman, and their constituents thought it was time for the league to declare victory, remove the salary cap, and live with the same free market principles that the owners embraced in all other facets of their businesses. The owners, needless to say, wanted the salary cap to stay. Indeed, Commissioner David Stern (and his general counsel and cap expert, Gary Bettman) wanted the new agreement to close up a loophole that some players' agents and teams had hit upon. In particular, teams were signing free agents for the low first-year salary available for this slot, but with guaranteed salaries escalating sharply in later years, pursuant to the Larry Bird exception.

Fleisher went to court to file an antitrust suit in the name of Bridgeman, claiming that the labor exemption of the salary cap expired with the collective agreement through which the union had consented to this "restraint on trade" in players' services. After the trial judge had rejected this theory, Fleisher simply collected signatures from all the union members authorizing him to decertify the union as bargaining agent if that was necessary to assert their antitrust claim. He then went back to the bargaining table with Stern to work out a compromise settlement that extended the cap for five more years, but with two significant changes. The revision secured by the owners placed a 30 percent ceiling on the annual escalation in salaries guaranteed by a contract, thus cutting back on the loophole noted earlier (and this "raise cap" is now down to 12.5 percent). The change secured by the union removed the prior team's right to match any contract terms offered by a new team to a free agent (a right of first refusal). In 1988–89 NBA veteran players enjoyed for the first time the same unrestricted freedom as MLB players to move to the new team of their choice—though not fully at the salary of their choice.

Meanwhile, football players' salaries were also rising sharply during the mid-1980s—from the $90,000 NFL average in 1982 to the $230,000 average in 1987, a higher percentage increase than in either the NBA or MLB. Even though NFLPA Director Ed Garvey had not been able to retain the free agency he had won in the *Mackey* litigation, the players had been the biggest beneficiaries of the emergence of the new United States Football League (USFL) in 1983 to compete in the ever more popular football marketplace. When a team like the New Jersey Generals was willing to pay huge amounts to sign up Herschel Walker and Doug

Flutie so that its owner, Donald Trump, could see his name in the sports pages rather than the gossip pages (and when other USFL owners were doing the same for their rookies like Steve Young and Reggie White), this inevitably had a large spillover effect on NFL salaries. Unfortunately for the players, though, the USFL folded in 1986, just a year before the NFL collective agreement was to expire. Thus Garvey's successor as NFLPA director, Gene Upshaw, placed at the top of his negotiating list some level of true free agency to generate a competitive market for players' services within the NFL's restored monopoly position.

The NFLPA first sought to use the traditional union weapon—the strike—to force the owners to compromise on this issue. This action produced the huge industrial relations defeat for the union that I described earlier, after a significant number of star players had crossed the picket line to perform in the owners' replacement games. After four weeks Upshaw called off the strike, sent all the members back to work, and sent his lawyers off to court in Minneapolis, within the Eighth Circuit where the *Mackey* decision had been rendered. In the *Powell* case (named after NFLPA President Marvin Powell), District Judge Doty adopted a view of the expiration of the labor exemption that was close to the union's position. The exemption for a restraint embodied in a collective agreement (here the *de facto* ban on free agent players moving to a new team) would expire when the parties reached an "impasse" in bargaining for a new contract. At that point, the owners would be free under labor law to make the necessary changes unilaterally; not only could they put their market restraints into compliance with antitrust law, but they could also remove any benefits (such as pensions) that the players had earlier enjoyed in return for that free agency limit. In late 1989, though, a divided Eighth Circuit upheld the NFL owners' appeal (with the author of the earlier *Mackey* ruling now dissenting). If the players' union had once agreed to a restraint on the players market, its labor exemption would survive as long as the union did.

The NFLPA, supported by President Bush's solicitor-general, Kenneth Starr, tried to get the Supreme Court to take the appeal of the *Powell* decision. But rather than await that eventually fruitless effort to get the Supreme Court to address this complex labor exemption issue, Gene Upshaw did what Larry Fleisher had done two years earlier. The football union members all signed slips that withdrew from the Association any authority to act as their bargaining agent under labor law. Instead, the

NFLPA was to function just as the players' litigating agent under antitrust law.

The NFLPA's lawyers did win the *Freeman McNeil* trial before a Minneapolis jury in 1992, and Upshaw was able to negotiate with NFL Commissioner Paul Tagliabue the *Reggie White* class-action settlement and a new collective agreement (see Chapter 7). While average NFL salaries had more than doubled from $230,000 in 1987 to $490,000 in 1992, they suddenly shot up to $650,000 in 1993, the first year of unrestricted veteran free agency within the league (led by Reggie White's move from the large-market Philadelphia Eagles to the small-market Green Bay Packers). This triggered the hard salary cap that guaranteed the players 63 percent of the owners' designated gross revenues. Recall that back in 1982 Garvey and Upshaw had been looking for a guarantee of somewhere between 50 and 55 percent of the much smaller NFL revenue stream. Not surprisingly, then, after Tagliabue had extracted the huge $2.2 billion-a-year television contract from the networks in 1998, he and Upshaw quickly agreed to extend their salary cap system to the year 2004.

The atmosphere surrounding the mid-1990s "season of the salary cap" was very different in basketball than in football: the NBA's owners and players were reopening their salary cap battles just as the NFL's were resolving theirs. On the surface, one would have expected this to be a period when the two NBA sides could be in harmony. At the same time as average player salaries were trebling (topping $1.5 million in the 1993–94 season), expansion franchises were quadrupling in price (from the $32.5 million paid by the Miami Heat and the Orlando Magic to bring NBA basketball to Florida in the late 1980s to the $125 million paid to bring it to Toronto and Vancouver in Canada in the mid-1990s). But the players now wanted to remove the cap entirely, while the owners wanted to harden it considerably.

While the *Powell* decision had permitted the NFL to maintain the current cap design to which the players had agreed earlier, this Eighth Circuit judgment would not exempt unilateral action by the NBA to tighten up the cap—such as removing a new loophole just invented by Chris Dudley and his agent. This time, Stern and the NBA's lawyers beat Fleisher's NBPA successors Charles Grantham and Simon Gourdine into the courtroom. They filed a lawsuit right at the end of the 1994 playoffs and the collective agreement, in order to get the case (with Association

President Buck Williams named as defendant) into the Second Circuit in front of the Yale law professor turned Judge Ralph Winter. Not surprisingly, Judge Winter's *Williams* opinion in early 1995 confirmed the soundness of that NBA legal tactic by articulating a broad version of the labor exemption. As long as players (or printers, to use the judge's other example) had a union, they could not use antitrust law to challenge restraints collectively imposed by the owners. It was that legal message that helped trigger Michael Jordan and Patrick Ewing's effort to decertify the NBPA that summer.

A year later the Supreme Court finally rendered its verdict on this crucial sports law issue, but in a dispute that did not make the headlines as had Buck Williams's or Reggie White's. Back in 1989, when the *Marvin Powell* litigation was still going on in football, the league had devised a new "development squad" to be added to each team's roster. This squad would consist of six players who had not been able to make the regular-season roster, but whom the team might want to keep for practice, talent development, and eventual replacement of regulars who were not performing well. The NFLPA, which was still functioning as a union (though without an agreement), approved this addition to team rosters, one that would eliminate the earlier tactic by which clubs stashed such players on their injured reserve list. But the NFLPA was firmly opposed to the owners' insistence that every one of these "development squad" players be paid a flat $1,000 a week (or $16,000 a season), rather than permitting each team to negotiate contracts with individual players—a practice that had generated salary averages of $4,000 a week ($64,000 a season) for the same type of players in the previous season. After bargaining had reached an impasse on this subject, the league unilaterally imposed this first-ever individual salary cap—actually, a huge salary *cut*—in football's history.

The union went to court and won a $30 million antitrust verdict in a class-action suit in which the named plaintiff was Tony Brown: ironically, Brown had been one of the replacement players who had helped the league break the union's 1987 strike. *Brown* was the only one of the outstanding lawsuits that was not part of the $200 million 1993 *Reggie White* settlement, apparently because the two sides could not agree on the appropriate damages figure. Instead, the NFL won its appeal in the D.C. Circuit, whose Judge Harry Edwards (a former labor law professor) applied the same broad-ranging labor exemption that Judge Winter had articulated in *Williams*.

The Supreme Court then took on *Brown* as its major sports law case of the 1990s. At that stage, the NFLPA not only had the support of President Clinton's solicitor-general but also hired as lead counsel President Bush's former solicitor-general, Kenneth Starr (who was now working on another rather notable case). However, when the Supreme Court's decision came down in June 1996, Justice Breyer and his colleagues essentially agreed with Judges Winter and Edwards. As long as the players had a union engaged in multiemployer bargaining with the league under labor law, they had to give up their right to challenge the owners' unilateral restraints on the players market under antitrust law. As Judge Winter had put it: "The players may not have it both ways. They may not avail themselves of the benefit of labor and antitrust law at the same time."

Brown's Consequences and Merits

This is the legal explanation for a little-noticed but rather strange sports event that took place in the winter of 1996–97. That summer Major League Soccer (MLS) had returned this sport to America, following the highly successful World "Football" Cup hosted by the United States in 1994. To make this new venture more attractive to investors (especially those who remembered the aesthetically pleasing but financially failing North American Soccer League of the 1970s), the MLS organizers created a salary cap. This cap was even harder than the NFL's, because it not only set a $1.1 million limit (up to $1.64 million in 1999) on the total team payroll but also capped the maximum amount that could be paid to a single player—initially $175,000 in 1996 and up to $250,000 in 1999. Needless to say, soccer players were delighted to welcome this new major league into their sport, especially in the home country of American players. But they were not enchanted to live with this owner-imposed constraint on the players market, especially if and when the league's popularity and financial returns rose. Thus Gene Upshaw and the NFL Players Association quickly organized the MLS players into an affiliate of the NFLPA to let them collectively challenge this (and other) MLS rules. However, Upshaw had the MLS players vote to form a *non-*

union soccer arm of the football players' union, so that they could make their antitrust claim in court without having to face the *Brown* labor exemption hurdle.

The continuing Major League Soccer litigation poses a complex question of substantive antitrust law: Does this league's version of the salary cap constitute an "unreasonable" restraint of trade in the sports market? We shall examine such questions about the appropriate design of the sports labor market in Chapters 11 and 12. The only legal question posed to the Supreme Court in *Brown,* though, was whether the fact that players had a union representative meant that they had no antitrust rights at all. Since that blanket exemption clearly runs counter to the antitrust objective of providing a reasonably competitive market, the exemption can only be supported on the grounds that it is necessary to accommodate the conflicting objectives of labor law. The labor exemption issue confronted by the Court in *Brown* did raise considerably more complex problems than the special baseball exemption asserted in *Flood.* Ultimately, though, the Court got it wrong in *Brown* as well, with potentially more damaging consequences in the broader labor market.

One reason is that by the time the *Brown* case reached the Supreme Court it was perfectly clear that antitrust law does protect *non-union* employees from their employers' combining to restrain trade in their services. A vivid illustration can be found in a different part of the sports world. In 1992 the NCAA created a new "restricted earnings coach" position, which had a $16,000 salary cap. This new rule drastically reduced the $70,000 salary of an assistant coach like Duke's Pete Gaudet, who earned just $16,000 when he took over as acting head coach of the Blue Devils after Mike Krzyzewski was laid up for the 1994–95 season. When the Tenth Circuit found this NCAA action to be a violation of antitrust law (in the *Law* class-action suit that produced a $67 million trebled damage award), no one ever mentioned the *Brown* labor exemption: the reason is that college basketball coaches are not unionized. The same judicial verdict would have been rendered on this labor exemption issue if, back in 1989, the NFL had created a new "designated earnings coach" as well as the "restricted player squad" position.

To subject a player like Brown to such qualitatively different legal treatment from a coach like Gaudet, just because Brown happened to have a union representative, would seem to undermine rather than to implement the policies of labor law as well as antitrust law. Recall that the key aims of the National Labor Relations Act are (1) to allow employees to unite in an organization that will give them somewhat greater equality of bargaining power in dealing with often giant corporate employers; (2) to encourage the two sides to bargain together to reach a mutually acceptable agreement about the terms of their employment relationship; and (3) to reduce labor unrest, in which work stoppages harm not only the immediate parties but also their customers and communities. The consequence of *Brown* is that players like Cal Ripken in baseball and Wayne Gretzky in hockey are told that they must go on strike, or Michael Jordan in basketball and Reggie White in football are told that they must go without a union, if they want to fend off a market restraint that was unilaterally imposed by the owners rather than collectively agreed to by the players. That result seems to run as counter to labor law as to antitrust legal policy. And, of course, a development squad player like Tony Brown had no real option of striking or decertifying the players' union if he wanted to follow the lead of a designated earnings coach like Pete Gaudet and challenge in court a league restraint targeted just at this small group of marginal players.

What about the judges' argument that players (and other employees) should not have the right to use both labor and antitrust law, because these dual legal rights would give them an unfair advantage at the bargaining table? Perhaps a sufficient answer to this argument is that there are now a host of legal regimes governing the American workplace— from the Fair Labor Standards Act of 1938, to Title VII of the Civil Rights Act of 1964, to the Occupational Safety and Health Act of 1970, to the Family and Medical Leave Act of 1993. No one suggests that employees who want to take advantage of these legal protections should have to give up their union that seeks to negotiate higher-than-minimum pay or safer and fairer working conditions.

What makes the application of antitrust law to unionized labor markets considerably more challenging than the application of employment law is the practice of multiemployer bargaining. For more than a century, employers have regularly organized themselves into associations that negotiate industry-wide contracts with their employees' unions. This practice is something that unions regularly embrace because it is conducive to their members' interest in having a stable labor market in which one firm does not undercut the others with lower pay rates. But once multiemployer bargaining has been consented to by both sides (as it must be under labor law), then the employers' group should be entitled to the same unified negotiating stance as the employees' union in seeking favorable terms in labor settlements.

In particular, the employers' association must be free (under antitrust law) to lock out the employees of all of its members—as the NHL and NBA owners did to their players in the 1990s. This *tactic* puts economic pressure on the employees to move closer to the employers' position at the bargaining table. The key premise to the judicial verdicts in *Brown* and *Williams* was that employers' groups like the NFL and the NBA should have exactly the same antitrust exemption when they collectively impose new contract *terms* on their players. As Judge Winter put it in *Williams,* if an employer's group in the printing industry is entitled to institute a 5 percent pay increase rather than the 10 percent increase sought by the printers' union, so also the NBA owners were free to establish a hard salary cap without any consent from Buck Williams and his labor teammates.

The judges, however, did not appreciate the qualitative difference between the basketball and football players in *Williams* and *Brown* and those hypothetical printers (as well as the real-world examples of the mine workers in *Pennington* and the meat cutters in *Jewel Tea*). Indeed, Justice Breyer in *Brown* misunderstood the point when he said that the fact that professional athletes had the kind of talent and reputation that gave them "superior bargaining power" would be an "odd" reason for fashioning special antitrust rights for them.

The true difference is that the printers and most other unions not only have consented to but have actually proposed the restraints on individual competition for their members' services and pay, because such competition drives *down* average workers' real pay (something that America has experienced over the last quarter-century). Given such union acceptance of the principle of standardized industry rates of pay, a printers' or a meat cutters' union would have absolutely no legitimate antitrust claim against the employers' action to set the same standardized rate at a lower level than the union members would like. In sports, by contrast, the players' unions have always sought to create a competitive free market for their members' services, and to eliminate and avoid such league-wide restraints as a reserve system or a salary cap. And this union objective is not unique to the sports world. Recall that the reason the Screen Actors Guild and other unions first arose in Hollywood in 1933 was to keep the studios from acting together through their MPAA to impose a hard salary cap on all their performers.

The aim of a labor exemption from antitrust should be to accommodate the sometimes competing policy objectives of labor and antitrust law. Certainly, the *Brown* rule serves no antitrust policies when it denies any role at all to antitrust in the labor market as long as a union is present. Similarly, it does not seem conducive to the basic labor law policies of employee self-organization and industrial peace for the law to tell players (and other performers) that they must either strike or decertify their union in order to challenge in court an owner-imposed salary cap (something the non-union NCAA "restricted earnings coaches" were able to do in *Law*). And on reflection, no true objectives of collective bargaining are served when, without agreement from the union (even as to the principle let alone the specifics), the multiemployer group creates and enforces on its own the kind of anti-competitive salary cut experienced by Tony Brown and his development squad teammates.

For better or for worse, though, *Brown* is the definitive ruling in this area (at least unless Congress ever brings itself to reform our law of labor relations). It is the reason the NFLPA organized Major League Soccer players into a *non*-union, so that it can litigate rather than negotiate about the league's efforts to harden its salary cap. *Brown* is also the explanation for one of the features of the baseball labor settlement in August 1996—that the MLB owners and players would jointly petition Congress to enact the Curt Flood Act. When the MLB lawyers read the *Brown* decision in June of that year, they were able to tell their clients that the owners could comfortably give up their special exemption from antitrust—though just for major league players who had a union, not for minor leaguers who had never organized into a union (or for fans, who have no labor law right to unionize as consumers). But the likely explanation of why the NBPA, with Patrick Ewing installed as president in 1998, did not decertify as a labor union so as to be free under *Brown* to file an antitrust suit against the owners' lockout effort to harden the salary cap is the topic of the next chapter.

11

HOW TO LEVEL
THE PLAYER FIELD

Whatever the legal reasons for the Supreme Court's decision to preserve baseball's unique exemption from antitrust law, a crucial motivating factor was the special place that baseball has long occupied in American life. This is how Justice Blackmun put it in his *Flood* opinion:

> Baseball has been the national pastime for over one hundred years and enjoys a unique place in our American heritage . . . To put it mildly and with restraint, it would be unfortunate indeed if a fine sport and profession, which brings surcease from travail and an escape from the ordinary to most inhabitants of this land, were to suffer in the least because of undue concentration by anyone on commercial and profit considerations. The game is on higher ground; it behooves everyone to keep it there.

Or, as Susan Sarandon put it in the film *Bull Durham,* "I believe in the *church* of Baseball!" A quarter-century later it is obvious that *Flood* did not restrain the commercialization of baseball. Nor will the Supreme Court's conferral (in *Brown*) of a full-blown labor exemption on salary restraints unilaterally imposed by any league's owners upon their *unionized* players.

I doubt that the Supreme Court would have formulated such a broad-based labor exemption for, say, an association of movie studios or television networks that had collectively imposed a substantial salary cut on neophyte actors, simply because they happened to be represented by the Screen Actors Guild or the American Federation of Television and Radio Artists. The sports labor market is special, though, and does need different treatment from those in the entertainment and other industries. While the actions of private team owners should not be given a blanket exemption from any public legal scrutiny, their judicial "rule of reason" appraisal under antitrust law—or bargaining with the union under labor law—must recognize and accommodate the distinctive nature of sports in a manner that serves the best interests of the game, not just the special interests of the parties.

I am now going to start spelling out my own verdicts about the major sports labor issues that have been sparking lawsuits and work stoppages for more than a century. Do restraints on player free agency and salaries serve to reduce the prices that fans must pay to watch the game? Was it the traditional reserve system or the more recent free agency that enhanced competitive balance and the quality of the game in baseball? Should leagues place a cap on each team's payroll, and if so, should there be the kind of "Larry Bird" exception that still exists in basketball? Or is a salary tax an even better way to address this dimension of sports, and if so, will Major League Baseball have to revise its initial version of this tax in the owners' upcoming bargaining round with the players' union? A final challenge for labor-management relations in sports (as in other industries) is to decide not just how to divide up revenues between owners and players but also how to distribute the players' share among their various constituencies. What is the best thing to do for rookies just being drafted, or for new players who are governed by the reserve system and may not yet have access to salary arbitration, or for veteran free agents, whether stars or journeymen?

Salaries and Ticket Prices

Sportswriters and fans are regularly appalled by the record-breaking financial deals being secured by free agent players. Opinion polls reveal that approximately three-quarters of Americans think athletes are overpaid. Indeed, people also assume that when "greedy" players (and their agents) use the threat of leaving town to force the home clubs to "show me a lot more money," this forces the teams to raise the prices that fans must pay to watch the games.

Unquestionably, professional athletes' earnings have soared since unionism and free agency came to sports. Recall that in the late 1960s the average major league player was paid between $20,000 and $25,000 a season. By the late 1990s the average player was paid $1.3 million (twice that in basketball). Whereas in 1967 the ratio of baseball salaries to those of American workers was less than 4 to 1, it is now greater than 55 to 1. So it is understandable that workers and fans whose real hourly earnings are *down* around 5 percent from their level a quarter-century ago may have somewhat negative feelings about players' unionism and free agency.

By contrast, when people go to a sports movie like *Jerry Maguire* they are not even aware of, let alone upset by, the fact that Tom Cruise was guaranteed a $20 million salary and that his ultimate return from that single project could top $50 million (as Tom Hanks's did from both *Forrest Gump* and *Saving Private Ryan*). Yet each year *USA Today* prints the salaries and payrolls of every baseball player and team, providing ammunition for the popular concern about the commercialization of our national pastime.

These very different emotional reactions are related to the fact that the typical fan has probably played the sport he or she now enjoys watching, whereas few have ever performed in a play or a movie. Fans who would find it a wonderful privilege to play baseball in Fenway Park or basketball in Madison Square Garden, who would gladly do it for free, are puzzled when professional athletes demand such huge salaries to play the same games there.

A more tangible concern of fans is that players' salaries appear to be tied to rising ticket prices. The average price to watch a first-run movie is under $6, even for the best seats in the house to watch *Titanic;* the average price to watch an NFL game is $45. A typical family of four going to watch an NFL game ends up spending nearly $250 (two full days' pay for the average American worker) for ordinary seats, parking, and something to eat and drink. If that family wants to preserve its season tickets, it often has to take out a bank loan. Most people assume that the highly paid players are responsible for those high ticket prices, which went up four times faster than the nation's Consumer Price Index during the 1990s.

This assumption is wrong. Professional athletes are the beneficiaries but not the cause of increases in ticket prices (or other sports revenues). A key principle of labor economics is that employer demand for employee services—that is, a firm's willingness to pay the asking price in a competitive labor market—is derived from consumer demand for the goods and services produced by these employees. Yet teams often cite a large salary they have just promised a player to explain why their ticket prices are going up. Although signing a new and high-priced player (or coach) may sometimes increase the demand for this more attractive team product, typically owners just use this as an excuse to make the price increase more palatable.

This is not, however, an excuse that the NFL negotiators made in the winter of 1998, when they extracted from the networks the all-time record in television deals—raising the league's annual take from $1.1 billion to $2.2 billion. (Even this is money ultimately paid by fans when they buy the products advertised during football broadcasts.) Disney agreed to such huge increases for its *Monday Night Football* on ABC and *Sunday Night Football* on ESPN, not because the NFL owners needed this money to pay their high-priced players, but because Disney had to pay these extraordinary amounts to outbid General Electric's NBC and Time Warner's TNT for these two valuable football time slots. (A little earlier NBC and TNT had agreed to pay an even higher percentage increase in broadcast fees to the NBA, from $275 million in 1997–98 to $640 million in 1998–99.) But when Disney's Anaheim Angels and Mighty Ducks, or Time Warner's Atlanta Braves and Hawks, set their ticket prices, they follow exactly that same consumer-demand strategy —indeed, just as Disney and Time Warner do for their movie prices. And once this ticket or television money is flowing into the team's coffers, the players in turn use whatever leverage they have in their sport's labor market to secure the maximum financial value that the teams place on their services.

This is not just a matter of economic theory: empirical investigation has documented that free agency and higher salaries do *not* cause ticket prices to go up. Recall that free agency came to baseball in 1976, and that in the next 10 years average salaries rose from $50,000 to $400,000. Yet during the same decade the average price of a baseball ticket actually dropped in *real* dollars. The owners were still making money because of increased attendance and box office receipts, substantial growth in national and local broadcast revenues, and the development of new merchandising and stadium revenue streams. Free agency certainly allows players to secure a higher proportion of team revenues from the owners. However, the true economic interaction of players and fans is that when ticket and other team revenues go up, this causes salaries to rise, rather than vice versa. And in 1995 when MLB gate and television revenues sagged substantially (largely because of fans' resentment about the 1994 baseball strike), average players' salaries also dropped by over $100,000 from the previous year.

American sports fans do face a significant economic problem, but it lies in the product market, not the labor market. Again, consider an example from the entertainment world. The reason fans could see *Titanic*—which cost $210 million to produce—for $6 a ticket was that it faced competition from a host of other movies, many being shown in the same megaplex theaters (including *Titanic's* Oscar rival *The Full Monty*, which cost just $3 million to make but charged the same admission price). So also, the reason the average baseball ticket costs $15, while basketball, hockey, and football tickets cost over $45 is that there are far more seats to be filled by fans in baseball than in the other sports because of its larger facilities and longer season. (There are around 120 million seats available in MLB each year, 24 million in the NBA, and 16 million in the NFL.) Even within baseball, the reasons the average price of Boston Red Sox tickets topped the league in 1999 at $24—significantly higher than, say, the prices of the much larger-market Los Angeles Dodgers—are that Fenway Park has considerably fewer seats than Dodgers Stadium and that the Red Sox do not face a local MLB competitor like the Anaheim Angels. The price of tickets is ultimately determined by the interplay of supply and demand in that consumer market.

As we shall see in later chapters, team owners cannot legitimately claim that they must have monopoly power in the players market in order to protect the fans in the ticket, television, and franchise markets. This would not be a credible reason for Rupert Murdoch and his Fox studio to claim that they needed to have "reserve clause" rights to Leonardo DiCaprio's services after he starred in the studio's *Titanic*. Similarly, it could not justify allowing Fox's Dodgers franchise to reserve the exclusive rights to its star catcher Mike Piazza rather than let him go in 1998 with free agency on the horizon.

Loyalty to the Home Team

While they cannot blame player free agency for the higher costs of watching sports, fans may have a more plausible claim that the new players market has undermined the quality of the game. On this score, sports and movies part ways: in 1999 the high-cost *Star Wars* was often playing in the same megaplexes as its low-cost rival *The Blair Witch Proj-*

ect, but they were never together on the same screen. Movie fans can pick which film they think is most worth viewing on a given night. But baseball fans who want to see the high-quality, high-paid Atlanta Braves or Cleveland Indians must watch them playing on the same field as, say, the low-paid, lower-quality Montreal Expos or Oakland Athletics.

Before we tackle this question of what free agency has done to competitive balance in sports, it is worth noting another concern felt by fans. The fact that so many players are leaving their current teams and cities in pursuit of more money elsewhere seems to have compromised an important feature of sports in American life. Fans who are loyal to their home team believe that players should be equally loyal to the community that gave life to that team and its players' careers. Baseball writers celebrate memories of Joe DiMaggio of the New York Yankees and Ted Williams of the Boston Red Sox, men who spent their entire playing careers with the clubs that brought them to the majors and to national recognition. Not only does this kind of commitment from players to their original teams now seem more the exception than the rule, but entire *teams* are now moving (or threatening to move) from their long-time homes in pursuit of lucrative stadium deals from taxpayers elsewhere. And fans blame this movement of teams, too, on free agency and its swelling of players' salaries.

A closer look at the history of both player and team movement reveals the misconception in these popular opinions. Indeed, we have already seen an especially vivid illustration of the fallacy in the claim that the traditional reserve system tied players to their home teams and towns. After Curt Flood had spent a decade living in St. Louis and playing for the Cardinals, he and his family wanted to stay there. It was the Cardinals' owner Gussie Busch who decided to send Flood to Philadelphia in return for the Phillies' star Dick Allen. The most notorious example of such action by an owner under the reserve system took place at the end of the 1919 MLB season. The owner of the Boston Red Sox, Harry Frazee, needing money to finance a Broadway musical for his lady friend, sold the game's best pitcher at the time, Babe Ruth, to the New York Yankees for $125,000. Of course, unlike what happened to Flood, when Ruth was moved to the Yankees he became baseball's greatest hitter ever, one who hit the sixtieth home run of his 1927 season in a Yankee Stadium "that Ruth built."

The Ruth and Flood cases are not isolated occurrences. A systematic empirical study of baseball revealed that from 1951 through 1976 an average of 4.7 players per team were moved each year from one club to another, through cash sales, trades, waivers, or the like. After free agency came to baseball in 1976, the next 18 seasons saw an annual average of 4.6 players moving from one club to another, with free agency moves initiated by the players largely replacing the sales initiated by the teams.

One obvious difference is that it was the owner of the Red Sox who pocketed the cash that the Yankees were willing to pay for Ruth, while it was Reggie Jackson who secured the financial premium that the Yankees placed on his services just after free agency came to baseball. So also in hockey, when the all-time great Wayne Gretzky was moved from the Edmonton Oilers to the Los Angeles Kings in 1989, it was the owner of the financially distressed Oilers, Peter Pocklington, who got the $15 million reward; but when Gretzky moved again, to the New York Rangers in 1996, the existence of some NHL free agency gave Gretzky the premium that the Rangers placed on his talent and drawing appeal even at that late stage of his career. A less obvious difference, at least during the first two decades of free agency in baseball, is that free agency moves by the players were more likely to be from the more talented to the less talented team than were sales of players under the reserve system.

There is another aspect to the Ruth saga that provides revealing lessons for the present-day concerns about sports. After being released by the Yankees following the 1933 season, Babe Ruth decided to return to Boston to serve as team vice president, as well as to play briefly, for the city's National League Braves. There Ruth hit the 714th and final home run of his career, leaving a record no one thought could ever be broken. Two decades later, though, the Braves brought in a young Hank Aaron, who would prove the experts wrong. But when Aaron joined the Braves in 1954, the team had recently moved from Boston to Milwaukee—the first such baseball relocation in the 20th century. In 1966 the Braves moved again, to Atlanta as the first MLB team in the South, and it was in Atlanta in 1974 that Aaron hit his 715th career home run, breaking Ruth's record. Just as Ruth had done in Boston, Aaron hit his 733rd and last home run back in Milwaukee, playing for the Brewers, who had moved there from Seattle in 1970 and had secured Aaron in a 1975 offseason trade with the Braves.

As we shall see in later chapters, such franchise movements pose a host of important issues of sports and public policy, especially when the moves are induced by luxurious taxpayer-subsidized facilities. Here, though, the key point is that franchise free agency came to baseball in 1953, long before player free agency did in 1976, and there have been no such MLB team moves (though many threats to move) since the latter date. The sport in which teams' desertion of their home towns has been the biggest problem is football—epitomized by the Raiders leaving their devoted Oakland fans to move to Los Angeles in 1982 and the Browns doing the same thing from Cleveland to Baltimore in 1995. Each of these NFL franchise shifts, as well as the six others over the last 15 years, took place when the league either effectively barred player free agent movement (as it did in the 1980s), or restrained it by a hard salary cap (established in the 1990s). The histories of both football and baseball (as well as hockey and basketball) make it clear that there is no real connection between moves by individual players and those by team owners.

Should it be the goal of the leagues to keep individual players with the teams and communities where they have been playing? If such player-fan allegiance is considered an important and independent value, then we should restrain not only moves initiated by players but also those sought by team owners—including both sales and trades of players. Many players (such as Tony Gwynn of the San Diego Padres) do not want to leave the area where they and their families have been living merely to extract the highest possible salary from the market. Yet team owners trying to improve their clubs' athletic or financial situation regularly send players elsewhere in return for other players, or future draft picks, or even cash.

The single biggest obstacle to moves instigated by either players or teams is a device developed in basketball: the Larry Bird exception to the NBA salary cap, which gives the player's current team a big financial edge in bidding for his services. Comparing the experience of basketball with that of baseball (and also football, given the NFL's combination of individual free agency and a hard salary cap) will help answer the question of whether facilitating or obstructing regular moves of players from team to team is better for the competitive quality of the game.

Competitive Balance

The most fundamental concern expressed about the shift in sports from the traditional reserve system to varying degrees of player free agency is that it has compromised the quality of the game, particularly in baseball. Team bidding for free agent players sends salaries soaring; high payrolls give an unfair advantage to wealthy owners of large-market teams; this advantage pressures small-market clubs either to resign themselves to mediocre team rosters and second-rate records or to move to another city (especially one offering a more lucrative stadium deal). It is true that sports faces a distinctive problem in the interplay of competition on and off the field. However, those popular concerns about player free agency contain far more myth than reality.

There is no question that the creation of free agency made a major contribution to players' salary gains, most dramatically in baseball, where the salary average jumped from $50,000 in 1976 to $1.57 million in 1999. Essentially the same trends took place in other sports, though there the picture is clouded somewhat by the fact that established leagues like the NFL faced competition for players from other leagues from the 1960s to the mid-1980s. However, a basic economic principle is that if several teams (whether from inside or outside the league) are bidding for a player's services, the player will be paid more than if he is locked in to a single club. And from the player's perspective this seems only fair, because he always faces other players competing for scarce major league positions during training camp (and the reserve system, of course, never committed teams to retaining their veterans).

But there is another important reason why players' salaries have climbed so high: team and league revenues have been rising at the same time. Even while real ticket prices in baseball actually dropped from the mid-1970s to the late 1980s, attendance at the games was surging. In 1976 the average major league baseball team drew 1.3 million fans to its games, up just modestly from 1.0–1.2 million in the 1950s and 1960s. Just a decade after free agency came to baseball, average team attendance had topped the 2 million mark, and it is now near 2.5 million. And television earnings went up even faster in the 1980s, while luxury suites and premium seats added to the league revenue pie in the 1990s.

The principal change wrought by free agency was that players began reaping a greater share of these team revenues. Again using baseball as the index, players' salaries represented approximately 40 percent of total league revenues in the 1930s, dropped under 15 percent by the mid-1950s, and moved up slightly to 17.5 percent by the mid-1970s. After that, aided and abetted by free agency, the players' share leaped to 41 percent in 1981. It then dropped to 32 percent by 1989, largely as a result of the owners' collusion that eliminated bidding for free agents even as box office and television revenues were going up faster than ever. But after free agent bidding returned to baseball in 1990, player payrolls topped 60 percent of the $2.7 billion in league revenues in 1999, and the players' shares in the other major sports were in roughly the same range.

So by the end of the century players' associations in all four major sports had established players markets that were channeling well over half of the game's revenues into the pockets of the major league players. This left less than half to cover the rest of the team's operating costs—coaching salaries, scouting and minor league player development, administrative staff, transportation expenses, and the like—not to mention some net return to the owner on his sizable capital investment in the franchise. Team owners regularly tell the press that the field of contract negotiations is unfairly tipped against them. However, "free" agency does not force any team to pay any player an amount it judges to be economically unsound. Though there are now 30-odd potential bidders for the services of any player (versus only one under the old reserve system), there are many more talented players who are competing for scarce positions on major league rosters.

Sports offers a revealing illustration of the basic principle of labor economics: in a competitive market, teams have a financial incentive to pay a player all—but *no more* than—the added value he can bring to the team, as compared to the value that would be added by his rivals for that position. And because play is far more individualized in baseball than in football, for example, labor economists have been able to use baseball to demonstrate the general validity of their "marginal revenue productivity" thesis.

Since "sabermetrics" emerged in the 1970s, baseball aficionados such as Bill James have collated and used statistics from every major league player since 1903 to determine how the productivity of individual players contributes to team accomplishments.* Building on the sabermetrics

---

* Measuring players' performance is not simple. In the case of hitters, for example, rather than the standard figures displayed on the sports pages (batting averages, home runs, runs batted in, runs scored), the ideal index is a combination of hits, total bases, walks, hit-by-pitches, steals, sacrifice bunts, and flies, minus caught steals and double plays, divided by the number of plate appearances. This number determines the run-making potential of the player in question (abstracting from the actual performance of his teammates). The number of runs the

data, labor economists figured out how to calculate the impact of team victories (from the prior as well as the current season) on attendance and gate receipts, and even on the size of new television and merchandising deals. The result of these calculations (and similar ones for pitching and fielding performance) is the marginal *revenue* productivity of particular players for particular teams. These figures can then be compared with actual salaries to determine how well the players market is operating.

What has been the empirical verdict on this score? In the mid-to-late 1960s, star players earned $100,000–$125,000 a season; they contributed an estimated 10–15 victories to their team's records; each extra team victory generated about $65,000 in additional team revenue; so star players in that era before free agency were paid between 10 and 20 percent of what they were worth to their teams in both wins and money. With the rising revenues that accompanied free agency, each additional victory was adding $200,000 to team coffers in the mid-1980s and about $700,000 in the late 1990s. Thus current stars are now clearly worth about $7–$10 million. Of course, a considerable number of the veteran free agents are paid substantially more than these figures. At the same time, though, a significant number of players—especially those not yet entitled to salary arbitration, let alone free agency—are still paid much less than the value of their contributions to team performance on the field and at the gate. The best judgment of sports economists is that, in the aggregate, the current division of baseball revenues between players and owners (after subtracting the other costs of team operations) is now much closer to the appropriate level than it was in the days of the reserve system.

We also have a market corroboration of that judgment: the capital market's assessment of the value of team profits. In the late 1960s, before

---

player can produce in turn determines the number of victories he can generate for a team. A similar measure of hitting productivity, and one that is easier for fans to calculate, is the *Wall Street Journal*'s SLOB index—a combination of slugging and on-base percentages. A little-known fact about the historic 1998 race for the home run record is that Mark McGwire's SLOB index was nearly 50 percent higher than Sammy Sosa's. But whatever index is used to determine the marginal relative productivity of a player's hitting, further adjustment must be made for both the player's position and his era. That is why the relative performance value of the shortstop Cal Ripken Jr. in the lower-hitting early 1980s was actually much greater than that of the first-baseman Mark McGwire in the high-hitting late 1990s.

free agency, baseball teams were being sold for $5–$10 million. By the late 1990s teams were selling for $100–$600 million—a 20- to 60-fold appreciation in franchise value during a period when the celebrated Dow Jones Industrial Average rose a "mere" tenfold. The likely explanation is that while free agency increased players' ability to extract salaries that better reflected their contributions, this freer movement of players also increased the value of the league as a whole—among investors as well as fans.

As a matter of general market principle, free movement of talent from one firm to another is likely to enhance the quality of the overall product being offered to consumers. A hypothetical from the entertainment world displays this point. Suppose a hit television series has a young and appealing performer in a supporting (and low-paying) role, who is attracted away to a higher-paying lead role on a new show. Although viewers of the original series will feel some regret at losing this character, the overall variety and quality of TV programming are clearly enhanced by a system that allows other networks to offer what is necessary to induce the performer to become the star in another series.

The same principle applies to sports. Indeed, one of the most vivid illustrations took place in football when free agency came to the NFL. For many years the San Francisco 49ers had been the dominant NFL team, with Joe Montana as their star quarterback. Sitting on the bench watching Montana out on the field was another rather talented quarterback, Steve Young; behind Young was Steve Bono. Faced with free agency in 1993 upon which a salary cap was to be imposed in 1994, the 49ers had to let Montana and then Bono go to the Kansas City Chiefs, where they revived that team and put it back in the playoffs. The same thing happened when Scott Mitchell left the Miami Dolphins' bench (behind Dan Marino) and moved to Detroit as first-string quarterback for the Lions, who also made it to the playoffs.

These stories show why freeing players to move from one team to another usually enhances rather than detracts from the quality of a sport. It is inevitable that the managers of some clubs are smart enough (or lucky enough) to draft and develop an array of top-flight players on their roster, while other teams end up with mediocre lineups. Under the reserve system, it is advantageous to the first club to keep that in-depth talent together—not just to make sure that a Young, for example, is there to play when a Montana gets hurt, but also to make sure that no rival team has access to the talent. From the player's point of view, clearly it is better to play in a starting rather than in a backup position, and to be paid (and praised) accordingly. The other teams (and their fans) are also better off if they are able to lure that player to a new situation where his talents will be fully utilized. This additional value to the new team will be displayed not only on the field but at the box office and in television ratings as well; this makes it economically rational and affordable for the owner of the new team to pay the free agent player the additional salary needed to induce the move. And from the league's perspective, a striking example of the competitive value of players' mobility is what happened with the NFL's 1995 expansion teams, the Carolina Panthers and the Jacksonville Jaguars. Just one season later, both teams had assembled enough talent to make it to the 1996 NFC and AFC championship games.

But what about the major concern expressed about free agency: that the best players will tend to flock to the larger-market teams that can afford to pay them the most, thus reducing competitive balance? Notice that the football teams just mentioned are in the smaller markets of Charlotte, Jacksonville, and Kansas City. Indeed, it was the smallest-market team of all, the Green Bay Packers, who secured the first top-flight NFL free agent, Reggie White, in 1993 (from the larger-market Philadelphia Eagles), and led by White the Packers returned to the Super Bowl in the 1996 and 1997 seasons.

In the NFL, those small-market clubs have always had the benefit of full-blown revenue sharing by large-market clubs, and the league has also established a hard salary cap to equalize the amount of money that teams are allowed to spend on their player rosters. Baseball, by contrast, has neither of these economic safeguards for small-market clubs such as the Kansas City Royals, which is why critics of free agency in baseball understandably focus on the competitive advantage this system offers to the New York Yankees. Equalizing the revenues and the payrolls of teams has a positive effect on the sports marketplace, though the NFL has gone a little too far with both of them. But even without those league-wide standards, the move to free agency in baseball did not give large-market teams anywhere near the level of competitive advantage that commentators assume that it did.

Recall that it was under the reserve system that the larger-market teams—particularly the Yankees, but the Giants and Dodgers as well—

dominated the pennant races and World Series for decades. Starting in the mid-1960s, smaller-market clubs such as the Baltimore Orioles, Oakland Athletics, and Cincinnati Reds became the major powers in baseball. However, these teams also dominated the NL and AL for several years in a row—just as has happened in other sports constrained by a reserve system (in hockey, for example, where the Edmonton Oilers won five Stanley Cups in seven years in the 1980s). If the key to competitive balance is that "each team has the opportunity of becoming a contender over a reasonable cycle of years" (to quote Judge Higginbotham from his *Philadelphia World Hockey* decision), it was *after* free agency came to baseball that MLB became the most competitive of all the major sports leagues. Over the next two decades 15 different teams won the World Series, culminating in the 1997 win by the five-year-old Florida Marlins. Perhaps the most remarkable such event took place in 1991. That season's World Series competitors were the Atlanta Braves and the Minnesota Twins, both of which had finished at the bottom of their respective divisions the previous season. They had then signed notable free agents, Terry Pendleton by the Braves and Jack Morris by the Twins, who in 1991 not only won MVP and Cy Young awards for themselves but took their teams to the World Series, which the Twins (and Morris) won in the tenth inning of the seventh game.

Again, systematic statistical analyses of baseball records have corroborated these examples. The gap between the winning percentages of teams at the top and those at the bottom has narrowed modestly since 1976, but the likelihood that teams will move to the top or the bottom has increased sharply. Major League Baseball does have the highest revenue disparity (as well as the lowest win/loss disparity) of any of the big leagues, but there has not been much correlation between size of market and winning percentages or championships. The reason has to do with another feature of the sports marketplace—one that makes the relationship between metropolitan size and the economic value of winning rather fragile.

Take attendance at games, for example. The fact is that the Kansas City Royals had season attendance comparable to that of the New York Yankees (or Mets). While there are far more people available to go to baseball games in New York than in Kansas City, there are also many more options available to New Yorkers for spending their leisure time and dollars. Game attendance depends far less on metropolitan size than on the degree of fan interest in the sport and on factors like the creation of new and attractive stadiums, which raised attendance dramatically in mid-sized (and previously low-attendance) Baltimore and Cleveland.

The real disparity between large- and small-market teams stems from their local broadcast deals. While there is much the same physical limit on how many people can watch a game in New York's Yankee Stadium and Kansas City's Kaufman Stadium, there is no such limit on how many people can watch the games on the screen at home. This explains why in the late 1990s the New York Yankees and the Atlanta Braves each earned approximately $60 million from local television and radio deals, while the Kansas City Royals and Pittsburgh Pirates took in just $6 million apiece.*

The exclusive control that MLB rules give each team over broadcasts in its home region is the principal source of the economic advantage that enables large-market baseball teams to pay large salaries. (In football, by contrast, small-market Green Bay could afford to induce Reggie White to move from larger-market Philadelphia, and Kansas City could lure Joe Montana from San Francisco, because the NFL sells all its television rights via league-wide contracts with national networks, then distributes the revenues equally among all the member clubs.) However, the fact that larger-market teams can better afford to spend money on players does not explain why they choose to do so. After all, rational economic analysis says that it makes sense to invest in high-priced talent to improve a team's winning record if—but only if—the enhanced record on the field would be matched by higher revenues off it.

Winning a championship certainly makes a significant difference in game attendance, though this is true in the smaller as well as the larger markets. Yet the television market displays only a modest link between team revenues and performance, again illustrated by the Yankees' experience. It was in the late 1980s, after quite an unsuccessful decade on the field, that George Steinbrenner extracted from MSG Network the largest local cable contract in sports history—nearly $500 million over twelve years. The lesson that financial analysts would draw from this and simi-

---

* The Braves are in a large *television* market but a middle-sized *attendance* market because in the mid-1970s (around the same time that free agency was coming to baseball), Ted Turner, owner of the Braves, used a combination of new technology and intellectual property law to turn his local WTBS-TV station into the country's first major superstation, transmitted by satellite and cable into homes from coast to coast.

lar sports examples is that it makes little economic sense to spend this big-market broadcast premium by putting more money into the players' pockets rather than the owners' bank accounts. Indeed, this premium is directly reflected in the capital value and purchase price of a team, explaining why Rupert Murdoch had to pay $310 million for the Los Angeles Dodgers while Claude Brochu's group paid just $80 million for the Montreal Expos. What this also means is that the additional "operational earnings" of the large-market Dodgers are largely offset by the higher cost of "amortizing" this large financial investment.

The Yankees and Steinbrenner are the example that automatically comes to the minds of sportswriters and sports fans lamenting the unfair competitive advantage enjoyed by large-market clubs. Yet one need only look at the Chicago Cubs to see an example of the modest difference that market size may make to team performance on the baseball field. The Cubs are owned by the Chicago Tribune media conglomerate, they play in historic and much-loved Wrigley Field, and their games are telecast nationally on the Tribune corporate family's superstation, WGN. But these large-market Cubs have not been one of the 15 teams that have won a World Series since 1977 under free agency (even with Sammy Sosa); in fact, they have not won a Series for nine full *decades*.

The clear lesson from baseball's experience, then, is that if we must choose just between the traditional reserve system and unrestricted free agency, the latter is a far better instrument for improving sports welfare—whether viewed as allocative efficiency in enhancing the quality of the game for fans or distributional equity in sharing the gains between owners and players. Certainly average MLB salaries have soared under free agency, but the gains in players' earnings have not triggered an increase in prices, for either tickets or broadcast rights. Instead, players' mobility has generated a considerably more competitive game, in which the gap in top-to-bottom winning percentages has dropped somewhat and the ability of teams to move from the bottom to the top has improved substantially. This enhanced competitive quality generated an increase in average team attendance from 1.3 million in 1976 to 2.4 million in 1999, with six new teams drawing fans since the earlier date. Television, merchandising, and stadium revenues have risen even more steeply. While player payrolls have grown from less than 30 percent of league revenues in 1976 to more than 60 percent in 1999, the 1977 Toronto and Seattle expansion franchises cost $7 million while the new

1998 Phoenix and Tampa Bay franchises cost $130 million (a figure only half the sale price that same year for the Texas Rangers and the Los Angeles Dodgers). Given this apparent win-win feature of player free agency, if Congress (or the Supreme Court) were to roll back baseball's special *Flood* exemption from antitrust laws, it would be a mistake for MLB owners to expect that restoring the reserve system could ever pass the antitrust "rule of reason" test.

Payroll Standards

Still, the fact that *full* free agency makes a sport better than it was with *no* free agency does not necessarily mean that unrestrained free agency is the best possible regime for professional sports. Again, baseball vividly displays the issues. Since the big labor battle in 1994, there has been a substantial upsurge in movement by players, in the form of team trades and sales as well as free agent deals. And there has been an apparent return to the traditional disparity in teams' performance and payrolls. In the 1997, 1998, and 1999 seasons, for example, the payrolls of all four of the teams that reached the AL and NL championship series were among the highest (although there were also teams like the Orioles and the Dodgers which proved that spending huge amounts of money does not guarantee a winning season). The gap between the top and bottom team payrolls jumped from $15 million in 1988 (between the Yankees and the Mariners), to $61 million in 1998 (between the Orioles and the Expos). In fact, in 1998 there were eight individual players who each made more than the $8 million the Expos paid its entire roster.

There is still substantial competitive balance among a large number of contenders, including a few traditionally viewed as smaller-market clubs—like the Mariners, the Indians, and the Padres. However, a growing number of clubs that were winning in the 1980s and early 1990s—not just the Expos, but the Athletics, the Pirates, the Twins, and others—are making the economic decision to reduce their players' payroll levels, at least until they can induce their local taxpayers to build them luxurious rent-free stadiums that will guarantee them even bigger profits.

This phenomenon is attributable to what truly is the distinctive feature of the sports marketplace—the fact that the winner takes the lion's share. Again, contrast sports with movies or television. A movie's Oscar for Best Picture makes only a modest difference in its total box office returns, and a television show's Emmy Award has even less effect on its Nielsen ratings. Not so in sports. While fans do enjoy watching their team win an individual game, winning the regular season and post-season races produces an order-of-magnitude greater exhilaration, boosting attendance and television ratings not only in the championship season but for years to come.

This financial payoff for the team is accompanied by huge personal gratification for the owner. Almost every local newspaper and television station has far more coverage of what's going on in the sports world than in the business world. A favorable *Wall Street Journal* article about the owner's other business ventures may increase his company's stock price and his own net worth; but when his team makes it to the World Series or the Super Bowl, his picture and life story appear on every television screen and newspaper, and he becomes a hero in the local community. Wealthy arts aficionados happily spend tens of millions to buy a Van Gogh or a Monet to hang in their living rooms, so it is easy to understand why billionaire sports fans are prepared to make the same kind of payment to win a World Series.

This combination of huge monetary and emotional rewards for an owner if his team is at the top rather than in the middle of the league makes standard "marginal revenue productivity" analysis fit somewhat awkwardly in the sports context. (Unlike Avis, the team that loses the Super Bowl does not celebrate being "#2.") In the standard labor market, the extra value gained by adding more star talent to a particular operation is significantly less than the value derived from the talent already in place. So, for example, when a movie studio pays $20 million to secure a big-name actor with worldwide audience appeal, it has far less incentive to pay anywhere near that amount to add even one more star with the same drawing power and price tag. By contrast, once a sports team has the kind of talent that makes it a serious competitor on the field (with the corresponding payoff at the gate), it has an even stronger incentive to invest in the additional talent that will secure the premiums attached to winning a division title and perhaps even the league championship. The owners of all clubs at that level feel essentially the same pressure, not only to acquire valuable free agents for themselves, but also to keep their race rivals from acquiring them. The payrolls of all of the serious contenders are apt to soar in pursuit of the big payoff, but just one of the teams will secure it. This unique feature of the competitive pressure in sports means that performance-enhancing payrolls create much the same kind of "collective goods" problem for owners that performance-enhancing drugs do for players.

But while the use of steroids, for example, by some athletes puts pressure on all their competitors to use them as well, this spending frenzy by some owners tends to send other teams in the opposite direction. Suppose that a team owner knows his roster is not talented enough to make the playoffs, and that he does not have the economic resources or emotional urge to try to change that situation in the foreseeable future. (Indeed, as leagues grow larger, the odds of making it to the championship series get correspondingly lower.) The rational economic strategy is not simply to refrain from bidding for free agent players but also to dispose of his own best and highest-paid talent in return for some combination of future draft picks, minor league prospects, and cash. This kind of sports "downsizing" is exactly what teams like the Expos, the Athletics, and the Twins have recently done with stars such as Pedro Martinez, Mark McGwire, and Chuck Knoblauch. The most egregious example is the total dismantling of the 1997 World Series champions, the Florida Marlins, to reduce their payroll from $54 million in 1997 to under $10 million by the end of the 1998 season, at which point they had become baseball's worst team.

Even if this lower payroll produces a worse team and lower attendance and television ratings, its owner will still make a profit. He gets the basic revenues that flow from having a franchise and offering games within the sport's major league, and from these revenues he has to deduct payroll costs that are only a fraction of what his league colleagues are paying. And if he can paint a picture for the sports press that the team is losing financially as well as on the field, the owner often succeeds in extracting from local politicians and voters a taxpayer-financed (and largely rent-free) stadium that confers a huge financial premium on him if and when he sells the team.

In almost any other product market, these divergent approaches to running a business are perfectly acceptable. If one person opens a restaurant staffed with top chefs, serving high-quality meals, and charging correspondingly high prices, while another hires less skilled and lower-paid kitchen talent, serves mediocre meals, but offers them at low prices, this restaurant market makes "food fans" better off because they now have a range of quality and price choices when they go out for dinner. But what makes sports fundamentally different from restaurants as well as movies is that when some owners decide to slash their team payrolls, this produces a phenomenon that in environmental contexts is known as the "tragedy of the commons."

In the sports world, one owner can make a rational, self-interested judgment to assemble and pay for a roster that makes his team either too much better or too much worse than other teams. The owner gets 100 percent of the additional benefit of having the best team or the cheapest payroll. He bears, however, only one-thirtieth of the harm that his decision inflicts on the collective league product, harm that often outweighs the sum of individual team gains. These costs to the sports "commons" are borne first by the fans of the other teams, who must watch far less competitive games and seasons than they thought they were paying for. These costs to fans are then transmitted to the league owners, whose overall revenue streams go down (or fail to go up), and finally to the players, whose economic value and pay eventually drop accordingly.

This "public goods" feature of the sports market does not justify restoring the old reserve system. Baseball today is certainly more competitive and more attractive than it was in the 1950s and 1960s, precisely because giving both players and teams the freedom to move talent to the sites where it was most needed generated a more rational and competitive allocation of the athletic resources (as well as a more equitable distribution of their share of the game's revenues to the players, whom the fans actually pay to watch and enjoy). The solution I favor, instead, is a set of league-wide payroll standards, negotiated between the owners and the players (through their union) that will provide an even more balanced allocation of talent among the teams. These standards should be implemented in a fashion that gives every club the incentive to invest to the level needed to build a competitive team, rather than spend too much on assembling a roster that is too strong or too little on a roster that is too weak. This kind of win-win approach would make the game better for fans, and consequently more rewarding for owners and players.

I have used the phrase "payroll standard" to distinguish my proposal from the terms "salary cap" and "salary tax" that often appear in the sports pages. As we saw earlier, a salary cap was first incorporated in the NBA collective agreement in 1983, but it limited only how much a team could spend on new players—whether free agents or draft picks—rather than on its own veterans such as Larry Bird or Magic Johnson. Ten years later the NFL owners and players agreed to "harden" that cap by having it govern the team's total payroll. And in 1997 the baseball owners and players ended their lengthy labor dispute by establishing a 35 percent tax on the amount that the top five team payrolls exceeded the sixth highest, again regardless of whether the money was spent on the team's current players or on a free agent coming from another club.

The term "cap" is something of a misnomer. What both basketball and football have adopted is the principle of revenue/salary *sharing*. Owners and players first designate a set of gross revenue streams, and then decide what proportion of these revenues is to be devoted to players (for both collectively negotiated benefits like pensions and individually negotiated salaries). That league-wide figure is then divided by the number of teams in each league to establish the appropriate payroll budget. In the NFL the current salary share figure is 63 percent; in the NBA, 48 percent. However, a significant portion of basketball facility revenues—from luxury suites and premium seats, though not from arena-naming rights—is included in the Basketball Related Income (BRI) base, while such stadium income is not part of football's Designated Gross Revenues (DGR). This means that the actual disparity between the share of league revenues spent on salaries in football and basketball is much less than those percentage figures indicate: the player payroll share of the real total of NFL revenues is approximately 55 percent. In addition, because the NBA has long had a soft version of that payroll cap, the actual average NBA payroll in 1997–98 was around $33 million, nearly 25 percent higher than the $27 million formal cap, and about 57 percent of total league revenues. It was these figures and trends that generated the owners' lockout of the players that almost cost everyone the 1998–99 season.

It is important to note that the NFL and NBA revenue-sharing systems not only established a *ceiling* but also a *floor* on each team's payroll. When they were fashioning the original version of this payroll-standards concept, NBA owners and players agreed that requiring clubs that had been spending too little on talent to spend more was just as vital to the quality of their game as was requiring teams that had been over-spending to cut back. The NBA owners even created a special fund to subsidize the payrolls of clubs that were not generating enough revenues on their own to cover this league-wide salary floor.

As a matter of principle some kind of revenue/salary-sharing regime appears to be the appropriate response to the collective goods problem in the sports world. Baseball would be an even better game if it were governed by standards that required the Orioles, the Yankees, and the Braves to reduce their $80–$90 million payrolls by giving up some of their valuable talent, but at the same time required the Expos, the Pirates, the Athletics, and now the Marlins to increase their $10–$25 million payrolls by investing in more talented players who would make their teams seriously competitive. Even from the point of view of the players, establishing payroll standards might well increase rather than decrease the total amount spent by the league on salaries. And if greater revenue sharing is necessary to make this better sharing of talent feasible, the owners can devise their own rules for distributing the revenues generated by the game.

One factor in particular has aggravated the recent situation in baseball. From the late 1970s to the early 1990s national television contracts emerged as a major source of league revenue, which was shared equally among all the teams. But since then local TV and cable contracts have become an even bigger revenue source. However, the games for which cable channels are paying the Yankees and Braves $60 million apiece also have teams like the Athletics and Expos playing on the field and being shown on the screen. These clubs, whose local television contracts are worth only $6 million each, do have a legitimate claim to a share of the television revenues generated by those games (at least in a manner I shall lay out in Chapter 18).

Understanding why sports has this distinctive need for payroll standards is only half the story: equally important is appreciating the complexities of their design and implementation. The emergence of salary caps has made lawyering almost as important as scouting in assembling team rosters for an upcoming NFL or NBA season. It was creative lawyering, certainly, that devised the "bonus payment" loophole that enabled the Dallas Cowboys to lure Deion Sanders away from the San Francisco 49ers and bring the Super Bowl back to Dallas in 1996 (a loophole on which NFL Commissioner Paul Tagliabue and NLFPA Executive Director Gene Upshaw put only modest limits afterward).

The major problem had existed in basketball, where the NBA's original cap design turned out to be extremely soft. In 1997–98, for example, the payrolls of the Chicago Bulls ($62 million) and the New York Knicks ($57 million) were 2.5 times as great as those of the Los Angeles Clippers ($24 million) and the Milwaukee Bucks ($25 million). Although this disparity was significantly smaller than the six-fold difference between the MLB Orioles' and Yankees' 1998 payrolls (over $65 million each) and those of the Expos and the Pirates (under $10 million), the harmful impact on competitive balance has been far greater in basketball than in baseball.

Take the ratio of win-loss percentage of the top and bottom three teams in the two sports over the 1995–1999 seasons. In baseball the top three teams had records around 50 percent better than the records of the bottom three; in basketball the top three teams' records were about 400 percent better. In other words, the NBA was *eight times* more imbalanced than MLB. (The huge 1998 gap between the Yankees' .704 percentage and the Marlins' unprecedented drop to .333 is very much the exception that proves this baseball rule.) Some might attribute this difference to the shorter length of the NBA's 82-game schedule, relative to the MLB's 162 games. That is the reason the NFL's 16-game schedule produces such large disparities in any one season, though often radical turn-arounds from one season to the next. But in the NHL, which has the same schedule length as the NBA, the gap between the top and bottom teams in the same years was only slightly larger than baseball's and far smaller than basketball's. And if one believes, as I do, that championship dynasties are an even deeper problem of competitive imbalance, the NBA's soft cap has generated the poorest experience of any sport on this parameter. Although in the 10 years preceding the cap seven different teams had won NBA championships, in the first 15 years of the cap just five teams won the league championship—the high-payroll Celtics, Lakers, Pistons, Rockets, and Bulls—and almost every one of these teams won its crowns in consecutive seasons. We basketball fans are now about to see whether the same thing will happen with the San Antonio Spurs, who took the NBA crown in the 1999 lockout season.

On the surface, this disparity in competitive balance between basketball and the other sports might also be explained by the much smaller basketball rosters and the much greater share of playing time by the five starters. But the fact that there is the same disparity in championship dynasties between the NBA and the NCAA Final Four means that the major explanation is to be found in the NBA's Larry Bird exception: this rule now functions as an even more restrictive version of the traditional reserve system in professional sports. This regime has certainly not denied

NBA players their equitable share of soaring league revenues. (Whereas MLB and NBA players both averaged around $20,000 when collective bargaining began in their sports in 1966–67, by 1998–99 the NBA average had hit $2.6 million under the soft cap while MLB's average was $1.6 million without any cap.) Rather, it has thwarted a more efficient allocation of talent among the NBA teams. Because only the player's "home team" could offer him an unrestricted salary figure, top-paid stars such as the Celtics' Larry Bird, the Lakers' Magic Johnson, the Pistons' Isiah Thomas, the Rockets' Hakeem Olajuwon, and the Bulls' Michael Jordan were able to remain surrounded by additional All-Star talent that sustained their teams' dominance.

The NBA's post-lockout revision of the salary cap did not address this fundamental need for competitive balance. It assuaged the owners' concern about excessive overall spending on players' salaries by creating an escrow system through which *all* players will repay *all* owners the amount by which total league salaries exceed 55 percent of Basketball Related Income. However, only when salaries exceed 61 percent of BRI must the top-payroll teams make special payments back to the league (in effect a 100 percent tax at that point). The underlying source of the problem of player immobility, the Larry Bird exception, remains fully in effect, with the payroll limit for signing other teams' players still calculated at 48 percent (not 55 percent) of league BRI. Indeed, the 1999 settlement actually accentuated this problem of competitive imbalance by establishing a cap on individual players' salaries that is significantly higher for a club's current players than for others. While the limits on the first year of the contract are the same (ranging from $9 to $14 million in 1999), the team can offer its own player a seven-year contract with up to 12.5 percent annual raises, while any other team, even if it has a much greater need for that player, can offer only a six-year deal with 10 percent pay increases.

So notwithstanding its huge labor battle, basketball still has not devised the right model for sports leagues to use to provide competitive balance for the benefit of fans rather than simply cost containment for owners. The NFL's hard salary cap performs much better on that competitive score. My ideal, though, is a meaningful graduated salary tax (*not* MLB's current rather spurious version). A well-designed tax system would provide incentives for every team to behave in the fashion that serves the collective good of the entire league, not merely benefits its own club. At the same time, such tax incentives would avoid the distorting effects that rigid legal regulation (even when privately created and enforced) tends to impose on the special situations and market needs of individual teams.

One tangible problem that arises when a league imposes a flat dollar cap on every team's payroll is that this cap makes absolutely no allowance for the difference in taxes assessed by various governments on players' salaries. This shortcoming imposes a major handicap on the NBA's Toronto Raptors and Vancouver Grizzlies when they are bidding for talent, since the income tax levied on highly paid employees in Canada is substantially higher than that in the United States. Even in the NFL, which has teams situated only in the United States, there is a tax-disparity issue: the combination of state and city taxes in California and New York, for example, can top 10 percent, while there is no such income tax at all in some states, such as Florida and Texas. This state tax gap means that actual take-home pay for players with the San Francisco 49ers or the New York Knicks is significantly less than for players with the Dallas Cowboys or the Miami Heat if their salary contract numbers are the same.

The way in which the labor market responds to such a tax difference—whether for NFL coaches or non-sports executives—is to have employers in the high-tax (and usually high-income) states raise salaries accordingly. In fact, baseball provides an illustration for players. In 1998 the Los Angeles Dodgers had to raise Gary Sheffield's $10 million annual salary by around $1 million to induce Sheffield to waive the no-trade clause in his Florida Marlins contract and move to—and thus be taxed by—the state of California. Yet this kind of market adjustment is barred by league-wide salary cap figures. At a minimum, if the NFL and the NBA really do want a level payroll playing field, they must reform their cap formulas to restrain only the *net* rather than the *gross* amounts the players receive from their teams.

Variable tax rates are just one of the multitude of locational advantages and disadvantages that every community has, including climate, leisure activities, personal security, media or merchandising opportunities, and the like. The general labor market also accommodates these other factors through the use of "compensating wage differentials." Employees are paid more or less for a given job in one community, based on that community's attractiveness compared with others where the same job opportunities are available. League salary rules ignore *all* of these features of a player's life, giving another advantage to teams that have a significant edge in this non-salary domain.

The flat payroll cap ignores the distinctive situations of teams as well as players. Some clubs, for example, may have a legitimate special need to add talent to their rosters. Bostonians experienced this disparate impact of the NBA cap when the Celtics' star Reggie Lewis suddenly died in the summer of 1993. The team had to count against its payroll limit the high salary guaranteed by Lewis's multi-year contract (and paid to his widow). Again, a solution to this problem would be to exclude from the cap calculation the amount that teams were still paying to players who were no longer physically able to play—although this policy could raise some complex questions about players who were retiring (with pay) because of a debatable physical disability. The more fundamental problem is whether a cap adjustment should be made for a team whose payroll is high but whose performance is unexpectedly low, because the current players' skills (though not their health) have deteriorated substantially from the level the team expected when it signed them. Certainly if competitive balance rather than salary containment is the justification offered for a cap regime, the league's welfare is not enhanced when teams are forced to keep using mediocre players until their contracts have expired and some cap room has been freed up for better ones.

These regulatory shortcomings of the cap system tip the scales for me in favor of the salary *tax* instrument. The comparative virtue of a tax over a cap is the flexibility it offers the individual team to adjust to the special features of its community and the special needs of its roster. And the comparative value of a meaningful tax over unrestricted free agency is the incentive it gives a team to respond to the league's broader need for competitive balance rather than simply reap the windfall profit the club derives from being an extravagant championship club.

MLB's salary tax regime suffers from two major deficiencies, though. The first is its very modest tax on excessive payrolls. This problem stems not so much from the 35 percent rate as from the fact that the taxable base is just the excess of the top five payrolls relative to the midpoint between numbers five and six. This means that if the top six team payrolls are all in the same financial ballpark, the top five will pay little if any tax, even if all six are spending far more than the remaining 24 MLB teams. That is why in 1998, when the Yankees spent $63 million in salaries (versus the Expos' $8 million), Steinbrenner paid less than $700,000 in league salary taxes to enjoy all of the financial and emotional benefits from his team's record-setting 125-win season and World Series sweep. If the baseball tax is to play anything more than its current symbolic role, it must have meaningful graduated rates—say, running from 10 to 50 percent or more—applied at different salary levels above the designated median point. The median figure in turn should be the players' agreed-to share of *all* the league's revenues (unlike the NFL's Designated Gross Revenues, which exclude the increasingly lucrative stadium revenue streams). Something like the current payroll share of league revenues would be an appropriate base for any initial agreement between the league owners and the players' association. However, the flexibility afforded by a payroll tax incentive rather than a rigid rule would regularly give the two sides the market information they need about the players' appropriate share as league revenues grow (or shrink).

The even bigger defect of the current MLB tax system is that it is not applied to the amount by which the lowest-payroll teams fall *below* the appropriate level. It is as counterproductive for baseball that teams like the Expos, the Pirates, and now the Marlins have payrolls (and talent) far below the league average as it is that the Orioles, the Yankees, and the Braves have payrolls far above average. Even a league policy for sharing revenue with small-market teams offers no guarantee that those clubs will spend the money on players who might make the team better on the field, but who the owner believes would not significantly increase local revenues off the field.* The best index that a league tax is intended to enhance the quality of the game rather than merely to contain players' salaries is that the same rates are applied to payrolls below the agreed-to line as to those above it.

The move to free agency has made baseball and the other major sports significantly better off than they were under the old reserve system. The

* In 1998, for example, the Expos' $8 million payroll was just half the club's $15 million share of league-wide television and merchandising revenues as well as what it received from MLB's explicit revenue-sharing regime created by the 1997 collective agreement. In other words, a big chunk of the Expos' (admittedly low) gate receipts and local television payments ended up in the pockets of the team's owners, giving them a much higher rate of return on their investment than the owners of much higher-priced franchises whose payrolls made them more successful on the field.

benefits have been secured not just by the players but also by the fans and even by the owners. To paraphrase the Supreme Court's comment in *Flood,* the game is *now* on higher ground; it behooves everyone to keep it there. However, baseball and the other sports could be raised to an even higher level by the establishment of a graduated salary tax, one that creates the same incentive for some clubs to spend more money on player talent as for others to spend less.

When labor negotiations between the MLB owners and players get under way early in the 21st century, let us hope that the two sides will not follow the lead of the NBA protagonists, who focused almost entirely on the share that each could extract from the existing pie—a posture that has always generated major industrial relations battles. Instead, baseball fans should root for the parties to work together to enhance the quality of the game, which will expand the size of the financial pie to be shared among them.

That win-win approach to collective bargaining requires owners to acknowledge that the justification for a league-wide constraint on individual player-team negotiations is to secure true competitive balance, not simply to constrain players' salaries. Players in turn must accept that certain distinctive features of the sports marketplace can lead to severe imbalances in team payrolls and talent levels, reducing not just the attraction of the game but also the amount that fans are willing to spend to watch it. Free agency tempered by a meaningful salary tax would address this problem faced by both owners and players, not merely the self-interest of one side or the other. Once this concept is accepted by the two sides, it may be considerably easier for them to settle on the actual tax numbers.

12

SALARY SHARING
AMONG PLAYERS

The major source of labor battles in sports has always been how to divide up league revenue streams between owners and players as a group. However, the 1998–99 NBA battle and settlement finally brought to the attention of the press and the public another important dimension of the players market: how the players' share of the revenues should be distributed among all the members of the union team.

Statistics from baseball again illustrate this feature of the players market. In 1967, when the players were just turning their associations into real unions, the MLB minimum salary was $7,000; the median, $17,000; the average, $19,000; and the top salary, $125,000. During the 1999 season the minimum salary was $200,000; the median, $495,000; the average, $1.57 million; and the top salary, $15 million. The salary of the median player (the one of whom exactly half the players are making more and half making less) used to be very close to the average, and the top salary used to be less than 20 times the bottom salary. Now, though, the median player makes less than a third of the average, while the top players earn about 70 times more than those at the bottom. Unionism in baseball, even more than in other industries, has done a remarkable job of increasing the players' overall share of league revenues, from under 20 percent in 1967 to over 60 percent in 1999. But that same collective action by players also has dramatically exacerbated the inequality in distribution of their share—particularly for the new and the journeyman players.

Of course numerical inequality in salary distribution is not by definition unfair. There should be a reasonable relationship between an individual player's productivity and his pay. Indeed, the presence of the reserve system and the absence of free agent bidding for players in MLB in the 1960s imposed the biggest market restraints on stars such as Hank Aaron and Willie Mays. Players like these were paid a mere fraction of their marginal revenue productivity (MRP) to the team that "owned" them, because of the absence of competitive bidding for their services. Three decades later free agency had transformed this situation: players entitled to free agency (after six years in the majors) were paid approximately 135 percent of their MRP; those entitled to salary arbitration (covering years four through six) made 60 percent of their MRP; and those still covered by the reserve system (from their first through their third years) earned about 20 percent of their MRP.

The MLB Players Association might respond that this salary distribution is the cumulative product of individually negotiated contracts, with almost every player represented by his own agent. In fact, along with negotiating valuable pension, disability, and other benefits, all players' unions have established minimum salaries for players at the bottom of the roster at levels that dwarf those in any other part of the American economy, including the movie world. The other noteworthy union accomplishment has been to establish varying degrees of free agency that now allow players to secure overall salary levels that far better reflect their contribution to the value of the team and the sport.

Yet the statistics we have just seen reveal the major source of the striking inequality in players' pay. Some of the disparity is probably attributable to the name recognition and popular appeal of many veteran players, as compared with relatively unknown newcomers. But most of it is explained by the fact that even individual player-team negotiations take place in the shadow of the league's privately fashioned labor "law," which defines the nature of the reserve system for different categories of players: first, newcomers are subject to the rookie draft when they seek to enter the league; next, players are reserved to a single team's roster during their first several years in the majors; later, in baseball and hockey (though not in basketball and football), players still reserved to a particular team eventually get the right to arbitration of their salary disputes with that team; and finally, at some point players become veteran free agents who are entitled to seek salary offers from other clubs. In this chapter we shall take a brief look at how the various leagues set up these player categories, and then consider whether and how the rules should be reformed to enhance the fairness (and quality) of the game.

The Rookie Draft

The rookie draft remains the sole feature common to every major league players market. In the NFL, the NBA, and the NHL the draft has been designed by the owners together with the players and incorporated in their collective agreements. In baseball the draft is still essentially in the form developed by the owners alone back in 1964. However, the labor agreement with the MLBPA now constrains owners from making unilateral changes in the draft. Since draft picks are transferred from the team that signs a free agent to the team that loses him, an arbitrator ruled that owners need the consent of the MLBPA to increase the value of rookie draft picks, because doing so would also have a negative impact on the marketability of veteran free agents.

Obviously the draft system has a direct impact on the marketability of rookies. Draftees have no chance to negotiate with and secure competitive bids from several teams; instead, each draftee is "reserved" to the single club that uses one of its picks to select him. Some events in baseball in the 1990s illustrated the financial impact of the draft. Guided by agents such as Scott Boras, top-flight draft picks threatened not to sign with the drafting team, a step that would cost the club that pick and put the player back in the following year's draft. This leverage served to push the signing bonuses of early picks up to $2 million apiece in the mid-1990s. But in the 1996 draft several teams mistakenly failed to make the minimum offer to their pick within 15 days of the draft: this meant that the player had not been reserved to the drafting team for even a year, and was free instead to sign with any team willing to pay him what he wanted. Soon afterward the expansion Arizona Diamondbacks and Tampa Bay Devil Rays agreed to pay two of these rookie free agents—Travis Lee, the #2 pick, and Matt White, $5—$10 million apiece for signing contracts.

The 1990s also witnessed several other efforts by draft picks and their agents—most prominently, Boras's client J. D. Drew in 1998—to locate and use loopholes in the MLB draft to enhance their negotiating leverage and bonus payments. The reason the MLBPA supported that kind of legal effort may have been to give its major league members a bargaining chip with which to extract some other tangible benefit from the owners. Certainly, if it can make some such tradeoff, the MLBPA should be amenable not just to preserving the current draft but to expanding and tightening it by eliminating the current $2 million (let alone $10 million) signing bonuses. Indeed, Mark McGwire and other Cardinals called Drew's $7 million deal with their team "outrageous" and said that baseball needed a $250,000 cap on draft pick contracts.

Under both labor law and the labor exemption from antitrust law, players' unions are entitled to reach a binding agreement that governs how new players begin their employment—analogous to the "hiring halls" that have long been controlled by building trades unions in construction and Actors' Equity on Broadway. As a matter of substantive sports policy, this is the one part of the traditional reserve system that I have always felt most comfortable with (as a matter of principle, though not necessarily as it is actually practiced).

From the point of view of allocative efficiency, the draft model that gives the worst team exclusive rights to the best new talent can make an important contribution to competitive turnarounds (by contrast with the veteran reserve system that kept both Steve Young and Steve Bono on the 49ers' bench for years, watching Joe Montana start at quarterback). And from the point of view of distributional equity, rather than let incoming players attract large signing bonuses based solely on their apparent promise, it is fairer to channel that payroll money toward the players who demonstrate their talent through their accomplishments in the major league games that generate the money they are being paid. The more revenue teams spend on signing bonuses, the less is available for other players' salaries, and vice versa.

Another fundamental problem in the current design and operation of the baseball draft—one that also will require the consent of the MLBPA before its terms can be changed—is illustrated by a rather gratifying event that took place in 1998. Orlando Hernandez, the older brother of Livan Hernandez, who had pitched the Florida Marlins to their 1997 World Series victory, fled Cuba on a tiny makeshift raft after Fidel Castro banned him from playing for Cuba's national baseball team (the regular Olympics champion). Although Hernandez was offered immediate asylum in the United States, he took the advice of his "baseball-immigration" agent and chose to go to Costa Rica, where he would be exempt from the MLB draft because it does not cover "foreign" players. That escape route permitted the New York Yankees to outbid the Cleveland Indians for Hernandez's services by offering him a $6.6 million contract, topping the $4.5 million package that his brother Livan had secured from the Marlins two years earlier.

This case highlights what has become an important gap in MLB draft coverage, with around 20 percent of league rosters now coming from foreign countries (including Japanese rookie "free agents" like Hideki Irabu, also signed by the Yankees). As a result, a team not only gets the picks reserved for it in the draft of North American players but can then add the cream of the foreign crop, as the Yankees did with Hernandez. And "El Duque" has certainly demonstrated the payoff to the team, leading the Yankees to two World Series championships in his first two seasons in the majors.

The flip side of this problem is what happened to Mike Piazza. When he finished high school, Piazza did not look like a serious major league prospect. However, his father, Vince Piazza, was a close friend of Tommy Lasorda, the manager of the Los Angeles Dodgers. As a favor to his friends, Lasorda had the first-place Dodgers select Mike Piazza as their 62nd pick in the 1988 draft. Piazza himself considered being made the 1,390th player drafted that year a "meaningless courtesy," but one that "would look good on my résumé." However, the young player surprised everyone by making it to the majors in 1993, being voted Rookie of the Year, and turning out to be baseball's best-hitting catcher of the 1990s.

The Piazza case is an extreme example (with a rather happy ending) of a general phenomenon. Especially when compared to the football and basketball drafts, the baseball draft is designed in exactly the wrong way for allocating new talent to the teams that need it most. By contrast with the NBA's two rounds and the NFL's seven rounds, MLB has only recently placed any limits on the length of its draft—and just to cap it at the fiftieth round.

Exacerbating the problem with these far-too-long baseball drafts is the fact that they are used to select talent that is usually far less developed than that in the football and basketball drafts. Football players are eligible for the NFL draft only after spending at least three years in college. And though basketball permits earlier eligibility—even after high school—that election is made by the families of players like Kevin Garnett and Kobe Bryant, who judge that their son's talent has reached a stage that suggests he really is ready for the big leagues. In baseball, however, it was the owners who decided that a team could draft any player when he was leaving high school. Of course, there is the occasional Ken Griffey Jr., who was the #1 pick in the 1987 MLB draft at 17, and who moved to the majors to star for the Mariners after just 75 minor league games. But a Griffey is very much the exception rather than the rule. About a third of first-round MLB selections (and about 45 percent of the pitcher picks) never even make it to the major leagues.* So rather than enhancing competitive balance in baseball, the supposed objective of the draft, this MLB system is more of a talent lottery.

Here is my prescription for solving that problem. First, the draft should be expanded to encompass all foreign players (like Irabu and Hernandez) who come to the United States to play in MLB. Second, the draft pool should include the entire array of players from the time they leave school until they reach the *major* leagues. Occasionally a team like the Seattle Mariners will still judge their best pick to be a novice like Griffey who has not even begun to play college, let alone professional, baseball. But after the talent of a Piazza has blossomed during his apprenticeship in minor league play, he should be available for selection by the club in last place at that time, the team that needs him most.

Next, the draft should last for a limited number of rounds—perhaps five—reflecting the number of players who typically make major league rosters each year. (Given the relative size of their respective rosters, the length of the MLB draft should be about halfway between the NBA's two rounds and the NFL's seven.) Players who are drafted by a team and do not make it to the major league club by the end of the season following that draft should become eligible for the next year's draft—by which time team standings and needs will probably have changed. Any player eligible for the draft who is not selected in these five rounds should be able to sign with any club as it puts together its roster for the upcoming year. And every rookie player coming into the league should be paid no more than the minimum salary established for all first-year players, thus preventing an apparently hot prospect like Travis Lee or J. D. Drew from holding out for far more.

The obvious objection to this proposed reform is that MLB clubs now stock and pay for the players on the minor league teams, while in foot-

* The following contrast provides evidence of the weakness of the MLB draft. Though baseball free agency is formally restricted by the rule that requires teams signing a Type A player (in the top 20 percent in performance statistics) to give up their next *first*-round pick to the team losing the player, this compensation system has had no depressing effect on the mobility and marketability of free agents. In that respect, MLB's experience is dramatically different from that of the NFL in the 1980s, where the prospect of giving up one or two first-round picks blocked the movement of a single veteran free agent for nearly a decade. That is why football greats like Walter Payton and Ken Stabler did not even get offers from other teams.

ball and basketball colleges now constitute the minor leagues.* If the teams that are making that investment in their farm clubs could not get the benefits of the star prospects developed in those clubs, they would seem to have no individual incentive to continue that investment (which now amounts to $7–$9 million annually per MLB team). The collective result for the game would be a drastic undermining of the future talent base.

Americans certainly benefit from the fact that major league owners rather than taxpayers or college tuition payers bear the bulk of the costs of developing professional baseball talent. The owners do so under an agreement between MLB and the National Association of Professional Baseball Leagues, which has the MLB teams pay the salaries of the players whom they assign to (and call back from) their designated farm clubs. The minor league teams have their own owners, who bear all of their teams' other costs and reap the benefits of their teams' rapidly growing revenues.

The relationship between major and minor league baseball has undergone several major transformations over the last century. If the major league teams want to improve the draft for their game, they should strike another new deal with the minor league owners. Under this agreement, MLB owners would provide the same amount of player-development money to the minor leagues, but the minor league teams would have the responsibility for distributing incoming players among their rosters in the way that enhances minor league competitive balance. (One side benefit of such a regime is that all major league teams would have to make the same contribution for development of major league talent, the Expos and Marlins as much as the Yankees and Dodgers.) In return, the MLB clubs would have the right to move players into the majors via their draft without paying any release fees to the minor league owners.

Establishing the most productive relationship between major and minor league baseball involves other complex issues that we cannot explore here. It should be clear, though, that at this drafting stage of its game, baseball should be moving closer to the football model. No one

* Baseball also draws upon college players, who are eligible to be drafted after their third year. J. D. Drew, for example, established his reputation and value while starring for the Florida State team. But the vast majority of major league players, including those who played in college, still do spend time in the minor leagues.

would ever suggest that either branch of football would benefit from employing the baseball system: imagine NFL teams drafting huge numbers of players coming out of high school; then sending those picks off to colleges chosen (and paid) by the teams to develop their (football) talents; and, when some of the picks turn out to be ready for the big leagues, calling them up immediately to join their NFL teams.* If achieving a competitive league is a legitimate rationale for a draft that reserves each rookie player to the single team that picks him, then the draft in any one year should include all—but only—those players whose talent has developed to the stage where they are ready to play for the team that selects them because it then really needs them.

Treatment of Reserved Players

Suppose that baseball owners could agree among themselves and with the players to reform their draft system so that the best *developed* talent would go to the major league teams that needed it most. One by-product of such reform would be the end of huge signing bonuses now paid for talent that is still underdeveloped but looks promising enough to justify an early pick. It is hard to imagine that the Players Association would agree to this new regime unless the bulk of the money saved on bonuses by the MLB teams was channeled into the pockets of major league players rather than kept by the owners.

Should such additional funds be expended principally on free agent stars like Mike Piazza, who in 1998 secured baseball's first-ever $90 million contract (though the record was very short-lived)? Or should the savings in signing bonuses be used to improve the situation of those younger players who have made it to the major leagues and are making a significant contribution to their team's performance, but who are still reserved exclusively to that team for several years?**

* Even in basketball, where the NBA draft can include high school graduates and college students who elect to be part of it, players who are not selected in one of the two rounds can still play in college. If a player's talent develops sufficiently during college play to make him a real NBA prospect, at the end (though not in the middle) of the NCAA season he can go back into the NBA draft for selection by the team that most needs him at this point.

** Another possibility would be for the MLB owners to compromise with the players on the "designated hitter" category. This 1970s innovation by AL owners has never been adopted in the National League. The rationale offered by NL owners is that their lineups should conform

There is a legitimate reason why all sports leagues have reserve systems for the first part of a player's major league career. The whole point of the draft system is to ensure that currently downtrodden clubs secure the best new talent to revive their team's performance. But in order for the draft system to play this role effectively, the drafting team must have the right to retain a player for several years after his rookie season, allowing the team to get a significant contribution from him once he has established major league skills. This may also lead the player and his family to develop an attachment to their home community that gives the original team something of an edge for re-signing the player even when he is free to leave. But these are benefits for the team and the league, which do not address the question of whether it is fair to subject players to a reserve system even for a limited number of years, thus giving the owners ultimate control over what the players will be paid.

Of course, it is customary to pay new and young employees less than their senior colleagues. For example, in teaching, including university teaching, the standard salary scale rests to a considerable extent on length of service. Analysts of the labor market regard basing salary at least in part on length of service as a rational mode of human resource management. True, at early stages in their careers junior employees are typically paid somewhat less than the value of their individual productivity, while veterans are paid somewhat more. Nevertheless, this kind of payroll distribution offers the right kind of incentive for beginners to develop their skills and make a commitment to their profession, because they can feel confident that they will eventually reap the benefit of their early effort. Many employers even offer an additional salary premium for seniority time in the firm itself because of the incentive this creates for employees to remain with the firm, promoting the collaborative efforts of the workplace team.

---

to the historical tradition of baseball, in which the manager must decide whether to pinch hit for his starting pitcher. I find rather strange the claim that regularly sending up to the plate someone who cannot hit the ball (especially with power) improves the game. No one advocates that the NFL go back to its traditional regime that required, for example, that running backs also be defensive backs. The true explanation is that the NL owners much prefer to have this position occupied by a bench-sitter paid $250,000 than by another starter paid $2.5 million. However, now that MLB has adopted regular-season interleague play, it is time to have the same rules defining player positions in both the NL and the AL. My hope (and advice) is that the owners will agree to make the DH the MLB lineup standard, in return for the players' allowing the owners to rationalize the draft system so as to enhance the sporting appeal of the game.

Two distinctive features of sports make it somewhat ill-suited to that standard salary rationale. The first is the huge size of its salary disparities. In baseball the starting minimum salary is only one-eighth of the overall average and a much smaller fraction of the veterans' average. Recall that, after controlling for actual performance on the field, MLB players in the first three years earn approximately 20 percent of their marginal revenue productivity (MRP), while players who are eligible for free agency earn approximately 135 percent of theirs. Second, and even more important, unlike careers in most other professions, careers in sports are inherently limited in length. Baseball players typically spend three to four years in the minors, and even if a player makes the majors, the median career is less than four years. This means that only a tiny number of professional baseball players make it to the free agency stage of their careers, when they can reap the full market value of their talent. Big-league career averages are roughly the same in the other sports, which, even more than baseball, bear significant risks of disabling, career-ending injuries from physical contact on the field, floor, or ice. Certainly by comparison with university professors, athletes face far more of a gamble than a guarantee that they will eventually reap the benefits of time invested in the reserve system.

Players' associations in the various sports have all been conscious of this problem and have addressed it in a variety of ways. In MLB the reserve system lasts six years, after which players are entitled to unrestricted free agency. For his first three seasons, a player's salary is effectively controlled by the team owner. During the next three seasons the player and the owner can have neutral arbitration of their salary differences. After evaluating the player's performance relative to those of others whose pay levels have already been set, the arbitration panel must select one of the final offers by the two sides.

In the NHL the initial reserve system lasts for just one to three years, depending on whether the player arrives in the league at age 24 or older, 22–23, or 18–21. Players are then entitled to a restricted version of free agency: in particular, their current team has the choice of matching a competing team's offer or taking draft picks from that team (picks that vary in quality according to the size of the salary offered). Unrestricted free agency is available only after the player reaches the age of 31 or if he has played 10 years of professional hockey but not yet reached the average salary level. In the meantime, many players are also entitled to arbitration of their salary disputes with their current team: after five years in the league if they started at age 20 or younger, and ranging to only one year if they started at 25 or older. Hockey uses the conventional version of interest arbitration, in which the arbitrator picks a salary number somewhere between the positions of the two sides and provides written reasons for his verdict. In return for the owners' dropping their push for a hard salary tax in the 1994 hockey labor battle, the NHLPA agreed to give each team (though not the players) the right to "walk away" from up to three arbitration awards every two years. If that happens, the player also becomes free to move to any other club willing to pay him more than his current one. It took five years before the Boston Bruins became the first—and still the only—NHL team to walk away from an arbitration award of $2.8 million to Dimitri Khristich, who then signed a four-year deal with the Toronto Maple Leafs.

Neither football nor basketball has ever had salary arbitration; instead they have somewhat shorter reserve systems constrained by their salary cap regimes. NFL players are entitled to restricted free agency after three years and unrestricted free agency after four years. The salary cap places a firm limit on the overall size of team payrolls, as well as a separate limit on rookie payrolls which applies only to the entire rookie payroll, not to individual salaries.

Basketball, by contrast, has set up a system of specified salaries for new players: these covered a player's first three years in the league under the initial 1995 deal, with a fourth year being added in the 1999 settlement. As of 1998–99 the salary figures ranged from $2.8 million for the #1 pick to $536,000 for the #29 pick at the end of the first round. These salaries go up by a total of 15 percent over the next two years, and teams have the option to retain a player for a fourth year (with a 26 percent increase offered to the #1 pick, rising to 80 percent for #29).

With that sketch of the systems as background, let us see what lessons can be drawn from the comparative experience of the various sports. While the NBA has most closely targeted the issue of newcomers' pay, it still ignores a more fundamental problem. To my mind, the most visible illustration came at the start of the 1998–99 season, when Kevin Garnett was to be paid $21 million for his then-unrestricted fourth-year contract and Tim Duncan $3 million for his capped second year. While Garnett certainly was a top-flight professional by that point, he was definitely not as valuable as—let alone seven times more valuable than—Duncan, who had succeeded Michael Jordan as the game's best player while giving San Antonio its first championship in any major sport. By then Duncan had spent five years developing his talent since high school, four in college and one in the NBA, while Garnett had spent just three years, all in the NBA. The 1999 NBA settlement did place a $9 million cap on how much future Garnetts (such as Allen Iverson) could make when they became free agents, but that settlement also extended the $3 million cap on #1 picks to their fourth year. So future Garnetts will still be paid three (rather than seven) times as much as future Duncans because of the NBA's dubious combination of eligibility rules for the draft and free agency.

This is not to suggest that the NBA should copy the NFL's bar on eligibility for professional football until after players have spent three years out of high school. (Indeed, it was not until 1989 that the NFL reduced its eligibility requirement from four to three years, thus enabling the Detroit Lions to make Barry Sanders their first-round pick that year.) I consider it rather unseemly for the NFL to tell young athletes that they must spend a minimum of three years playing in college for no pay before they become eligible to be paid for playing in our one major (professional) football league. Golf certainly would not have been better off if the PGA Tour had told Tiger Woods that he had to complete three years at Stanford before joining the Tour, nor would tennis have improved if the Women's Tennis Association (WTA) had told Venus and Serena Williams to get through college (or even high school) before turning professional. Unlike the PGA Tour or the WTA, the NFL and its rule are insulated from any legal challenge because the rule is incorporated in the collective agreement with the NFLPA. However, the league's actual motivation has always been to offer college football programs the exclusive rights to young players, in return for the colleges' providing free minor league training to the NFL. (MLB, by contrast, now spends about $260 million a year on its minor league managers, coaches, and players.) Yet thinking about players like Kevin Garnett, Ken Griffey, and Wayne Gretzky, all of whom were major league successes as teenagers, does highlight the unfairness of the NFL's denying that same access to football prospects, just so they can receive a college "education."

The NBA has done the right thing in permitting young male players to come into the league when they are good enough to make a team (though the owners did a very questionable thing when they decreed that *female* players must complete four years of college to be eligible for a professional basketball career in the new WNBA). However, the problem in the NBA labor agreement is the way this has skewed the choice to be made by high school players and their parents. The family's "advisor"—at that stage *not* an "agent"—will tell the parents that if their son is talented enough to be drafted by an NBA team (a draft that lasts only two rounds), then it is in his strong economic interest to opt in to that year's draft. If picked, the player will receive a sizable salary even for his four years in the reserve system, with the numbers determined by the point in the draft at which he is selected. At the end of those four years, when his talent is likely to have blossomed, the player becomes an unrestricted free agent asking for an annual salary ranging from $5 million to $10 million. Even if the player is not picked in the draft, he can go to college for a year or two, more clearly establish his talent and reputation, and then opt in to the NBA draft once more. If a player follows the lead of Stephen Marbury, for example, and leaves college for the NBA after one year, he will get to free agent status three years earlier than a Tim Duncan who invests three more years in college. Not only are these disparities unfair to the players; they can also be counterproductive for the league. Avoiding any play in college, or leaving college very early to go professional, means that players come into the NBA without getting all of the competitive experience and reputational value of college ball.

The solution to this basketball problem can be found in hockey. Under the NHL-NHLPA agreement, eligibility for both salary arbitration and (restricted) free agency is triggered not just by the number of years spent in the NHL but also by the number of years it has taken to get there. The specifics of this NHL contract rest on a player's age, but the NBA would be better off using the number of years since a player finished high school—in particular, years he spent playing in college. In that event, a player like Kevin Garnett who came to the NBA directly after high school should have to wait six or seven years for free agency, while a Tim Duncan who spent four years playing in college could have that same freedom after two or three years. This kind of formula would produce much fairer treatment of these categories of new players.

Changing the rules governing eligibility for free agency in this way to fit better with draft eligibility would, however, add to another fundamental though less visible problem in the NBA's current salary scale. The salary scale numbers during the four-year reserve system are based on a player's position in the draft. Obviously, a player is picked early or late in the draft depending on how team management expects he will perform when he enters the league. Yet past experience shows that there is no firm connection between how well a player has performed in college (or perhaps just in high school) and how well he will do in the NBA. Draft position, reflecting nonprofessional basketball accomplishments, is the only viable index for first-year NBA pay. After his first year, though, it should be the player's actual contribution rather than simply his earlier promise that determines his salary base for later years—especially if the eligibility period for free agency is extended for early-entry players. In order to establish the appropriate pay-for-performance figures for those players, the NBA should draw upon MLB's salary arbitration model to resolve disagreements between the team and the player's agent.

Recall that the key difference between the MLB and NHL versions of salary arbitration is that the NHL regime allows the arbitrator to choose a figure somewhere between the two parties' positions, while MLB says that the arbitrator must select one of the final offers the two sides have made. The virtue of the NHL's model is that it allows the neutral decisionmaker to arrive at the most appropriate verdict after the parties have fully debated and explained the issues at a hearing. The virtue of the MLB's version is that it forces each side to make an offer that it believes is very close to what a neutral arbitrator will judge to be the most reasonable position (whereas in conventional arbitration each party is likely to take an extreme bargaining position so that the compromise verdict will be closer to what it really hopes to get). The arbitration panel may believe that neither side's final offer is the absolutely "correct" one, but since the case concerns just a single salary figure (typically for a single year), there is little downside to the MLB's arbitration regime.

There is, however, a large upside: once the parties on both sides of the contract-negotiating table feel compelled to put forth salary figures that reflect a reasonable appraisal of the player's performance, they generally find that the numbers are close enough together that they can readily reach a voluntary amicable settlement. The experience in MLB offers the best real-world corroboration of the theoretical expectation for this type of arbitration. In some winter baseball seasons more than 150 cases have entered the arbitration system, but fewer than 10 percent have gone all the way to an arbitration verdict. With the few that have not been settled, the teams have won around 55 percent and the players around 45 percent.

Of course, both the parties and the arbitrators need to have criteria for determining the appropriate salary amount, based on various indexes of player performance. The ideal reference point would be the salaries negotiated by teams with free agent players, since these reflect market competition among teams appraising the true relative value of different players, who are themselves competing for positions with those teams.

Leagues object to such a standard because (with the consent of the players' association) newcomers are supposed to be paid less than established veterans, even if they have made similar contributions to their team's performance.* But there is a ready solution to that problem. The arbitrator (and thus the negotiators) should be instructed first to assess the relative performance and value of the player in question and to calculate what an appropriate salary would be if he were at the free agent stage of his career. That salary figure should then be discounted by percentage amounts agreed upon by the league and the union for different seniority levels. For example, if free agency began in the sixth year, a fifth-year player might get 85 percent of his free market value, a fourth-year player 70 percent, and so on down to the second-year player. The owners and players would have to agree on both the length of their reserve systems and the rate at which salaries were to progress based on performance. But this basic model is much more sensible and equitable than either the NBA's current salary scale, which rests merely on draft pick promise rather than on actual performance, or MLB's current eligibility for salary arbitration, which produces a huge pay increase for players simply for moving from their third to their fourth year in the major leagues.

* That at least seems to be the assumption of the MLB's arbitration system, which directs the arbitrator to compare the player's performance and pay with those of others who have played at most one more year than he has. Hence only a player entering his sixth and last reserved season should be able to draw upon the free agent numbers from the seventh season and beyond. But the arbitration rules make an explicit exception for players with "special accomplishments," and the very nature of the arbitration regime transmits the free market figures throughout the entire group. In other words, the sixth-year arbitrated salary can be and is compared to the seventh-year free agent negotiation figures, the fifth-year arbitration to the sixth-year figures, and so on down the line. The huge quantitative jump takes place between the third and fourth years, when the player goes from having to persuade the team owner that he deserves that comparative salary to having to persuade a neutral arbitrator.

Should the Star Take the Lion's Share?

This brings me to the last—though certainly not the least—controversial issue posed by the sports labor market, and one that the NBA owners and players were also the first to tackle. We finally have a sports salary regime that not only places a cap and floor on the total team payroll but also places a rising cap on the amount that can be paid to individual stars and a rising floor on what must be paid to their journeyman teammates. After becoming free agents following their fourth year in the league, the top NBA players can now be paid no more than 25 percent of the team payroll cap figure in their fifth and sixth years, 30 percent in their seventh through ninth years, and 35 percent in their tenth and later years. On the other side, the minimum salary ranges from slightly under $300,000 in the first year to $1 million by the tenth year in the league.

While I believe this to be the right system, my reasons are quite different from the ones that led to its adoption in the NBA. When the owners realized early in the 1998 lockout that they were not going to be able to get rid of the Larry Bird exception, they sought to place limits at least on the amount that could be paid to star players, in order to alleviate some of the particularly intense competitive pressures felt in the winner-takes-the-lion's-share sports market. For that same reason the Players Association fiercely resisted this idea until it looked as though the entire 1998–99 season was going down with the lockout.

If the parties in MLB were to follow the lead of the NFL rather than the NBA, and establish true standards for overall team payrolls—though preferably with a meaningful tax rather than a rigid cap—then they should apply that same salary standard to the amount that can be paid to any one player, regardless of his level of talent, popularity, or service. Again, by contrast with the NBA version, any such limit in individual baseball salaries should be set on the net *after-tax* pay, so as to avoid giving an unfair advantage in the free agent market to teams based in no-tax states.

The differences in the performance of individual players should still be substantially reflected in their relative salaries. But the current gap in pay between stars and journeymen is far greater than any realistic assessment of the disparity in their performance. Every single player on a major league roster has already demonstrated the exceptional talent needed to make it to the big leagues—a prize that even selection to a college All-

American team does not guarantee. Yet stars' salaries are 55–75 times higher than those of backups and 10–15 times higher than those of other regulars. While stars play significantly better than do other regulars in their lineups, the fact that one player is batting .325 and another .275 does not seem to warrant the former being paid 20 times as much as the latter (say, $8 million versus $400,000).

This disparity between performance range and salary range is the product of yet another feature of the players market—the huge disproportion between the number of players in the journeyman and star categories. There now are many players with enough talent to be serious contenders for one of the scarce positions on a major league roster, where, for example, they could hit .250 over the season, or perform at an equivalent level in other sports. The number of such players gives clubs a significant bargaining advantage in constraining the salaries they must pay to the players who win one of the coveted positions on the team. (These amounts would be even lower than they are now if all the players' associations had not established minimum salaries, along with salary arbitration in baseball and hockey.) At the same time, only a tiny number of stars can hit .350, and there are many clubs competing for their services. This intrinsically limited pool of star talent allows the players who meet that standard to extract a large salary premium when they sell their talent to a particular club instead of one of its competitors.

A star's value and bargaining leverage get another boost from the name recognition factor. Players who are at or near the top in a season's performance statistics enjoy far more media coverage and public attention than do teammates whose performance ranks somewhat lower. This factor weighs heavily in a club's decision about how much it can afford to pay to attract or avoid losing a free agent, a decision made during the off-season when the team owner is trying to sell season tickets and television contracts. It is this competitive edge that stars can supply to a team both on and off the field that enables agents to convince teams that their clients are worth somewhere between 10 and 75 times the pay of their teammates.

This disparity is not unique to the sports world: it is even more endemic to the entertainment world, where a Tom Cruise or a Jim Carrey is guaranteed $20 million to make a single film because of his worldwide name recognition and marketability, whereas key supporting players in the movie gladly accept $200,000 and are grateful for the role and the pay. Still, much more than movies, baseball and basketball are supposed to be *team* enterprises—with everyone collaborating to try to win games and championships for the club, rather than just trying to win individual hitting or scoring titles and the resulting publicity and salary payoffs.

But why should stars' salary premiums (and lucrative endorsement deals) be considered a problem for the other players and their unions? After all, it's the team owners who ante up these $10–$15 million salaries. In addition, paying the stars more does not mean that fans must pay a higher price, because the owners are already using their power in the sports consumer market to charge whatever ticket prices and television fees they can get. There is a labor problem, though: the more money that is paid to the stars, the less is available for their journeymen teammates.

This is even true of a sport like baseball that lacks a meaningful salary cap or tax on overall player payrolls. Even if the league has no uniform rules in this area, any individual team has its own payroll budget based on its market setting and anticipated revenue stream. Especially now that the payroll figures have risen so high, any economically rational team owner has to decide how much money should be made available for signing up the team's entire roster, at whatever competitive level the owner is looking for. So after two or three stars have consumed the lion's share of that payroll budget, the general manager has to tell the other regulars that only a limited amount remains for them, salary figures that they will have to take or leave. And, for almost any player, leaving the sport (rather than just changing teams) would mean taking a significant drop in pay, even from the minimum MLB level.

Notwithstanding this distributional impact of stars' salaries, it probably would be a mistake for the MLBPA to seek to establish a limit just on top individual salaries. For one thing, a considerable share of that star premium does come from the pockets of owners—driven by the urge to win a championship rather than merely make money from a business. In addition, the new salary heights reached by stars have some tendency to pull up the salary figures of others who can draw meaningful comparisons between their performance and that of the stars (a point the agent can make in both salary arbitration and informal negotiations). Only if the owners were providing a significant new benefit in return would it make sense for the players' association to agree to establish a cap just on individual salary amounts.

Football, even more than basketball, should be the clear exception to that union judgment. The basic owner-player exchange was already made back in 1993, when the players got free agency plus a guaranteed share of the league revenues, in return for giving the owners a hard payroll cap. The NFL is now the only league that does have an enforceable ceiling on every team's payroll. (While many fans believe that a Deion Sanders–like signing bonus makes an end-run around the cap, this is largely an illusion, because these bonuses are just up-front payments of what otherwise is a non-guaranteed contract amount.) This ceiling means that when a team's star quarterback or defensive lineman uses his free agency leverage to extract a large salary premium, the amount that the league permits the team to pay to all the other players on its roster goes down.

True, the salary disparities are significantly smaller in football than in other sports—ranging from the $8 million star salaries to the NFL's $400,000 top veteran minimum. But this is still a large gap in a sport in which regular team rosters number around 55 (including players on injured reserve) and in which there are 22 starters playing on totally distinct offensive and defensive teams, as well as the specialists in punting, place-kicking, and the like. In addition, whereas hitting and pitching in baseball are fundamentally individual performances, the passing and rushing statistics of a quarterback or a running back are heavily influenced by the quality of his offensive line, just as individual quarterback sacks or pass interceptions are dependent on the way the entire defensive team plays. Yet even in football the very few players who are considered stars extract the lion's share of NFL payrolls, and this definitely comes at the expense of their teammates.

To address the interests of its overall union team, then, the NFLPA should establish a maximum salary in tandem with the minimum—set at around 10 percent of the team payroll cap. This star ratio should be much less than it is in the NBA, because the team rosters there are only a quarter the size of those in football. Now suppose that baseball were eventually to move to a meaningful graduated salary tax imposed on total team payrolls (both for being too high and for being too low according to league standards). Then the players should agree to apply that same tax standard to high individual salaries, to generate the same financial disincentives for teams to invest too much money in a few stars at the expense of their teammates as well as the owners. And the fans should not worry that the prospect of earning a "mere" $5–$10 million salary (depending on the league) would reduce incentives for future players to star on the field. Even setting aside the huge emotional payoff from leading a team to the league championship as Most Valuable Player, the player's agent can assure his client that such an accomplishment will bring him a lucrative endorsement reward.*

The lack of negative reaction among fans to the NBA labor agreement imposing a cap on how much money an individual player can be paid by his team was a pleasant surprise to me. Several conservative commentators, however, portrayed this part of the cap as an inappropriate form of regulation of the free market, one that would redistribute pay from the people at the top who seemed to have earned the right to have it.

I have two answers to that concern. First, what makes sports special is that we do not and should not have an entirely free and unregulated players market. The "public goods" dimension of the league venture and product means that a host of constraints can and should be imposed on individual player-team negotiations. It would be in the best interests of baseball and the other sports to draw upon past experience and serious analysis to design better versions of the rookie draft and limited-time reserve system and the payroll cap or payroll tax. The parties must appreciate, though, that once such a regulatory regime has been fashioned to enhance the quality of the game, it also has significant distributional consequences for various categories of players: drafted rookies, reserved newcomers, and journeymen. It is not only legitimate but desirable, then, that baseball owners and players follow the lead of basketball and

---

* Owners and players in the other sports should follow the lead of basketball and agree to channel much of the money saved on top players into a higher *graduated* minimum salary— one that rises by a certain amount (say, $50,000) for each year of service in the league. There is a fundamental problem with any rule that requires, for example, that a first-year player be paid at least $200,000 but that a 10-year player be paid at least $1 million. Even if a veteran had somewhat better skills than the rookie competing with him for a position on the roster, this rule would induce some teams to keep the less skilled but considerably cheaper player. The NBA came up with the solution to that problem: the *league,* not the team, picks up much of the *additional* service-based amount of the minimum salary. So individual clubs can select the players whose present and prospective talents offer the best contribution to their lineup, while teams share the cost of the extra reward for longer service in the league (as teams do now for service-based pension and disability benefits). In return, the NBA teams all get the benefit of the cap on individual star salaries.

focus some of their attention on determining the appropriate slice of the league pie to go to those players who have been skilled, dedicated, and lucky enough to become veteran stars.

Second, sports offers a unique role model for American life. This kind of collaborative effort in the players market might well convey a valuable message to our broader political economy. In view of the massive gap that has been developing between the pay of executives and workers in the American labor market, ordinary workers-fans might learn from the experience in sports that a collective effort is the key to securing a more level playing field in their own employment settings.

———————

There is no question that being a part of a union team has made a major difference in the lives of players. Professional athletes now receive a much larger—and fairer—share of league revenues than they did back in the "good old non-union days." And a major move in that same direction was taken in the Women's National Basketball Association (WNBA) in 1999, after unionization came to women's sports for the first time. Even though the American Basketball League (ABL) had suddenly gone under, leaving the WNBA owners with both monopoly power and a large array of talented and unemployed replacement players, the Players Association was able to secure major improvements in its members' pay and benefits just as the third successful WNBA season was to begin.

A less obvious but equally important contribution of collective bargaining to sports is the way it has enhanced the quality of the game, not simply the personal interests of players. The reserve system first established in baseball back in the 1870s, and one that governed all sports leagues until the 1970s, may have served the financial interests of the owners who created it, but it was detrimental to the competitive balance sought by fans. The situation in baseball was substantially improved when free agency finally appeared a quarter-century ago, though our national pastime would be made even better if payroll standards were developed to ensure relatively equal quality in rosters across the entire league. The best way for this to happen would be for the parties to replace MLB's currently very soft payroll tax with something like a meaningfully graduated tax.

Ideally such a system will be the product of a peaceful, win-win kind of deal between MLB players and owners. Indeed, a set of meaningful standards that established exactly the same kind of floor on what all clubs must pay their players would actually make the middle-level players better off. Not only would it rechannel a good part of the money that is now going to and from the wealthiest clubs to spend on their stars; it would also block future Wayne Huizengas from using a "race to the bottom" payroll strategy to make their franchises more profitable for the owners. And in the longer run, even if one side happens to give up an edge it now enjoys in negotiating individual players' contracts, making the game a better one means that we fans will spend even more money to watch and enjoy it—thus increasing the total size of the pie to be divided up among players and owners.

III

OWNERS VERSUS
OWNERS—AND FANS

13

THE BRAVE NEW WORLD OF
FRANCHISE FREE AGENCY

The New York Yankees experienced perhaps their most memorable season ever in 1998. On the field, the team won 125 regular and postseason games, culminating in a four-game sweep of the World Series. Nearly 3.5 million fans, another record-breaking number, went to the Bronx to watch the Yankees play and win in the 75-year-old stadium known as "the house that Ruth built." And the following year witnessed a full-blown return of the Yankee Dynasty, with the team securing its third World Series Championship in four years after winning 12 Series games in a row.

Off the field, the Yankees' owner George Steinbrenner was having an even more exhilarating time. He entered into a new partnership deal with the NBA New Jersey Nets that valued the Yankees at $600 million. One key reason for that financial windfall was the expected huge increase in the team's record-setting $500 million television deal, since the incumbent Cablevision would have to outbid Rupert Murdoch's new Fox Sports to keep the Yankees on its local MSG cable channel.

Even more important for the value of the franchise, New York City Mayor Rudy Giuliani was saying that he wanted to spend several hundred million public dollars to build a new Yankee Stadium. Why did Steinbrenner want the city to replace the historic ballpark, which had opened in April 1923 with a Babe Ruth home run? He considered a new facility essential for reducing overall seating capacity while devoting much more of the scarce and valuable space to luxury suites and premium seats. Mayor Giuliani was also advocating public financing of a second expensive new ballpark, a modern replica of Ebbets Field to be built in Queens for the New York Mets. The mayor (and candidate for governor) believed it was vital to the economy as well as the culture of

New York to keep both these teams from moving across the Hudson River to a New Jersey ballpark, as the NFL's New York Giants and Jets had done a quarter-century earlier.

Sports fans and commentators are generally unaware of the underlying legal factors that enable teams like the Yankees, or leagues like the NFL, to secure their extremely generous contracts from television networks or product manufacturers. Americans are very conscious, though, of what has been going on in the franchise and stadium markets. While the move of a player, even a star, to another team is reported only in the sports pages, when Steinbrenner intimated that he might have to move his Yankees out of New York unless he got the kind of new stadium he wanted, his potential use of "franchise free agency" made the front pages of the *New York Times*. Certainly Clevelanders felt aggrieved when Albert Belle left the Indians in 1997 for a five-year, $55 million contract with the Chicago White Sox. But just the year before they had felt totally betrayed when the owner of their Browns, Art Modell, moved the entire team to Baltimore in return for a $250 million stadium deal from the state of Maryland.

The Saga of the Browns

The Browns were born in Cleveland in 1946 as part of the new All-American Football Conference (AAFC) that was started just after World War II had ended. The appearance of the Browns impelled Dan Reeves, the owner of the Cleveland Rams in the struggling NFL, to move the Rams to Los Angeles, where they were the first major league team to make its home in California. Meanwhile, the Browns were the first team to make a commitment to play in Cleveland's Municipal Stadium, which the city had built on the banks of Lake Erie in an unsuccessful effort to outbid Los Angeles as host to the first Olympics in the United States.

Cleveland's baseball Indians played briefly in Municipal Stadium in the mid-1930s, but it was not until 1947 that they felt comfortable playing the whole season in a facility built to hold 80,000 fans. Yet in those years just before television became the centerpiece of American home life, the Indians regularly packed the stadium, especially in 1948 when Lou Boudreau, the player-manager, Larry Doby, the American League's first black player, and Satchel Paige, an aged reliever from the Negro

League, led the team to a World Series triumph over the Boston Braves. The football Browns—both coached by and named after Paul Brown— had an even more spectacular record on the field. Led by Otto Graham, Marion Motley, Lou Groza, and several other stars, the Browns won four consecutive AAFC championships. However, their overwhelming success ended up killing the AAFC: even Cleveland fans showed by their rapidly declining attendance that they did not want to know beforehand who was going to win a game they were paying to watch and enjoy. So the AAFC folded in 1949, shifting the Browns (as well as the San Francisco 49ers and the Baltimore Colts) to the NFL. There the Browns won the 1950 championship by beating the Los Angeles Rams.

The Browns remained at or near the top of the NFL throughout the 1950s. In 1961 the franchise was sold for $4 million to a partnership headed by Art Modell, a young man from Brooklyn who initially put up just $250,000 of his own money to secure the position of managing partner and eventual majority owner. After taking control, Modell dismissed Paul Brown as the team's coach, but he retained Jimmy Brown, the NFL's best-ever running back, who led the Browns to their last league championship in 1964.

Since then the Browns have never appeared in a Super Bowl game, though occasionally they have come close. In stark contrast to the MLB Indians, though, the Browns retained one of the NFL's best bases of home-town fans. Attendance consistently averaged 70,000 or more per game; Cleveland's Nielsen ratings for NFL telecasts were the highest in the country; in merchandise sales the Browns were usually second only to the Dallas Cowboys; and the passionate "Dawg Pound" fans in the end zone at Municipal Stadium reinforced football's image as the favorite sport of America's working middle class.

But in Modell's eyes his Browns were seriously handicapped by Municipal Stadium—dubbed by many the city's "mistake by the lake." True, the value of the Browns' franchise had soared by the early 1990s. *Financial World* estimated that in 1994 the Browns' annual *net* operating revenues were $6 million, and the book value of the franchise was $165 million—a rather nice return on Modell's initial $250,000 investment. But unlike much wealthier NFL owners like the 49ers' Eddie DeBartolo and the Jets' Leon Hess, Modell lacked a major independent source of cash flow that would allow him to live at ease in the NFL's new era of player free agency (even limited by the hard salary cap). It was understandable, then, that, like so many other franchise owners, Modell sought to cash in on the latest sports "gold mine"—a lucrative stadium deal.

Modell's stadium fantasies were undoubtedly fueled by the experience of Cleveland's MLB Indians and NBA Cavaliers. In May 1990 the county voters approved (by a narrow margin of 51–49 percent) an increase in the tax on public services like parking, as well as a new "sin tax" on cigarettes and alcohol, to raise the money to build a new $460 million Gateway Complex. Gateway included a baseball-only Jacobs Field for the Indians, a Gund Arena for the Cavaliers, plus parking and office space for the teams and their fans. The clubs contributed only modest amounts to the construction costs (funds raised by selling personal seat licenses or PSLs to fans who wanted to be season-ticket holders) and would pay a low rent. In return, each team kept all the revenues generated by its facility—gate receipts, luxury boxes and club seats, concessions, parking, and advertising—as well as the fees charged for non-sports events held in their facility. Public officials and voters were prepared to make that huge investment on behalf of the Indians (and the Cavaliers) because MLB Commissioner Fay Vincent had told them that the franchise met baseball's standards for relocation: attendance was consistently low (though team performance was as well); the team was playing in an unattractive ballpark; and a negative vote on the tax referendum would be viewed as a lack of community support.

Following the great success of the Indians in Jacobs Field, the mayor and business leaders of Cleveland campaigned vigorously for passage of a November 1995 referendum that would extend the "sin tax" in order to pay for a $175 million renovation of Municipal Stadium for the Browns. Municipal Stadium was to be redesigned as a football-only stadium, with seats moved closer to the field; it would feature more attractive luxury suites as well as 4,000 new club seats; and the Browns would reap all the revenues while paying no rent at all. But even this plan was not enough for Modell: he wanted a brand-new, more luxurious, and partially domed football stadium to be erected downtown for the city's beloved Browns.

Unfortunately for the Cleveland fans, Modell had a very attractive alternative waiting in Baltimore. Maryland had been the trend-setter in baseball when it erected a beautifully designed Camden Yards, which became a huge financial asset for the Baltimore Orioles. Baltimore fans had long lamented losing their NFL Colts to Indianapolis in 1984, and then losing (along with St. Louis) the 1993 NFL expansion finals to Charlotte and Jacksonville.* So state and local officials were interested in expanding on the state's special lottery fund, which had paid for Camden Yards, to build a new football-only stadium. Several other NFL teams, including the Buccaneers, the Bengals, and the Rams, had been exploring the possibility of moving there, but, in a secret airport meeting in late October arranged by his new partner, the billionaire Alfred Lerner, Modell leaped in and grabbed the Baltimore deal. After playing for three rent-free years in Baltimore's Memorial Stadium, the Browns would move into a new $225 million facility with 70,000 seats, including 7,500 club seats and 108 luxury boxes. The team would receive all stadium revenues from football games and the bulk of revenues from other events like concerts. In addition to a $15 million training facility also financed by the lottery, Modell received a $75 million signing bonus for "relocation expenses," paid for by the sale of PSLs to eager season-ticket seekers.

The next several weeks were a turbulent time. At that Sunday's Browns game (a game that Modell wisely stayed away from), Dawg Pound fans brandished placards saying "Rot in Hell, Modell!" On election day the following Tuesday, county voters approved the referendum authorizing the $175 million investment in stadium renovations for the Browns. And NFL Commissioner Paul Tagliabue entered the fray, expressing his disapproval of the Browns' leaving Cleveland, the

---

* The Colts had begun play in Baltimore in the early 1950s, in a brand-new Memorial Stadium that had been built to lure baseball's St. Louis Browns to town as the Orioles. In that first decade the Colts were far more successful than the Orioles, with John Unitas and Alan Ameche leading the team to victory over the New York Giants in the 1958 championship. This was probably the most important game in NFL history: it displayed the competitiveness and popular appeal of *professional* football in the midst of the television season, at a time when TV sets were appearing in every American home. Thus, rather than baseball's World Series or college football's New Year's bowl games, the NFL championship (eventually called the Super Bowl) was about to become the most heavily watched and highest-priced sports event on television (with spillover effects on regular-season TV deals, players' salaries, and franchise values). And I should also note that this 1958 Colts victory over the Giants took place in the same Yankee Stadium that the owner Jacob Ruppert—and Babe Ruth—had built for $2.5 million back in the early 1920s, and that Steinbrenner was wanting to tear down in the late 1990s.

#13 television market with the country's highest NFL ratings, for #23-ranked Baltimore, where attendance at Colts games had dropped to under 50,000 in the early 1980s.

The City of Cleveland went to state court to try to block the Browns from leaving town before the team's 25-year lease expired in 1998 (a lawsuit that posed some difficult legal problems because of Modell's carefully designed lease terms). At the same time, the Maryland Stadium Authority went to its local federal court to lodge an antitrust claim against the NFL, based on an Oakland Raiders legal victory against the league in the early 1980s. (As we shall see, it was the *Raiders* decision that had prompted the NFL to allow the Colts' owner Bob Irsay to move his team to Indianapolis in the middle of the night in March 1984.) On another front, members of Congress were vigorously debating a number of legislative proposals designed to place substantial legal restraints on franchise free agency.

By February 1996 the sports law battle over the Browns was essentially resolved. Modell was allowed to move his team to Baltimore, but he had to leave the Browns name and logo behind in Cleveland. From the $75 million realized from PSL sales in Baltimore, he agreed to pay $10 million to Cleveland to settle the dispute about the stadium lease and approximately $25 million to the other NFL owners for taking over the vacant Baltimore franchise site. And the league guaranteed that Cleveland would get a new Browns team by 1999. In return the city would have to put up at least $230 million for a brand-new facility like the one Modell had wanted. The NFL agreed to provide the additional $50 million of the estimated $280 million construction cost, money that league authorities quickly raised through the sale of PSLs to Cleveland fans who wanted to reserve Browns season tickets for the future.

In the summer of 1998 Commissioner Tagliabue conducted an auction for ownership of the new Browns franchise. Seven groups were bidding, each controlled by hugely wealthy businessmen like the Jacobs brothers whose Indians franchise had been greatly enriched by Jacobs Field. Several of the groups also included a former Browns player, such as Jimmy Brown, Don Shula, Paul Warfield, or Bernie Kosar. The ultimate franchise winner was Modell's ex-partner Al Lerner, who had just sold off his 5 percent share of the Browns-turned-Ravens for $32 million. Lerner's minority partner was Carmen Policy, who returned to his native Ohio to try to build the same kind of talented club that he had built as president of the San Francisco 49ers. But the major financial winners from this venture were the other NFL owners, who split the franchise sale proceeds of $530 million—nearly four times the record-setting amount of $140 million paid five years earlier for the expansion Carolina Cougars and Jacksonville Jaguars.

The Setting for the Browns

Cleveland's loss of its original Browns had triggered a national wave of stadium referenda. Elsewhere in Ohio, in the spring of 1996, Cincinnati voters approved a 20 percent increase in their general sales tax that would raise $500 million to build not one but two stadiums to replace Riverfront Stadium, erected in the early 1970s. One was to be a baseball-only park for the Reds, the other a football-only stadium for the Bengals, a team that Paul Brown had created after Modell fired him as coach of the Browns. In the spring of 1997 voters in the state of Washington approved a set of specialized taxes to build a retractable-dome football stadium for the Seahawks. With an open-air facility also being built for the Mariners, the Washington taxpayers were spending nearly $700 million to replace the Kingdome that they had built for $70 million just two decades earlier. Another paradoxical feature of the Washington vote is that the $325 million in public funds was to be used to build a new football home for a Seahawks franchise that was being purchased by the second-wealthiest person in the world: Paul Allen, co-founder with Bill Gates of Microsoft.

The attention of fans and taxpayers in Seattle and elsewhere had been focused on this stadium problem by a wave of franchise relocations in the mid-1990s. This wave had been precipitated by the Los Angeles Rams rather than the Browns. As noted earlier, while the Rams had first played in Cleveland, the appearance of the AAFC Browns in that city had led Reeves, the Rams' owner, to move his team to Los Angeles to play in the 92,000-seat L.A. Coliseum, which had originally been built for the 1932 Summer Olympics. The Rams became a very successful venture on and off the field in the flourishing Southern California environment.

By the late 1970s, though, the Ram' new owner Carroll Rosenbloom had become somewhat disenchanted with his team's situation at the Coliseum, and he decided to move the Rams down to Orange County to play in Anaheim Stadium, originally built for Gene Autry's baseball Angels. The league had no problem with this move, since Anaheim was within the 75-mile Los Angeles region that made up the exclusive territory of the Rams under NFL rules. (That had also been true of the Giants' move from New York to the New Jersey Meadowlands in the early 1970s.) However, the fact that the Rams' departure left the Coliseum and the City of Los Angeles teamless precipitated the extremely controversial move of Al Davis's Raiders from Oakland to Los Angeles in the early 1980s, with far-reaching legal consequences. But Rosenbloom was not destined to witness the *Raiders* litigation. He drowned while swimming in Florida in the spring of 1979, leaving the Rams to his widow, Georgia, who was soon remarried to Domenic Frontiere, a young Hollywood composer.

By the 1990s the Rams were not doing very well in Anaheim, either on the field or at the box office: the 4–12 Rams averaged only 42,000 in attendance per game in 1994. This kind of fan infidelity was not unusual in the Los Angeles area, which by then had a total of eight major league teams. When the Rams, the Lakers, or the Kings were strong contenders, they enjoyed large attendance and high television ratings, but when their performance dropped, so did team revenues (the Dodgers being the sole exception). Rather than try to improve the quality of her team in the NFL's new regime of player free agency, Frontiere decided to explore the prospect of a more lucrative stadium deal through franchise free agency.

The most attractive offer came from St. Louis, a city eagerly seeking to regain an NFL franchise after having lost its Cardinals to Phoenix in 1988 when St. Louis elected not to build a new football-only stadium. After finishing out of the race for expansion NFL franchises in 1993, St. Louis was determined not to lose again. So it was that in January 1995 Frontiere and her Rams were offered a new domed stadium that would cost the taxpayers nearly $300 million. For an annual rent of $250,000 the Rams would receive all the football-related revenues (and two-thirds of the other revenues) from 65,000 regular seats, 6,500 club seats, 113 luxury boxes, concessions, parking, advertising, and even the multi-million-dollar annual fee paid by TWA to name the stadium after the airline. Finally, St. Louis football fans paid $75 million through the sale of PSLs for 52,000 season-ticket sites, ranging from $250 to $4,500 apiece.

This pending move by the Rams set off a struggle within the NFL owners' ranks over franchise free agency: should it be allowed, and if so, how should the $75 million in new PSL revenues be divided? The initial league vote in March 1995 denied the Rams permission to move by a 21–3 margin (with 6 abstentions). Faced with the threat of a $2 billion lawsuit by the team and the city, and enticed by a sweetened offer from the Rams, the NFL voted a month later to approve the relocation (by a 23–6 margin, with the Raiders abstaining). The Rams agreed to pay approximately $35 million as the league's charge for moving into the vacant St. Louis territory; to reimburse the league up to $12.5 million for any rebate demanded by Fox Television if its overall NFL TV ratings dropped (if Fox lost more viewers in the #2 Los Angeles market than it gained in the #17 St. Louis market); and to waive its per capita share of any expansion fees over the next 10 years, with the sole exception being fees for any new team placed in Los Angeles, which the Rams were leaving open. In the 1995 season the Rams began playing in St. Louis, doing not that much better on the field but with attendance at 99 percent of capacity (and Fox did not have to claim a ratings rebate).

The Rams' successful move to St. Louis not only inspired the Browns to move to Baltimore in 1996 but also stimulated the Raiders to return to Oakland that same year. The Oilers followed suit in 1997, leaving the Houston Astrodome for a $300 million facility offered by Nashville. Daunted by all of these precedents, and by warnings from the Broncos' owner Pat Bowlen that he would let the Super Bowl champions move to Los Angeles or Houston, the voters in Denver agreed to ante up hundreds of millions of dollars to keep that team (even minus John Elway) in town.

The ability of team owners to extract this kind of money from city and state authorities has driven up franchise values even more steeply than players' salaries. In the early 1960s NFL players earned an average of $15,000 a season, while in 1999 they were paid around $1.1 million—73 times as much. Back in 1961 the Cleveland Browns went to Art Modell's original ownership group for $4 million. In 1998 Al Lerner paid $530 million for an expansion Browns franchise to replace the team that Modell had moved to Baltimore—135 times the value of a franchise in the same city in 1961. A year later Bob McNair broke the expansion price record when he bid $700 million to bring professional football back to Houston—1,166 times the $600,000 that had been paid four decades earlier to bring the NFL to Texas with the Dallas Cowboys.

One major source of this dizzying rise in teams' value (as well as in players' salaries) is the increase in broadcast revenues: the NFL's first television contract, with CBS in 1962, generated $4.6 million, or $330,000 per club; in the 1999 season the four national and cable contracts generated $2.2 billion, or $75 million per club. But the City of Cleveland's agreement to erect a luxurious $280 million stadium to house the new Browns was the principal reason that franchise sold for $530 million while the Minnesota Vikings went for a "mere" $250 million the same year. And the fact that the taxpayers in Houston were prepared to put up $200 million for a new football stadium is the reason McNair was able to outbid the Los Angeles billionaire team and restore the NFL in the nation's eleventh-largest, rather than its second-largest, market.

One key reason for this dramatic surge in the amount of money being spent on sports is the much greater fan interest in the games and championship races. The full magnitude of these numbers, though, is also attributable to the legal regime that now governs the sports world, one that has secured monopoly power to be wielded by the league at the national level and by individual teams at the local level. It is not surprising that the producers of this monopoly sports product have been able to extract a large premium from its consumer-fans. In particular, during the 1990s state and local governments felt compelled to spend more than $10 billion in taxpayer dollars on luxurious new homes for professional teams, conferring such lavish public largesse on well-to-do figures such as Paul Allen, the owner of the Seattle Seahawks, and Ted Turner's Time Warner, the owner of Atlanta's Braves and Hawks.

We have seen that the move to player free agency substantially enhanced the quality and appeal of the game, at least by comparison with the old reserve system created by owners. However, the winner-takes-the-lion's-share character of the sports market means that all the leagues would be even better off if they had the kind of payroll standards produced by collective bargaining in football—though a meaningful graduated tax would be a better instrument than the NFL's somewhat inflexible salary cap. Franchise free agency, too, can sometimes enhance the quality and appeal of sports across the country—at least when team shifts take the form of the Dodgers' 1950s move from Brooklyn to Los Angeles, rather than the 1990s moves of the Rams and Raiders out of America's second-largest metropolitan area. But the nature of the current franchise/stadium marketplace is now making the team owner literally the winner-takes-all from any such relocation. Leagues like the NFL and MLB must reform their internal revenue-sharing systems to ensure that any such moves actually do serve the private interests and quality of their sport. But it is the American public that must unite to replace the current stadium taxes with a "stadium cap" if we want to avoid a replay of the 1990s in the 21st century.

14

HOW FAR HAVE
WE TRAVELED?

Since the early 1980s franchise free agency has created its biggest waves in the NFL, but it is not unique to football. In the National Hockey League, the Minnesota North Stars moved south to Dallas, the Quebec Nordiques headed west to Denver (winning the Stanley Cup in their first season as the Avalanche), the Winnipeg Jets jetted to Phoenix, and the Hartford Whalers relocated to Raleigh, North Carolina, all in the 1990s. One key difference from the attitude in the NFL was that the other NHL owners and Commissioner Gary Bettman actively supported this shift of several league franchises from smaller northern cities to larger vacant markets in the South and the West.

No baseball teams relocated in the 1990s, though there was a very close call with the Giants. Clear intimations that such moves might take place prodded the people of Cincinnati and Seattle to erect luxurious baseball stadiums to replace their relatively new multi-purpose public facilities. In the fall of 1997, when the citizens of Minneapolis–St. Paul and Pittsburgh reversed the referendum trend and rejected publicly funded separate stadiums for the MLB Twins and Pirates (as well as the NFL Vikings and Steelers), Commissioner Bud Selig made it clear that baseball would endorse rather than oppose relocation of these teams to North Carolina, Tennessee, or other areas willing to provide such tax-payer subsidies. That threat prodded politicians in Pittsburgh (though not in the Twin Cities) to offer the Pirates and the Steelers around $350 million to build new facilities to replace Three Rivers Stadium, which had been the home for both teams since the early 1970s. Only the NBA franchises seemed stable in their current locations—a remarkable change from the earlier peripatetic nature of that league, which had experienced more moves than any other from its formation in 1949 until the mid-1980s.

Growth of Franchises and Facilities

The NBA teams, like their counterparts in other sports, were benefiting from the surge in public spending on professional sports facilities. By the end of the 1990s there were 120 franchises in the four major leagues. More than 75 of these teams were playing in 65 facilities built or rebuilt in the 1990s. Thirteen of the arenas were shared by basketball and hockey teams playing in the same city; Oakland's renovated County Stadium was shared by the NFL Raiders and the MLB Athletics. The total cost of these construction projects was around $15 billion, over 70 percent of which came from the public coffers. And many other teams, such as the Yankees and the Mets, were actively exploring new facility deals with their home cities or with bidders from elsewhere.

It is now quite customary for a team to make some financial contribution to its public facility, often with money extracted from fans through the sale of PSLs, or for the city to make a significant contribution to a private team project, usually by assembling and donating the land and preparing the infrastructure. The following figures categorize each facility by its *principal* funding source: of the 36 new football or baseball stadiums erected in the 1990s, only 4 were principally privately built (by the NFL Dolphins and Redskins and the MLB Giants and Tigers). Of the 25 new arenas built in the United States, 15 were primarily publicly and 10 privately financed. Of the latter, 6 are shared by NBA and NHL teams, in the large-market areas of Boston, Chicago, Los Angeles, Philadelphia, and Washington-Baltimore and the smaller-market Denver; the exceptions are private Portland and Salt Lake City facilities for NBA teams and Columbus and St. Louis facilities for NHL teams. The remaining 4 new professional arenas in the 1990s were built in Canada, and were all paid for by the teams rather than by the taxpayers.

The large number of new sports facilities in the 1990s dwarfs the figure of 8 franchise relocations in the same decade—although the threat of relocation tends to trigger such public investment to keep the team at home. Many of these new facilities were built for expansion franchises, of which there were 17 in the 1990s: 3 in the NFL, 4 in MLB, 2 in the

NBA, and 8 in the NHL. But the interplay of league expansion, team re-location, and public construction that was so much in the news during the 1990s had actually been going on for several decades.

Any sports league is quite fragile in its early days. Even if the league survives the start-up phase, many of the franchises will move several times, and quite a number will simply fold. This was the pattern of the various baseball leagues in the late nineteenth century, until an alliance of the National League and the American League in 1903 established baseball's dominance for the next half-century. Faced with MLB's control of the larger markets, the NFL, the NBA, and the NHL put down their original roots in smaller cities in the Midwest; in the NHL's case, farther north in Canada. The basic 6-team structure of the NHL was firmly es-tablished in the 1930s, as was the 12-team NFL in 1950, following its absorption of the Browns, 49ers, and Colts from the AAFC. The NBA was formed through a 1949 merger of the National Basketball League and the Basketball Association of America. In the next few years the 17 original NBA teams were reduced to 8: most of the teams that folded had been based in tiny sites like Sheboygan, Wisconsin; Waterloo, Iowa; and Tri-Cities, Illinois.

By 1957, when the Pistons moved from medium-sized Fort Wayne, Indiana, to large-market Detroit, the NBA's 8 teams, along with MLB's 16, the NFL's 12, and the NHL's 6, made up the core of professional team sports. These league franchises were almost all based in the northeastern quadrant of the United States and Canada's nearby Montreal and To-ronto; the one exception was in the NFL, which had established bases in Los Angeles and San Francisco just after World War II. Football was able to take this step because its teams played just one game a week, and thus could feasibly travel across the country by train during that risky infancy of the commercial airline industry.

In what kind of facilities were the teams playing? In 1950, 5 of the 12 NFL teams (the Browns, Rams, Colts, 49ers, and Packers) played in *public* stadiums, as did 5 of the 11 NBA teams (in Philadelphia, Minneapo-lis, Fort Wayne, Rochester, and Syracuse, though the last 3 small mar-kets were about to lose their teams); only 1 baseball team played in a public stadium (the Indians, in the Municipal Stadium they shared with the Browns), and none in hockey. By the end of the 20th century only 3 of the 31 NFL teams (the Patriots, Dolphins, and Redskins) were playing in essentially *private* facilities, as were 7 of the 30 MLB teams, 13 of the 30 NHL teams (9 of the 24 U.S. teams), and 12 of the 29 NBA teams (10 of the 27 U.S. teams). Boston was the only American metropolis that could watch all of its teams (including the Patriots) play in privately paid-for facilities.

The Dodgers Go West

What triggered this transformation of the sports facility world over the last half-century? In the eyes of many, the fateful event was the move of the Brooklyn Dodgers to Los Angeles in 1958. At the time, the Dodgers' owner Walter O'Malley was even more reviled than the Browns' Art Modell would later be for wrenching a team away from its faithful hometown fans. Yet even now few Americans realize the critical difference between the two cases.

O'Malley, a Brooklyn lawyer, took control of the Dodgers at the end of the 1940s, paying slightly over $1 million for the franchise. During the 1950s the Dodgers were the most successful team in the National League, to a large extent because Branch Rickey, O'Malley's minority partner and team general manager, had broken the racist bar against blacks in baseball by bringing in future Hall-of-Famers like Jackie Robinson, Roy Campanella, and Don Newcombe. Though fewer fans could get seats for a World Series game at Ebbets Field than in the much larger Yankee Stadium, the community passion for the Dodgers far outshone fans' enthusiasm for the Yankees. The Dodgers had become the standard-bearers for Brooklyn's name, identity, and reputation after the city was absorbed into Greater New York in the late nineteenth century.

In spite of the intensity of Brooklyn's community feelings, attendance at Dodgers games dropped steadily from a 1.8 million average in 1946 and 1947 to just over a million in 1955. Although that was the year Jackie Robinson, Roy Campanella, Duke Snider, Don Newcombe, and their teammates finally brought the World Series title to Brooklyn, the attendance-leading Milwaukee Brewers outdrew the Dodgers by nearly a million in their home games. Walter O'Malley accurately diagnosed at least part of the problem as the small size and decrepit condition of Ebbets Field, then nearly 50 years old. He was prepared to build and pay for a new and more attractive ballpark, which he proposed to locate in

Brooklyn at the intersection of Atlantic and Flatbush Avenues, right beside subway and metropolitan transit stations.

O'Malley was aware of an important episode in the building of Ebbets Field itself, shortly before World War I. Charles Ebbets, the Dodgers' owner at the time, had gone far over budget on the project because the costs of buying the land had spiraled—and the reason was that those landowners who had not sold early were able to hold out for an exorbitant premium. As a lawyer, O'Malley was also aware of the potential solution to this problem now faced by his far more popular Dodgers team. The city could use its power of eminent domain under Title I of the Federal Housing Act of 1949 to take the land for his new ballpark site, while paying the owners "just compensation"—the fair market value of their property. The city would then resell the land to O'Malley for the same market price and he would build the facility out of his own pocket.

While O'Malley had many political supporters for his idea, including Mayor Robert Wagner, he faced an insuperable obstacle: Robert Moses, the all-powerful head of planning and development in this metropolitan region. As a matter of development principle, Moses much preferred suburban traffic on highways to urban traffic on public transit, and as a matter of development politics, he wanted the city to build and control the new ballpark that he had planned for Queens. So Moses rejected the idea of using the law to take land from one private owner in order to transfer it to another.

But O'Malley was adamant about owning his team's stadium, and Los Angeles was more than happy to provide him with an opportunity to do just that. So O'Malley first traded his Dallas minor league team and stadium to the Chicago Cubs in return for their Pacific Coast franchise and ballpark site in downtown Los Angeles. Los Angeles County had earlier acquired land in Chavez Ravine on which to build public housing. However, after county voters expressed their disapproval of that project, the county decided to resell the property to private developers for ventures that officials judged to be in the public interest. The politicians believed that bringing major league baseball—especially the celebrated Dodgers —to Los Angeles easily satisfied the public interest test. In a referendum, voters approved the Dodgers plan by 52–48 percent, and the Supreme Court of California ruled that providing facilities to professional sports teams did serve a "public purpose." But in stark contrast to Art Modell,

Georgia Frontiere, and other present-day team owners, O'Malley spent $20 million of his own money to build the new Dodgers Stadium on Chavez Ravine land that was appraised as slightly *less* valuable than the downtown site he gave to the county in exchange.

In hindsight, O'Malley certainly made a valuable private investment. Not only did the Dodgers continue as one of baseball's leading teams on the field, but they regularly were the MLB leader in home attendance—the first to top 3 million seats sold in a season. Four decades later Rupert Murdoch and his Fox sports arm paid a baseball record $310 million to acquire the Dodgers' team and stadium. The Dodgers' move clearly demonstrated what a team could gain by moving out of a metropolitan area, even a giant one like New York, that felt crowded with three MLB teams, to a teamless city like Los Angeles, which was soon to become the second-largest metropolitan area in the country. Only a couple of years after the Dodgers' move, the NBA's Minneapolis Lakers also moved to Los Angeles, where they found a lot more fans (though far fewer lakes).

The Dodgers story was not an entirely happy one from the perspective of sports fans. Understandably, the people in Brooklyn felt bereft and angry when the Dodgers deserted their long-time home. But the people in California—and soon in other western and southern states—were made better off by becoming part of major sports leagues that were now using the new technology of airplanes and television to blanket the nation. Of course, relocations are not the only way for a league to spread across the country; they can expand by forming new teams, as the American League soon did with the California Angels, rather than by taking popular teams like the Dodgers away from their home-town fans. But from the point of view of taxpayers' welfare, there is no doubt that Los Angeles was left far better off by Walter O'Malley than by Georgia Rosenbloom-Frontiere: O'Malley built, operated, and paid for the place where his Dodgers would play. An owner makes a far more credible long-term commitment to a community when he invests his own money in a physical facility, not just in a league franchise that he can easily move.

Evolution of Stadium Construction

O'Malley's construction of Dodgers Stadium was a throwback to the past rather than a wave of the future. The future was taking shape 400 miles to the north, where the City of San Francisco was building Candlestick Park for Horace Stoneham's Giants, who had also left New York to move west. In doing so San Francisco was following a trail blazed by Milwaukee, Baltimore, and Kansas City, which had built new stadiums in the early 1950s to attract the MLB Boston Braves, St. Louis Browns, and Philadelphia Athletics to their respective cities. Cities were also putting up stadiums for expansion teams—among them New York, building a ballpark for the Mets, and Anaheim, for the Angels. Associated with this shift in financial responsibility from the team to the community was a remarkable change in the cost, quality, lease terms, and life expectancy of ballparks.

These examples track the trend in stadium costs:

- Ebbets Field, Fenway Park, Wrigley Field, and other new concrete stadiums were built in the early 1910s at an average cost of around $500,000 (a huge jump from the $50,000 typically spent on the initial wooden, small, and unsafe ballparks of the late nineteenth century).
- The larger and more elaborate Yankee Stadium of the early 1920s cost just over $2 million.
- The even larger multi-purpose Los Angeles Coliseum and Cleveland Municipal Stadium each required an investment of $3–$4 million to compete for the 1932 Olympics.
- Baltimore's dual-purpose Memorial Stadium and Milwaukee's County Stadium cost $5–$6 million in the early 1950s.
- Dodgers Stadium, Candlestick Park, Shea Stadium, and others were built in the early 1960s with a $20–$25 million price tag.
- Similar open-air facilities such as Pittsburgh's Three Rivers Stadium, Cincinnati's Riverfront Stadium, and Philadelphia's Veterans Stadium each cost around $50 million in the early 1970s.
- Several cities jumped on the domed stadium bandwagon, following the lead of the 1960s Houston Astrodome. The Seattle Kingdome, the Twin Cities Metrodome, and the Pontiac Silverdome cost around $65–$75 million; the cost of the New Orleans Superdome in the mid-1970s soared from an initial $40 million estimate to $170 million.
- With the return to single-purpose outdoor facilities in the late

1980s and early 1990s, the total costs of Chicago's Comiskey Park, Baltimore's Camden Yards, Cleveland's Jacobs Field, and Dallas–Fort Worth's Arlington Park were each in the $150–$200 million range.

- The bills for the wave of baseball and football stadiums begun in the late 1990s in St. Louis, Seattle, Detroit, Hartford, and elsewhere were running between $300 and $500 million apiece.

This dizzying spiral in stadium costs is also captured in the overall figures for each decade. The total amount spent on stadium and arena construction in the 1960s was approximately $500 million; in the 1970s and again in the 1980s, $1.5 billion; and in the 1990s, around $15 billion.

Obviously a significant part of this cost spiral reflects general inflation: costs of construction are now 30 to 40 times higher than they were in the early 20th century. But inflation is just a modest part of the explanation for Seattle's spending $500 million for a qualitatively better Safeco Field, within which Mariners fans hope to see the World Series finally come to the Pacific Northwest (though probably not with Ken Griffey Jr. on their side).

Another possible explanation for the cost hike is an increased seating capacity. It is true that Boston's Fenway Park, the oldest big league facility, now has a short life expectancy because its 33,000 seats make it the smallest MLB ballpark. But the situation is more complicated than that. Why did Seattle, Cincinnati, and other cities feel compelled to spend $500–$800 million on *two* stadiums to replace the single multi-purpose stadiums they had built a quarter-century earlier for $50–$75 million? The reason is that the older facilities were considered too small for football (for which the ideal seat number is 70,000) but too large for baseball (ideally 45,000). Teams want to create a certain degree of ticket scarcity for all their games, since a shortage of seats is what promotes pre-season sales at higher prices; but this means there must be different numbers of seats for the 8-game football and 81-game baseball seasons. By contrast, because of the similar 40- or 41-game home schedules in hockey and basketball, dual-purpose arenas are much more economically viable for those sports.

Along with these box-office considerations, teams want to make the fans' experience at the games more enjoyable. That is another reason football and baseball teams now insist on separate facilities, since the distinctive layouts of the playing fields for the two games call for corresponding differences in the location of seats with the best sight lines. In addition, new ballparks offer a host of other amenities—convenient parking, escalators and elevators, more attractive concession stands and lavatories, as well as restaurants and children's play areas. For fans who are willing to pay the price, a much fancier array of club seats and luxury suites are situated in the prime viewing sites. And starting with Toronto's $500 million Skydome for the Blue Jays, retractable roofs are now being erected to guarantee fans either a pleasant sunny day or at least protection from rain and snow when they come to watch a game.

These elaborate new features make present-day sports facilities more expensive as well as more enjoyable. They also turn the buildings into far more productive revenue-generators, completely separate from the home team's huge television and merchandising revenues. Even for basic bleacher tickets, prices are pumped up: fans are prepared to pay a higher admission price to watch the Indians play in Jacobs Field than in the old Municipal Stadium; likewise for Orioles fans now going to Camden Yards rather than Memorial Stadium. The very expensive club seats and luxury suites also fill up quickly—with well-off spectators who enjoy having waiters at their beck and call, and who usually write off at least some of the price as a corporate expense. More convenient parking and more elaborate concessions, restaurants, and bars seduce spectators into spending more money as well as more time at the game. And companies have discovered that advertising displays inside the stadium and arena are an even better way to catch the attention of consumers than TV commercials: fans won't take their eyes off an ad if it is visible right behind the catcher or the goalie. Another new and lucrative advertising device is putting the corporate name on the stadium or arena itself. At the start of the 1990s there were only four major league facilities bearing business names, but by the end of that decade almost 70 teams had negotiated such naming deals, with companies paying prices up to $5 million a year to have the facility identified with their business rather than the team or the community.

Yet another revenue source emerged in the early 1990s—personal seat licenses (PSLs). These give their purchasers the right to buy (and pay for) season tickets for those seats for future seasons (either indefinitely or for a specified term).* This is a lucrative innovation: the NFL's expansion Carolina Panthers used PSLs to raise $150 million to build their new stadium in downtown Charlotte. Football is especially conducive to the use of this financial instrument because its fans are willing to make the up-front investment ($250–$5,000 a seat) to acquire the right to buy scarce season tickets that cost much less per year than in baseball, for example, because there are far fewer games in a football season. And when the Panthers made it to the 1996 NFC championship game in only their second season, fans were delighted both to have seats for that game and to realize that the financial value of their PSLs was higher than what they had paid four years earlier.

This transformation in the revenue streams, as well as in the quality and expense, of sports facilities has been accompanied by an equally stark change in the terms of the leases that teams are signing. In the 1950s and early 1960s more and more American cities became willing to build stadiums and arenas that would attract and keep professional teams in their communities. In return, the teams agreed to pay a reasonable rent for a period set to cover the time needed to repay the facility bonds. In addition, the stadium's (not the team's) owner kept much if not all of the secondary-use revenues—from parking, concessions, advertising, even rental of luxury suites.

Even with these various sources of revenues, financial analysts calculated in the early 1970s that taxpayers were providing significant public subsidies in building $25–$50 million stadiums and arenas, after accounting for all the capital amortization and interest costs as well as operational expenses. By the late 1990s the owners of some teams were making a significant investment—say $50–$100 million—in their teams' new facilities, though their contributions were dwarfed by the $250–$500 million in total construction costs. Much more important, these owners now keep for themselves almost all of the lucrative stadium revenue streams—not only from sports but also from other types of events like music concerts and trade shows. Indeed, in 1999 the Pitts-

---

* This device was first developed in college sports under another name. Colleges told their alumni and team boosters that if they wanted midfield seats at football games, for example, they had to make a substantial financial contribution to the school. This has long been an effective fundraising tool for Division I-A schools. And making that seat license fee look like a tax-deductible donation to a nonprofit educational institution means that U.S. taxpayers are now unwittingly helping pay to put wealthy people in the best seats at college football games.

burgh Penguins and their Hall-of-Famer and new managing partner Mario Lemieux used federal bankruptcy law to extricate the team from a lease whose less generous terms had been considered attractive by the prior owners when they signed it years earlier. Surprisingly, the principal adversaries wrangling with individual owners over who should get this money are not city officials and taxpayers but the league's other team owners.

Even while the quality, cost, and revenue potential of sports facilities have soared, their life spans have been drastically shortened. The most telling example is Miami Arena, built in 1988 for $60 million to house the NBA's expansion Miami Heat and the NHL's expansion Florida Panthers. By 1997 both the Heat and the Panthers had announced that they would be leaving the Arena for two new $200 million facilities, one being built in neighboring Dade County for the Heat, the other in Broward County for the Panthers. Likewise, the Seattle Kingdome, the Pontiac Silverdome, and most of the sports facilities built in the 1970s were felt to be antiquated and were being replaced in the late 1990s.* Although the physical quality and safety of sports facilities have steadily improved, they now can quickly become economically obsolete.

In the 1990s American cities, counties, and states spent or committed approximately $11 billion to erect 65 or so new stadiums and arenas, whose total costs were in the $15 billion range. Boston and Massachusetts are the only city and state sticking to the principle that new facilities for all four of their major league teams must be paid for by the clubs themselves, with taxpayers limiting their (legitimate) contributions to the surrounding roads and other infrastructure that are needed to make any major building project accessible to the public. Though these facilities provide a much more enjoyable experience for local fans cheering for their teams at the games, they also provide a far more expensive experience for local taxpayers. The amortization and interest costs alone

---

* Needless to say, the Houston Astrodome, unveiled as the "Eighth Wonder of the World" in the mid-1960s, was deemed an ancient relic in the 1990s: by the Houston Oilers, who left it for a $300 million football stadium in Nashville; by the Houston Astros, which used the threat of moving to extract from Houston taxpayers a $250 million baseball stadium to keep the team at home; and then by the NFL owners, who granted Houston a new franchise only after the taxpayers had agreed to put up $200 million to build a new football stadium.

are over $1 billion a year for the 25- to 30-year life of the bonds issued to finance construction, and the life of the bonds now often exceeds the life of the facility. And under the usual lease, further public expenses for operating and maintaining the facility significantly exceed the amount that the public stadium authority receives from the facility's revenues.

Issuance of the facility bonds is usually tied to a specific tax source— some version of the sales tax. Sometimes it is an increase (20 percent or so) in the existing sales tax rate, sometimes a "sin tax" on alcohol and cigarettes, sometimes a "visitors' tax" on hotels and car rentals, sometimes a "fun tax" on bars and restaurants, and sometimes a "voluntary lottery tax." Alternatively, political leaders in a number of communities simply tell their constituents that most or even all of this sports investment will be covered by the rise in general tax revenues generated by the increased economic activity flowing from the presence of a major league team.

That contentious economic view of the team as a generator of business and revenues we will examine in Chapter 16. But first we must explore the contribution that the law has made to this new sports marketplace—one in which Walter O'Malley's move of the Dodgers should look rather different from Art Modell's move of the Browns.

15

WHAT THE LAW SHOULD DO
WITH *RAIDERS*

The greatest "credit" for inspiring franchise free agency is usually given to Al Davis and his (once-again) Oakland Raiders. Though Davis was inducted into the Football Hall of Fame for what he accomplished on the field, among sports fans he is probably even more notorious than Walter O'Malley and Art Modell for what he accomplished in the courts. Davis was the first, and is still the only, franchise owner to obtain a judicial ruling that his team could move against the will of the league. That judgment set off a wave of franchise relocations that eventually cost Los Angeles both of its NFL teams. How much this had to do with the law, rather than with team owners, is a complicated question, as we are about to learn.

How to Win the Raiders

Like those other notorious owners O'Malley and Modell, Al Davis came from Brooklyn. Though he was not a star football player in college, Davis quickly became a successful coach—beginning at the age of 24 as an assistant coach of Carroll Rosenbloom's Baltimore Colts, next with the USC Trojans, and then with the San Diego Chargers in the new American Football League. In 1963 Davis was brought to Oakland as head coach to try to save the Raiders.

Oakland originally secured an AFL franchise in 1960 only because the NFL had wooed away another prospective AFL site, Minneapolis–St. Paul, by awarding it the expansion Vikings franchise. The Raiders initially did very poorly on the field and at the gate, especially in competition with the NFL 49ers across San Francisco Bay. In fact, before Davis arrived, the Raiders were seriously considering a move to Seattle. But with Davis at the helm as coach and then general manager, the Raiders were transformed as a team and enjoyed huge popularity in Oakland. The city quickly erected a dual-purpose Coliseum for them, one that also became the home of the MLB Athletics when Charles Finley was lured to Oakland from Kansas City.

In the mid-1960s the football war between the NFL and the AFL intensified. Davis was installed as AFL commissioner, and within four months AFL teams had signed up seven of the NFL's 14 starting quarterbacks (including the 49ers' John Brodie, who would be competing against the Jets' Joe Namath instead of the Packers' Bart Starr). This AFL initiative helped persuade NFL owners to make peace with their rival, through a 1966 merger that had to be blessed by Congress to avoid antitrust challenges. In this newly integrated league, the Raiders and the Jets paid a total of $18 million to the 49ers and the Giants for invading their "exclusive" NFL territories.

Pete Rozelle stayed on as NFL commissioner, and Davis returned to Oakland, this time as part owner and managing partner of the club. With John Madden and Tom Flores as head coaches and Kenny Stabler and Jim Plunkett as starting quarterbacks, Davis's Raiders won three Super Bowls, compiled the NFL's best overall record for the next two decades, and enjoyed the league's top attendance percentage in the Oakland Coliseum. The Raiders' first Super Bowl victory took place in 1977 in Los Angeles, a city about to be vacated by Carroll Rosenbloom's Rams. The Rams' move 30 miles south to Anaheim posed no problems for the league, because the new location was within the Rams' 75-mile territory. The eye-opening sports law controversy began soon after, when L.A. Coliseum officials sought to fill the gap left by the Rams by attracting Davis and his Raiders to come play close to the glamour of Beverly Hills and Hollywood. After a bidding war between the L.A. and Oakland stadium people, the Raiders agreed to move to Los Angeles in return for a $15 million low-interest *loan* for stadium improvements—in particular, for erecting 99 luxury suites—and a $4 million relocation fee. Strange as this seems now, back in 1980 that was considered a very generous offer by a city to a team.

Davis still faced the challenge of getting the other NFL owners to approve this relocation—to agree to send their teams to Los Angeles rather than Oakland to play the Raiders. Commissioner Rozelle appointed a special committee, chaired by Art Modell, to assess the pros and cons of this move. The committee's verdict was that the Raiders' move would not be in the best interests of the league, and that judgment was endorsed by the owners in a 22–0 vote, with other teams (including the Rams) abstaining. Davis said that he refused to vote as a matter of principle: that without agreed-upon objective standards to rely on, the league had no business telling individual owners whether and where they could move their teams. Then the Raiders joined with the L.A. Coliseum to sue the NFL under antitrust law for, in effect, restraining trade in teams.

The Raiders were blocked from moving at least until a trial verdict had cleared the way. So it was with mixed emotions that Oakland fans watched their Raiders win yet another Super Bowl, this time against the Eagles. After the first trial was aborted in 1981 because of a hung jury, a second trial took place in the spring of 1982—and, against the strong objections of the NFL, again in Los Angeles. The six members of the jury were all women who disclaimed any particular interest in football. This jury returned with a quick verdict for the plaintiffs, awarding the Raiders $11.5 million and the L.A. Coliseum $4.5 million for having been denied the right to operate together over the past two seasons. The total antitrust verdict against the NFL, after damages were trebled, amounted to $48 million.

While the league immediately filed an appeal, this time its lawyers did not ask for a stay of the decision, given the risk of several more seasons of treble damages if they lost the case. Ironically, the Raiders' move to Los Angeles for the 1982 season was facilitated by a lengthy NFL players' strike that canceled most of the games in the first two months while the Coliseum was being refurbished for football. The Raiders' 8–1 regular season record topped the AFC that year, though they were upset by the Jets in the playoffs. But the following year Marcus Allen led the team to another Super Bowl win, this time against the Redskins—the first and only Super Bowl victory for an L.A. team. Pete Rozelle had to hand the trophy to his courtroom opponent, Al Davis, with 100 million fans watching on television. It was even more galling for the commissioner a month later when he read the Ninth Circuit decision upholding Davis's jury victory, in the first and still the most extensive appellate court exploration of franchise free agency under antitrust law.

What the Law Really Did in *Raiders*

In popular (and political) discussions the *Raiders* decision is usually depicted as a clear-cut judicial endorsement of franchise free agency. This judicial ruling has been the standard explanation offered for the NFL's failure to block later moves by the Colts and the Cardinals in the 1980s and by the Rams and the Browns in the 1990s. But when one actually reads the majority opinion, the legal situation turns out to be much more complicated.

While holding the NFL to be a "joint venture" of independently owned and operated franchises, and thus obliged to pass antitrust's "reasonability" test for its restraints of trade, the *Raiders* judicial panel agreed that sports is quite special for any such legal inquiry. Any sport requires that all clubs agree to abide by rules necessary to offer a competitively attractive product for the fans. Even dividing up territory among teams could be accepted as "ancillary to the main purpose of protecting NFL football" to the extent that the league was "competing in the entertainment market." However, the court said, granting each team exclusivity within its territory could be justified only if the legitimate benefits this would create for the league could not be achieved "by less restrictive means."

The court also accepted the facial validity of the benefits that the NFL claimed would flow from league control over teams' relocation, even into another club's territory. Such control gives the latter club's owners some financial stability to protect their investment in the franchise; it distributes teams on a more rational basis across the diverse national market (especially on television); it protects the local communities' substantial expenditures on stadiums and other facilities; and it fosters fan loyalty and support for teams in a league that shows it is committed to the home communities. But the appeals court accepted as defensible (though not necessarily correct) the jury's finding that these factors were not sufficiently in play in this case. The Rams had already spent 35 years in Los Angeles, ample time to recoup their initial investment; there was no significant benefit to the NFL in the television market from having two teams in the San Francisco Bay area rather than in the Greater Los Angeles area; and there was considerable evidence that the league had previously given informal approval to teams that threatened to leave their home-town fans in order to extract a better stadium deal from the community. The basic message from the *Raiders* court was that to protect itself from adverse jury verdicts a league like the NFL had to adopt a set of objective standards that were clearly tailored to legitimate procompetitive factors, along with procedural mechanisms designed to make sure that these were the real reasons for any rejection of a proposed franchise relocation.

An intriguing legal sidelight of the Raiders saga was played out in a different domain of the law. At the same time as the Raiders were joining the L.A. Coliseum's antitrust suit in federal court in Los Angeles, the City of Oakland filed an "eminent domain" claim in a local state court. The city asserted its prerogative to "take" the Raiders franchise under state law, while paying "just compensation" for the taking as required under the federal Constitution. In this case the Raiders lost the first legal battle, when the Supreme Court of California rejected the team's argument that no "public purpose" was served by a city's seizing a sports team. After rereading its earlier decision that had permitted the city of Los Angeles to take land in Chavez Ravine to use as the site for Dodgers Stadium, the court said that if owning and operating a sports stadium is a "permissible municipal function," so also is "owning and operating a sports franchise which fields a team to play in the stadium."

Oddly enough, the combination of the *City of Oakland* and *Raiders* decisions precipitated the next move by an NFL team. The Baltimore Colts had been pressing the Maryland Stadium Authority to renovate Memorial Stadium and give the team a more generous lease, using the threat to go elsewhere as an inducement. In early 1984 the Maryland legislature passed a statute that explicitly conferred on cities such as Baltimore the right to take and keep professional teams like the Colts. However, before that bill could be moved from the floor of the state senate to the office of the governor for his signature, the Colts' owner Bob Irsay sent a dozen Mayflower moving vans into the team headquarters at midnight. Before dawn, all of the teams' equipment, records, and other materials were on the highway on their way to Indianapolis. A federal judge then ruled that when property has legally crossed a state's border—even intangible property such as a sports franchise—the state or local government cannot reach out and take it back. Having lost its appeal of the $50 million *Raiders* antitrust verdict only three days before Irsay's midnight move, the NFL decided to accept the fact that the Colts would be playing their future home games in a newly erected Hoosier Dome.

The City of Oakland did not face such an extraterritorial obstacle: not only had the city filed before any move, but the Raiders had just gone south to Los Angeles within the same state. In the California Supreme Court decision, Chief Justice Rose Bird reluctantly acquiesced in the remand of this case to the lower courts, though she did express serious qualms about a community's being able to "condemn any business that decides to seek greener pastures elsewhere." The lower court responded to that concern by erecting a new "dormant commerce clause" barrier to cities' taking a sports franchise that seeks "greener pastures" elsewhere, even within the same state. In the eyes of this court, what made a league like the NFL special in regard to this federal constitutional barrier to state action was its "interdependent character . . . [as] a joint venture of its members organized for the purpose of providing entertainment nationwide." Echoing the views of the Supreme Court of Wisconsin, which had struck down a state law forbidding a move of the Braves from Milwaukee to Atlanta in the mid-1960s, the California court said that to allow local governments to use their taking power to control the location of a team would "threaten the welfare not only of individual teams but of the entire league."

The NFL had in fact supported this "taking" action by the City of Oakland on the understanding that the city would resell the franchise to a local owner who would agree to keep the Raiders there. But the court in *City of Oakland* wanted to guarantee that such an integrated league venture would not be subject to any dislocation by local public authorities. Of course, the federal court in *Raiders* had said it wanted to preserve some measure of private owner control even if this did conflict with overall league policy. But the state court in *City of Oakland* seemed most concerned about the possibility that a mere threat of eminent domain action by a city—even though it had to pay fair market value for the team—"would seriously disrupt the balance of economic bargaining on stadium leases throughout the nation."

How to Lose the Raiders

Al Davis and the L.A. Coliseum Commission were totally successful, then, in their joint battle to pry the Raiders away from their original home town. (The Coliseum eventually collected $30 million from the NFL, and the Raiders $20 million, for damages caused by the league's delay of the move.) However, these legal allies were never able to establish an amicable partnership at their new site.

The immediate problem related to renovation of the Coliseum, which had been erected for the 1932 Olympics and was not particularly well suited for professional football. The stadium had no luxury suites, a revenue source that had originated in the late 1960s with the Dallas Cowboys. Many of its regular seats were located too far from the playing field for good visibility, in part because the field was surrounded by a large running track. And the Coliseum's 92,000 seats were simply too many to be filled except at the occasional special game, such as the first Raiders-49ers match-up, the USC Trojans against the Notre Dame Fighting Irish, and, of course, the Super Bowl when played there. Al Davis expected to get a more manageable 70,000-seat capacity with closer and better views, one that would motivate fans to keep buying their season tickets even when the team was doing poorly, along with a large number of luxury boxes that could be sold at much higher prices in Los Angeles than in Oakland.

But the original 1980 understanding about the revamping of the Coliseum was never implemented. The first obstacle was the extensive litigation that had held up the move. Even after the Raiders arrived in 1982 and Davis was given his $19 million renovation loan, he could make only minor immediate alterations, because the 1984 Olympic Games, to be held in Los Angeles, required that the Coliseum remain in essentially the same shape. By the end of 1984 Davis's expectations about the stadium had risen, but the willingness of the new L.A. political leaders to invest in refurbishing had declined. Major stadium surgery did not take place at this site.

Instead, Davis explored a host of free agency options, using the bargaining leverage that his lawyers had secured for him in both federal and state courts. The Coliseum Commission forgave its loan to Davis when he agreed to sign a short-term lease at the Coliseum in its existing state. The little town of Irwindale, east of Los Angeles, gave him a $10 million bonus just for agreeing in principle to a stadium project that its officials were never able to develop. The cities of Sacramento, Oakland, and Los Angeles all made increasingly generous stadium proposals, but each fell through: the 1989 Oakland proposal because of the Bay Area earthquake, the 1994 Los Angeles offer because of L.A.'s own devastating earthquake.

As the Rams were in the process of moving to St. Louis in the spring of 1995, Davis was discussing relocation with several other cities, as close as Hollywood and as far away as Baltimore. But he decided that the safest step for the Raiders was to move back to Oakland, with a 16-year low-rent lease that required the city to spend approximately $225 million in major stadium changes (with about $40 million given to the Raiders to spend as they wanted). The money was to be raised by selling PSLs (at prices ranging from $250 to $4,000) to fans seeking season tickets that were priced much higher than before the Raiders' departure (averaging $50 in 1995 versus $11 in 1981), as well as by charging a separate club membership fee for those in club seats and a $50 annual seat-maintenance fee for every season-ticket holder. As the California court should have acknowledged in *City of Oakland,* not just the presence but also the *absence* of eminent domain power over league franchises has a serious effect on "the balance of economic bargaining on stadium leases."

The NFL approved the Raiders' move back to Oakland by a 23–0 vote (with 7 abstaining). They did so even though league owners and officials were concerned about leaving Los Angeles without any football franchise. In fact the NFL has approved every single relocation request when the team has insisted on it: the Colts in 1984, the Cardinals in 1988, the Rams and Raiders in 1995, the Browns in 1996, and the Oilers in 1997. This has happened even though the league dutifully revised its Rule 4.3 to incorporate the kinds of relevant factors noted in *Raiders* (the level of fan attendance and team revenues, stadium quality, community support in the current location, and the value of the metropolitan area and facility in the proposed new area). The league owners reluctantly accepted Georgia Frontiere's move of the Rams to St. Louis, even though on its face this relocation reduced the level of local competition (from two teams in L.A. at that time to just one in St. Louis). NFL owners were worried enough about even a slim prospect of losing an antitrust suit—in which the damages to be trebled are now an order of magnitude higher than they were in *Raiders*—that they would not take such a risk even to protect fans as loyal as the denizens of the Dawg Pound in Cleveland.

Tampa Bay Woos the Giants

The Raiders' move in the 1980s and the Browns' move in the 1990s generated both storms of popular protest and political debate and serious scholarly analyses of franchise free agency. Everyone agrees that something has to be done about the current state of the law. There is strong disagreement, though, about even the nature of the problem, let alone its appropriate solution.

The most obvious element of the problem is the emotional trauma inflicted on long-time fans of the Raiders, the Browns, the Dodgers, and other teams with which a community has identified itself. Alienating local fans may also undermine the support enjoyed by the league as a whole, as it seeks national television and merchandising markets that include territories abandoned by such teams. On the flip side of the coin are the sports devotees in regions where an owner has finally brought them the big league club they had long hoped for—as the Oilers' Bud Adams recently did for Tennessee football fans and the Dodgers' Walter O'Malley originally did for Southern California baseball fans. In the 1990s the interests and concerns of taxpayers in both the winning and losing cities also came to the fore, since huge numbers of scarce tax dollars are now required for either attracting or keeping a team—and without even a guarantee of how long it will stick around.

Various solutions have been proposed for this sports problem. One point of view would preserve and even expand the franchise free agency rights of team owners to let the market tell them which city places the highest value on their product. The opposite position espouses the same free market sentiment but contends that the members of the league should have the authority to decide where to assign or relocate the franchises in their joint venture, free of outside legal scrutiny by judges and juries. A more populist position places less trust in the incentives and commitments of either individual owners or leagues as a whole, especially when it comes to protecting the financial and emotional investments made by communities in "their" teams. Congressional advocates of this position have introduced numerous bills that would give leagues control over teams' relocation, but would allow such relocation only if it complied with a list of objective standards that certainly were not satisfied when the Raiders left Oakland or the Browns left Cleveland, and that were quite doubtful in the other NFL (though not necessarily the NHL) moves in the 1990s.

In appraising these options for reform of sports law, we should be conscious that the prospect of an antitrust claim was just one aspect of a significantly larger social and economic problem in sports. Another sports controversy that arose in the early 1990s allows us to see what happens when owners assume they are *not* governed by antitrust. This was when the baseball Giants nearly moved from San Francisco to the Tampa Bay area.

The Giants had come from New York to the San Francisco Bay area in the late 1950s. Unlike Walter O'Malley with his Dodgers, the Giants' owner Horace Stoneham had the citizens of San Francisco build him a $20 million Candlestick Park. Candlestick was located on a beautiful site on the bay, but one that was often in a pocket of uncomfortably cool and wet weather, especially during the summer baseball season. Over the next three decades the team performed erratically both on the field and at the box office. In spite of the presence of such all-time greats as Willie Mays, Willie McCovey, and Juan Marichal, the Giants often fared poorly in competing for fan support with their American League rival in that metropolitan region—the Athletics, who had moved to Oakland in the late 1960s.

After Reggie Jackson, Catfish Hunter, and their A's teammates had won three World Series in a row in the mid-1970s, Stoneham came close to selling the Giants to Labatts Brewing, which planned to move the team to Toronto. But a white knight in the form of the San Francisco financier Robert Lurie came forward with $8 million and a vow to keep the team in his home city. Lurie's Giants also had their ups and downs, the downs culminating in the loss of the 1989 World Series to the Athletics—in a four-game sweep that was punctuated by an earthquake during the first game at Candlestick. On the stadium side, Lurie also lost four voter referenda for public funding of a new facility in the area. Finally he decided to sell the Giants, with no restraints on where the buyer would locate the team.

The sole attractive bid came from Tampa Bay, an area that had been pursuing a major league baseball team for a decade. The original Tampa Bay Baseball Group, headed by the local businessman Frank Morsani, had engaged in serious discussions about buying the Minnesota Twins in 1984, the Oakland A's in 1985, the Texas Rangers in 1988, and the Seattle Mariners in 1991. In tandem with that effort by the business community, the city of St. Petersburg in the Tampa Bay region erected a $140 million stadium, the Suncoast Dome, on the theory "build it and they will come." The city officials did this even though MLB Commissioner Peter Ueberroth had emphatically asked them not to make this huge speculative investment.

Tampa Bay had come closest to acquiring a franchise with the Chicago White Sox and their principal owners, Jerry Reinsdorf and Eddie Einhorn. In the mid-1980s the Sox were pressing the city and the state to build a new stadium to replace the old Comiskey Park, which was especially unattractive by comparison with the charming Wrigley Field in north Chicago that was regularly filled by fans of the lowly Cubs. Reinsdorf and Einhorn were reluctant to take the White Sox out of the city, in part because such a move would probably cost Reinsdorf his new role as managing partner of the Chicago Bulls. However, the two signed a tentative agreement to move to the Suncoast Dome and become the first big league baseball team in Florida unless they secured a stadium commitment from the state of Illinois by mid-1988. Illinois Governor Jim Thompson, who had been a classmate of Reinsdorf and Einhorn at Northwestern Law School, said that he would "bleed and die" before he let the White Sox go, and was able to get the stadium funding bill passed in the middle of the night of June 30. (Governor Thompson and the House Speaker had to turn their watches back to 11:59 P.M. to satisfy the state constitutional requirement that the legislature adjourn for the year on June 30.) So the White Sox did stay in Chicago to play in a new, $150 million Comiskey Park that opened in 1991.

In 1992 Tampa Bay experienced a replay of the White Sox scenario, while across the country the San Francisco Bay area avoided a replay of the Raiders saga. Tampa Bay had just lost out in baseball's 1991 expansion finals to Miami and Denver, so its current baseball search group, headed by Vincent Naimoli, made an offer to Robert Lurie to take the Giants off his hands for $115 million, 14 times what Lurie had paid for the team 16 years earlier. Residents in the Tampa Bay area began hoping that they would finally be going to major league baseball games in the regular season, not just in spring training.

But this sale could not go through unless the Giants were allowed to move to the Suncoast Dome—a relocation that under MLB rules required the approval of three-quarters of the NL teams. Most of Lurie's fellow owners had serious reservations about the move. None of them liked the idea of leaving the #4 metropolitan market solely in the hands of the American League and its Athletics; the Dodgers did not want to lose their century-old rivalry with the Giants, initially in New York and then in California; the West Coast teams did not want to be playing their division games on the East Coast, since these would be broadcast while their local fans were still coming home from work; and the newest NL owner, Wayne Huizenga, did not want his expansion Florida Marlins to make their debut in Miami during the same season in which the well-established Giants would be moving in across the state. Emboldened by their belief that baseball was immune from antitrust, the National League rejected the Giants' proposed move to Tampa Bay by a 9–4 vote.

Unlike the Raiders' Al Davis, Lurie was not particularly perturbed by that NL decision. While events had been unrolling in Florida, a San Francisco group, headed by Safeway's Peter Magowan and including other wealthy local investors such as Charles Schwab, had offered to buy the Giants for $100 million and keep the team in San Francisco. Not only was Lurie prepared to accept an offer that was $15 million lower than the Tampa Bay price, but he even lent $10 million of the money back to the purchasers' group to facilitate the sale. Having won the Giants because of the apparent absence of franchise free agency in baseball, Magowan immediately went into the player free agent market and wooed Barry Bonds away from Pittsburgh for what was then baseball's highest-ever salary.

Meanwhile, a number of lawsuits had been filed against Major League Baseball, notwithstanding the antitrust barrier erected by the Supreme Court in *Federal Base Ball* and *Flood*. The most intriguing of these suits was filed by two of Vincent Naimoli's original partners in the Giants' deal, Vincent Piazza (father of Mike Piazza) and Vince Tirendi. The National League Ownership Committee that investigated the planned sale of the team had requested the removal of Piazza and Tirendi from the group for "security reasons," which was assumed to mean a connection to organized crime. Piazza and Tirendi sued the league for defamation and other personal torts and also for violation of antitrust law. As to the latter claim, the federal district judge delivered a potentially important ruling: *Flood* should be read as confining baseball's unique and anachronistic antitrust exemption to its player reserve system (which had certainly been the focus of *Flood*), not as encompassing the entire "business of baseball." Rather than pursue this case further, the owners settled with Piazza and Tirendi, extending to them an apology and a multi-million-dollar payment.

Roll Back *Raiders?*

Florida's attorney general dropped the state's antitrust suit as soon as Tampa Bay was granted the Devil Rays expansion franchise. Other affected individuals are, however, still pressing their antitrust claims, and so far the Florida courts have continued to utilize the *Piazza* ruling to permit these suits to proceed against MLB. As I explained in earlier chapters, there is absolutely no justification for giving baseball the unique exemption that it has long enjoyed from any antitrust scrutiny of its league-wide policies and restraints. Indeed, Congress rolled back this immunity by the Curt Flood Act of 1998, though just from suits by *major* league *players*. Not only minor league players but also the fans of both major and minor league ball still have no explicit protection from restraints of trade in baseball, even though they seem to deserve such protection even more than major league players. But to avoid any such broader congressional reversal of *Flood*, baseball spokesmen have regularly pointed to owners like Al Davis and decisions like *Raiders* as reasons that the sport should be protected against "greedy" owners' taking advantage of judicially created franchise free agency to extract huge stadium subsidies from taxpayers.

So even if the Supreme Court were to endorse *Piazza* or the Congress to override *Flood* entirely, the essential question remains of whether there should be any antitrust liability when a baseball (or other) league blocks a team like the Giants from moving to a community like Tampa Bay. Or, to put it another way, should the Court or Congress roll back *Raiders* as well as *Flood*?

It is important to note that the Giants' situation did not involve one key brand of market competition that the court found—questionably—to have been restrained in *Raiders*. Like the Raiders, the Giants were leaving a San Francisco Bay area that had two baseball teams; but unlike the Raiders' move to Los Angeles, which already had the Rams, the Giants' planned move was to Tampa Bay, where they would be the only MLB team. (It would be a real stretch to include the Miami-based Marlins in a statewide baseball market, but even if a court did so, the Giants would be leaving behind intrastate competition from the Dodgers, the Angels, and the Padres in southern California.) So to the extent that the antitrust value in franchise movement is securing or preserving team competition within local markets, the National League decision to block the Giants' move to Florida would have enhanced rather than reduced that brand of sports competition. The opposite effect was generated by the NFL's decision to let the Rams leave the Los Angeles football market—in which the Raiders were still playing—and go to a vacant St. Louis. With the sole exception of the Browns' move from single-team Cleveland to Baltimore (very close to the Redskins), the other recent team moves have been neutral in terms of that local-competition factor: they have all been from a one-team city (like the NFL Oilers in Houston and the NHL Whalers in Hartford) to another one-team city that seemed financially more attractive (Nashville for the Oilers and Raleigh-Durham for the Whalers).

The standard reading of *Raiders,* however, is that the court also wanted to protect competitive bidding by cities and their stadium authorities for scarce teams in a national market. In other words, St. Petersburg with its Suncoast Dome and St. Louis with its new TWA Stadium should enjoy the same right that Los Angeles and its Coliseum secured in *Raiders:* to seduce the Giants and the Rams respectively by offering them better deals than they had at Candlestick Park and Anaheim Stadium. The presence of the NL bar to the Giants' move and the absence of an NFL bar to the Rams' move had a clear-cut effect on their respective franchise values: the Giants' Lurie had to settle for $15 million less from a San Francisco purchaser than he had been offered by the Tampa Bay group, while *Financial World* found the value of Georgia Frontiere's Rams to have jumped by $90 million immediately after their move.

These eye-opening financial figures illustrate why an agreement among league owners to place an obstacle in the way of one of their members' engineering a better stadium deal is *not* the type of anti-competitive harm that antitrust law should prohibit in the sports world. In the aftermath of *Raiders,* individual team owners have seen their franchise values soar, to a considerable extent because more and more owners have been able to exact huge stadium premiums from local taxpayers—most of them from the teams' home communities, which have felt forced to outbid other cities that have tried to woo their teams away. There is probably no other legal example in the entire marketplace that is farther away from the core aim of antitrust policy: preventing groups of producers from bonding together so as to enhance their market power at the expense of consumers (or workers or other suppliers). Fans and taxpayers would be somewhat better off if the league had both clear authority and responsibility to decide whether a particular franchise relocation was in the best interests of the game—viewed by owners as a group, not merely by the individual owner who would be the principal beneficiary. As Senator Arlen Spector proposed in his 1999 Stadium Financing and Franchise Relocation Act, *Raiders* should be reversed.

Can Franchise Movement Enhance Sports for Fans?

We should not be under the illusion that giving legal authority over franchise relocation back to the leagues would produce a sharp reduction in team movement. Well before the *Raiders* decision apparently created free agency for individual owners, teams had been moving with the approval of their fellow owners.

It was always common for a team to shift to a new city in the early days of a league. When the NBA was at that development stage in the 1950s, it saw several teams move, as well as other teams fold. Most of the relocations were from smaller cities like Fort Wayne to larger metropolitan areas like Detroit that had become excited about pro basketball. In that same period, though, the long-established baseball leagues, in which there had not been a single team relocation for 50 years, were about to witness 10 such moves in two decades. This phenomenon may have been facilitated by a 1953 amendment to MLB relocation rules that required a three-quarters, rather than unanimous, vote of approval by fellow owners. The baseball emigration waves began with the shift of the Braves from Boston to Milwaukee, the Browns from St. Louis to Baltimore (renamed the Orioles), and the Athletics from Philadelphia to Kansas City. In each of these situations the losing city kept its better-performing, more popular club (the Red Sox, the Cardinals, and the Phillies). Even losing the Dodgers and the Giants left New York with the Yankees, who were winning most of the World Series in that era. By contrast, most of the moves in the 1960s came from single-team cities (now including Milwaukee, where the Braves had done very well) to other cities (here Atlanta, where long-term prospects seemed even more promising). In the early 1970s baseball's last relocation saw Washington lose its Senators for the second time, to Dallas–Fort Worth.

This pattern was mirrored in basketball, where nine relocations took place from the early 1960s to the mid-1980s, when the teams finally stabilized in their current settings. The second-to-last NBA move, by the Clippers from San Diego to Los Angeles in 1985 (which was followed by the Kings' transplant from Kansas City to Sacramento in 1986), was the only relocation that had not been approved in advance by the league. The trend in the NHL was just the reverse. From the late 1920s until the early 1990s there were only four team moves—two of them by the Devils on their way to New Jersey—but that tally was matched in the next five years, all with the endorsement of the league. The principal impact of the *Raiders* decision appears to have fallen on the NFL. After the league had stabilized in the early 1950s, only one franchise shift occurred over the next 30 years: the Cardinals went from Chicago to St. Louis. But six more owners have now followed the trail blazed by Al Davis (including the Bidwell family's Cardinals' going on to Phoenix) and moved their teams to new, smaller-market sites, something their fellow owners have accepted only reluctantly.

Putting the current controversies in that historical context makes it clear that player free agency has had very little to do with franchise movement. The vast majority of the moves in baseball, including the Dodgers' migration to Los Angeles, took place before players even had a union, let alone free agency, and at a time when average salaries were in the $10,000–$15,000 range and made up less than 30 percent of team budgets. Even now, football, in which so many teams have moved, enjoys a *hard* salary cap, whereas basketball, with no recent moves, still has a rather *soft* one. In fact, the major explanation for the divergence of franchise and league positions on team relocation in football (by contrast with hockey, for example) is the nature and breadth of NFL revenue sharing (see Chapter 18).

That same historical perspective helps explain why the vast majority of the sports reform proposals introduced in Congress not only would formally confirm the authority of the league over team relocation but also would require league standards and procedures that would make league approval difficult to obtain. In effect, franchise shifts would be reserved for cases in which the home site displayed a serious lack of fan and community support for the team, after taking account of its performance on the field. It is easy to understand the popular and political support for imposing such conditions on team moves, considering the bitter disappointment of fans in Oakland and Cleveland, for example, when their beloved teams deserted their long-time homes. Nevertheless, such judicial or administrative supervision of leagues' judgments on this score is probably misguided—principally because it stresses the interests of the fans at risk of losing a team and largely ignores the interests of fans who would benefit from gaining a team.

Allowing teams to move serves overall consumer welfare in a number of ways. Recall that professional team sports originated in the northeastern quadrant of the United States, dominant at that time in both popula-

tion and economic activity. But after World War II the country and the
economy began to move west, and after the Vietnam War they also
moved south—and sports franchises have followed suit. That is why
New York should not have had the legal right to block its Giants from
moving to San Francisco, or Cleveland the right to stop the Rams from
relocating to Los Angeles. Likewise, San Francisco and Los Angeles
should not be empowered to bar any of their teams from moving to
places like Tampa Bay and St. Louis. Ultimately the decisions about
shifts in team location should turn on the league's judgment about what
makes the most sense for the continuing evolution of its sport in response to changes in population and fan interest.

The Giants' story had an unusually happy ending for all sides. In 1995
Major League Baseball granted the Tampa Bay area an expansion franchise: the Devil Rays. Naimoli and his group paid MLB $130 million for
the team to play in the Suncoast Dome, and the Devil Rays began play
in 1998, after baseball's fierce labor struggles had ended (for a while).
Meanwhile, the Giants' owner Magowan agreed in 1997 to spend $300
million—20 times more than the $15 million "discount" he had secured
in buying the team after the league had nixed the move to Florida—to
construct a new San Francisco stadium, which will be the first privately
built ballpark since Dodgers Stadium.

I do want to underscore that overturning *Raiders* would achieve only a
modest improvement in the current state of franchise free agency. As the
Chicago White Sox case illustrates, baseball owners have long threatened to move to vacant sites like Tampa Bay, in order to get the taxpayers
to pick up the bill for expensive new facilities. In the late 1990s baseball
and its commissioner, Bud Selig, conveyed that warning—pay or risk
losing your team—to voters and politicians in San Diego, Pittsburgh,
and elsewhere, to persuade them to approve new publicly built ballparks
for their teams. Protecting taxpayers from this kind of extortion by owners has to be done through public finance law, and we are about to discover how.

16

STADIUM SOCIALISM OR A STADIUM CAP?

As we have seen, the true problem of franchise free agency is not the fact that a city is losing its team, because its loss is another city's corresponding gain. The test of whether a particular move secures a net benefit for the sport and its fans is whether the level of interest is significantly higher and better located at the new site than at the current one. The real sports problem stems from team movements (or threats to move) that are intended to force taxpayers to build new and expensive facilities for the profit of the team owners. Giving the league clear legal authority over team relocation would provide something of a hurdle to that social harm. The most unseemly cases (like those of the Raiders and the Browns) would be blocked by a league that did not want to risk such harm to the integrity and appeal of its sport.

But overturning *Raiders* is by no means a sufficient response to what took place in the 1990s, when approximately $11 billion of taxpayers' money was spent on new sports facilities that offered huge financial benefits to the owners (and their players). It would be naive to expect owners as a group to prevent one of their individual partners from making a credible threat to move unless such a facility is built for his team: after all, this is a role each owner already has played or is likely to play in the future. The only way to protect American taxpayers from a replay of the 1990s is through collective action on our part—via elected representatives who focus on public finance and tax policy, rather than on antitrust law.

The Federal Tax Subsidy for Stadiums

Until recently only insiders were aware of the most egregious feature of the current regime—the fact that taxpayers in Cleveland, for example, made a significant contribution to the erection of the new stadium in Baltimore that lured the Browns away from their birthplace.

The source of that contribution is a long-standing federal policy that exempts from federal taxes the interest paid to purchasers of bonds issued by state and local governments to finance their policy objectives. This tax rule means that the interest that must be paid on state and local bonds is lower than that on commercial bonds because the after-tax return to investors (especially those at the top of the income scale) is higher. To give a rough estimate of the magnitude of this federal contribution to a stadium or arena that is funded by state or local bonds, if the total facility costs $300 million and the bond term is 30 years, the federal revenues lost on the tax-free interest will be $60–$120 million (depending on whether the interest gap between public and commercial bonds is closer to two or four percentage points at the time). And of course the federal tax revenues lost from this part of the financial market must be made up for in Washington by increases in other taxes or cuts in public benefits.

Until 1986 public borrowing for sports facilities was routinely included in this category of tax-exempt bonds. Indeed, some facilities (including Texas Stadium, home of the Dallas Cowboys) were financed with public bonds in order to lower their capital costs, even though under the terms of the facility leases the bonds were effectively paid off from revenues generated by the team (not only through seat sales but also from concessions, luxury suites, and the like). In 1986 Congress passed and President Reagan signed a major Tax Reform Act intended to cut back sharply on general tax rates (such as reducing the top income tax rate from 50 to 28 percent) by eliminating a host of tax loopholes. One of these loopholes was the sports facility bond. After 1986 such a stadium bond could be tax-free only if no more than 10 percent of the facility's *use* was by private actors or if no more than 10 percent of its *debt service* (both interest and principal payments) came from the facility's revenues.

Ironically, a key author of this tax reform bill was then-Senator Bill Bradley, who had once been a Rhodes Scholar at Oxford as well as a Princeton and New York Knicks basketball star. What Bradley and his co-sponsors did not realize was that the more and more popular sports teams would still be able to force local governments to issue these bonds, and then sign leases that allocated at least 90 percent of the revenues derived from the facility (from non-sports as well as sports uses) to their teams in order to qualify for the lower financial costs of tax-free bonds. That is how Cleveland taxpayers helped pay for the new Baltimore home of the Browns-turned-Ravens (and Baltimore taxpayers reciprocated for Cleveland's new Jacobs Field for the Indians and Gund Arena for the Cavaliers). It is also how taxpayers in the Dakotas, who have no team in any major league sport, are contributing to the $15 billion worth of new facilities built in Cleveland, Baltimore, and elsewhere around the country.

In his final term in office in the late 1990s, New York Senator Pat Moynihan tried to persuade Congress to enact a new Stop Tax-Exempt Arena Debt Issuance Act (STADIA) that would remove from "qualified" tax-free status any bonds issued for erection or renovation of a "professional sports facility" that would cost more than $5 million. That proposal faced a federalism problem: it seemed to intrude on the autonomy of state and local governments to decide what kinds of public investments they wanted to finance with tax-exempt bonds.

The more sensible approach would be to remove the 10 percent cap on stadium revenues used to repay the bonds, which would give cities the freedom to extract a greater share of that money from the team—to the extent that they have the leverage to do so. But these financial instruments should then be included in the broader category of bonds for "private activities" that qualify for tax-exempt status, a category for which the federal government imposes a cap on each state. This more flexible federal approach would require politicians and voters in each state to decide whether they wanted to spend a given year's tax-free bond amount on building a stadium or arena for a team, or on Industrial Development Bonds (IDBs) for small firms, or on mortgages for first-time homebuyers, or on other public investments in "private activities." Whatever judgments states or local communities made on this score, such a measure would mean that federal taxpayers around the country would no longer face an unlimited bill for subsidizing investments that individual cities chose to make in their sports teams.

Should state and local governments invest their own taxpayers' dollars, as well as their limited shares of this federal tax subsidy, in sports facilities rather than in other "private activities" (such as IDBs), or in public schools, parks, and the like? For example, should the citizens of Seattle and its surrounding areas have contributed $750 million to new facilities for the Seahawks, Mariners, and Supersonics? Certainly the principal motivating factor behind such sports investment is the popular and political pleasure gained from having a big league team in one's home town. Only a small proportion of residents actually go to watch games, by comparison, for example, with movies. These games, however, get far more attention than movies on television and in the newspapers, and the team typically makes a significant contribution to the community's sense of identity.

Still, opinion polls usually indicate that a majority of the affected population does not approve of their government paying for an expensive facility for a professional team. Yet most referenda pass anyway, though almost always by a very narrow margin with low voter turnout; predictably, fans with an intense interest in getting or keeping a team are much more likely to take the time to go out and vote. Such stadium projects are almost always strongly supported by politicians and the business community, and usually by the media. Indeed, even if the referendum loses (as it did in Seattle in 1995 and Pittsburgh in 1997), the local powers that be may simply devise another measure for channeling public funds to the project. And the proponents of such an investment justify it by claiming that it will confer a large economic (as well as emotional and cultural) benefit upon the city—and thus will more than pay back the amount the city has to spend.

In evaluating this economic argument, we need to appreciate the scope and dimensions of financial expenditures on a sports facility. The cost items include the capital investment in assembling the land, preparing the infrastructure (including special access roads), and erecting the building, as well as the continuing expenses of operation, maintenance, and renovation. A new $300 million facility requires approximately $25–$30 million a year for interest payments, amortization of the bond, and regular operating and maintenance expenses. In a metropolitan area of 2–3 million people, this sum amounts to $30–$50 a year paid by the average four-person family. If a city such as Seattle or Cleveland does this for separate baseball and football stadiums, as well as for a two-sport arena, the family's cost is over $100 a year. Why should the typical working middle-class family be asked to make even such a modest contribution to a venture whose immediate beneficiaries are wealthy team owners (and their players)?

One possible answer lies in what took place in Atlanta, where more than $500 million was spent on new facilities for staging the 1996 Olympic Games. Those expenditures made economic sense because the city's Olympic authority received even more than that amount in its direct share of the gate receipts, parking, concessions, and worldwide television and sponsorship deals for those Games. But in the present-day world of professional sports, the team keeps almost all of these revenue streams and pays little or no rent for the facility, which must then be paid for from the general tax budget. The standard rationale offered for these public expenditures is that the presence of a major league team creates a whirlpool with a ripple effect on the regional economy. This, in turn, brings in additional tax revenue for the community that more than matches its up-front investment. These are the key components of that argument:

- Operation of the team is a significant business activity that generates a host of jobs, salaries, and income taxes, with a further multiplier effect as the highly paid players and other team employees spend their earnings in the region.
- Staging the games has a significant spillover effect, because many fans go to lunch or dinner before or shopping or to nightclubs after the game.
- The games draw tourists to visit the city, rent cars or use taxis, stay in hotels and eat their meals in surrounding restaurants, shop in the city's stores, and add to its overall attraction and economic performance (the most-used example of this is Camden Yards in Baltimore).
- The mere presence of a major league team attracts owners and executives of non-sports businesses, who will choose to locate in a major league city where they will be able to watch their favorite sport.

At first blush, all these points seem quite plausible. In fact the usual prelude to the vote on a stadium or arena tax is a document prepared by a management consulting company which provides the numbers to demonstrate that the facility will more than pay for itself in greater business activity and government revenues. If there is one proposition, though, that sports economists all agree upon, it is that this "spin-off benefit" argument is *dead wrong*. These are the fundamental misconceptions that have been identified:

- Sports teams are actually small businesses, with average annual revenues ranging from $40 million in hockey to $100 million in football—less than the revenues generated by a single Wal-Mart store, let alone a Ford or Boeing manufacturing plant.
- As for the income taxes paid on the $25–$60 million average team payrolls, no one would suggest that the state and local income taxes paid by employees of a new Wal-Mart store should be treated as *extra* revenue for the government, which could be used to build and pay for the store. After all, the purpose of taxes is to provide such public services as police and fire protection, education for children, and highways and subways for travel, all of which are available for use by the store's employees along with everyone else. Surely the local government should not give players, coaches, and other team personnel a "free ride" on the same public services (which sometimes may have to address crimes by, rather than against, players) by reserving their payroll taxes to pay for a luxurious new team facility. After all, it is this financial subsidy that helps put even larger salaries in the pockets of the players, as well as sharply increase the profits and franchise value for the owner.
- The same aggregate payroll level in a Wal-Mart store would actually generate a somewhat greater spillover effect than the one created by the team's payroll. The vast majority of sports salary money is paid to players, coaches, and a few executives, while other employees work in low-paying, often part-time, jobs such as selling tickets and concessions or cleaning the seats and the field. Because of this much more unequal payroll distribution, the federal government takes a higher tax share of the overall salaries of employees of sports franchises than of department stores, the players save and invest a much higher proportion of their annual income for their post-sports lives, and much of their immediate expenditure occurs outside the team's home city—often in another community that is the player's permanent home.
- Few tourists actually come to a city and stay in its hotels simply to see a game. Almost all football, basketball, and hockey seats are bought by season-ticket holders, and a large majority of baseball tickets are bought by local residents. Visitors to the city may attend games, but they usually do so as the guests of family, friends, or businesses they would be visiting even if there was no game.

- Even visitors who come from out of town to go to games (say, from Washington, D.C., to Baltimore to see the Orioles play at Camden Yards) typically behave like local residents and do almost all their spending inside the sports facility itself rather than in the surrounding businesses. And while that is not true of football fans who go to Miami or San Diego for the Super Bowl, these fans are just a different group of tourists from those who would be going to Florida or California at that time of the year anyway.
- As for residents of the metropolitan area, who make up the overwhelming majority of fans at the regular-season games, their game-related expenditures are also not an addition to but rather a substitution for other spending. Families have limited time and money to spend on entertainment. If they cannot go to see a major league game, they may go to a minor league or college game, or to a movie, concert, or play, as well as to a restaurant or bar near that event. The presence of a team does influence where people will spend their entertainment budget, but not how large this budget will be.

In sum, a major league sports franchise may well be a big part of a community's social life, but it is only a tiny part of its economic life. The typical sports franchise is a small ($80 million) business with little multiplier effect, which cannot possibly generate the additional $25–$30 million a year to pay for and maintain a luxurious sports facility. Indeed, when we take into account the "dead-weight business loss" engendered by the higher taxes (especially sales taxes) needed to pay for the facility, the real economic result of such a public sports subsidy may well be to *reduce* rather than *enhance* business activity in the region. If the government wants to spend tax dollars on a site for spectator sports, it can justify doing so only as an investment in community leisure and pleasure—like building a public park.

Needless to say, there is an important difference between New York's building historic Central Park and building a new Yankee Stadium for the Yankees and a new Ebbets Field for the Mets. Anyone who wants to walk around and relax in a public park can enjoy this pleasure for free. Anyone who wants to go watch the Yankees, the Mets, and other teams play in a ballpark has to buy an (often expensive) ticket to enjoy that pleasure.

Of course, an even larger number of fans watch games on television without having to pay for a ticket. They also regularly read about the games in the newspaper sports pages and talk about their favorite team's performance with family at home and friends at work. And if the hometown team makes it to the World Series or the Super Bowl, the resulting community exhilaration extends far beyond the regular fans. These public benefits might seem, then, to warrant public expenditures on a facility that makes the games possible.

But here too there is more fallacy than accuracy. First, the people who watch games on television do pay for that privilege, either through advertising costs added to the prices of products that appear in commercials or through cable fees for the channels that now broadcast most local games (other than football). Second, people spend much the same amount of time talking to family and friends about other kinds of entertainment events—such as the appearance of a new *Star Wars* or the final episode of *Seinfeld*. Yet no one suggests that the government should help pay the $150–$200 million costs of movies like *Titanic* or *Star Wars* or the even higher costs of a TV series like *Seinfeld* or *ER*. People know that the producers of these entertainment works are large private businesses that sell the works to cover their costs and, if the works turn out to be hits, to reap large profits as well. Exactly that same policy judgment should have been made when Time Warner's Ted Turner went to the city of Atlanta asking it to "donate" a $200 million Olympic facility (now renamed Turner Stadium) to his Braves, or when Microsoft's Paul Allen secured the huge stadium subsidy for his Seattle Seahawks. Private profitability is the second big difference between a Central Park and a Yankee Stadium.

A third characteristic of professional sports that makes it even less entitled to public subsidies than movies is that even big movie hits are shown in theaters around the country at local ticket prices that range from $4 to $9, with a theater charging the same price for every seat. So any American who wanted to see a *Titanic* or a *Star Wars* could do so sitting in seats that were readily available at a very affordable price, and even more so on home video. By contrast, the vast majority of seats (and all the very good seats) at major league games are reserved for a small number of season-ticket holders, many of whom also pay a premium of up to $5,000 for the PSL to acquire those seats. The price of going to a game now averages over $45 in football, basketball, and hockey, and around $15 in baseball, which has far more seats to fill in a season than any other sport. More and more middle-class season-ticket holders must take out bank or credit card loans if they want to hold on to their family's long-time, well-located seats, whose current prices are even higher than the averages. And of course the principal reason for the $15 billion spent on construction of new facilities in the 1990s was to dedicate the best space to luxury suites and premium seats. These are occupied by truly wealthy Americans, almost all of whom write the huge rental costs off as a business expense paid for by their customers—and, to the extent this expense is deductible, by taxpayers.

This brings us to one final regressive feature of the recent surge in public stadium subsidies, which in the 1990s amounted to around $11 billion. Almost all of the financial benefits go to rich team owners and their highly paid players. The largest share of the entertainment benefits goes to well-to-do Americans who have season tickets in the very good seats and to wealthy Americans who relax in the luxury suites. However, presumably to try to preserve the image of sports as something that transcends divisions within a community, no one has ever asked voters to approve the funding of a new ballpark through a more progressive income (or capital gains) tax. Instead, the only tax that is used for this purpose is the apparently uniform but actually regressive sales tax, whether general or targeted at specific goods.

A few states have found another financial instrument that seems to avoid the negative connotations of any tax. This is the state lottery—used, for example, by Maryland to fund the building of Camden Yards for the Orioles and the Ravens Stadium that lured the Browns from Cleveland. NFL Commissioner Tagliabue has advocated that governments use this tool rather than taxes to finance expensive new facilities for football teams. True, a lottery is not a tax in the sense of a forced extraction of money from those who choose not to participate in it. But from those who are attracted (perhaps even addicted) to this kind of activity, the states do extract money: they have used their monopoly control of legal lotteries to generate a 50 percent "take" on these bets, far more than the 8 percent take of casinos or racetracks. And the bulk of lottery revenues comes from lower-income Americans, few of whom are able to go to big league games and many of whom do not even watch the games on television. Earlier, when we were examining the position taken by sports authorities toward gambling athletes like Pete Rose, we learned that gambling has become a major and rather troubling feature of present-day American life—and that this began in the early 1960s with New Hampshire's invention of a "voluntary sweepstakes tax." But to the extent that state voters believe that it leaves their community better off to raise funds for public services through this device, spending a significant part of those scarce dollars to build a ballpark rather than a public park raises exactly the same distributional concerns that we have been discussing.

Even given these concerns, it would not be fair for politicians simply to substitute a surcharge on the income tax for one on the sales tax as the source of stadium funding. Many well-to-do citizens are also not sports fans and do not want to watch—let alone pay for—games played in a local stadium. They should not have to pay to build a stadium in which committed fans watch games. And in fact the sports world has developed a feasible and fair alternative: paying for construction with revenues from the stadium itself.

The Case for a Stadium Cap

The annual cost of building and maintaining a new sports facility is now in the $25–$30 million range. Average stadium revenues alone are in that same range, and for some clubs (such as the Dallas Cowboys and the Cleveland Indians) they are twice as high, around $50 million. Stadium revenues are a team's income from the stadium over and above the basic ticket price. They include luxury suite and club seat rentals, concessions, parking, advertising, and "naming" and "pouring" rights, with the prospect of new tie-ins (such as virtual reality games featuring the players) in the near future. In fact, paying for the facility does not require anywhere near all of these revenues. As the Carolina Panthers proved in Charlotte, all the costs of construction can be covered instead by a special PSL fee charged to fans who choose to purchase the right to have season tickets for the games. Indeed, because the fans who obtain the best seats pay a higher price for that right, PSLs function as a progressive, rather than regressive, sales tax instrument.

Thus it is now perfectly feasible for the clubs that use sports facilities to build and pay for new and more attractive replacements if they believe this investment makes sense. Clear corroboration of this point can be found in the beautiful new stadium built by the U.S. Tennis Association in New York for its annual U.S. Open, which was fully paid for by the USTA out of such revenue streams as luxury suites, club seats, and attractive food courts, and was named after Arthur Ashe, not a corporate paymaster. Requiring clubs to select which part of their stadium revenue streams should be used for facility construction is also probably the best way to ensure that total construction costs are economically sound from the point of view of the fans who ultimately pay for, as well as enjoy, the facility. And because the team owner has made the up-front investment in the physical facility, there is some assurance that team moves will take place only when there is substantially greater consumer demand for the team in a new community than in the current site. There is, however, a huge practical obstacle to the use of this economically sound and fair technique in the sports world.

Once these stadium revenue sources were developed and their financial value demonstrated in the capital markets (as when the Baltimore Orioles sold for $175 million as soon as they were installed in Camden Yards), owners such as Art Modell and Georgia Frontiere used their leverage under franchise free agency to extract almost all of these revenue sources (including PSL sales) for themselves, while letting the taxpayers pick up the bill for their new stadiums. After a significant number of teams have secured these lucrative revenue streams, and have spent that money to attract the best players, who help the team win and make even more money, the other team owners feel severe economic pressure to secure similar deals from their local governments and taxpayers. Whether free agency is permitted by the law or by the league, the ability of a team's owner to extract a generous offer from another city or state seeking a scarce team places heavy pressure on the team's home town to provide a luxurious taxpayer-built facility.* The same performance-enhanc-

* That pressure is now being directed by American cities at the people in Canada. Governments in that country became much less receptive to publicly financed facilities after building the hugely expensive Montreal Olympic Stadium in the 1970s and Toronto Skydome in the 1980s. All four of Canada's major league facilities of the 1990s were privately funded: by the Montreal Canadiens, the Ottawa Senators, the Toronto Maple Leafs and Raptors, and the Vancouver Canucks and Grizzlies. In that same decade, though, Canada had the sad experience of seeing the Quebec Nordiques and Winnipeg Jets move to Denver and Phoenix respectively (with the top-flight Nordiques team quickly winning the NHL Stanley Cup as the Avalanche). There are serious risks that the Montreal Expos, Ottawa Senators, and Vancouver Grizzlies will follow suit. From the perspective of fan interest alone, one can understand why baseball's Expos might leave Montreal, where average attendance has dropped to around half of what it

ing competitive pressures in the sports world that led to the *salary cap* in the players market now require a *stadium cap* in the franchise market, to create a more level playing field for fans and taxpayers.

How do we get to a stadium cap? One way to establish this socially optimal situation—in which users pay for the facilities—would be for the league itself to place a limit on permissible taxpayer subsidies. We should assume that even the L.A. Coliseum lawyers and the *Raiders* court would not find this brand of collective self-restraint by owners to be a violation of antitrust law. The NFL has actually adopted a new "G-3" plan to lend money to large-market teams like the New England Patriots to help them pay for their own new stadiums rather than move to much smaller markets like Hartford, Connecticut, and reap the benefits of a $400 million facility taxpayers were willing to put up to lure the Patriots there. But neither the NFL nor other league owners would ever impose a broad-based cap on any taxpayer subsidies going into their pockets, any more than the players volunteered to create the salary cap.

Another theoretical possibility would be for municipalities to organize themselves into a single national body that bargains collectively for the stadium cap, just as the players and owners did to secure both free agency and the salary cap. Indeed, this kind of "stadium union" could lock the teams out of all the current public facilities (the vast majority of playing sites) until and unless the leagues agreed to this proposal. Such united—but very unlikely—municipal action would require Congress, rather than the Supreme Court, to create a sports-facility exemption from the antitrust suits that would immediately be filed by the league owners.

Pennsylvania Senator Arlen Spector recognized in his proposed Stadium Financing and Franchise Relocation Act of 1999 that simply reversing *Raiders* and restoring league authority over franchise free agency is not nearly enough to protect taxpayers such as those in his state, who

---

was in the early 1980s while overall MLB attendance has been steadily rising. But lack of fan interest certainly has not been a problem with Canada's hockey Senators and basketball Grizzlies. Thus if any such team move south of the border were to be significantly influenced by an American state or city's offer of a new taxpayer-subsidized stadium or arena, such government action would seem to constitute a violation of the principles of the North American Free Trade Act Agreement (NAFTA) between the world's biggest trade partners, which is supposed to preclude a government's conferral of such competitive advantages on its constituents within an international *private* industry.

have been forced to spend nearly one billion dollars building new stadiums for its four football and baseball teams. Thus Senator Spector (and his Republican and Democratic co-sponsors) would require the leagues themselves to contribute 50 percent of the cost of new stadiums (surprisingly, though, not of new *arenas*) from their national television deals, with the individual team owners putting up at least 25 percent and local taxpayers no more than 25 percent.

This proposal is an important political step in the right direction. In my view, though, Congress should not be telling league owners how to divide up the costs of new construction among themselves—for example, forcing the Green Bay Packers to help pay for the new stadium that the New York (actually, New Jersey) Giants are now seeking. All that Congress need do in representing American taxpayers is to pass a law that bars the use of *any* tax funds to build new facilities for professional sports. The Dodgers' Walter O'Malley, not the Rams' Georgia Frontiere, should be the owners' role model for the 21st century.

There should be one important exception to any such federal rule. A state should be able to finance a facility through a tax imposed on those who use it—on ticket prices, concessions, parking, or perhaps even local pay cable broadcasts. Any such user tax is, of course, simply a substitute for the amount that team owners would be likely to charge fans to watch the only football (or baseball, basketball, or hockey) game in town. But team owners may prefer—if only for marketing reasons—to have the government, not the team, be the apparent source of this higher price. If local politicians are prepared to absorb this reputational cost to gain a fancy new facility, the federal government should certainly allow them this freedom.

However, with respect to the tax dollars now being extracted from Americans generally (especially sales taxes that are principally paid by ordinary working Americans), it is not enough for Congress to bar only the use of federal tax subsidies for local facilities (the focus of Pat Moynihan's STADIA proposal). What we need is a national standard that will protect American taxpayers whose local governments now all face a classic Prisoner's Dilemma posed by teams' playing off one community against another. This dilemma is whether to accept the *poor* outcome of spending $300 million or more of scarce public funds to keep a team, or risk the *terrible* outcome of no team at all if another city gives in to the temptation to pay the owner that $300 million inducement to move.

Only a national standard can produce the *best* outcome of decisions about team location made on the basis of fan interest rather than taxpayer subsidies. Absent such federal action, Americans will experience (probably in the 2020s) yet another wave of stadium/arena construction to replace the $15 billion worth of facilities built in the 1990s alone.

Even those who agree that it is poor public policy for governments to spend so many tax dollars on luxurious stadiums for professional teams may be concerned about letting the federal government bar local bodies from doing what they want with their money. These doubters should appreciate that this kind of federal action would actually allow the people of America to use one arm of our government to protect ourselves from undue pressure felt by other arms of government in the current sports marketplace.

The legal reason that local governments now cannot protect themselves from that Prisoner's Dilemma is that the courts have accepted the owners' argument that states cannot use either their power of regulation (as in the case of the Braves' move from Milwaukee to Atlanta) or eminent domain (as in the Raiders' move from Oakland to Los Angeles) to block their home teams from pursuing more lucrative stadium deals elsewhere. In any event, it would be just as impossible for the taxpayers in Pittsburgh and Minneapolis–St. Paul, for example, to establish a fair stadium cap that would bind them but not their competitors in Atlanta or Baltimore, as it would be for the Pirates and the Twins to establish a team payroll cap that did not govern the Braves and the Orioles. While we can still debate the pros and cons of public stadium subsidies, we must accept the fact that if there is to be a rational public policy on this score, it must take the form of a national standard governing a sports industry that itself is intrinsically national in shape and scope.

One important question about my proposed stadium cap remains unanswered. Why should the federal government single out professional sports as the sole branch of private business that is prohibited from receiving public subsidies from local government? Actually, much of my analysis of taxpayer subsidies of the sports business also applies to other American businesses—such as auto manufacturing in the 1980s and software production in the 1990s—that have played one state off against another to secure generous public payments for locating their plants there. My personal view on this score is that Americans as a whole would be much better off if the federal government used its authority over interstate commerce to block such artificial local intervention in the private business world, intervention that confers no net benefit on the overall economy because whatever one locality may gain from its payoff another locality loses. But the special feature of the sports world that definitely requires federal action here is one we have not yet focused on: the monopoly status of the major sports leagues. This crucial aspect of the economic and legal structure of sports is what we shall be exploring in the next three chapters, before we render a final verdict on the stadium cap.

17

SPORTS IN
INTELLECTUAL SPACE

Most media coverage of off-the-field struggles in sports has focused on the battles between players and owners over player free agency, and between cities and owners over franchise free agency. These seem to be the sports wars that inflict the greatest emotional and financial damage upon both fans and taxpayers. Much less visible, but in many ways more significant, are the relations of owners with broadcasters and merchandisers. Television is by far the largest source of sports dollars, and commercial use of team and league logos is now one of the fastest-growing revenue streams. Understandably, then, pursuit of larger shares of this money pool has triggered major conflicts within the leagues—most prominently between the NFL and the Dallas Cowboys' owner Jerry Jones, and between MLB and the New York Yankees' George Steinbrenner. Just like Al Davis and Art Modell, Jones and Steinbrenner have been portrayed as greedy owners seeking to enrich their own clubs at the expense of the solidarity of their league and the quality of their sport. What people do not realize, though, is that league restraints on the ability of individual clubs to license use of their intellectual property in space are quite expensive to fans—not just to broadcasters and merchandisers—and that these restraints are the least warranted for preservation of the integrity of the game.

The New Sports Market

It is ironic that franchise free agency—the freedom of teams to move to more lucrative locations—emerged as a major sports issue in the late 20th century at a time when the physical location of teams seemed to be much less important than in the past. When professional baseball first appeared in the late nineteenth century, followed by football, hockey, and basketball in the early 20th century, it was through live attendance at the game that fans enjoyed and teams profited from the sport. The same was true in the general entertainment world—for example, at live theater and concerts.

The invention of recording and filming technology at the turn of the century transformed the economics of the entertainment industry. People could watch and listen to stories and songs without having to attend the actual performance. It took the emergence of radio in the early 1920s and television in the late 1940s to produce the same effect in sports, because games are live events that people want to experience as they are being played rather than after reading who won in the next day's newspaper. However, once broadcasting stations and networks were established, fans could cheer for their favorite teams while sitting in their homes instead of in a stadium or arena–even if they lived far from the cities where the games were played. This is what turned sports leagues into national rather than local experiences and ventures. But, as we have seen, nationalization—even internationalization—of spectator sports has intensified the passion of local residents and politicians to have their own home team, so that their community will be viewed as truly "major league."

Notwithstanding the surge in stadium revenues over the last two decades, broadcasting is by far the biggest financial feature of the sports business. Back in the early 1950s, when television was first appearing, the MLB earned less than $6 million—and the NFL less than $1 million—per season from broadcasts of games. In the early 1960s, when the leagues began negotiating national contracts with the three well-established networks, baseball's revenues from broadcasting were nearly $20 million, and football's $7 million (for the NFL and the AFL combined). By the end of the 1990s, when there were many over-the-air and cable networks, football had soared to the top, averaging $2.2 billion a year from four network contracts. Baseball was also flourishing, with its broadcast total of $900 million made up of around $350 million from Fox and ESPN national contracts and $550 million from the dozens of contracts between clubs and local stations and cable channels.

Football and baseball differed sharply in the way they distributed those revenues. The NFL's equal sharing of television revenues means that each franchise receives over $70 million a season, while baseball's

$550 million in local television contracts ranges from the Yankees and Braves at around $60 million apiece to the Royals and Expos at under $6 million.

The NBA's total broadcast revenues were as high or higher than baseball's, but considerably more evenly distributed among clubs. This is because much more of the basketball total comes from the league's national contracts with NBC and TNT/TBS, which had soared in value by the time of the 1998–99 lockout season. The NHL was still far behind the other sports, especially in its $50 million national contracts with Fox and ESPN for the 1998–99 season. However, because of the considerable progress hockey had made since its mid-1990s lockout, and with even more expected after the expansion and relocation of clubs to the southern and western regions of the United States, ABC and ESPN agreed to pay the league $120 million beginning with the 1999–2000 season.

Merchandising became a source of revenue for sports (as well as movie studios) in the 1960s. Teams and players grant licenses for the use of their name, logo, and image for display on clothes, shoes, glasses, and other merchandise, or in advertisements for these and a host of other consumer goods that sports fans are likely to buy and enjoy. The players were the sports pioneers in this area: individuals like Arnold Palmer endorsing golf clubs and clothes, and the MLB Players Association granting collective licenses from all its members for their display on baseball cards and the like. In the 1970s teams began to follow suit, with league organizations (such as NFL Properties) eventually controlling almost all of the licensing. Of the $70 billion in annual sales of licensed merchandise in the late 1990s, sports accounted for $16 billion, second only to entertainment at $17 billion. The NFL led the leagues at $3.5 billion in sales, with the NBA close behind. Of these sales figures, approximately 7–8 percent is paid to the leagues, clubs, and players for licensing use of their names and logos on the product or in the commercial. The approximately $250 million earned by NFL Properties is first used to fund league operations and then divided equally among the clubs (the same is true in the other sports). By contrast, players keep all the revenues from their individual licensing deals—now totaling more than $550 million annually. Throughout the 1990s Michael Jordan was the leader at more than $40 million a year, with Tiger Woods second at around $25 million.

It was precisely this contrast between owners' and players' rewards for their individual merchandising value that led to the Dallas Cowboys' owner Jerry Jones to condemn the NFL system as far too "socialistic," and to picture himself as America's Gorbachev who would bring capitalism back to sports. In 1982 Clint Murchison, Jones's predecessor as owner of the Cowboys, had agreed with the other clubs to assign all team names and logos to an NFL Trust, which in turn gave NFL Properties the exclusive authority to license use of all club as well as league marks. A decade later Jones lamented the fact that his Cowboys, "America's Team," were generating 30 percent of NFL merchandising sales but were collecting just one-thirtieth of what he believed to be far too low a total return. While teams like the Packers and the 49ers also generated substantial shares of total league sales, they received no more than the Buccaneers or the Oilers, whose sales were then just a fraction of one percent of the total. Among the many merchandising deals made by NFL Properties were agreements with Reebok, Coca-Cola, and Visa that gave them exclusive rights to use all NFL club identities in their product areas. In the summer of 1995, though, Jones (through his marketing arm, Pro Silver Star) sold to Nike, Pepsi, and American Express the sponsorship and advertising rights in Texas Stadium, where the Cowboys played their home games.

Jones's well-publicized actions produced an immediate $300 million lawsuit by NFL Properties, claiming that they violated the letter as well as the spirit of the Cowboys' agreement with NFL Trust. Jones defended his actions on the grounds that the identity of Texas Stadium was qualitatively different from that of the Cowboys—though the stadium logo just happened to have on it the phrase "Home of America's Favorite Team." He also filed a $750 million countersuit against the league and his fellow owners, asserting that when the clubs agreed to permit only a single merchandising arm to do all the licensing for all the clubs, this amounted to an illegal restraint of trade under antitrust law. By the end of 1996 both Jones and NFL Commissioner Tagliabue had decided that it was in their best interests to drop their respective suits: this preserved the core of NFL Properties' domain, while allowing a few clubs to exploit potential loopholes in it.

Early 1997 saw a similar controversy arise in baseball, when George Steinbrenner's Yankees secured a 10-year, $95 million sponsorship agreement with Adidas. In baseball individual teams did retain some merchandising autonomy within their own "Home Licensing Territory," though far less than in their home *broadcasting* territory. When the MLB executive council sought to place some significant limits on the scope of the Yankees-Adidas contract, the Yankees went to court not just to contest the specific issues but to challenge the whole baseball system under antitrust law. Again, this suit was amicably settled early in the Yankees' great 1998 season, with neither side wanting to undermine the current status of the game in the merchandising market.

A longer-lasting dispute between the NBA and the Chicago Bulls did require the court to address—though not ultimately resolve—the key legal issues. This legal battle was triggered by an early-1990s decision by NBA owners to cut back (and later to eliminate) the number of games by Jerry Reinsdorf's (and Michael Jordan's) Bulls that could be broadcast on the Chicago station WGN; the reason was that WGN had become a superstation carried across the country.

Superstations emerged as a key feature of the television world in the late 1970s, following HBO's development of a satellite distribution system that made it feasible for local cable systems to carry programs appearing on national cable channels, not just on over-the-air stations in the local area. Ted Turner, who had just bought the Atlanta Braves in baseball and the Hawks in basketball, also owned WTBS, a local independent station in that city. Turner hit on the idea of having his local signals transmitted by satellite to cable systems around the country, which could then show their viewers baseball games via the Braves, and basketball via the Hawks. Even better, the satellite (and legal) system permitted WTBS to carry local advertising on the signals reaching Atlanta over the air, but much more expensive national broadcasting on its cable signals covering the country.

Atlanta's WTBS was soon followed by New York's WWOR (with the Mets and Nets) and then by Chicago's WGN (with the Cubs and Bulls). By the 1990s, when Michael Jordan, Scottie Pippen, and Dennis Rodman made the Bulls the best and most popular team in basketball, the other NBA owners became concerned about the effect of Bulls broadcasts both on national NBA contracts (now not just on NBC but also on Turner's TNT and WTBS) and on each team's local contracts in its home territory. The NBA first placed a 20-game cap on "superstation" broadcasts, and a couple of years later barred them altogether. The Bulls and the Nets were the lone dissenters, since the Hawks' Ted Turner now had national contracts with the NBA to carry games on his TNT and WTBS. The Bulls and WGN filed suit against the NBA, and this litigation has produced as voluminous a body of rulings as *Raiders*. While much more sophisticated in its analysis than the *Raiders* panel, the *WGN* court is still undecided about this area of sports law.

Intellectual Property Underpinnings

Before tackling the question of whether the NBA's restraints on the Bulls (or MLB's limits on the Yankees or the NFL's on the Cowboys) square with antitrust doctrine and public policy toward sports, it is useful to explore at least briefly the legal underpinnings of the rights asserted by the Bulls (or Yankees or Cowboys) in the first place. Why should the Bulls be able to extract any payments from cable viewers, or the Yankees and Jones from buyers of athletic clothing, for enjoying the teams' games and names?

There are no inherent *physical* limits to how many people can enjoy a single game or team name in intellectual space. While only 20,000 or so people can fit into the seats in the United Center to watch the Bulls play in person, the fact that one family tunes its television set to WGN to watch the game creates absolutely no obstacle to millions of other families who want to do the same thing. So also, if one person is wearing a T-shirt adorned with the Cowboys or Texas Stadium logo, this does not keep other people around the country (or around the world) from wearing the same adornments. When the Boston Marathon had its 100th anniversary on the streets of Greater Boston in 1996, all the television stations in the area were able to send over the air the pictures they filmed beside the road or from above via helicopters. And while there are physical limits to how many broadcasters can fit into United Arena to film a Bulls game, once WGN has sent its signals up into the air, any number of cable services and viewers can draw that picture down with the appropriate satellite dish technology.

But there is a *legal* limit: an elaborate body of law that confers private property rights on these otherwise public intellectual goods. The core of this legal regime has an obvious and compelling rationale. Major upfront investments are required to write a book, make a movie or recording, or produce and transmit a television program. Such investments make sense only if the authors of such creative works can realistically expect to be paid by their ultimate readers, viewers, or listeners. If other people can simply swoop in and take the contents of this work through a form of intellectual piracy, they can sell it at much lower prices that do not reflect the original creative investment. Such a result is grossly unfair to the original authors because it deprives them of a return on their efforts. It also is eventually harmful to consumers, because far fewer works will be made in the future. That is why the United States and all other industrialized countries have created and conferred intellectual property rights on the authors of creative works, which allow the authors to determine who can distribute or view the work in question and at what price.

Sports events themselves are not "authored" for purposes of this branch of the law. However much planning and practice takes place beforehand, a football or basketball game is a competitive event, not a scripted play. Even the carefully crafted routines of a figure skater cannot be copyrighted to block others doing the same thing at the Olympic Games. Nor is what takes place at the game the exclusive property of its participants. Sportswriters and newscasters have as much right to say who won a horse race and why as they have with a political race. It is only these creative depictions and descriptions of the game that are protected by the law.

At about the same time that radio sets were appearing in homes across the country, Ronald Reagan was beginning his first career—as a Des Moines broadcaster of baseball games played by the Chicago Cubs and White Sox. The technique Reagan used was to sit beside a Western Union telegraph receiving agent who would hand him a piece of paper stating, for example, "#12, out, 4–3." Young Reagan would then vividly describe to his listeners how the Cubs second baseman had fielded a hard-hit ground ball and just barely thrown the Cardinals hitter out at first. In his presidential autobiography Reagan recalled a challenge he had faced when the telegraph receiver suddenly went dead during a game. Reagan slowly recounted what ended up as the all-time record in foul balls, until finally the receiver went back on—with news that the batter had grounded out on the first pitch.

By the late 1930s, when Reagan had gone off to Hollywood for his second career as a movie star (and then as a *liberal* labor leader), the lower courts had moved in to give baseball teams, boxing promoters, and other sports bodies the legal right to block such "unfair competition" through "misappropriation" of their live games. Three decades later the courts also created and conferred on teams—and players—the exclusive right to determine who could use their names and identities, not just their games. In the case of players, judges took a branch of the common law termed *privacy*, rights that were designed to protect individuals from the emotional distress of seeing their persons and lives inappropriately displayed in public, and expanded it into a branch of law now called *publicity*: an affirmative right to license (often for huge fees) the use of celebrities' names and likenesses in commercials or on products.

This publicity branch of the law began with a 1950s sports case, one that ruled that baseball players had a property right in use of their names, pictures, and statistics on baseball cards that were sold with packages of chewing gum. It had reached such a state by the late 1990s that an appeals court allowed Kareem Abdul-Jabbar to sue General Motors over a commercial aired during the 1993 NCAA Final Four which celebrated the fact that Oldsmobile had just been selected by *Consumers Digest* as its Best Car Buy for the third year in a row. As lead-in to this commercial, viewers were asked, "Who holds the record for being voted the MVP in the [NCAA] tournament three times in a row?" The answer on the screen was UCLA's Lew Alcindor from 1967 through 1969; this had happened before Alcindor changed his name to Kareem Abdul-Jabbar and went on to basketball's Hall of Fame with the Bucks and the Lakers. Indeed, Kareem Abdul-Jabbar not only sued GM for using his old name for commercial reasons but also sued and blocked the Miami Dolphins' Karim Abdul-Jabbar from using his current name in endorsement deals. This was a name that Sharman Shah had adopted in 1995 while a star running back at UCLA, for what Karim said were the same Muslim religious reasons that had moved Kareem to change his name. And Tiger Woods has followed Abdul-Jabbar's lead and sued an artist for putting Tiger and his graceful golf swing in the foreground of an artwork called "The Masters of Augusta."

The courts later conferred a similar windfall on teams (and entertainment firms) by expanding the scope and use of federal *trademark* law. The original aim of this body of law was to allow the producers of goods and services that had become identified with a particular name (such as Oldsmobile or Coca-Cola) to block other companies from putting that name or logo on their product in ways that might confuse consumers about who had created the products they were thinking about buying.

The immediate protection of consumers from such product deception would also encourage competitors to create equally high-quality products with their own identifiable brand names.

That is why Nike, for example, is and should be able to block a new sports-apparel company from attaching to its products Nike's famous "swoosh" symbol of the "winged victory." What is not so clear is why the Cowboys (or the NFL) should be able to block Nike or Reebok or Adidas from attaching the symbols of the Cowboys to those same pieces of clothing. The legal answer stems from a decision of the Fifth Circuit, one that granted the Boston Bruins and other NHL teams an injunction against a company that was manufacturing and selling embroidered emblems with team names and logos, which hockey fans could sew onto their own clothes. The court said it was not enough that the emblems carried an explicit disclaimer of any authorization or sponsorship by the teams. While the circuit court acknowledged that its decision "may slightly tilt the trademark law from the purpose of protecting the public to the protection of the business interests of [NHL] clubs," it concluded that even if purchasers knew they were not buying a product that had any connection with or endorsement by the NHL, they should not be sold any product that fans identified with their favorite team (at least without securing and paying for the consent of that team's owner).

A vivid demonstration of how far trademark law has journeyed since then took place right in the midst of baseball's 1994–95 labor dispute. The owners' marketing arm, MLB Properties, took legal action to block the use of Little League uniforms labeled with the names Yankees, Dodgers, and the like, unless the manufacturer (and thus the purchaser) paid a licensing fee. Needless to say, the parents of Little League players were *not* confused about who was sponsoring their teams and uniforms (which did not say *New York* Yankees or *Los Angeles* Dodgers). As *USA Today* put it, the "kid-league gougers" were simply trying to extract a licensing fee of approximately $6 for any uniform that had one of "their" names on it. And contrary to the assertions of MLB Properties, all or most of that $6 charge would be passed on to the families buying uniforms for the approximately 2.5 million children who play on Little League teams.

The *Abdul-Jabbar* and *Little League* cases are revealing examples from the sports world of how far the courts have expanded intellectual property law in order to confer exclusive control over commercial use of names, likenesses, and identifying symbols. In my own view, we have taken this part of our law far beyond its original and legitimate core (which was to ensure that celebrated products or performers did not have their names and images used to convey the impression that they were endorsing someone else's goods and services) to what is now a brand of extensive government intervention and regulation for the benefit of private entities and individuals who are least in need of it. A movie like *The Lion King*, which is a huge hit at the box office and on home video (earning more than a billion dollars from these domestic and foreign sources), has the right to make hundreds of millions of dollars more from merchandise licensing. A basketball star like Michael Jordan, who in 1997–98 earned (a well-deserved) $33 million from the Bulls, reaped another $47 million from various endorsements. There is far more myth than reality to the legal rationale that such huge bonuses for these already richly rewarded productions or performers are a necessary incentive for the development of movies or basketball talent. They are actually just another illustration of the winner-takes-the-lion's-share features of our legally shaped marketplace.

League Restraints on Team Licensing

There is a crucial difference between the ways in which players (or movie studios) and league owners sell their merchandising rights. When a studio like Disney tries to get a sponsorship deal from McDonald's or Burger King for a movie such as *The Lion King*, it competes in that market with Warner Brothers and its *Batman*, or Universal and its *Jurassic Park*. So also Michael Jordan faced competition from Shaquille O'Neal and Dennis Rodman in the sports shoe market, and Tiger Woods from Greg Norman and John Daly for golf-club endorsements. Unlike studios, league athletes can and do engage in group licensing of their names and likenesses on collective products such as baseball and football cards. However, such group action is legal only if conducted in a reasonable and non-exclusive fashion; this means that the MLB Players Association cannot bar a Ken Griffey Jr. from granting individual licenses.

The same sports policy ought to prevail in marketing by owners. MLB Properties should be able to grant Little Leagues a collective license for use of team names and logos (assuming the teams do have trademark rights in them). But the league should not be able to bar an individual team like Steinbrenner's Yankees from licensing its own name to specific Little League clubs, perhaps at a lower price than Murdoch's Dodgers are looking for. It is the contrary league practice of, in effect, a private group monopoly in the sale of legally conferred individual monopolies that one would have hoped to see struck down in the *Jones* and *Steinbrenner* lawsuits against NFL and MLB Properties in connection with their Nike and Adidas deals.

In fact, back in the 1950s a judge did use antitrust law to remove some of the restraints that the NFL had placed on telecasts of games of the Browns, for example, into the home cities of rival teams. This was an era when both television and professional football were trying to establish themselves as significant features of American life, dominated until then by movies and baseball. By the early 1960s the value of professional football on television had risen, triggered especially by the dramatic overtime win by the Baltimore Colts over the New York Giants in the 1958 championship game. In the early 1950s NFL teams had received an average of $65,000 for their TV rights. By 1961 the teams were averaging $250,000, with the Giants at the top at $370,000 and the new Minnesota Vikings at the bottom at $120,000. But the NFL was now facing a competitor for this fan interest—the new American Football League, which had signed a network television contract with NBC. In order to free the NFL from the federal judge's antitrust injunction, Commissioner Pete Rozelle went to Congress in 1961 and persuaded it to pass a new Sports Broadcasting Act (SBA) which immunized from antitrust challenge all league-wide television contracts. With that legal backing, Rozelle (and his new Browns owner and television specialist Art Modell) negotiated a much improved $4.6 million contract with CBS for the 1962 season. Another key feature of this new regime was that each of the 14 teams got the same amount: $330,000. This was somewhat less than what the Giants or Browns had been making, but a large increase for the Vikings and the small-market Green Bay Packers, which Vince Lombardi had then made the best team in football. Even the Giants would quickly be rewarded by this new league approach: the $14 million NFL contract for the 1964 season paid every team $1 million.

In the next chapter we shall investigate whether and to what extent such equal sharing of television (or merchandising) revenues is a good practice in sports. As a practical matter, though, only in the NFL, with its small number of regular-season games, can the central league office effectively negotiate contracts for all its games to be shown on national TV networks. (Even in the NFL, the courts have ruled that the SBA does not exempt from antitrust scrutiny the league's DIRECTV Sunday Ticket package, which, for $139 a season, lets fans around the country watch any Sunday game they want.) MLB, the NBA, and the NHL have contracts with network and national cable channels for telecasts of a selected number of games each season. But the vast majority of these league games are broadcast under contracts that individual teams negotiate with their local stations and cable channels.

A long-established condition of both league rules and their national television contracts is that no club will license broadcast of its games on other networks or cable channels shown outside its territory. But as we saw earlier, Ted Turner devised the superstation loophole to that league regime. His Atlanta Braves and Hawks games were broadcast on what seemed to be his local WTBS station, but one whose signals (with nationally tailored commercials) were picked up by satellite for transmission to local cable systems around the country. Turner and his Braves eventually agreed to pay a special superstation fee to MLB, which was distributed to Turner's fellow baseball owners. In basketball, Turner's TNT, and then his WTBS, secured the national cable contracts from the NBA, and thus it was in their interest as well to drop the Hawks' other games from WTBS. However, to address the significant ratings and revenue challenge posed by the dominant Chicago Bulls on the WGN superstation, the NBA first capped and then barred any team contracts with superstations. The Bulls' owner Jerry Reinsdorf and WGN sued the NBA in the biggest sports broadcasting case of the 1990s.

On its face, that NBA superstation restraint (like other league broadcasting controls) seems to be rather suspect under usual antitrust policy. Obviously it is not a threat to the "integrity of the sport" to have the broadcasts of one team's games coming into another team's home territory. NBA games are regularly broadcast into areas where college teams are playing, just as major league games are transmitted into minor league towns. What leagues are really trying to do through their rules is to protect each member from the competitive threat of other members' games when they are all trying to sell their own broadcast rights (or even season tickets). But many fans would have preferred to watch the Bulls play their games, rather than be limited to watching a home team at or near the bottom of the standings (as were the Boston Celtics, for example, during the Bulls' 1996–97 championship drive). Indeed, if basketball fans in Boston (or Philadelphia or Dallas) had regularly been able to watch the Bulls (or the Jazz or the Heat), this would have placed strong competitive pressures on the Celtics, the 76ers, and the Mavericks to improve the quality of their product and/or lower its price. Thus District Judge Hubert Will was twice persuaded that the harm done to the welfare of sports consumers made this NBA policy an illegal restraint of trade. On the second round of appeals, however, the noted antitrust jurist and theorist Judge Frank Easterbrook was sufficiently impressed by several of the NBA counsel's counterarguments that he overturned the lower court's "quick look" finding of illegality and remanded the case for a full-scale "rule of reason" trial. By this time Judge Will had passed away, and the parties settled their five years of litigation with a *de facto* victory for the NBA: a 15-game cap was imposed on national superstation telecasts, and the league was given a substantial share of the advertising space on any such broadcasts.

All of the judges and lawyers agree that there are three crucial legal issues in such a sports antitrust claim (issues that were also raised by the Cowboys-NFL and Yankees-MLB suits about a league practice that is not insulated by a special sports *merchandising* act). The first issue is whether §1 of the Sherman Act, which bars "combinations" of independent parties who come together to impose unreasonable restraints of trade, applies at all to sports leagues which claim that they are a "single entity"—akin to Wal-Mart, for example. We will take up this question in the next chapter. The second issue is whether these league policies actually "restrain" trade in a television market in which the NBA's product does not have any special and significant market leverage. The third is whether league restraints that may have significant market impact are nonetheless "reasonable" because they are vital to the viability of the league that creates and offers this sports product to its television fans.

The last two substantive questions about the application of antitrust to leagues provide complex insights into the sports world. The question of whether the NBA has significant market power turns largely on the way in which one defines the relevant market. If the scope of the market is professional basketball, then the NBA clearly is the one dominant force. However, the NBA (like other leagues) believes that it is really a tiny share (ranging from $1.5 to $3.5 billion) of the broad entertainment world (at roughly $400 billion a year) that includes all the other shows on television as well as movies, plays, concerts, gambling casinos, and the host of other ways in which Americans now seek to have fun.

But the existence of such a broad and plausible entertainment category is by no means a sufficient answer to the charge that a league is illegally restraining trade in its specific product. A combination of airlines could not defend an antitrust suit against, say, an agreement to give each airline exclusive control over its "own" airport by claiming that airlines are just a small part of a transportation sector that also includes cars, buses, trains, boats, and the like. The technical legal inquiry is about how much "cross-elasticity" of consumer demand there is among more or less "substitutable" products. Suppose the airlines got together and gave each one of them control of its respective airport, and then their average fares went up 5–10 percent. They would not face a corresponding loss of passengers who decided to shift to cars and buses instead of flying. The same is true even within the entertainment industry: people do not find concerts and plays the same kind of easy substitute for movies that a McDonald's is for a Burger King.

What about basketball as compared with hockey, football, and baseball, or sports as compared with movies, concerts, and plays? This may depend to some extent on the context. With respect to live attendance, there seems little cross-elasticity of demand. Teams regularly raise their ticket prices by 20–25 percent with no discernible effect on attendance. The fact that Baltimore had not only the Orioles playing baseball but the Baltimore Stallions playing in the Canadian Football League did not ease any of the pressure the city felt to offer a $225 million stadium deal to the Browns' Modell, one key part of which was the sale of expensive PSLs to fans who saw big-time NFL football as the only game in town (at least in the fall). Consumers exhibit essentially the same reactions in the merchandise market. There are very few customers who would choose between Bulls, Packers, and Yankees T-shirts (let alone Batman or Bart Simpson shirts) solely on the basis of price rather than personal identification and allegiance.

However, as the NBA rightly pointed out in *WGN*, the television market is significantly different. There a key figure is the advertiser that buys commercial time on the program and is principally interested in what the Nielsen ratings reveal about how many viewers it is getting for the price it is paying. Thus, while the NBA may have restricted the ability of Bulls games to be viewed in Boston or Philadelphia, advertisers in those cities have hundreds of other television programs from which to choose, an option that the NBA said placed sufficient constraints on the size of the licensing fees charged by the Celtics or the 76ers.

But the broadcast market is much more complex than that, and advertisers are by no means the only key players. Indeed, the availability of Bulls games on cable television in Boston or Philadelphia would place some limits on the ability of the Celtics and the 76ers to raise the price they charged for pay cable broadcasting (perhaps even for tickets) of their home games. In addition, the networks, local stations, and cable channels often are prepared to pay a substantial premium to get sports on their screens. That is why Fox made a record-setting bid to win the 1994–97 NFC contract, a time span in which Fox was trying to establish itself as a major network. (For example, Fox hoped that late-Sunday-afternoon football viewers would keep this channel on until *X-Files* was shown.) So also, WGN was able to use the Bulls and Jordan (as WTBS used the Braves) as the lever with which to secure one of the scarce channels in local cable systems around the country, and thus was able to sell national advertisements on all their shows.

Even advertisers are interested not so much in aggregate numbers as in the demographic makeup of a program's audience, which it hopes will buy its products. The same economic reasons that prompt companies like Nike or Budweiser to place their commercials on sports events rather than on situation comedies (let alone talk shows or Saturday morning cartoons) also explain why these other types of programs are not part of the same market as sports for antitrust purposes. In other words, Michael Jordan, Jerry Seinfeld, and Jay Leno sell different products to different audiences. The Supreme Court ruled in the 1980s that college football was a distinct and significant part of the television market (in a case we will read about shortly). By the late 1990s, certainly, NBA basketball had reached that level.

The fact that leagues such as the NBA and the NFL exert collective control over broadcasters' and advertisers' access to their distinctive audiences is the reason sports revenues from television have soared as more and more networks and cable channels have emerged to bid for this scarce resource. Suppose, for example, that all the broadcasters delegated to their National Association of Broadcasters (NAB) the authority to bargain collectively with each league for an overall television deal that allocated teams and games to channels that wanted them at the price they considered reasonable to pay. The leagues would immediately sue the NAB for illegally restraining trade in this service in order to reduce broadcast prices and team revenues below the level that would be set by a competitive market. But it is only if the 30 or so teams within each league also have to compete with one another for access to the networks, superstations, cable channels, and other outlets (just as producers of situation comedies or action dramas now do) that consumers will get the benefit of the true marketplace that public policy is supposed to provide in the interplay of the sports and television industries. And a further fact must also be appreciated: it is the people who buy the products advertised during NBA games (or the apparel bearing NFL team logos) who end up paying the higher prices that the leagues are now able to extract for their broadcasting and merchandising licenses.

This brings us to the most plausible defense advanced by the NBA in the *Bulls* case (and by the NFL and MLB in the *Cowboys* and *Yankees* suits). What makes sports special is that the league is a joint venture among franchise partners who have to collaborate in creating a single athletically competitive product to offer to fans (on television as well as at the game). The Bulls, for example, were America's favorite basketball team of the 1990s, but they had something to sell to WGN and their other customers only because other teams were playing those games with them. While basketball fans across the country applauded when Jordan and his teammates won games and championships, they were most pleased (and prepared to watch) when other clubs like the Seattle Supersonics or the Utah Jazz put the Bulls to the test in a closely fought race to the wire. To be successful in the longer run, the NBA needs a system which precludes future Bulls from taking the lion's share of the game's revenues and using this money not only to enrich the Bulls' owner Reinsdorf rather than his league partners but also to attract too many stars from other teams so that the Bulls are never seriously threatened with losing.

While these league objectives are valid, the superstation cap (or a bar on separate team merchandising deals) is not the most appropriate (let alone the "least restrictive") means for achieving them. Take, for example, the claim by other NBA teams that they are just as entitled to the television revenues generated by league games as are the Bulls, who happened to get this windfall profit from WGN because of the team's stature in the league in the 1990s. The answer to this argument against "free-riding" by currently popular teams is systematic revenue sharing. This would give the small-market Sacramento Kings or Charlotte Hornets a fair share of what WGN is paying not just to televise Jordan and the Bulls by themselves but to display them playing the Kings, the Hornets, and other league teams. Indeed, that is precisely what Ted Turner and his fellow baseball owners agreed to do with some of the extra revenues generated by WTBS superstation broadcasts of Braves games.

Such a television revenue "tax" must not be set so high as to be the functional equivalent of a superstation *ban,* because otherwise the price is paid by sports fans who are denied enjoyment of the games they really want to watch. And the best test of whether the owners themselves judge the revenue-sharing rate to be reasonable rather than restrictive is to have them assess that same share of every team's *local* broadcast revenues. While the Kings and Hornets do have a legitimate claim to a share of the Bulls' revenues from WGN, they have exactly the same claim to a share of the Knicks' and the Lakers' revenues from broadcasts in their very large local markets. The same is true in baseball, regarding the claims of the Royals and the Expos, for example, to the local broadcast earnings of the Yankees as well as the superstation earnings of the Braves. If the league owners' true objective is to distribute their revenues equitably and sensibly among all the partners in this joint venture, rather than to restrain competition in certain market categories (such as those generated by superstations), adopting that broader sharing principle is the way to do (and prove) it.

Revenue sharing is a legitimate and valuable feature of a competitive sports league. Deciding how to share it is a far more complicated challenge than indicated by the usual rhetoric (such as contrasts between socialism and capitalism). I will address these complexities in the next chapter, which will explain, among other things, why football has too much and baseball too little. However, for our purposes here, the core claim made by the NBA in *WGN* (and by all sports leagues in response to all antitrust attacks on league policies) is that we need to preserve competitive balance on the basketball court as well as in the law courts. The answer is that even revenue sharing, let alone broadcast restraints, is not needed for that purpose. Instead of a superstation cap, leagues can adopt a player salary cap or tax that is targeted precisely at this problem. Because the owners can (and do) address this issue through labor negotiations with the players, they must not be permitted to use competitive balance on the field or the floor as an excuse for imposing significant restraints on competition in the consumer market (including dealings with broadcasters and merchandisers) and thus extracting an even greater monetary premium from fans who deeply want to watch and enjoy the game.

Learning from College Sports

Happily, this is not just speculation by a legal academic. We now have the experience of a 1984 Supreme Court ruling that struck down the NCAA's even more restrictive limits on telecasts of college football games.

Ironically, when Congress was passing the 1961 Sports Broadcasting Act, it asked the NCAA if it wanted the same antitrust exemption as the NFL. The NCAA declined, saying that it was already immune as a combination of not-for-profit universities. The NCAA confidently went ahead and fashioned its own broadcast policy, in which it negotiated a small number of television contracts with networks and cable channels. Revenues were shared among all school members (even those without football squads), and the NCAA also placed a cap on the number of games in which a team could appear on television. Notre Dame, for example, could have no more than six games televised over *two* seasons, with only four receiving national coverage.

However, while annual college football television revenues rose from $5 million in the early 1960s to $75 million in the early 1980s, these restraints on school and conference autonomy as well as earnings produced a lawsuit by the universities of Oklahoma and Georgia. Not only did the NCAA learn from the Supreme Court that public and private colleges are governed by antitrust law; it also discovered that college football was a distinctive product in the television advertising market, one whose attraction gave the NCAA substantial market power in this sector. What about preservation of competitive balance on the field? This, the Court believed, was more than adequately preserved by NCAA rules about how much (or how little) schools could pay their "amateur" student athletes.

Whatever the pros and cons of that NCAA scholarship pay cap, the key lesson for us here is the difference the Court's *NCAA* decision made in the college football television market. In 1984, the first year in which schools and conferences could license telecasts of their games on their own, the number of televised college football games went up to nearly three times its 1983 amount, and the average price per game dropped from about $1 million to $250,000. And notwithstanding the far greater number of telecasts, attendance for these games actually rose slightly from 1983. There are few, if any, more vivid illustrations than *NCAA* of the contributions that antitrust enforcement has made to consumers' welfare.

By contrast, the immediate byproduct of the *WGN* verdict reversal and litigation settlement was that the NBA secured a 240 percent increase in its contracts with NBC and TNT. Annual payments leaped from $275 million in 1997–98 to $660 million in 1998–99, even though the people involved assumed that Michael Jordan was going to be leaving and a big labor dispute was coming to the game. Shortly afterward NFL Commissioner Tagliabue and his negotiators used bidding wars between CBS and NBC (for Sunday afternoon AFC games), NBC and ABC (for Monday night games), and ESPN and TNT (for Sunday night cable games) to raise the league's annual television revenues from $1.1 billion to $2.2 billion. The prices charged by ESPN and TNT to local cable systems immediately went up, as did the network's prices for commercial time during football and basketball games. We fans of professional sports are the ones who ultimately pay both these higher cable fees and the higher prices of products advertised on all these networks and cable channels. We should be allowed, then, to enjoy the benefits of a more competitive sports marketplace, one that now tells us to "show them the money"—as well as our allegiance.

18

WHAT SHOULD LEAGUES BE LIKE?

The combination of a properly designed salary cap (or tax) with free agency is the best instrument through which leagues can fairly distribute player talent to establish a level playing field in the games viewed by fans. This instrument also removes the principal defense that owners have always offered for restraining competition among themselves in dealing with television networks, merchandising firms, and stadium authorities. In addition, the ability of players to organize themselves into effective labor unions ensures that players can receive a fair share of the financial value of their individual talent and team commitment displayed on the field.

Of course, any legitimate set of salary standards must contain not just a *cap* but also a *floor* on how much any club is paying to assemble a truly competitive team. But an owner-player labor agreement that limits both how *much* clubs like the New York Yankees and the New York Knicks can pay their rosters and how *little* clubs like the Montreal Expos and the Los Angeles Clippers can pay theirs generates a further problem among the teams. How can we be sure that the Expos, the Clippers, and their counterparts will have the funds to pay for more talented rosters—especially without having to extract the money from local taxpayers to build them lucrative new facilities?

That problem raises some practical questions about the extent to which revenues secured by one team should be shared with its partners in the league. The more fundamental analytical question concerns the very nature of the league. In particular, are teams like the Yankees and the Expos separate entities engaged in a joint sports venture, or just different branches of a single MLB conglomerate?

The Nature of the League

Owners are correct in the claim they often make to the courts and Congress: a sports league is a unique form of organization. Carefully designed league rules are required to define the nature of the product that teams collectively offer to fans on the field. A central body is also needed with the authority to tell individual teams whether they can play a Roberto Alomar (who once spat in the face of an umpire), a Pete Rose (who always bet on his Reds—to win their games), or a Steve Howe (who regularly used cocaine). Some combination of league rules and administrative authority also seems necessary to spell out what member clubs can do in their off-the-field dealings with players and their agents, with cities and their stadium authorities, and even with television networks like NBC and merchandising firms like Nike. At the same time, though, the other participants in the business of sports also need the appropriate use and protection of labor law, tax law, intellectual property law, and antitrust law to ensure that league rules established and enforced by owners (and their commissioners) actually do respond to the broader interests of fans. The inevitable tension between these private and public legal regimes makes the job of leveling the playing field a complex one, often with some surprising solutions.

There is an issue that comes up in almost all of these controversies: What is the true structure, and therefore the legal status, of a sports league? In particular, §1 of the Sherman Act bars only *combinations* in restraint of trade; this implies that the parties involved are all separate persons or entities that have come together to place unreasonable restrictions on what should be market competition among them. A key argument that league lawyers have advanced against any such antitrust attack on their rules is that the league is actually a single entity designed to create a single product: a competitive race to the championship in its sport.

Everyone in this field agrees that what makes the sports industry different—and sports law fascinating—is that leagues have to be closely knit partnerships among teams and their owners. The sports product will be attractive to spectators only if it reflects a shared understanding about a host of matters that are crucial to the game's nature and appeal. What are the rules of the game as it is played? How many games are there in a season and where and when are they scheduled? Who gets into the playoffs and how does the champion get crowned? Many of these decisions affect not only the internal content of the sport but also the interests of outside parties. The size of rosters and the use of special roles like designated hitter determine how many jobs there will be for players with what kinds of skills. Timeouts or instant replays or visits to the pitching mound influence the time the game takes over the air as well as at the stadium or arena. A rule that suspends players who merely leave their benches when a scuffle breaks out among their teammates can determine which team wins a playoff series. With respect to these and a host of other issues, the sports marketplace requires a league procedure for setting the governing rules, and a central commissioner's office for their administration.

Sports is unique in the degree to which it requires such agreements among the responsible parties, but it is by no means the only example of industry collaboration in the creation of such a product. In 1997 Twentieth Century Fox and Paramount studios combined to finance, produce, and distribute *Titanic,* a course of action that is becoming quite common in the increasingly expensive and risky movie business. In the 1980s General Motors and Toyota, two of the auto giants, found such a partnership to be the best way to produce and market their Nova car. A century ago newspapers across the country established the Associated Press to gather news from around the world to be shared with all members for publication in their local papers.

Courts have long recognized the legitimacy under antitrust law of such "joint ventures" that fashion a new product for the benefit of consumers. But the law also insists that the partners agree to rules and restrictions that are reasonably necessary for production and distribution of their joint product, but not to additional restrictions that may reduce competition in the broader market. That is why the Associated Press and its members were found to have violated the Sherman Act when access to the AP product was barred to new papers entering the local markets of existing AP members. This is also why Fox and Paramount's *Titanic* venture could not have incorporated an agreement between the studios to cap their performers' salaries for that entire movie season. Most relevant for our purposes, the Supreme Court applied its *Associated Press* precedent in the *NCAA* case to find the universities who were parties to this particular joint venture to be a §1 "combination" that had agreed to *reasonable* restraints about what could be done on the college football field, but also to *unreasonable* restraints about which games would be shown on television and at what price.

Proponents of the single-entity position have long argued, though, that a professional sport is qualitatively different from the college version. A year after *NCAA* came down, in *Copperweld,* a case not related to sports, the Supreme Court issued another opinion in this area, in which the Justices made it clear that there could be no antitrust "combination" between a parent company and its wholly owned subsidiary corporation, because for all practical management purposes the two were a single entity. This is the legal precedent that the NFL, the NBA, and other leagues cite when arguing that they too are single organizations, whose terms are defined by the league constitution and whose operations are controlled by its central office (not just the commissioner but also the executive board on which sits each team owner or delegate).

Under this theory, it is these league-wide bodies and rules that ultimately determine which teams are created, where they play, and who plays for them. True, with respect to many of these matters, leagues will conclude that it makes sense to delegate to individual partners the autonomy to make the judgments about issues that are closely tied to "their" team and community. The team "owners" decide which players, coaches, and other personnel they will hire and at what salary; in which facilities the games will be played, on what lease terms, and at which ticket prices; what local television or radio stations will broadcast the games for how much money; and the like. However, these individual team decisions must be made in accordance with overall league rules that define the league's common product, and the league has the right to take back from local owners one or more of these team prerogatives when league authorities judge this to be in the best interests of the sport. From this perspective, professional sports leagues are said to be the functional equivalents of a national retail chain such as Wal-Mart or an accounting firm such as Arthur Anderson: single entities that delegate considerable autonomy to those responsible for running their local stores or offices.

The truth of the matter is that both professional football and basketball (under the NFL and the NBA) and college football and basketball (under the NCAA) are quite different from either a clear-cut single entity such as Wal-Mart or a clear-cut joint venture such as the Associated Press. Unlike members of the AP, a news-gathering operation created and controlled by publishers of many separate papers, the NFL, NBA, and NCAA members collaborate in creating a single, fully integrated sports product. Unlike a Wal-Mart store, each partner-member of a sports body owns and operates its team, takes in the profits (or absorbs the occasional losses) that show up on the team's balance sheets, and keeps for itself the (usually huge) capital gain realized in the sale of the team. And those key financial rules cannot be changed by the league without the consent of every league member.

It has always been possible to design a sports league that is the functional equivalent of a Wal-Mart and thus gets the benefit of the *Copperweld* antitrust immunity. In fact that was the original design of the lawyers who fashioned the new Major League Soccer venture of the 1990s. A single MLS corporate entity would own and operate all the teams around the country, with financial investors owning shares in MLS and sitting on its board of directors to set basic league policies. But the MLS commissioner's office would actually run the teams—not just by setting prices for all local tickets, concessions, and broadcasts, but also by deciding which players, coaches, general managers, and other personnel would be hired and assigned to which teams. That would ensure that everyone's salary would be capped. The league would pay all the local teams' costs and collect all their revenues (along with national television and merchandising revenues); after corporate taxes were paid, any balance would be distributed to the investors as corporate dividends. Unquestionably, that kind of league design would and should pass the *Copperweld* test as a "single entity" immune from §1 challenge to restraints on player or franchise free agency.

However, that legal design for the new MLS did not pass muster with its potential investors, who included Robert Kraft, owner of the NFL's Patriots, and Lamar Hunt, owner of the Kansas City Chiefs. Wealthy sports fans are not likely to provide millions and millions of dollars in start-up costs for such a risky league venture, just to be faceless investors in a league whose visible powers that be are all in the head office. A major attraction of any such sports investment is the pleasure a person gets from running a team that he is committed to seeing win in his own home community. As we saw back in Part II, the emotional benefit the owner gets from winning a championship (something only one team in a league can do each year) is a key justification for league salary standards that facilitate fair distribution of talent among the teams. The prospect of such exhilaration and popular recognition for owners is also why sports franchises always sell for considerably more than what analysts calculate to be their economic value, based simply on financial profits. In the end, MLS had to make a radical change in its structure to give Kraft, for example, special status as "investor operator" of the New England Revolution, wielding much the same control over this team as over his Patriots—including the right to keep its annual profits or pay its losses and reap the ultimate increase in value of the Revolution franchise.

The one exception to the authority of the MLS "investor operators" is with respect to players. The league wanted to avoid a replay of what had happened to the North American Soccer League of the 1970s, a league that had been dominated by the big-market New York Cosmos, whose owner Steve Ross (also the major figure in Time Warner) used a huge salary deal to lure from Brazil the Babe Ruth of soccer, Pelé (to join such other all-time greats as Franz Beckenbauer, Carlos Alberto, and Giorgio Chinaglia). Thus the MLS constitution makes the league the formal "employer" of all players, who are paid from league coffers pursuant to salary cap rules, and are selected by and assigned to the teams. Now that MLS players have challenged the salary cap, the league will not be able to make any better single-entity claim than could the NFL. Certainly Kraft and his family believe and say that they "own" the Revolution as much as they do the Patriots.

We should also remember that the Patriots, along with twelve other teams, came to the NFL from independent leagues, and the same is true of numerous members of the NBA, the NHL, and MLB. Each team enjoys the benefits of its individual location and success and pays the price of failure. For example, when the Pittsburgh Penguins made their very exceptional sports bankruptcy filing in 1999, no one ever suggested that the other NHL teams would be responsible for "their" Penguins' unpaid debts, as Wal-Mart would be if one of its stores failed. (Those debts included the $30 million in deferred salary owed to the Hall-of-Famer Mario Lemieux for what he had done in twice bringing the Stanley Cup to Pittsburgh before becoming disabled and retiring. Indeed, Lemieux has now become the Penguins' post-bankruptcy managing partner.) Thus, on reflection, the Atlanta Braves, owned by one entertainment-sports conglomerate, Time Warner, and the Los Angeles Dodgers, owned by another, Rupert Murdoch's Fox, seem to be even more "separate entities" than the Georgia Bulldogs, Oklahoma Sooners, and other partners in the college sports joint venture that the Supreme Court found subject to (and in violation of) antitrust because of the NCAA's restraints of trade in the sports television market.

The fact that a league (or tour) policy is subject to meaningful judicial scrutiny does not necessarily mean it is illegal as economically anti-competitive. The crucial feature of sports as a joint venture in athletic competition must be given serious weight by courts (or legislators) when appraising the reasonability of the policy in question. Indeed, even judicial and scholarly proponents of the single-entity defense for professional team sports have been prepared to give that argument more weight in some markets (such as "downstream" sales to stadium authorities and/or television broadcasters) than in others (such as "upstream" purchases of players' services). However, what is crucial to the appraisal of a league rule is not its position in the market stream; rather, it is whether the rule's principal role is to preserve the integrity and quality of the product being offered in the marketplace or instead to extract an economic premium for the owners from other parties affected by that rule.

The most pro-competitive cases in favor of league rules are those targeted to the midstream: the definition of the product itself. For example, league restraints on the type and quality of equipment used in the games —allowing just wooden rather than aluminum bats in MLB—should definitely be legal. A significant, though less compelling, claim can be made about a league's relations with its upstream players market—the allocation of talent among teams. As I explained in earlier chapters, these restraints must be designed as a revenue/payroll-sharing arrangement among players and clubs that serves the interests of competitive balance in sports, rather than the traditional reserve system, which principally served the interests of owners by lowering players' pay.

The least defensible joint-venture argument relates to the downstream market with fans. These are the people who are being asked to pay more and more to watch their favorite team live or over the air, or to wear a T-shirt with the team's name and logo on it. The *de facto* monopoly status of the NFL, MLB, the NBA, and the NHL in their respective sports markets has allowed them to extract a large economic rent from fans in these markets by eliminating significant competition among themselves. And the fact that the owners and players have the ability to design internal revenue- and salary-sharing arrangements that can fully and effectively deal with concerns about competitive balance on the field is the reason sports courts must now seriously address these downstream markets and not be diverted by the "single entity" illusion.

Revenue Sharing

My bottom-line conclusion is that all of the major professional leagues are properly characterized as partnerships among distinct team owners, rather than as single corporate entities whose branches may be locally managed but are centrally controlled. Antitrust law does need an either/ or answer to this key question of whether league restraints of trade are subject to *any* external review. However, while the NFL and MLB, for example, share that legal status, they are located at quite different points along the spectrum of coordinated league policies and shared revenues. The vast majority of fans and commentators believe the NFL model is the preferable one; indeed they would like to see football integrated even further. As we are about to see, this issue is also more complex than it seems at first glance.

The best index of league coordination is revenue sharing. Baseball has huge disparities in team revenues: by the end of the 1990s, while the league average was over $85 million, a few teams like the Yankees, Orioles, and Indians were averaging $160 million while the Expos, Twins, and Pirates were averaging just $40 million. In football, by contrast, the Cowboys, Redskins, and Dolphins, then at the financial top of the ladder, averaged $115 million while the Colts, Bengals, and Jaguars averaged only $70 million at the bottom. The standard assumption is that such disparities mean that small-market teams cannot afford to pay and keep their stars in the current world of player free agency. This not only costs their fans (and those of the league as a whole) the chance to see competitive teams matched up on the field but also puts the home city in grave danger of losing its team to another location through franchise free agency. This is why editorial writers across the country were supporting the NFL and MLB efforts to block separate and lucrative merchandising deals between the Cowboys and Nike and the Yankees and Adidas.

But in truth sports consumers are made better off by a league design that gives each team the right to sell its television and marketing rights wherever fans would like to watch or buy its product. The better way to address the problem of disparity in team revenue is through sharing of such revenues among all league partners. Thus, even if Congress were to repeal the Sports Broadcasting Act so that the NFL no longer had the *exclusive* right to license broadcasts of team games, substantial (if not full-blown) sharing of the money thus earned by individual teams such as the Cowboys would seem essential to preserve the appeal of the football product being offered on television.

The case for the NFL's style of revenue sharing is not so clear. First, the impersonal operation of capital markets eliminates much, if not all, of the apparent disparity in the ability of the Orioles and Pirates, for example, to invest in talent and so perform well on the field. At the same time, the manner in which a league redistributes its revenues can actually harm rather than help the team and its home city. Indeed, this NFL revenue-sharing system is a major reason Los Angeles lost the Raiders and Rams and Cleveland the Browns. Just as we know from other areas of institutional governance, sports leagues have to be designed in a fashion that not only fairly distributes the existing financial pie but also generates an expanding pie—again for the benefit of fans as well as owners and players.

Let us look at how the four major leagues divide up the revenue streams that flow into their sports. In football, well over half of the NFL's $3.6 billion in annual revenues comes from broadcasting, with the key national television contract divided equally among each of the teams: the Green Bay Packers receive the same $70–$75 million as the New York Giants. This is also how the $250 million in NFL Properties revenues from merchandising deals are divided. Regular gate receipts are shared on a 60–40 basis between the home team and the visiting team in each game. The biggest source of the $50 million or so gap between the Cowboys and the Vikings, for example, is stadium revenues—luxury boxes, club seats, concessions, parking, advertising, naming, and the like.

Both basketball and hockey have significantly higher revenue disparities. Of the NBA's approximately $2 billion in revenues, the Knicks and Bulls average around $105 million, more than twice as much as the Bucks and Clippers at $45 million. Very little of the gate receipts and none of the arena revenues or local television contracts is shared with visiting teams. But the NBA's national television and merchandising deals (second only to the NFL's in size and in proportion of overall league revenues) are shared equally among the clubs, reducing somewhat the disparity between large- and small-market teams. The NHL's system is essentially the same as the NBA's (though no gate receipts are shared at all). However, both shared national and unshared local television and merchandising revenues make up a much smaller portion of hockey's $1.3 billion in total revenues. That is why the NHL has a disparity of 2.3–1 between, for example, the earnings of the Detroit Red Wings (at $80 million) and those of the Edmonton Oilers (at $35 million).

The disparity in Major League Baseball is more deeply embedded, as shown by the way MLB divided up its $2.7 billion annual total in the late 1990s. Part of the 4–1 gap between the $160 million average of the Yankees, Orioles, and Indians and the $40 million of the Expos, Twins, and Pirates was due to (very modestly shared) gate receipts from the usual sellouts of Yankees, Orioles, and Indians games. Even more of the revenue gap comes from television. While the 28 teams collectively earned about $900 million, just $340 million came from national contracts, which are shared equally. The remaining $560 million came from local contracts, which are only modestly shared, and which ranged from around $60 million for the Yankees and Braves to less than $6 million for the Expos and Royals. While it certainly was beneficial to owners (and players) as a whole that local television revenues soared from $30 million in 1971 to $560 million in 1997, the current 10–1 (or $54 million) gap between the Yankees' and Expos' contracts has increased dramatically from the 4–1 ($1.8 million to $450,000) difference between the Dodgers' and Pirates' broadcast contracts in 1971.

The emergence of player free agency in the late 1970s not only produced far higher salaries for players but also made this item a significantly greater portion of overall league revenues (55 percent by the mid-1990s). This accentuated the concerns of small-market club owners about the way the total league pie was being divided. Baseball had a specific revenue-sharing plan, but in the early 1990s only $25 million of approximately $1.2 billion in local team revenues was redistributed. Thus, as a prelude to the 1994 labor negotiations in which the owners' Player Relations Committee set out to force the Players Association to agree to cap players' salaries, a caucus of small-market owners also sought to extract a somewhat greater share of the large market's money. These capitalists had convinced themselves that redistribution of wealth, at least among league *owners,* is not un-American.

The "union" of small-market owners had devised a technique to get the large-market owners to adopt that same principle. The Royals, the Expos, the Padres, and others announced that they would lock out of their home stadiums the television crews coming to broadcast Yankees games on the New York MSG cable system, Cubs games on the WGN superstation, and others. And they were able to do that because the television-access agreement among the owners was expiring at around the same time as their labor contract with the players.

After a year of intense negotiations, the Yankees, the Orioles, and other large-market clubs did agree to share more of their revenues with their smaller-market partners. However, such owner revenue sharing was conditional on the players' also agreeing to some system of salary restraint. It took another three years of conflict before labor peace finally came to baseball in December 1996, with a very modest form of salary tax. A somewhat more substantial revenue-sharing regime was also endorsed by the players, one that channels approximately $70 million of local gate receipts, broadcast earnings, and stadium revenues (minus stadium costs) from the 13 highest- to the 13 lowest-revenue clubs— taking around $9 million from the Yankees and giving $8 million to the Expos.

———————

The supposed beneficiaries of revenue sharing are the fans, rather than the owners of small-market clubs. Sharing of league revenues enables smaller-market teams like the Royals and the Pirates to attract and keep higher-quality (and thus higher-paid) players, making them more competitive with the larger-market Yankees and Dodgers. Indeed, this is why league salary-sharing agreements with the players, which establish both a cap and a floor on each team's salary budget, must be accompanied by revenue sharing among owners. The NFL, for example, requires teams like the Kansas City Chiefs and the Pittsburgh Steelers to pay roughly the same total salaries as do the New York Giants and Chicago Bears; for this reason, the NFL needs corresponding sharing of team revenues among owners, covering every component of Designated Gross Revenues (DGR) that figures in the salary-sharing deal with the players.

Revenue sharing not only produces those apparently fairer results after the fact but also creates new incentives for team actions before the fact. Pure revenue sharing is likely to make owners as a group better off vis-à-vis the players, because it serves as a drag on players' overall salaries.

From a business perspective, at least, the reason the Yankees and Dodgers believe it makes sense to invest more money in star players is that winning more games and championships attracts more fans to watch their games at the ballpark or on television. Suppose, though, that substantial parts of these added team revenues must be shared with other teams, but that all of the players' salaries come out of the team's own budget. This combination significantly reduces the owners' incentive to bid more for players who will enlarge their financial returns. In fact, absent a salary floor, the same skewed incentive effects are felt by small-market teams. If instead of keeping the money received from the Yankees for themselves, the Pirates' owners spend it on better players who increase their team revenues, this will reduce the amount the club receives from the Yankees in future years. These salary-depressing effects are most likely to be felt when the revenues being shared come from gate receipts, which are most affected by team performance, rather than from television contracts, which are most affected by market size.

Of course, team revenues and profits are not the only factors that influence decisions by owners—who often have lots of money from outside sources—about how much to spend on players. The personal pleasure and popular acclaim that the winning owner experiences when he receives the Super Bowl or World Series trophy on national television is *not* shared with fellow owners. The principal instrument for distributing player talent in a manner that preserves competitive balance among teams has to be a revenue/salary-sharing arrangement among owners and players, one that has built into it the sharing of enough revenues among teams that each can meet its salary floor. But revenue sharing by itself does not solve this problem—at least unless teams like the Pirates or the Expos, which get significant amounts from the high-earning and high-paying Yankees and Orioles, are required to add that money to their payrolls rather than to their owners' bank accounts.

Taxpayers can be affected even more than players by the way league revenue sharing alters owners' incentives and decisions. The single biggest reason the Rams and Raiders left Los Angeles vacant (as the Browns also did to Cleveland) was the NFL's revenue-sharing system. Just like the Giants and Jets in New York, the Rams and Raiders in Los Angeles collected only one-thirtieth of the league's television and merchandising revenues, much of which was attributable to the very large L.A. market. And the Browns received just one-thirtieth of the value of Cleveland's very high football Nielsen ratings. At the same time, the Rams, Raiders, and now-Ravens collected and kept almost all of the stadium revenues offered by the smaller-market cities of St. Louis, Oakland, and Baltimore in seeking to attract a free agent franchise. These stadium revenues also are not included in the NFL labor agreement's Designated Gross Revenues (DGR) that serve as the base for players' salaries. This means that whatever the owners may have said to the media, teams like the Browns and the Rams were *not* pressured by the players market to move their teams in return for huge taxpayer subsidies.

From the point of view of individual owners like Frontiere, Davis, and Modell, it makes more business sense to sharply enlarge a team revenue source of which they keep around 95 percent than to preserve a much higher league revenue source of which they each receive just over 3 percent. This NFL experience graphically demonstrates how important it is that league revenue-sharing systems treat all revenue streams in a coherent and coordinated fashion, not just on the basis of when and how each stream happened to come on the scene. And of course the example of Frontiere, Davis, and Modell in moving their teams then served as the lever by which the Seattle Seahawks, the Cincinnati Bengals, the Denver Broncos, and other NFL clubs extracted huge stadium subsidies from their home taxpayers. Whatever the impact of this revenue source on the integrity of the sport, one should not expect football owners to start treating it differently on their own. American taxpayer-voters must have Congress take the necessary step to protect the integrity of the public purse.

Even from the point of view of the sport itself, a more rational NFL regime would extract a substantial share but by no means *all* of a team's stadium revenues. Perhaps the most sensible regime would apply the same formula to luxury suites, concessions, and parking that it now does to regular gate receipts. At the same time, there should be a *reduction* in the division of revenue from national television and merchandising. As we saw in the previous chapter in connection with the *Bulls/*

WGN, Cowboys/Nike, and *Yankees/Steinbrenner* lawsuits, the fans of each of these sports will be better off if individual teams can and do compete with one another for a larger share of the national market for broadcasting and sponsorship contracts: fans will then get the chance to experience more of the product at a smaller price per item. There are good reasons for the Bulls' Reinsdorf, the Cowboys' Jones, and the Yankees' Steinbrenner to share a portion of their added revenues with their league partners. However, full-blown revenue sharing—anything near 100 percent of merchandising and television dollars—would be the functional equivalent of restraints placed by the league on this trade. If a league wants to make sure that it is not creating inappropriate economic disincentives for individual teams, it should simply use the same 35–40 percent corporate tax rate imposed on these same owners in their outside business activities.

Excessive revenue sharing may not only deter the Cowboys from competing in the national market but also reduce the incentive of franchise owners to make their teams more attractive in their home markets—both on and off the field. An especially graphic illustration is the experience of the Tampa Bay Buccaneers. This team came into the NFL in the mid-1970s for a $16 million expansion fee. For the next two decades the Bucs were one of the worst-performing and least popular teams in the league (with a fleeting exception in the late 1970s). Notwithstanding that history, the Culverhouse family was able to sell this team in 1995 for $200 million, at the time the highest price ever paid for an NFL club. The reason the team's poor performance had little effect on the value of its franchise is that capital markets do not object to a balance sheet that displays low expenditures by the team itself but large revenues flowing in from the league as a whole—revenues due, in this case, to the fact that the owners of the 49ers, Cowboys, Dolphins, and other teams were expending money, time, and skill to make their teams so good and the league so popular. That is precisely why the Browns' league-high television ratings while in Cleveland should have secured for them a higher share of the league's overall television revenues than was going to the Buccaneers. For the sake of its own quality, a league should reduce excessive revenue sharing to a more moderate level in order to avoid replays of the experience of the Buccaneers (at least until their current owners took over and installed Tony Dungy as head coach) and other low-paying, low-performing, but high-earning clubs.

Adjusting the level of revenue sharing is just as important in other sports, particularly in Major League Baseball, which has too little sharing of club revenues even since the 1996 agreement among owners and players. But it is not enough to require the Yankees and Orioles to pay more into a league pool because they are large-market, high-paying teams. As I have noted, a corresponding salary tax should be levied on the lowest-paying clubs such as the Pirates and Expos—that is, a "stingy" tax as well as a "luxury" tax. A similar revenue-sharing assessment should be made on large-market teams such as the Philadelphia Phillies or Detroit Tigers, whose lack of quality has often led them to underperform in their home markets with negative spillover effects on the sport's overall popularity and profits.

The test for this revenue assessment should begin with how well the team does in attendance, television ratings, merchandise sales, and the like, including at games played in other teams' home cities. These numbers should then be adjusted by the size of the team's market—the difference, for example, between the large-market Boston Red Sox and the small-market Kansas City Royals. (In the case of New York, Los Angeles, Chicago, and the San Francisco Bay Area, the markets should be divided in two to adjust for the presence of two teams.) The aim is to share revenues from high-earning teams to the extent that these revenues come from the large market that the league reserves for them as the home team, while at the same time taxing clubs in similarly large markets if they fail to generate revenue for that redistributional pool.

One lesson that would be driven home by this economically sound system is the crucial difference between a small-market team and a small-earning team—the latter epitomized by the Montreal Expos. By contrast with the Kansas City Royals, the Expos generate very low revenues in a medium-sized market, one that is actually larger than those of the high-earning Atlanta Braves and Cleveland Indians. Perhaps baseball owners would then ask themselves why the Orioles, whose home town of Baltimore is smaller than Montreal, should be paying substantial parts of their revenues to an Expos team located in a community that is committed to hockey (and its Canadiens) rather than to baseball.

How to Pay for Revenue Sharing

A properly designed revenue-sharing system enhances the quality of the game being offered to fans. This is, however, a feature of league organization that should definitely be left up to private agreements reached among owners and between owners and players, rather than imposed on the league by the law. But there is a major financial barrier to reaching a consensus about revenue sharing. How can one initiate a change in league policy that requires large-market teams such as the Yankees and the Orioles to transfer a significant part of their revenues even to small-market teams like the Pirates, let alone to small-*earning* teams like the Expos?

Consider the situation of Peter Angelos and his fellow owners of the Orioles, who bought the team for $175 million in 1993, not long after Claude Brochu and his partners bought the Expos for $80 million and three years before the Kevin McClatchey group purchased the Pirates for $85 million. Angelos paid that huge premium to Eli Jacobs, who had bought the Orioles in 1988 for just $70 million. The reason the price of the Orioles rose so high in just five years was that in the meantime the people of Baltimore had built Camden Yards for the team—a beautiful new ballpark that sent attendance and revenues soaring.

We have seen that it is poor public policy for taxpayers (or lottery gamblers) to have to spend scarce government dollars on wealthy franchise owners such as Eli Jacobs. But once this has been done, as it was for Jacobs's Orioles, it is poor league policy to require a Peter Angelos, after he has paid for that subsidy, to donate a significant part of its value to very well-to-do owners such as Brochu and McClatchey who paid correspondingly lower prices for their franchises. And the NFL would have to follow exactly the same principle in order to make a fair transition toward better sharing of its stadium revenues—ideally, at the same 60–40 ratio now applied to gate receipts. It would be totally unfair to require Daniel Snyder, who in 1999 paid $800 million for the Washington Redskins housed in their luxurious privately built stadium, and Bob McNair, who that same year paid $700 million for a new Houston franchise, to be lodged in an equally luxurious but publicly funded stadium, to "donate" much of their high stadium revenue streams to Red McComb, for example, who that same year paid $250 million to acquire the very talented Minnesota Vikings playing in an "ancient" 1982 Metrodome.

The key lesson from this example is that financial markets quickly and efficiently work into a team's franchise price the current capitalized value of its expected streams of revenues and profits (or losses). Some of the owners bought their clubs long before the sport's popularity and earnings shot upward: George Steinbrenner and his partners, who paid just $10 million for the Yankees in the early 1970s, have now reaped a $600 million valuation of this franchise in their 1999 partnership deal with the owners of the New Jersey Nets. But as teams are sold and resold over time, the new owners of teams with higher operating revenues have higher capital costs, while the new owners of teams with low operating revenues have correspondingly low capital costs. One must assume that the Pirates and the Expos were worth what their new owners chose to pay for them, which was less than half what Angelos paid for the Orioles and only a quarter of the $310 million that Rupert Murdoch paid for the Los Angeles Dodgers. These differences in franchise price are why such "poor" teams should be able to afford to pay their players roughly the same as the "wealthy" Orioles or Dodgers are paying.

This capital-value feature of the sports marketplace is crucial to a full understanding of the complexities of revenue sharing. There remains, however, a solid case for redesigning the systems in each sport to better address the longer-run substantive issues discussed in this chapter—in particular, we should have more revenue sharing in baseball and less in football. To facilitate that transition, the owners who "lose" from this change must be paid "just compensation" by the other owners who are "taking" a substantial share of their revenue stream. Exactly that same step must be taken if, for example, the NFL were to reduce its revenue sharing system to a more efficient model, and thus leave more money with owners of the larger-earning clubs at the expense of the small-earning teams. And calculating the current amounts is something that the owners should find easy to do. Whatever their levels of expertise in evaluating players on the field, almost all owners of sports franchises have had a great deal of success in evaluating business revenues off the field.

19

EXPAND OR BREAK UP
THE BIG LEAGUES?

The design and adoption of a revenue-sharing system is something that should be left to the leagues themselves rather than imposed by Congress or the courts. The changes I have proposed would make a considerable difference in the quality of the product leagues offer to fans. That is precisely why owners as a group should be motivated to address the problem of revenue disparity: if they solve it, they will reap the financial benefits of a more attractive sport.

But we should not assume that greater sharing of stadium revenues is the answer to the problem of taxpayer subsidies. After all, to the extent that any revenue policy reduces the incentive of individual owners to insist on such subsidies, it correspondingly increases the incentive of other league owners to press for precisely this step. The best way to lighten the heavy burden now being imposed on American taxpayers is through congressional action designed to protect the broader public rather than just owners and players.

There is one feature of the stadium subsidy problem that I have not yet addressed in any detail. Why do so many cities feel so strongly compelled to spend large amounts on new stadiums—whether to lure the Browns from Cleveland to Baltimore or to keep the Seahawks from moving from Seattle to Los Angeles?

One part of the answer is the shortage of franchises available (especially in football and baseball) to meet the demand of fans who are convinced that their cities deserve major league status. Recall that it was because the NFL did not award expansion franchises to Baltimore and St. Louis in 1993 that two years later these cities took the Browns and the Rams away from their long-time homes. The other part of the answer is that in football, as in baseball, basketball, and hockey, there is only one major league. This is why the NFL felt able, first, to deny football teams to Baltimore and St. Louis (whose level of fan support in 1995 and 1996 clearly satisfied any objective standard of eligibility), and second, to relinquish its franchises in powerful markets such as Cleveland and Los Angeles.

Indeed, in the summer of 1998 the NFL was able to play off against one another half a dozen partnerships—each comprising both a financial billionaire and a football great—that were bidding for the privilege of restoring big league football to Cleveland. The resulting franchise price of $530 million was nearly four times what had ever been charged for an expansion team in any sport, and that record lasted just one year, until Bob McNair put up $700 million to return the NFL to Houston rather than to Los Angeles. What makes the NFL and every other established major sports league unique in the entertainment and business world is that there was no other league to compete with the NFL to fill the market gaps left by the departures of the Browns, Oilers, Rams, and Raiders. This diagnosis of the underlying sources of the compulsion to provide stadium subsidies suggests two possible remedies. The first would require that the monopoly league in each sport expand into every city that seeks a franchise and meets objective qualifying criteria based on its comparative size, fan interest, and other features. This requirement would be imposed on a sports organization that, in the eyes of the law, is the "essential facility" that new competitors must use to enter this field.

A second, more broad-reaching but less regulatory government action would break each league into several competitors—three or four leagues with 8 to 10 teams in each. These separated leagues could still play a national championship game at the end of the season, just as the top teams in each college conference now participate in the NCAA's basketball Final Four or football Bowl Championship Series. In all other respects, the leagues would compete against one another for access to the various sports markets, rather than preserve the artificial scarcity that now allows league members to extract large premiums from their fans—not just in stadium subsidies but also in television contracts, ticket prices, and the like. Such a sweeping, once-and-for-all transformation of the world of sports into something resembling the rest of the entertainment world would render unnecessary many of the rules and regulations discussed in this book.

How Much Can Leagues Expand?

The scarcity of league franchises is not confined to football and Los Angeles. There have been equally striking examples in baseball, the most recent of which involved Tampa Bay. Recall that Tampa Bay, the 13th-largest metropolitan area in the United States, had built the Suncoast Dome to demonstrate a passionate year-round interest in baseball. The presence of that vacant stadium had allowed a half-dozen team owners to make credible threats to move to Tampa Bay as part of their dealings with their home cities. Indeed, the Dome came very close to enticing Jerry Reinsdorf to move his Chicago White Sox down south, until the Illinois legislature stepped in to build a new Comiskey Park. Next Tampa lost out to the smaller cities of Miami and Denver for the two expansion franchises awarded in 1991. Then the owner of the San Francisco Giants agreed to sell his team to a Tampa Bay group that would move the Giants east to the Suncoast Dome. But the other National League owners (including Miami's Wayne Huizenga) blocked that move, precipitating a wave of lawsuits and legislative proposals to strip baseball of its antitrust exemption. To try to contain that legal damage, the MLB owners finally decided to give Tampa Bay, along with Phoenix, an additional expansion franchise that began play in 1998.

Note that all the participants in this battle, including those in Tampa Bay, saw their one plausible legal claim as relating to the move of the Giants out of San Francisco and across the country. No such antitrust suit was filed when baseball denied Tampa Bay a new franchise, even though one reason for the denial was the benefit that current owners were getting from a *vacant* Suncoast Dome in dealing with their own home-town politicians and taxpayers. The same was true in football, where both St. Louis and Baltimore filed (or threatened to file) suits only when the league blocked moves of the Rams and Browns, not when the two cities lost out in the 1993 expansion contest. What happened shortly afterward demonstrated that in the eyes of MLB and NFL owners as well as city residents, Tampa Bay, St. Louis, and Baltimore were fully qualified to have major league teams. Yet everyone assumed that the law gave a city a right only to take someone else's team, not to create its own new team within the league.

The explanation is to be found in another important decision: *Mid-South Grizzlies*. The Memphis team in the World Football League (called the Southmen) had been one of the few successful franchises in that short-lived league challenge to the NFL. When the WFL folded midway through its second season in 1975, the owners of several WFL clubs assembled their best players on a single team named the Mid-South Grizzlies and applied for an NFL franchise—one that would be the region's first major league team in any sport. The league rejected the application, saying that it did not want to add a third club to its pending expansion into Seattle and Tampa Bay. The Third Circuit rejected the Grizzlies' antitrust claim—principally on the ground that there was no anti-competitive harm taking place. Unlike the Raiders' move to Los Angeles within 30 miles of the Rams in Anaheim, the closest team with which the Grizzlies would be competing for fans was the St. Louis Cardinals, nearly 300 miles away. In fact, the court expressly qualified the scope of its ruling to state that a different verdict might well have been reached if the rejected application had been for a franchise in New York, where it would have been competing with teams already established in the area.

Like *Raiders,* though, *Grizzlies* has been given a considerably broader reading, one that bars any affirmative antitrust claim to expansion, by contrast with relocation. This may be why, a decade later, Donald Trump did not seek an NFL franchise in New York after the USFL folded and left his New Jersey Generals with the Heisman Trophy winners Herschel Walker and Doug Flutie but with nobody to play against. The combination of those two decisions (with the Ninth Circuit following *Grizzlies* to dismiss an NHL expansion bid by the Seattle Totems) has produced the best of all possible legal worlds for team owners. Each franchise has a plausible *relocation* threat to make against the city to secure a more lucrative stadium deal, but the city has no viable *expansion* counter-threat, no matter what its size and fan interest in the sport.

For this reason, then-Senator Al Gore opposed the NFL's bid for a Professional Sports Community Protection Act of 1985 which would have restored league control over relocation but granted no right to cities like Memphis for expansion. In Gore's words: "The fundamental cause of franchise instability in professional football is scarcity of franchises. The NFL has refused to expand to meet legitimate demand and this has occasioned intense bidding by cities to lure and maintain existing franchises. Professional team owners are positioned to extract enormous benefits and subsidies from municipalities and they are taking advantage of these opportunities." A dozen years later, Vice President Gore could celebrate the arrival of his home state's first NFL franchise. He surely had the same qualms, though, about the way this had come about: by taking the Oilers out of Houston and taking $300 million from the Tennessee and Nashville taxpayers to build a luxurious new football stadium as inducement for the move.

Another reason offered by the Third Circuit for dismissing the *Grizzlies* antitrust claim was that adding Tennessee to the NFL would have reduced the likelihood that another fully competitive league would emerge in professional football. Whatever may have been the situation in the 1970s, by the end of the 1990s there was no realistic prospect of a rival league to challenge the NFL. Given its *de facto* monopoly status in this sport, the doctrinal question is whether qualified cities should have a right of access to the NFL (or other major leagues) so that their residents can also enjoy the big league experience. In several decisions over the last century the Supreme Court has read antitrust law as imposing such an access obligation on "natural monopolies": on a group of railroads who controlled the only way by which railroads could cross the Mississippi in the early 1900s; on the large newspaper alliance behind the Associated Press, which was generating wire service news stories during World War II; on broker-dealers with the only system that generated instantaneous data on stock sales and prices in the early 1960s; and on the Aspen ski resort that was located in the center of a planned multi-mountain skiing route in the early 1980s. Should the NFL (or MLB, NBA, or NHL) also be judged a natural monopoly that had to admit a Memphis, a Baltimore, or a Tampa Bay that met the relevant qualifications?

Whatever the prior scope and application of this feature of antitrust law, the courts are unlikely to extend this doctrine to the creation and inclusion of entirely new franchises in current sports leagues. Congress could do so, perhaps as a future President Gore's alternative to the stadium subsidy cap that I advocated in Chapter 16. On its face, giving both sides the necessary leverage to decide whether public or private financing of new sports facilities is in their mutual interest would seem to be a better route to a level playing field than a general legislative bar on any such public subsidies, whatever the apparent needs in a particular setting. If both city officials and current home-team owners knew that if a team left town a new team could take its place, a city like Seattle, for example, might decide it did not make good business sense to offer

Paul Allen more than $300 million to build a new stadium to keep the Seahawks in town. But whatever the apparent virtues of such an abstract right to expand, how would it work in practice, and would it have any serious negative effects on the sports in question?

For the near future, at least, it does seem feasible to formulate and apply a meaningful standard to judge whether a particular city is qualified for a major league franchise. The test should be whether the applicant has at least as large a population, television market, and fan commitment as displayed by several other cities in the league in recent years. (For that purpose Green Bay should be deemed part of the Milwaukee metropolitan area.) The best test of fan commitment to the sport is whether the fans are prepared to put the money up front for personal seat licenses, club seating, luxury suites, and the like to generate the funds needed to construct a satisfactory sports facility. There would also have to be an ownership group that was willing and able to pay the appropriate expansion fee and had the financial resources to absorb the initial start-up costs and any potential future losses.

Applying these standards would initially qualify a significant number of new cities. Thus any such expansion would have to be phased in carefully—perhaps two new teams every two or three years. But over the next two decades, one could imagine the NFL rising to 50 teams, the NBA and MLB to 40–45, and the NHL to 35 or more. (One reason football is viable in significantly more locations is that there are only 10 games a season that have to be sold out—something a relatively small city like Jacksonville has proved to be quite easy to do.) And as long as cities knew that even if they did not win an expansion franchise this time they were sure to win one soon, cities like Baltimore and St. Louis would no longer feel compelled to offer owners like Modell and Frontiere financial bonanzas to move their teams from their long-time homes. The financial value—and redistribution of wealth—of franchise free agency would drop sharply.

This raises the question of whether such an expansion right would trigger a dilution in player talent, and thus reduce the quality of the sports product being offered to fans throughout the league. In appraising this concern it is useful to recall some of the history of league expansion. By the late 1950s the four established major leagues had a total of 42 teams—16 in baseball, 12 in football, 8 in basketball, and 6 in hockey. Over the next dozen years all four leagues expanded dramatically, largely because of the presence (or threat) of rival leagues. By the beginning of the 1970s the NFL had 26 teams (10 from the AFL), MLB had 24 (4 from the threat of a Continental Baseball League), while the NBA had 16 and the NHL 14. This was also the period when consumer interest in spectator sports began to soar; average game attendance rose sharply, and television viewership far more so. Yet over the last three decades only basketball and hockey have grown significantly—by 13 and 14 teams respectively, with each league absorbing 4 clubs from the rival ABA and WHA. Meanwhile the NFL and MLB have each grudgingly added just 6 clubs, in large measure because of felt legal and political pressures. Indeed, at the start of the 21st century, baseball—our supposed national pastime—has teams in 24 U.S. cities, one fewer than the NBA and just one more than the NHL. This certainly is not due to any shortage of talented players.

In fact, for several reasons, the level of talent has expanded and is likely to keep expanding much faster than the available teams and roster positions. The U.S. population has grown at roughly the same pace as the size of the NFL and MLB over the last three decades. However, in baseball, basketball, and hockey (though not in American football), the worldwide supply of talent has grown dramatically. Hispanics have now overtaken blacks in their share of MLB positions (with both ethnic groups making up significantly larger shares of MLB players than of the U.S. population), and more and more players are now coming from Japan, Canada, Australia, and other countries. This is even more true in basketball, which now draws upon southern Europe and Africa, and in hockey, which has drawn upon both northern Europe and the northern United States to reduce the dominance of Canadians on NHL rosters from 95 percent in the 1960s to under 60 percent in the late 1990s.

Even in the case of American-style football, which has only modest participation in other countries that concentrate on their "soccer" version, the amount of talent has risen sharply. Youngsters begin playing with decent coaching and training in elementary school, and by the time they go to college they are competing for 85 scholarships (and numerous "walk-on" positions) at more than 100 universities engaged in big-time Division 1-A football. The simple explanation for that kind of career selection and training is that average NFL salaries have risen from approximately $15,000 in the late 1950s to around $1.1 million by the late 1990s. And while we do not have obvious and objective tests of the improvement in talent in team sports, we do have such indexes for track and field. Here, although there are nowhere near the financial incentives felt in football and other sports, only a few of the American athletes who won medals at the 1960 Olympic Games in Rome would even have qualified for the team in the 2000 Games in Sydney. During that same time frame, total attendance in the four major team sports soared from the approximately 20 million fans who went to games played by the 42 teams in 1960 to the 125 million fans who went to watch 115 teams in these same four leagues in 1998.

Undoubtedly, then, the major leagues could expand significantly from their current levels. In stark contrast to relocation, expansion would add to the welfare of fans by giving more people in more cities games to watch, to the welfare of players by giving them more positions to play in (even if average salaries did drop somewhat from their current lofty levels), and to the welfare of taxpayers by reducing the political pressure to subsidize owners (and players and fans). In fact, if a league really were a single entity all of whose assets were owned by one group of investors, expansion would clearly improve the investors' welfare as well (just as in other business sectors). The league's corporation shareholders would secure the financial returns from this larger consumer-fan market without having to share it with new owners. But the skyrocketing of NFL expansion fees from the $600,000 paid for the Dallas Cowboys in 1960 to the $700 million paid for the new Houston team in 1999 demonstrates that even present-day owners can be well reimbursed for admitting more members into their dominant sports power. Certainly, a legal mandate in favor of expansion of the current league monopolies would be far more responsive to broader social welfare than a rule obstructing moves of existing franchises to communities that display a greater interest in their sport.

Along with these obvious advantages, however, there are some significant practical questions concerning the creation of an abstract legal right to an expansion franchise. One is whether a metropolitan area like Philadelphia, whose population is in the 6 million range, should have the right to a second team before an Oklahoma City, at just over 1 million, gets its first team. While there is far more personal and political passion in the communities that have not yet been admitted to a major league, from the point of view of satisfying consumer welfare there may be a better case for taking away the Phillies' monopoly power in their far larger market. Then again, since much of the enjoyment of a home team comes from watching the games on television and talking about them with friends, the 6 million fans in Philadelphia may derive sufficient consumer welfare from a single team, in which case the greater marginal increase in welfare will come from bringing the first home team into a much smaller but still virgin territory such as Memphis or Oklahoma City.

Another question is where the expansion would end. When a smaller city (such as Jacksonville or Nashville) acquires a big league team, its neighbors (say Orlando and Charleston or Memphis and Birmingham) feel significant pressure to claim that same right. To my mind, the NFL's experience in growing from 12 teams in 1959 to 26 in 1970 demonstrates that it could also grow from 31 in 1999 to 45 in 2010. But I feel real qualms about requiring a single major league to reach 100 teams by the year 2050—even though we are already reaching that number of channels on our home cable systems.

How Much Can Leagues Compete?

There is a possible solution to this regulatory problem: the generation of competition *between* leagues, rather than *for* teams. This would resolve the question of whether we are getting too little or too much league expansion, and it would also address many of the other issues we have encountered in this book (such as player reserve systems). The only feasible route to interleague competition would be through government action to break up the existing big leagues. If it worked, this step would eliminate most of the future need for lawsuits and legal controls regarding specific league decisions.

There is a potentially large hurdle to reaching that brave new sports world. However, before addressing this perhaps insurmountable problem, it is valuable to lay out what we are missing in the current sports world.

Think first about franchise free agency. In a multi-league environment, Los Angeles would never have lost all of its football teams, or Cleveland its Browns. One reason is that St. Louis and Baltimore would never have been denied expansion franchises in the first place. These markets would have been occupied by at least one of the competing football leagues, and Los Angeles undoubtedly would have had teams from more than one league. Because different leagues would be competing to occupy scarce space in more and more cities that have fans willing to pay to watch their games, city politicians would feel little pressure to spend huge amounts of taxpayers' money to attract teams, and an owner like Bob McNair would not have to spend $700 million for the right to have a new football franchise in Houston.

Indeed, even more than individual teams, the leagues as a whole would feel the economic motivation to move into more cities. Leagues want not just to attract fans to watch games in the stadium or arena, but even more to induce television networks or merchandising firms to offer lucrative contracts. However, national league exposure, especially (though not exclusively) in the larger markets, is crucial to the value of this intellectual property asset. If there were several leagues competing for contracts with the various national and cable channels, each would need a base and fan allegiance in every significant region across the country. The leagues would then be competing for access to city stadiums, rather than cities competing for teams, and there would be little of the kind of anti-competitive restraint in the broadcasting and sponsorship markets that we saw in the *Bulls/WGN* and *Cowboys/Nike* cases. In that respect, sports would experience much the same economic life as every other part of the entertainment world.

Finally, many of the problems of the players market would be resolved by competitive pressures rather than have to be challenged through lawsuits or strikes. A Curt Flood would not have to choose between leaving baseball and being traded under the National League's reserve system; he would have the option of moving to an American League team offering a better deal. Time Warner, Disney/ABC, and Fox do not impose strict salary budget limits on all their films, whatever the immediate attraction of such a cost-saving device; the studios know that if they did so they would not be able to attract stars such as Tom Cruise, Jim Carrey, and Leonardo DiCaprio, who are crucial to the appeal and financial value of their movies (not just in the United States but around the world). The same would be true of the sports franchises—the Hawks, the Braves, the Mighty Ducks, the Angels, and the Dodgers—owned by these same entertainment conglomerates, if they were divided into different leagues having to compete for stars like Tim Duncan, Mark McGwire, and Eric Lindros.

Of course, the movie world has also displayed the winner-takes-the-lion's-share phenomenon of a vast inequality of earnings between stars and the very talented but lower-profile performers in their projects. The solution to that problem in both movies and sports is for the performers' union (for example, the SAG or the MLBPA) to agree to a salary cap that includes both an overall movie or team budget and a limit on the share that can go to any one performer. Inter-league (like inter-studio) competition would guarantee that the owner-employers could not come together and unilaterally establish the kind of unconscionable salary *cut* that the NFL owners imposed on Tony Brown and his fellow development-squad players. This talent pool would have easily been attracted away by an independent American Football League that offered fair market value for the players' current talent and future prospects.

The foregoing claims are not just speculative theorizing. At some time in the last century, each of the established sports has experienced strong inter-league competition. Whenever there have been just two big leagues in each sport, overall players' salaries have risen significantly, even in the face of an intra-league reserve system that the courts have ruled is not enforceable against players' movement to another league. So also, the major source of expansion in sports has been the appearance (or threat) of another league on the scene. At the same time, serious competition has quickly induced the owners of the rival leagues to settle their differences through some form of merger or integration or financial payoff—thus restoring to the surviving major league its monopoly status in the player, franchise, broadcasting, and other sports markets.

Major League Baseball has not faced a competing league since the early 1900s. As we have seen, the National League, born in the mid-1870s, faced a series of rivals over the next three decades. The biggest challenge came from an American League organized by Ban Johnson in the Midwest, which lured future Hall-of-Famers such as Nap Lajoie and John McGraw away for a time. The two leagues agreed to end their bidding war for players and managerial talent in a 1903 settlement that created a single major league reserve system and the World Series. From the current antitrust perspective, this baseball deal would seem to have been a clear-cut agreement to restrain market competition. However, in those infant years of the Sherman Antitrust Act, this federal law was used principally by employers to attack unionized actions by their employees. Thus nobody even raised questions about the new baseball monopoly.

A decade later, when antitrust had been deployed against corporate giants such as John D. Rockefeller's Standard Oil and business alliances such as Thomas Edison's Motion Picture "Trust" (whose break-up let the movie industry blossom in Hollywood rather than in New Jersey), another challenger appeared on the scene: the Federal Base Ball League. This new contender (which was organized as a true "single entity") generated not just player movements and contract claims but also antitrust suits. In the end Federal Base Ball folded in return for a $700,000 payment by MLB and an invitation to several of its owners to take over AL or NL teams. In a suit filed by the Baltimore Orioles, who had been left out of some of the attractive features of the settlement deal, Justice Oliver Wendell Holmes of the Supreme Court wrote the *Federal Base Ball* opinion that granted baseball a special exemption from antitrust.

The reaffirmation of the *Federal Base Ball* decision in the *Toolson* case after World War II meant that there was no antitrust risk in baseball's response to another possible challenger in the late 1950s, a proposed Continental Baseball League. This venture, initiated by New York Mayor Robert Wagner and led by Branch Rickey and the corporate lawyer William Shea, was precipitated by the moves of the Dodgers and the Giants from New York to California, and its investors hoped to capitalize on both the vacancy left in New York and others in Los Angeles and elsewhere. When MLB owners heard this was happening, however, they undertook the first expansion of the 20th century. Four new teams were added—the NL New York Mets and Houston Astros and the AL California (Anaheim) Angels and Washington Senators. (This last franchise was placed in the nation's capital to replace the team of the same name that had just been moved to Minneapolis–St. Paul as the Twins.) Shea advised New York officials that it was better to take a new team in the established league rather than take a chance with the new league, and as his reward the Mets' new home was named Shea Stadium. It took the new players' union, operating under labor rather than antitrust law, to gain relief for players from baseball's continuing monopoly power over their services.

Football's history was somewhat similar. The NFL was created in 1920, and like baseball's National League it struggled for three decades to establish itself as a serious presence in the sports world. Until at least the late 1950s, college football was the dominant version of the game. The NFL did beat back the post–World War II challenge of the All-American Football Conference, and in 1950 it absorbed the AAFC's

Cleveland Browns, San Francisco 49ers, and Baltimore Colts into a twelve-team league. A decade later, after the NFL resisted requests to expand into Dallas, the extremely wealthy Hunt family organized a new American Football League. This immediately prompted the NFL to expand into both Dallas and Minneapolis–St. Paul, which blocked the AFL from putting a team in the Twin Cities and forced Lamar Hunt to move his AFL Dallas Texans to Kansas City (as the Chiefs) after two years. Although the AFL did not win the antitrust suit it filed as a result of the NFL's expansion, the league was able to survive and even to expand (for example, into Miami with the Dolphins).

After Al Davis became AFL commissioner and a serious bidding war began to lure star quarterbacks out of the NFL, Pete Rozelle and his NFL owners decided that their best tactic was to merge what were now two dozen teams rather than to keep the league rivals fighting for players. Such a new football monopoly posed a serious antitrust problem that did not enjoy baseball's special judge-made exemption. But the NFL and AFL owners went to Washington and got Congress to grant their merger an antitrust exemption through an amendment quietly added to the Sports Broadcasting Act.

As the popularity and financial value of professional football soared, the NFL faced two more challengers: the World Football League in the 1970s and the U.S. Football League in the 1980s. Both of these ventures were successful in attracting some star players, but not in attracting enough fans. With its lawyers having read the judicial ruling in the AFL lawsuit, the NFL was careful to delay expanding when either of these competitors was around. Thus it was not until after the WFL had folded in its second year in 1975 that the NFL announced its plan to create new teams in Seattle and Tampa Bay, and it was not until a decade after the demise of the USFL in 1985 that the NFL expanded with two more teams into Charlotte and Jacksonville. But a look at its past reveals that more than half of the NFL's current 32 franchises were added as a result of competition from or mergers with rival football leagues.

Much the same history unfolded in both basketball and hockey, though I will not recount the details here. Suffice it to say that the threat and then the presence of an American Basketball Association in the late 1960s created not only the three-point shot and the Connie Hawkins–Julius Erving slam dunk but much of the NBA's expansion, including its absorption of four ABA teams when that league folded in 1976. So also, the NHL took in four teams from the World Hockey Association of the 1970s, one of which, the Edmonton Oilers, brought along Wayne Gretzky, Mark Messier, Paul Coffey, and other prospective Hall-of-Famers to make it the dominant hockey team of the late 1980s. These franchise absorptions (rather than full-blown mergers) were accepted by the respective players' associations, though they threatened to eliminate the large salary hikes that players such as Rick Barry and Bobby Hull had gained from inter-league competition for their services. The basketball union leader Larry Fleisher got the NBA to agree to player free agency within this enlarged league monopoly (later modified by a soft salary cap), but hockey's Alan Eagleson took just a modest pension increase. In neither case did the Justice Department seriously scrutinize these deals from the point of view of the public's interest in a competitive sports environment.

By the end of the 1990s one league had a *de facto* monopoly position in each of these sports. No new major league has appeared for 15 years, and there is no realistic prospect of such a new league surviving even if one does appear. Now that players' associations in all four sports have secured substantial free agency, these workers do enjoy the benefit of a competitive labor market in which clubs within the league compete for attractive talent with generous contract offers. But there is very little such intra-league competition in the stadium, broadcasting, and merchandising markets; and whenever there is, the league authorities take action to stamp out such threats from maverick owners such as Reinsdorf, Jones, and Steinbrenner. The fact that there are a growing number of cities, television networks (including cable channels), and merchandising firms deeply interested in the sports product means that members of established leagues have been able to extract an even larger economic premium from each of these sources.

Ironically, it is this combination of player free agency and league monopoly that makes the entrance or survival of new leagues almost impossible. The interplay of game appeal and monopoly power in the various sports markets enables owners to secure spiraling stadium subsidies, television contracts, and merchandising deals that ultimately are paid for by taxpayers and fans. But because of the competitive bidding regime established by their unions, players now receive the majority of these league revenues in the form of salaries and benefits. The NFL, for example, with the hardest of all salary caps, has ensured that its players will end up with more than 60 percent of its Designated Gross Revenues. The top stars now earn $6 million or more per season in football, $10 million in hockey, $15 million in baseball, and $22 million in basketball. Even top rookie draft picks now get multi-million-dollar signing bonuses. In order to provide a meaningful challenge to an established league whose annual revenues now range from $1.2 billion in hockey to $3.6 billion in football, owners of a new league have to be able to pay enough money to hire the player talent that will in turn attract patronage and payments from cities, networks, merchandisers, and fans. The problem—the vicious circle—is that new leagues cannot get stars until they have lucrative television and stadium deals, and they cannot get those deals until they have the stars.

The long-time absence of a second league effectively competing with the established league in baseball or football or other sports means that there is no realistic prospect of new league competition in the future. The only way for fans and taxpayers to get the benefit of such a competitive sports market would be for the law to break up the current dominant leagues into three or four rival leagues with 8 to 10 teams in each. As past experience demonstrates, that is a viable number for league play. This initial body would also serve as a launching pad for expansion by each league to a dozen or more cities that provided sufficient exposure across the country. The leagues would be permitted to collaborate in staging a national championship series at the end of their seasons— something that would require coordination in the rules that they use on the field of play, such as designated hitters, three-point shots, or instant replay. Professional sports would to some extent follow the model of American college sports, in which universities collaborate in an NCAA championship but conferences (and even individual schools such as Notre Dame) compete for fans, television contracts, and merchandising deals and do not expect local taxpayers to finance expensive sports facilities.

There is no legal possibility that the courts will impose such a breakup on the professional leagues. While §2 of the Sherman Act does constrain economic monopolies, this provision bars not their mere existence but only improper actions taken to create and preserve such monopoly power. Because over the last century both Congress and the courts have endorsed the critical actions taken to establish these sports monopolies, judges cannot legitimately step in now and say that these endorsements were legal mistakes—they cannot, for example, strike down the 1903 merger agreement between the National and American Leagues. If any such step is to be taken, it will have to be taken by Congress.

While there is obviously a massive political barrier to any such congressional action, there is no constitutional barrier. The federal government can do what it believes necessary to establish a competitive market in an industry that is clearly part of interstate commerce. In the early 1980s the Justice Department secured an analogous result when it broke up AT&T by requiring divestiture of long distance from local phone systems. Over the next 15 years, with competition among AT&T, MCI, and Sprint for the allegiance of long distance customers, the number of phone calls soared and the average price per call dropped sharply. Exactly the opposite price trends were taking place in both local telephone and cable systems, each one of which was controlled by a single Baby Bell or cable system operator. The hoped-for result of the 1996 Telecommunications Act is to create competition in these two monopoly markets through technology that allows companies to offer long distance, local, and cable services to their subscribers at a lower price for a higher quality.

A competitive sports market offers fans the same upside potential. For example, if there were separate leagues competing for television networks as well as networks competing for leagues, prices would almost certainly drop, and each league would feel much greater pressure to take steps that would make its games more enjoyable to fans. (Baseball, for example, might finally have to figure out a way to make its games shorter.) And as each league felt the need to locate a team in the larger markets, not just the largest ones (say in Boston as well as in New York), the prices charged for tickets, luxury suite rentals, concessions, and the like would probably go down. Owners and players might have to give up some of the lavish increase in franchise values and salary levels they have enjoyed over the past quarter-century—but there would be considerably more owners and players reaping the benefits of this larger number of leagues and teams. True, sports lawyers would have much less legal business in trying to persuade judges that a league's internal rules were reasonable and thus legal under antitrust law, because a competitive external market is the best judge on that score. This effect on lawyers would surely enhance the popular appeal of this radical action.

Needless to say, there remain huge political obstacles to the federal government daring to touch, let alone to break up, the professional leagues. These obstacles are not likely to be surmounted in the foreseeable future—certainly not until fans as well as taxpayers appreciate the price they are now paying to preserve the monopoly status of their favorite leagues. There is also a significant policy problem: the arguably *natural* monopoly status of any major league sport. If a sport (or any other economic activity) is inherently monopolistic, any effort to break up the existing dominant entity will be short-lived, because one of the competitors will soon regain monopoly status by putting the other contenders out of business.

It was long assumed that both telephone and cable systems were natural monopolies whose products and prices had to be controlled by regulation rather than by competition. This standard version of the natural monopoly—based on the large up-front investment in the *physical* transmission system—clearly does not apply to a sports franchise like Bob Irsay's Colts, which, in the middle of the night in 1984, he moved from Baltimore to Indianapolis with a dozen Mayflower vans. Instead, the big investment is now required to purchase a team in the existing monopolies, whose $250–$700 million franchise prices reflect the stadium, television, and merchandising deals in the currently tilted market.

The puzzle, then, is why not one of the 20th-century contenders against the established leagues was able to survive as an independent rival. It is true that a few star players in an established league are tied up by expensive long-term contracts. But there are always numerous free agent veterans, and there are also younger "reserved" players who would be free to move to a new league after their contracts expired at the end of the season, as well as a regular flow of new talent into the professional game from college or the minor leagues. Perhaps the explanation lies in the special legal treatment given to the sports mergers and absorptions over the last century. But no such treatment aided the NFL's besting of the WFL in the 1970s and the USFL in the 1980s, and so far as I know, no other nation in the world has two or more major leagues in its favored sport.

The more likely answer is found in the word "major." What most fans especially want to see are major league, not minor league, games. This is true at the gate in larger cities and on television in all cities. The *major* league is the one that fans consider to be the best—the league that has the talent to win a Super Bowl or World Series that matches up champions from otherwise independent leagues.

In this respect sports is very different not just from standard business markets where the quality-price ratio is crucial (as in AT&T's competition with MCI and Sprint), but even from the entertainment world where there are annual awards for best performances—Oscars in movies, Emmys in television, and Grammys in music. Such an artistic honor gives considerable prominence and economic value to the winner. But the fact that a studio wins the most Oscars, or a network the most Emmys, even for several years in a row has absolutely no impact on movie attendance and very little on Nielsen ratings for its other films or programs. By contrast, if one league regularly wins the championship title, fans will judge it to be *the* true big league in the sport—with corresponding effects on all its teams' home attendance, television ratings, and stadium deals. And once a league gains even a modest edge in these markets, the substantially greater revenue allows it to pay more to attract free agent talent from the other league, which not only reinforces but is likely to make irreversible its initial edge. Eventually owners in the other leagues will decide that it makes no sense to keep losing money as well as championships, and their folding will restore a monopoly in that sport.

The late 1990s provided a test case about whether that historical experience would remain the norm for sports. Title IX's transformation of college sports for women produced a level of player talent and fan interest in women's basketball that made possible the formation of not just one but two such professional leagues—the American Basketball League (ABL) and the Women's National Basketball Association (WNBA). The WNBA was a spin-off venture by the NBA owners, who were able to use their clout in the basketball market to secure double the ABL fan attendance at games and a far bigger advantage in television and merchandising deals. Some of that WNBA money was used to lure the top women players coming out of college or becoming free agents in the ABL, to reinforce in fans' minds which was the truly "major" women's basketball league. The ABL people got the message: in December 1998, just a month into their third season, the ABL investors folded their league venture into bankruptcy.

It is likely—though not inevitable—that much the same scenario would take place if Congress were to require the break-up of the NBA (and the NFL, the NHL, and MLB), with current teams distributed among three or four new league entities. Even though each of these leagues would begin with fan recognition of their former major league status, that image would probably be a fragile one. And as soon as even a modest disparity emerged in levels of talent, the most prominent league would be able to use its control of that major league image off as well as on the field (as the WNBA did versus the ABL). The risk would be even greater if the break-up law envisaged the leagues competing in a Final Four–like championship. While in the short run such a match-up would be what the fans (and voters) wanted, in the longer run if a single league won several championships in a row, this would undermine the economic base for a competitive market in that sport. The possible antidote to such a race to the top (and the bottom) in each sport may be found in the world of college sports.

College teams and conferences have long competed in the marketplace as well as on the field or floor in NCAA championships. The NCAA has its own version of a salary cap (actually a salary ban) that permits each of the 300 members in Division I, for example, to offer only scholarships (for tuition and room and board) in their competition for high school stars. This far too rigid formula for compensation of players has probably generated more single-team dominance in college sports than most of us would like to see, because there are a few schools whose name, sports history, coaching staff, and even educational reputation are most attractive, and less prestigious schools are not allowed to outbid them by offering more money for a fair share of playing talent. But the Big Ten, Pac Ten, SEC, and a few other conferences have all managed to survive in people's minds as major leagues in college sports, where football and basketball, especially, have a long-time image as qualitatively different from the professional leagues. By analogy, then, if breaking up the big leagues is to endure for the benefit of fans, there has to be a single salary capping (and salary sharing) system that governs *all* the leagues.

This is a step that players and their associations would feel very ambivalent about. On the one hand, the presence of three or four leagues would considerably expand the number of teams, and thus the number of major league positions available. On the other hand, embracing a single salary cap that covered all the teams in all the leagues would remove a valuable lever for free agent players in their contract negotiations and for unions in collective bargaining about the nature and limits of the free agency for players in each league.

The owners in any one league could not afford to unilaterally impose an unacceptable cap on their players and risk losing their best talent and then their major league status to other competitors. If all the leagues agreed among themselves to impose an across-the-board cap, this action almost certainly would enjoy no labor exemption—because the players' association would not have agreed to participate in such multi-league bargaining—and would face a risk of trebled antitrust damages if a jury found the cap to be an unreasonable restraint of trade. Most important of all, both owners and players would realize that by agreeing to a multi-league salary cap designed to preserve the existence of competing leagues, they were eliminating the financial premium that the current league monopoly was extracting in ticket prices, television contracts, and stadium subsidies and then sharing among the owners and players. If Congress really did seek to break up the big leagues for the benefit of fans, it would probably have to mandate a salary regime that gave each new league a real chance to preserve its major league status.

My bottom-line judgment about a legal break-up of the big leagues is essentially the same as (though more emphatically felt than) my view about legal expansion. A once-and-for-all intervention to break up each current league monopoly into three or four competing leagues would provide the ideal solution not just to problems of franchise free agency but to many of the other policy problems examined in this book. However, even if we ignore the political obstacles to initiating any such break-up, there remains the crucial practical question of whether competition among major leagues can endure over the longer run. Still, I have always found that reading and reflecting about this issue is valuable because of the window it offers into the way that the big leagues have evolved to their current dominant status. At this stage, I am affirmatively endorsing just the more moderate and feasible legal reforms investigated in earlier chapters, which I will synopsize in the next chapter.

20

A BETTER WORLD FOR FANS

The saga of the Browns had a reasonably happy ending. The NFL granted Cleveland an expansion (rather than a relocation) franchise that began playing in the 1999 season. The league also managed to save the treasured Browns name and logo for the Cleveland team. And by contrast with the people in Oakland experiencing the return of Al Davis with the Raiders, the fans in Cleveland's Dawg Pound did not have to welcome back Art Modell.

The owner of the new Browns, Al Lerner, did have to pay $530 million for membership in the NFL, or 135 times what Modell paid back in 1961. The biggest source of this massive increase in franchise prices is the NFL's latest television deal—negotiated under the protective umbrella of the Sports Broadcasting Act—which pays each team around $75 million a season, or 225 times the $330,000 each team received from the league contract that Modell helped negotiate with CBS in 1962. But another factor is that taxpayers in Cleveland put up $250 million to build a luxurious new stadium where Browns fans would again watch and enjoy NFL games—needless to say, at much higher ticket prices.

Football is the clearest illustration that players' salaries are *not* why team owners "need" such "donations" from taxpayers. The NFL has a hard salary cap that imposes stringent limits on the total amount each team can pay its roster. So even if a club like the Browns gets local taxpayers to provide rent-free use and control of a facility that generates much greater revenue, the team's owner cannot use this extra money to lure better talent away from a "stadium-deprived" team (such as the Vikings), in order to enjoy the personal pleasure of winning the Super Bowl in front of more than 100 million television viewers. The worth of a luxurious new football stadium is displayed in the value placed on the franchise in the capital markets, not in the team's success on the field.

Under the NFL's revenue-sharing and salary-cap rules, a team's stadium revenues are not shared, either with other owners or with players. Luxury suite rentals, naming rights, and other stadium income sources are not included in the Designated Gross Revenues used to calculate the total payroll permitted for each team. These rules are embodied in the collective agreement negotiated by the union that football players formed in the 1960s and that finally established a productive relationship with NFL owners in the 1990s. This labor contract limits players to 63 percent of the league's $2.2 billion in television revenues and the same share of gate receipts, merchandising deals, and the like—a "limit" that has sent average football salaries up from $15,000 in the late 1950s to around $1.1 million by the end of 1999.

I hope that the two sides in baseball will also be able to negotiate a constructive reform of their far-too-soft salary tax, along the lines of the meaningful, progressive, and two-way payroll tax that I proposed in earlier chapters. Meanwhile, NFL owners should negotiate a more sensible system of revenue sharing among themselves. One key element should be the distribution of the huge new stream of stadium revenues along the same lines as traditional revenue sources. Treating the return on luxury suites in the same fashion as that on gate receipts would remove the distorted incentives that now prod football owners to desert their teams' long-time homes in pursuit of taxpayer-financed bonanzas around the country.

In all major professional sports, both the owners and the players have organized themselves into bodies that effectively serve their interests, and that often can work out constructive deals between the two sides. But this kind of organization is not available to protect the interests of fans, who generate the flow of revenue into the league that benefits both owners and players—either directly or through the intermediary of television networks, merchandising companies, and stadium authorities.

The crucial feature of the sports world that generates this social problem is that every major league is a monopoly in its own sport. It is this monopoly power that enables owners to extract a large premium from the growing number of markets within which their league operates. Since it is athletically questionable, not just politically improbable, to try to split up dominant powers like the NFL and MLB into several competitive leagues, America will retain the traditional monopoly status of the major leagues well into the next millennium of sports. American fans, then, will have to use the legal system to gain fairer treatment in this branch of the nation's economy.

Congress should take a serious second look at the Sports Broadcasting Act, which was passed in 1961 without any serious reflection or debate. After four more decades of experience with major league sports as a real *business,* we need a new Sports Broadcasting and Merchandising Act. There is fierce competition between networks like CBS and NBC or product manufacturers like Nike and Reebok for the right to telecast league games or use team names. On the other side of the business table, Congress has authorized leagues to bar meaningful competition between teams such as the Cowboys and the Packers in the sale of their television rights. While the even stronger league restraints on trade in the sports merchandising market have no such special immunity, the only challenges to these restraints—by Jerry Jones's Cowboys and George Steinbrenner's Yankees—have quickly been settled by owners in a fashion that preserves their group's special market clout.

There is an important lesson to be drawn from our examination of the interplay of the player and product markets. For the same reason that leagues can and should create a combination of free agency and a payroll tax (or cap) to ensure a truly competitive set of lineups on the playing field, owners can and should be required to compete with one another when dealing with television and broadcasting competitors in these other branches of the sports marketplace. Just like other participants in the "intellectual property" business—including the players' association when it sells its members' publicity rights to card manufacturers—leagues should be free to make *group* deals about television merchandising. However, they must not be permitted to make those league contracts *exclusive,* thus insulating themselves from any competition from individual teams in the national market. (The league should be free to require sharing of the revenue from these national team contracts, but only on the same basis as it does the revenue from local contracts.) What Congress must do is put an end to a sports marketplace that has allowed MLB Properties to extract for wealthy baseball owners a monopoly premium from the parents of Little League children. While parents now do get the personal pleasure of seeing the Yankees or Dodgers team name on their children's uniforms, they should also enjoy the economic pleasure of paying a fair price, as they would if the Yankees and Dodgers were competing to sell their trademark licenses.

Having the law produce intra-league competition by clubs in the television and merchandising markets would not solve the biggest social problem we have encountered in this book: stadium subsidies. As we have seen, the principal reason the NFL Cleveland Browns sold for $530 million in 1998 and the Minnesota Vikings for $250 million that same year is that Cleveland had agreed to put up so much public money to build a $280 million football-only stadium for the Browns. Earlier in the 1990s Cleveland spent another $400 million on separate new facilities for its Indians and Cavaliers, but it was topped by Seattle, whose citizens spent $750 million on their three teams. Throughout the decade, taxpayers across the country contributed about $11 billion of the $15 billion in sumptuous new facilities being created for major league teams.

This problem is not likely to go away. When state and local governments were anteing up around $3 billion to build a large number of stadiums and arenas over the previous three decades, no one would have predicted how short-lived those facilities would turn out to be. As we start the new millennium, then, it is high time for our national government to take action to block a replay of that social and economic misplay.

The economic mistake does *not* consist in a team's moving from one city to another where the owner and the league believe there is greater untapped fan interest. The overall level of sports welfare was enhanced when, after the Browns began playing in Cleveland in 1946 (in the AAFC), that city's NFL Rams moved out to Los Angeles and took major league sports to the West Coast for the first time. It was likewise good for sports in America when the Brooklyn Dodgers left three-team New York City to introduce major league baseball to California—especially since Los Angeles (unlike New York) was prepared to allow Walter O'Malley to build and pay for a new Dodgers Stadium himself. And even I, born and brought up in Canada, admit that it was good for the NHL to allow Winnipeg's Jets to move south to the Phoenix area, where there are far more people available—including Canadians on winter holidays—to pay to watch the games.

The true *economic* problem is that so many of our scarce taxpayer dollars are being spent to facilitate consumption in the sports branch of our leisure life, rather than on more productive investments such as the effective education of our children. It is time that both politicians and voters start listening to independent economists rather than to team consultants, and realize that the presence of a professional team in a stadium has no more economic impact on an area than the presence of a movie theater megaplex.

One important element of the *social* problem is that it is ordinary Americans who are putting up the money (via regressive sales taxes) to build the luxurious new ballparks, and yet in these ballparks, by contrast with movie theaters, the vast majority of attractive seats are reserved for the affluent Americans who can afford the steep ticket prices. Another element is that, by contrast with any revenue that public authorities may collect from publicly owned parks (or concert halls or art museums), the revenue flowing into professional sports ends up in the pockets of highly paid players and extremely wealthy owners. And we should all have learned from the steep rise in the overall revenues generated by our more and more appealing sports that more than enough private money is now available to build any needed professional sports facility.

Understanding the nature of this problem is, admittedly, a rather difficult challenge. But once we grasp these key features of the present-day sports world, the solution is clear. America needs to establish a stadium cap that will replace the current spiral in stadium taxes.

The major leagues all exercise monopoly power within their respective sports. One important use of that power has been to preserve an artificial scarcity in the available number of franchises, thus making politicians in vacant cities feel the need to bid with taxpayer dollars to attract a team. The cities of Baltimore and St. Louis spent so much public money to lure the Browns from Cleveland and the Rams from Los Angeles precisely because they had been refused new franchises by the NFL in 1993, in favor of much smaller Charlotte and Jacksonville. A radical form of federal regulation of that league monopoly power would require a league to expand into any geographic area that satisfies basic standards of fan demand for this "essential" feature of our leisure lives. My more moderate proposal to Congress is simply to prevent members of the monopoly league from playing one local government off against another, by barring any government from rewarding an owner who agrees to move to (or stay in) a particular community.

The bottom line, then, is that the Yankees' owner George Steinbrenner (and the Mets' Nelson Doubleday and Fred Wilpon) should be required to follow the path of the Dodgers' Walter O'Malley, who built Dodgers Stadium himself, rather than the path of the Giants and the Jets, who took money from New Jersey taxpayers to move across the Hudson River into the Meadowlands. The Yankees (and the Mets) should first decide whether there really is a better place to build a more attractive facility for their fan base. (Like the Giants and Jets, the Yankees and Mets certainly would not give up their New York name and identity.) The owners can then prove that their decision is a reasonable one by using a share of their team's increased revenues to pay for the new ballparks themselves.

There is a major political figure who can explain to Americans why this would give us a much fairer sports market. In 1989 George W. Bush, son of our then-President George Bush, put together a group that bought the Texas Rangers for $83 million; George W. himself put up around $600,000. Just three years later Bush and his partners persuaded Arlington County (which includes Dallas–Fort Worth) to build the Rangers a grand new stadium financed by a higher sales tax. In 1998, after George W. had moved up from managing partner of the Rangers to governor of Texas, his group sold the club for $250 million, with the governor's share $15 million.

Mark McGwire should *not* be condemned for using currently legal Andro to help set the new home run record in the 1998 season. It is equally understandable why, as the Rangers' managing partner, George W. Bush wanted to use the taxpayer-built Ballpark in Arlington to enhance the financial as well as the athletic performance of his Rangers—one that allowed the team to break the American League franchise price record that year. (Unlike McGwire's 70 home runs, though, the Rangers' $250 million mark was topped a year later by the $320 million price for the Cleveland Indians in an equally luxurious Jacobs Field.) But now that George W. is seeking to follow his father into the White House, he should be explaining to America why there is no need to use scarce taxpayer dollars to build such lucrative facilities. Truly "compassionate" political leaders, especially those who advocate caps on progressive income taxes, should also be blocking the use of regressive sales taxes to build luxurious new stadiums that confer a windfall profit on wealthy owners (and then on their players). A national stadium cap is the only way to create a level playing field in a better sports world for fans.

EPILOGUE

A PERFORMANCE-ENHANCING
LAW FOR SPORTS

Our world of sports is constantly on trial. Leagues and players' associations, teams and communities, and athletes in professional and amateur sports regularly battle in front of judges, arbitrators, labor boards, civil rights agencies, and even federal and state legislatures. This trend has furthered the professional careers of fans who also happen to be lawyers; but has it also conferred benefits on ordinary fans who simply want to enjoy a game being played rather than litigated?

Two decades ago, when my Harvard law students and I began studying the way the legal system shapes the sports world, *Sports Illustrated* published a noteworthy series with a title that still captures popular sentiment—"Money: The Monster Threatening Sports." As the authors saw it, this central feature of the nation's culture had become "moneyball." Revenues of the four major leagues had passed the $600 million mark, average players' salaries had gone up from $10,000 to $75,000 in the preceding 20 years, and franchise values were as high as $10 million. But consider the situation at the end of the 1990s: total revenues of the four leagues were over $9 billion; average players' salaries were over $1.3 million; and franchise values ranged from $100 million to $1 billion (Jerry Jones's Dallas Cowboys).

These figures are actually an index of the growing popularity of sports rather than proof of the existence of a game-threatening "monster." Total attendance at major league baseball games is now double what it was a quarter-century ago. The number of games that fans are watching on television (especially on cable networks, which did not even exist back then) is up several more times than that. Many new teams have been added to the established major leagues, new leagues have been formed in soccer and women's basketball, and players (as well as fans) have experienced a surge in opportunities at both the college and professional levels.

The more enthusiastic fans feel about watching games, the more they are willing to pay for that pleasure. And the more money fans send into the sports world, the more resolutely its participants will compete to get a bigger share—almost always using lawyers to advance their cause. In some significant respects the law has done much to improve the quality of the game, as well as to divide up the money among the protagonists. This is especially true of the elimination of the traditional reserve system and its replacement by enough free agency to allow players to move from their current teams, which often do not really need them, to others that do. And in a different context, adoption of Title IX gave American women a real chance to display their love for and talent in sports—initially in college and now in the professional ranks.

Just as in free competitive labor markets, so also under Title IX there are many complicated questions about how to apply the general principle of "equal opportunity" to determine the number of team positions, scholarships, and so forth to be allocated to "separate but equal" women's college sports. The distinctive features of the sports world present a constant challenge to the legal system whenever it is asked to shape a truly level playing field.

One of these distinctive features is the inherent "joint product" nature of sports. As leagues regularly tell judges, this is why there has to be a governing body to define and enforce the rules of the game. For example, we need the USGA or the PGA Tour to take up the problem raised by powerful new titanium golf clubs. Certainly we amateur golfers find it exhilarating to be able to hit the ball farther and farther off the tee thanks to these high-tech clubs. But if we want professional competitors to have to use the full array of shotmaking skills on the fairway, while preserving venerable golf courses such as Augusta National or Pebble Beach, we do need somebody with the authority to establish a power cap on golf clubs (or balls, or tennis racquets, or other athletic equipment).

Historically, though, once such an authority has been established to preserve the quality and integrity of the game on the field, the powers that be naturally feel inclined to use their monopoly leverage to extract more money from fans and pay less to players—thus leaving larger sums in their own pockets. For example, not only has the NFL taken advantage of the Sports Broadcasting Act to secure $2.2 billion a year from television networks, advertisers, and consumers, but MLB Properties has used the *Flood* case to extract a significant premium from every family whose children are playing on a Little League team named after an MLB club.

Some analysts suggest that the law should respond to these two characteristics of sports by dividing up league authority in a corresponding fashion. With respect to the game on the field, the league and its commissioner should have broad autonomy to define rules to make the game more attractive: for example, to require wooden rather than aluminum baseball bats, wielded by designated hitters rather than pitchers at the plate. But events that take place off the field should be shaped by the same full-blown market competition that operates in every other industry.

That apparently natural division of authority faces a major challenge because of the third and least visible characteristic of sports. By contrast even with other parts of the entertainment world, sports is unique in the extent to which the winner takes the lion's share—not just the financial but also the emotional payoff from being champion. The resulting competitive pressures force all participants either to pay a large premium in their efforts to be named champion—a title that only one team can hold—or to save money and pay the other price of finishing at or near the bottom of the race.

It is not only owners who face that Prisoner's Dilemma in making their financial decisions. Players must make a similar physically risky call in deciding whether or not to use performance-enhancing substances, be they illegal anabolic steroids or legal Andro. The willingness of some athletes to use these substances to win an Olympic gold medal or break a home-run record puts strong pressure on other athletes to do the same. This pressure is felt even though there are significant long-term health risks for every user but only one will win the gold or set the record. That is why anti-drug policies in sports should give priority to performance-enhancing Andro (let alone steroids), rather than performance-detracting cocaine (let alone marijuana).

Athletes play a special role as models in American life, especially for young fans. For that reason, even if some of our laws are rather dubious public policy—such as criminalizing marijuana use or betting with bookies—leagues may be justified in setting their own penalties for players who break these laws. But the test of whether MLB (or NCAA) authorities are really committed to the principle that athletes must respect the law is whether they impose at least as strong a penalty on an athlete like Lawrence Phillips who batters a woman as they do on an athlete like Steve Howe who buys drugs from an undercover DEA agent.

Performance-enhancing payrolls create an analogous problem for the teams. Elimination of the owners' traditional reserve system has definitely made sports more appealing to fans as well as more equitable for players. Freer access to talent around the league is what enabled the 1993 expansion Florida Marlins to win a World Series just five years later. But by the late 1990s baseball was displaying the vices as well as the virtues of unrestricted bidding for free agents. This was vividly displayed by the huge disparity in 1998 payrolls and performance between George Steinbrenner's Yankees and Wayne Huizenga's Marlins, but we should be even more concerned about the apparent return of an enduring Yankee Dynasty by the end of the 1999 season.

The special nature of sports justifies a system of salary standards designed to foster competitive balance across league lineups. The ideal instrument for achieving such balance is a meaningful graduated tax on team payrolls. The owners in the NFL and other sports also want the benefit of cost certainty from a hard salary cap, even at the price of less flexibility in responding to their teams' needs for talent. However, the key virtue of what the owners and players agreed to in football was not so much the *cap* placed on how much the Dallas Cowboys or the San Francisco 49ers could pay to try to win another Super Bowl as the equally hard *floor* placed on how little the Tampa Bay Buccaneers and New Orleans Saints could pay *not* to win. Major League Baseball needs to follow exactly the same principle by imposing the same payroll standards on the Florida Marlins and Montreal Expos as on the New York Yankees and Atlanta Braves.

If the MLB owners and players should reach such an agreement in their upcoming negotiations, this would improve the competitive quality of the game even more for fans in the stands. Such a labor solution could also improve the economic situation for fans, who have to pay the price (direct or indirect) of watching games on television or buying products displaying their favorite team's logo. Now that sports leagues have shown that they can secure competitive balance through the players market, there is no justification for the NBA's blocking the Bulls' home games from being telecast in Boston to compete against the Celtics, or the NFL's blocking the Cowboys from selling their team name to Nike to compete against a potential Packers deal with Adidas. Team owners and players should be entitled to reap the full market value of their sport, as measured, for example, by the relative Nielsen ratings of *Monday Night Football* and *ER*. But that value must be determined by the same free market competition among teams that NBC now faces in its competition with ABC or the Disney studio in its competition with Warner Brothers.

Such intra-league competition will not solve the problems of franchise free agency and stadium subsidies. Because there is no foreseeable prospect of any dominant major league's losing its monopoly power, the scarcity of available franchises will persist. As their sport becomes ever more popular, team owners, speaking from their protected position, now regularly tell their local communities that a luxurious, taxpayer-financed new facility is essential to improve the quality of the team on the field. Even in baseball, there is much more fiction than fact to that claim, especially after we think through the way the new Ballpark in Arlington, for example, dramatically increased the price that the new owners had to pay to buy the Texas Rangers from George W. Bush and his partners. Football most clearly demonstrates the fallacy in that claim. Even though the NFL owners do have a true payroll cap that does not share any stadium revenues with players, they have secured at least as much public money as baseball owners to build separate new facilities for their teams. The extremely generous "donation" that Art Modell received from the State of Maryland for moving the original Browns from Cleveland to Baltimore certainly increased the financial value of Modell's franchise. It did not, however, do anything for the performance of the Ravens on the field.

Leveling the competitive pressures felt in this franchise and stadium marketplace is something that we Americans can and must do for ourselves. The only way to avoid a regular replay of the experience of the 1990s is to have Congress pass a law that bars redistribution of middle-American taxpayers' dollars into the pockets of wealthy Americans like George Steinbrenner. In earlier chapters I used the debates about the morality of athletes' behavior to suggest that the country as a whole would be better off with a marijuana tax and a gambling cap. Whatever one's views about these complex social issues, I hope my readers now understand that as fans we would be better off if our favorite sports had the combination of a salary tax and a stadium cap.

ACKNOWLEDGMENTS

Since Red Auerbach and I began that informal course on sports law two decades ago, many notable sports lawyers have come to Harvard to teach my students and me about the complexities of the issues.

Among the key people on the league owners' side have been David Stern, Commissioner of the NBA; Jeff Pash, who has played the same executive vice president role for the NHL and now the NFL; Sandy Alderson and Rob Manfred, who now have vital responsibilities for Major League Baseball; and Brian Burke, who was one of my original group of Harvard students in this field and went on to become vice president of the NHL and now president of the Vancouver Canucks.

On the players' side, I am especially indebted to Larry Fleisher, who created the NBA players union right after graduating from Harvard Law School; Dick Moss, who played a similar key role in bringing the players' union and free agency to baseball; Don Fehr, who succeeded Moss as general counsel and then Marvin Miller as executive director of the MLBPA; Dick Bertelson, the long-time general counsel of the NFLPA with Gene Upshaw; Jeff Kessler, who has performed as outside legal counsel for players' associations in all the sports; and Bob Woolf, who just after he graduated from law school became the pioneering agent negotiating contracts for individual players.

Of course, I must absolve all these experts—many of whom I also go to games with—of any responsibility for the verdicts I offer in this book. But as a long-time Red Sox season-ticket holder, I certainly hope that in their crucial next round of baseball labor negotiations, my friends Don Fehr and Rob Manfred will be able to negotiate a peaceful win-win settlement along the lines that I develop in Part II.

One person to whom I owe a special debt is Rick Horrow. Rick had graduated from Harvard Law School just before I arrived there as a professor, and he eventually became a consultant to NFL Commissioner

Paul Tagliabue, as well as to other leagues and teams seeking to get new stadiums and arenas built with some private, but a lot of taxpayer, money. In the dozen years that I have taught Sports and the Law, Rick has always come back for at least one class in which we debate the stadium funding issue (which has about ten times as much money riding on it now as it did when my course began). Needless to say, Rick does not subscribe to the crucial final piece of advice I give in this book about how to level the playing field for taxpayers. But when the two of us go out on the golf course or to a Super Bowl together, we talk about who should be winning the games, not the lawsuits.

I have the same kind of fun with my close friend and partner in *Sports and the Law,* Gary Roberts. Gary and three other top legal scholars in this field—Roger Abrams, Michael Harper, and Steve Ross—read the manuscript for this book and gave me a host of valuable suggestions for improving its content and my judgments. I want to thank all of them for their great help, even on those issues where our ultimate verdicts may differ.

Preparing and revising the manuscript also required a great deal of time and effort from my administrative assistants over the last five years—Tasha Hansen, Michelle Eichelberger, Ed Upton, Leslie Sterling, and now Wendy Moore. And as with my other books published by Harvard University Press, I received indispensable advice from its editorial people. Michael Aronson has helped shape *Leveling* ever since we began discussing the project a half dozen years ago. And I had very helpful editing from Camille Smith to make my presentation of the policy issues posed by sports readable by fans who are *not* lawyers.

The people who taught me most about how to enjoy sports are my family, especially my father, brothers, and sons. (My mother, sister, and daughters made sure I had an equal interest in entertainment.) That is why I dedicated both *Sports and the Law* and *Entertainment, Media, and the Law* to members of the Weiler family. But this book is the first I have dedicated to my wife's family, in particular to my father- and mother-in-law, Sidney and Natalie Darwin.

I have always celebrated the fact that my wife, Florrie, is not only a Harvard Law School alumna but the only person ever to have been both an editor of the *Harvard Law Review* and a cook in several top restaurants in Paris. I reap the benefits of her expertise both at the dining table and at the writing table. As with my earlier works, Florrie played a crucial editorial role, enhancing the readability and the content of *Leveling*. Meanwhile, I have long enjoyed watching games with Florrie's dad and playing them with her brothers and their wives. And when I visit the Darwins, Nat sets aside a nice little porch on which I can work on my books (especially during the halftime break). Thus I want to express my appreciation to Nat, Sid, and their family for everything they have done for me since I joined the Darwin clan. And we are all hoping that the powers that be in sports will follow the advice I give in *Leveling the Playing Field* and make the games even better for Darwins, Weilers, and all other fans in this new sports millennium.

Index